Prais
JIVAMUK

"Jivamukti has been a big influence in my life. I've read this book twice and expect to read it many more times. It's the bible of my spiritual practice."

—RUSSELL SIMMONS
CEO of Rush Communications and cofounder of DefJam Records

"David and Sharon are great teachers in the fullest sense of the word—as guides and mentors they challenge and inspire. Their book gives readers a glimpse of the power of yoga to transform lives."

—TRUDIE STYLER
Cofounder of the Rainforest Foundation

"Sharon and David sing the essence of yoga in their new book *Jivamukti Yoga*. Their book is amazingly accessible without being compromising to the tradition of yoga. In the same breath I applaud them for their courage to be creative and daring in expressing their unique and gifted voices."

—RODNEY YEE

"Sharon and David have been able to touch so many people through the dance of life. Embracing the true sense of yoga: the union of mind, body, and spirit. They have the unique ability to create a space in New York and for New Yorkers where one is able to balance the outer craziness with the inner calming world. At the same time, they are able to captivate and enhance their own creativity and share it with so many others."

—DONNA KARAN

"David and Sharon have given us a profound gift in this very readable, tangible road map that provides a means to experience our own unlimited potential, our true selves. It also allows us to see god, even if just a glimpse. May all beings go on to experience these gifts, and apply them to every facet of their lives. God bless."

—MIKE D
Beastie Boys

more . . .

"If you're not fortunate enough to study with David and Sharon, here's perhaps the next best thing. A book filled with their personal reflections and philosophy. The knowledge expressed in this book instructs and inspires."

—Willem Dafoe

"Sharon and David make a great gift with this book; they open up the world of yoga in a personal and down-to-earth way that makes it live for today, while bravely sharing their holistic vision of yoga as transforming union with absolutely everything, bringing together body, mind, loving spirit, society, all beings, the divine, and the divinely human."

—Robert A. Thurman

Author of *Inner Revolution*

Translator of *The Tibetan Book of the Dead*

"Purifying, liberating, uplifting: the gentlest, most knowing guide from two most gentle, knowing gurus. They clear away all the tangly bits from the path to pure joy. Can you imagine: enlightenment made easy for anyone who wishes to discover the best in themselves and the hidden happiness in life!"

—Ingrid Newkirk

Cofounder and president of People for the Ethical Treatment of Animals (PETA)

"This wonderful book, the Jivamukti method for the ancient art of yoga, is the next step in an authentic and living lineage, from two great teachers who really care about their tradition and—most important—about their students."

—Geshe Michael Roach

Director of the Asian Classics Institute

Author of *The Garden* and *The Diamond Cutter*

"*Jivamukti Yoga* is a treasure-house of insights and information that can be of great help to anyone seriously following a yogic path."

—John Robbins

Author of *Diet for a New America* and *The Food Revolution*

"David and Sharon aim to teach yoga for liberation, in all ways, and this book is their manifesto for liberating yoga from the fetters of the humdrum, the predictable, the conventional."

—Dr. Robert E. Svoboda

Leading Ayurvedic scholar and bestselling author of *Ayurveda: Life, Health and Longevity*

JIVAMUKTI YOGA

Also by Sharon Gannon and David Life

Cats and Dogs Are People Too!
The Art of Yoga

JIVAMUKTI YOGA

SHARON GANNON AND DAVID LIFE

Ballantine Books
New York

A Ballantine Book
Published by The Ballantine Publishing Group

Published in the United States by The Ballantine Publishing Group, a division of Random House, Inc., New York, and simultaneously in Canada by Random House of Canada Limited, Toronto.

Grateful acknowledgment is made to the following for permission to reprint previously published material:

Alternative Tentacles Records: excerpt from "Baghdad Stomp," False Prophets. © 1986 Not for Prophed Music. Alternative Tentacles Release.

Baba Bhagavandas Publication Trust: excerpts from THE TEXTBOOK OF YOGA PSYCHOLOGY by Ramamurti S. Mishra, M.D. (Shri Brahmananda Sarasvati), pages 409 and 205, Baba Bhagavandas Publication Trust (Monroe, New York). First published by Julian Press (New York, 1963); TERRESTIAL & CELESTIAL MAGNETISM by Shri Brahmananda Sarasvati (Ramamurti S. Mishra, M.D.), pages 4–5, Baba Bhagavandas Publication Trust (Monroe, New York, 1996); NADA YOGA by Shri Brahmananda Sarasvati (Ramamurti S. Mishra, M.D.), pages 16–17, George Leone Publication Center, Ananda Ashram (Monroe, New York, 1989).

EMI Music Publishing/Magnetic Music: excerpt from "Fragile" music and lyrics by Sting. © GM Sumner (1987), published by EMI Music/Magnetic Music.

Jowcol Music & US Copyrights: excerpt from liner notes for *A Love Supreme* by John Coltrane. Reprinted by permission of Jowcol Music & US Copyrights.

Meta Records: excerpt from H.H. the 14th Dalai Lama's quote from the liner notes of *Life-Space-Death*, Meta Records 2001.

Roderick Romero: excerpt from the lyrics of "Chickaboom Cocktail," *Seeds,* Collective Fruit, by Sky Cries Mary. Reprinted by permission of Roderick Romero.

Triloka Records: excerpt from the liner notes of *One Track Heart*, Krishna Das, Triloka Records, 1996; Live on Earth, Krishna Das, Triloka Records, 1999;

www.ballantinebooks.com

Library of Congress Catalog Card Number: 2002090184

ISBN 0-345-44208-3

Cover design by Min Choi
Cover photo by Martin Brading

Manufactured in the United States of America

First Edition: April 2002

10 9 8 7 6 5 4 3 2

Book design by H. Roberts Design

To all Jivamukti students
past, present, and future

Contents

Foreword

T*he middle of the night, somewhere over the north Pacific in the back of a DC-10 at 35,000 feet . . .*

The plane is empty but for my band, the crew, and me—forty tired guys sleeping off too many working nights in a row. Each night a different city, sometimes a different country or even a different continent. None of us has slept in our own bed for months, but nine hours in a DC-10 is as good a place as any to catch up on some sleep.

Only I'm not sleeping. While my crew and bandmates are snoring and dreaming of home, I'm standing on my head between the bulkhead and the empty economy section.

The stewardesses have been giving me strange looks since I began my yoga practice an hour ago. Now, don't get me wrong, I'm as tired as everybody else is. But when I saw that space on the floor, I knew how I wanted to use my time. I wanted to practice yoga.

I can see the full moon out of the little window. I feel the vibrations of the engines through the floor from my head up to my feet. It sounds like OM to the power of six thousand horses. I'm vibrating with it upside down with an inverted smile on my face. This is truly flying.

They say when the pupil is ready, the teacher will appear. My yoga journey began in 1990. My first teacher, Danny, walked into my studio in London and asked if I wanted to learn about yoga. I had no idea what yoga was but I was intrigued enough to ask him to show me. Which he did. I was impressed by both his quiet confidence and the strength and flexibility that he demonstrated. I was even more impressed after I had tried to emulate some of his movements.

I had always thought myself as fit. My job demands it. I was an athlete when I was younger and ran every day. But could I bend forward and lay my palms on the floor with straight legs? No way. Nor could I complete a simple sun salutation without huffing and puffing like an old train. This teacher's breath had been smooth and effortless. I asked him to come to my house the next day and teach me.

Not so coincidentally, my house in London used to belong to Yehudi Menuhin, the violin maestro. It was Mr. Menuhin who first brought Mr. B.K.S. Iyengar to London in the 1950s to teach yoga. The garden where they practiced daily overlooks a vast park with huge old trees. Menuhin even wrote the foreword to Mr. Iyengar's book *Light on Yoga* in 1966.

I feel blessed to practice in that house and partake of the accumulated *sadhana*, and of their knowledge of and dedication to yoga. I'd like to think that some of their dedication has rubbed off on me, as I have now been practicing yoga six days a week for ten years. And I believe that yoga has provided me with energy and focus that I would not have possessed otherwise.

My work as a performer is physically demanding, and my work as a songwriter challenges my imagination. Yoga practice has enhanced my capacity in both areas. My duties as a husband and a father, as well as my ability to deal with other relationships, have all been enhanced by a yoga practice that has become inextricably bound to every aspect of my life.

Through yoga practice I've sought to know my Self and have managed to gain a number of insights. For example, I now *feel* that my body carries within it a holographically complete record of everything it has experienced in fifty years. My fears, my prejudices, and my doubts are all somehow reflected in the structure and musculature of my body. Where it is closed and unyielding, resistant to change, I find that I am holding fast to emotional wounds suffered in the past. When I am confident, fearless, and open, this, too, is reflected in the ease with which my body moves.

My yoga practice has given me tools for facing and processing aspects of the unconscious that otherwise could remain hidden and frustrating for a lifetime. It has been a task in my practice of yoga to feel the unlimited aspects of Self as well as to explore and challenge the physical aspects—both pleasant and painful.

This challenge is emotional, intellectual, psychological, physical, and spiritual. I feel that there is an interpenetration between the mind, the body, and the spirit of God within. What I think about affects the subtle bodies as well as the physical body, and, in turn, the physical functioning affects mind, emotion, intellect, and what I call soul. There is no separation. This I have learned.

We have entered a new millennium and I'm happy to be called on to express my strong belief in the Jivamukti Yoga method. In his book, Iyengar brilliantly enumerated the minutiae of expressions of the body, mind, and breath. In this book, David and Sharon reconstruct the flowing dance of life in both outer and inner yoga practices. They have been friends and teachers to Trudie and me for many years now. David and Sharon have inspired and encouraged us to think of yoga not just as a system of exercises but also as a door to the infinite. The book you are holding in your hand is a result of a lifetime of experience, knowledge, and passion and is a manual for living that is deeply meaningful and profound. It is a royal gift to the world.

I feel a subtle change in the vibration of the airplane. We are starting our descent as the first light of day pierces the eastern horizon. The lights of New Orleans sparkle below us and I give thanks for the new day. I give thanks for my teachers and their lineage. I give thanks for all of those who will read this book and continue their journey to Self-knowing and Bliss.

Namaste,
Sting

From left to right: Sting, Sharon, David practicing yoga in Jaipur, India, 1998.
Photographer: Martin Brading

Introduction: Putting It All Together

It's kind of fun to do the impossible.
—Walt Disney

It is said that two people cannot satisfy their thirsts from the same fountain and have a different taste in their mouths. There is only one yoga, even though there are many brand names for it. Some "brands" of yoga are based on breaking apart the various yoga practices, such as *asana* (postures) and *pranayama* (breath restriction), and studying them individually. This can help the beginning practitioner build a sound foundation. But if our practices are only deconstructed, how will the joining of the mortal and finite small self to the eternal and infinite Self that is the true aim of yoga take place?

Jivamukti Yoga is our brand name, but our method is not based on deconstructing the yoga practices. Jivamukti Yoga is our attempt to reintegrate the physical, psychological, and spiritual aspects of yoga for Western practitioners. We are dedicated to teaching yoga as a spiritual practice, and to reminding our students that they are committing themselves to a demanding mystical journey toward enlightenment. We have created a yoga method that provides direction for this journey.

When you were a child, perhaps you took apart a clock or a radio, or some other mechanical device. You probably soon realized that it was easier to take it apart than to put it back together again! In general, taking things apart is easier than putting them back together—but you don't *really* know how something works until you can put it back together. In this book we are going to put yoga practices back together that were taken apart (some were even discarded) by curious Americans when yoga was first brought to the United States.

Swami Vivekananda introduced yoga to the West in 1893 at the World Parliament of Religions in Chicago. He described practices developed thousands of years ago by sages called *rishis* who were seeking to experience a blissful state they called "Yoga," meaning union with God. The practices they developed helped them experience Yoga by shifting identification from body and mind toward the Divine or Cosmic eternal Self. (The identification with body and mind is called "ego," and constitutes the small self.)

The rishis were seeking Self-realization, which is also called God-realization, enlightenment, *samadhi,* or bliss. They wanted to put themselves back together.

Although many great Indian teachers visited the United States after Swami Vivekananda, they found it difficult to communicate the full physical, psychological, and spiritual scope of yoga to a culture in which the existence of God was a debatable subject. Some of the yoga practices did take hold, though. The practice of asana postures, for example, was accepted as a useful exercise program that could increase flexibility and mobility, rehabilitate injuries, and encourage weight loss. Meditation was promoted as a stress-reduction technique. But the true aim of yoga was glossed over.

Spiritually, we Americans were children when the yogis came to show us their practices, and, like children, we took them apart to examine them. In doing so we discovered some useful exercises that can improve one's quality of life. But studying yoga as disparate useful exercises is rather like taking a camera apart and wondering why the disassembled parts aren't enabling you to take a picture.

We hope to encourage you to move beyond studying the various interesting shapes and attributes of the yoga practices and start fitting them back together. After all, the aim of yoga is not a better body or a calmer mind, even though the practices may improve your body or calm your mind. The aim is enlightenment, the state in which everything fits together.

From our earliest classes, we have tried to teach a living translation of the Indian system of yoga that Western minds like ours can comprehend. It is this translation that we have set down in this book. That is why you'll find chapters here about asana and meditation, as well as chapters about equally important practices like *ahimsa* (nonviolence) and *bhakti* (devotion). Don't be concerned if you are not familiar with these Sanskrit words, because by the time you finish this book, you will understand them and many others. (This book includes a comprehensive glossary. Words, except for proper nouns, included in the glossary are italicized the first time they appear in the book.) You will also become familiar with the great range of inner and outer yoga practices that the rishis developed to help us reach the state of Yoga, or union with the Divine Self.

The chapters on asana don't focus on teaching individual asanas—plenty of books already exist that do. Instead, we teach *vinyasa krama*, the art of sequencing asana postures. Asana sequences are illustrated with photos and integrated into classes you can practice on your own, beginning in Chapter 6, "Prana: Freeing the Life Force." This book also gives instruction for specific techniques for pranayama (breath restriction), *kriya* (purification), and meditation. We do recommend, however, that you study concomitantly with a qualified yoga teacher.

We became teachers because we were driven to communicate something extraordinary about human potential. Our passion is to teach yoga as a spiritual practice. We are both artists, so we believe that teaching can be an inspired, creative act. The creative desire to lift people out of the mundane that first inspired us as artists became the foundation of the Jivamukti Yoga method.

When our informal classes had outgrown a friend's apartment on Avenue B in Manhattan's East Village, we decided to open the Jivamukti Yoga Center in 1989. We chose the name Jivamukti (pronounced Jee-va-mook-tee) Yoga to reflect the true aim of yoga, which is liberation.

Jiva means individual soul and *mukti* means liberation. The exact transliteration of the Sanskrit word from which we derived Jivamukti is *jivanmuktih*, which means liberation *while* living. The name Jivamukti Yoga reflects the fact that it is possible to have a beneficial and fulfilling life in the world, and also progress spiritually—perhaps even attaining liberation (samadhi) while living.

Yoga provides practices for the body and mind that can liberate the individual soul. Yoga frees the soul to merge with God and realize that it is not separate from any other thing. Yet even in modern India, as we discovered on our extensive travels there, yoga is rarely practiced with liberation as its goal. Most modern Indians consider yoga merely a collection of exercises for increasing flexibility and losing weight. You

Jiva, the individual soul, is bound by *maya*, the world of forms, phenomena, and time. The experience of jiva is the experience of birth, growth, and death. You were born, you are now growing and changing, and one day you will die. Birth and death are for the physical body. After death the individual soul is free from its present physical body and will pick up another one, according to its *karma*. This process of birth, growth, and death is called *samsara*. Samsara is the wheel of life and death. Samsara means suffering the condition of individualization. Samsara goes on and on until liberation. What is liberation? It is when the jiva realizes that it is not individual, but that it is Absolute. With enlightenment there is automatic liberation from all karma. The jivanmukta is freed from all past, present, and future karma—all actions from beginningless time are dissolved.

cannot journey to India, as some students have assumed, to find the "original Jivamukti Yoga Center."

We, on the other hand, have believed from the beginning that liberation is the *only* reason to practice yoga! By immersing ourselves in the ancient scriptures that form yoga's philosophical foundation, and through meditation, contemplation, and the encouragement of the great teachers we were blessed to meet, we have been graced with insights that have enabled us to create a yoga method that combines contemplation of the yogic scriptures and meditation with a challenging Hatha Yoga practice.

Perhaps because we are musicians, we also believed from the start that music could play an invaluable role in a yoga method dedicated to enlightenment. That's why we play uplifting music during asana practice and teach our students to sing Sanskrit chants.

Jivamukti Yoga is also our attempt to offer a form of ethical social activism. This activism is not aimed at overthrowing existing governments or even critiquing them. Jivamukti Yoga is the practice of internal revolution, of liberating the only prisoner you can really free: your soul.

Yoga philosophy states that liberation and happiness are available to each being, regardless of species, race, sex, or religion. Deep inside, we all instinctively realize this, but this realization is typically obscured by our thoughts, which tend to argue otherwise. The aim of yoga, therefore, is not to change the world but to change our minds. That is a more profoundly political act than overthrowing any government.

Some people will say that they don't want to be political. Well, you can't help but be political. Every action, every choice you make affects us all. To say that you are political is to say that you care about the world we all live in. Caring for others will bring you closer to liberation sooner than anything else will. And yoga provides a wonderful template for responsible action.

Will there be a movement of cool heroism in America? Will we be able to produce and support such leaders here? If so, could he or she win power? What would be the campaign strategy in line with the politics of enlightenment? How do we as individuals develop cool heroism ourselves? How do we engage in the politics of enlightenment on the day to day level?

—***Professor Robert Thurman,* Inner Revolution**[1]

The yoga practices use the body and mind as tools for liberation because these hold clues to all the mysteries of the universe. But why do you want to change your body and your mind? What are your motives? As Krishna the chariot driver tells Arjuna the prince in the ancient yogic text, the *Bhagavad Gita*, we must act perfectly and devote the fruit of our actions to God. This means that our actions must not be selfish or self-absorbed, because most of the world's problems stem from selfishness.

When we relinquish selfishness as our motivating principle, the potential for true happiness opens up. From compassion toward others you will realize happiness for yourself. Through service to all beings you will experience the bliss of the end of suffering for yourself.

Replace the question "What will yoga do for me?" with "How may I serve thee, Lord?" Let love be your guide. When you love what you do, the means to do it will be revealed to you.

The practices of yoga are ethically sound. They enhance the physical body, refine the emotions, challenge the intellect, and reveal the soul. As long as your primary motivation is concerned with what yoga can do for you, however, your suffering will continue unabated and your yoga practice will be binding, not liberating.

Yoga practices clean the mind. The dirt that is cleaned away is the dirt of *avidya*—ignorance of your true identity, which is the Divine Self. In this way, yoga helps us bridge the separation between our individual souls and their Divine Source. It helps us trace our way backward from where we are now to where we came from.

The Greek word *apocalypse* means to uncover, to reveal. The result of yoga practice is enlightenment, which is an apocalyptic event. Enlightenment is the uncovering of the self that reveals *Atman*, the I-Am, the God in you.

Jivamukti Yoga is not a passive practice. The life of the *jivanmukta* is not normal. A normal life is one spent trying to avoid pain and seek pleasure. The jivanmukta, on the other hand, experiences pain and pleasure with equanimity, understanding that everything we experience is the karmic result of past actions. The jivanmukta realizes that even though the past cannot be undone, he or she can affect the future by what he or she does here and now. The jivanmukta never loses sight of joy as the goal.

We hope that you will use Jivamukti Yoga to progress toward liberation. We want to foster independent practitioners who are curious and excited and who are not looking for someone to stroke them and control their lives. The method of yoga is practical. The proof of the method is in its results. You can test it for yourself. We encourage you to read scriptures that form yoga's philosophical base, such as Patanjali's *Yoga Sutras* and the *Hatha Yoga Pradipika*, and form your own opinions.

If you reflect on the texts, you will start having your own insights. They will come to you in magical little explosions that will feel like things you've always known but didn't know how to express.

Consciousness is chemical. Physiologically speaking, all the yoga practices lay the groundwork for such insights to occur by stimulating the endocrine glands, altering the brain chemistry, and helping you develop psychokinetic skills that promote contemplation. But the longing for liberation that you will uncover was always within you.

From joy all beings have come, by joy they all live, and unto joy they all return.
—Taittiriya Upanishad[2]

Part 1

What Is Yoga?

Introduction

Yoga Is Your True Nature: Union with the Divine Self

The Sanskrit word *yoga* is derived from the root *yuj*, which means to yoke. The yoga practitioner seeks to yoke his or her individual soul with cosmic consciousness.

When oxen are yoked they are still separated, held slightly apart, but they walk in the same direction, on the same path. The various yoga practices are like the yoking mechanism: they put you on the path, and direct you as you walk toward God. They make you available for the possibility that you might experience a graceful dissolution of the yoke and the merger with the Divine called samadhi.

In a sense, this is what we request when we say this prayer: "Not my will, but Thy will, be done." We are requesting that the yoke be put around our necks. We are seeking to merge our own will with that of the higher Self, which is the Divine. We are attempting, through these practices that have been developed over thousands of years, to yoke our individual experiences as small selves with the Source of our being, so that we can overcome the illusion of separateness from that Source.

The teachings of yoga are Self-revealed and prehistoric. No one invented union with the Divine; in fact, Patanjali, who compiled the Yoga Sutras over five thousand years ago, wrote that these teachings are available in the natural world around us. We can observe them ourselves if we are willing to look with the detachment of a sage. We can experience them through the yoga practices.

Yoga practices such as asana enable us to *feel* that there's something animating our physical form. Yoga practices such as meditation enable us to watch our minds think, to realize that we must be more than the mind, if we can sit back and watch it generate thoughts. This is the power of these practices: they show, rather than tell, us who we really are. When you feel the pulsation of the life force during asana practice, you can begin to let go of your identification with your physical body. When you can watch your mind, your identification with it will begin to subside. All yoga practices enable us to feel that there is something animating our physical form and to watch our minds at work and realize that we must be more than the body and mind.

Yoga practices help us to achieve spiritual understanding and to integrate that understanding into daily life. Sometimes people confuse yoga practices with various New Age methods of integrating body and mind in pursuit of "health." Although these methods can improve health, the body and mind represent only a portion of the five bodies—physical, vital, emotional, intellectual, and bliss—that yoga practices integrate. Your idea of what is possible limits your possibilities. Why settle for just physical results when you could have Cosmic Consciousness? Why settle for a banana when you could have nirvana?

"I'm interested in the mind-body connection," a reporter once told us.

"The mind and body are intimately connected," we replied. "They were both born, and both will die."

What will not die is the soul, the spiritual Self, which is beyond body and mind, beyond personality, beyond ego. Our goal as yoga practitioners is to free ourselves from selfishness and strengthen our connection to this Self. Yoga is the joining of the separate self with the universal Self; it is a process of synthesis.

Most people are not truly interested in disturbing the illusion of separation between the small self and the universal Self. It can be frightening to contemplate the dissolution of your personality, of your ego, of yourself. Our culture provides us with so many tools we can use to further that separation. We can use analysis, language, religion, science, and even yoga practice to strengthen our small selves.

We Westerners are very attracted to breaking things apart. We have this notion that doing so will yield "the truth." This approach can have a negative effect on our yoga practice, however. It can tempt us to divide the asanas into the ones we like and the ones we don't like. Or to separate our good days from our bad days, and practice only on our good days. The true goal of yoga practice, however, is *to perceive the sameness in all, simultaneously with our experience of all differences.*

We also have a habit in this culture of giving less credibility to the unseen than the seen. Yet we are all profoundly affected by the unseen all the time. We suffer from anxiety, sadness, depression, despair, and confusion, for example. The practices of yoga equip us with tools for transcending this suffering—and for transcending our moments of happiness, too. Even moments of elation, contentment, and joy carry the future pain of their termination, after all.

The practices of yoga will help you maintain equanimity in all situations by teaching you to become transparent, able to allow both joy and sorrow to flow through you without destroying your peace of mind.

No one can "do yoga." Yoga means union with God. Yoga means *eternal* happiness, bliss, joy, and unconditional love. Yoga is who you are. It is your natural state. What we *can* do are practices that, by revealing to us our resistance to existing in our natural state, may lead us to it. But the intention underlying all our practices must be clear. The motivation underlying the yoga practices must be Yoga, union with the Divine Self. For any practice to be a yoga practice, one must consciously and continuously cultivate a desire for Self-realization. When we experience Yoga, we experience freedom from suffering and pain here and now, freedom that does not end.

Where are you, but here and now?
—Sky Cries Mary, "Chickaboom Cocktail"

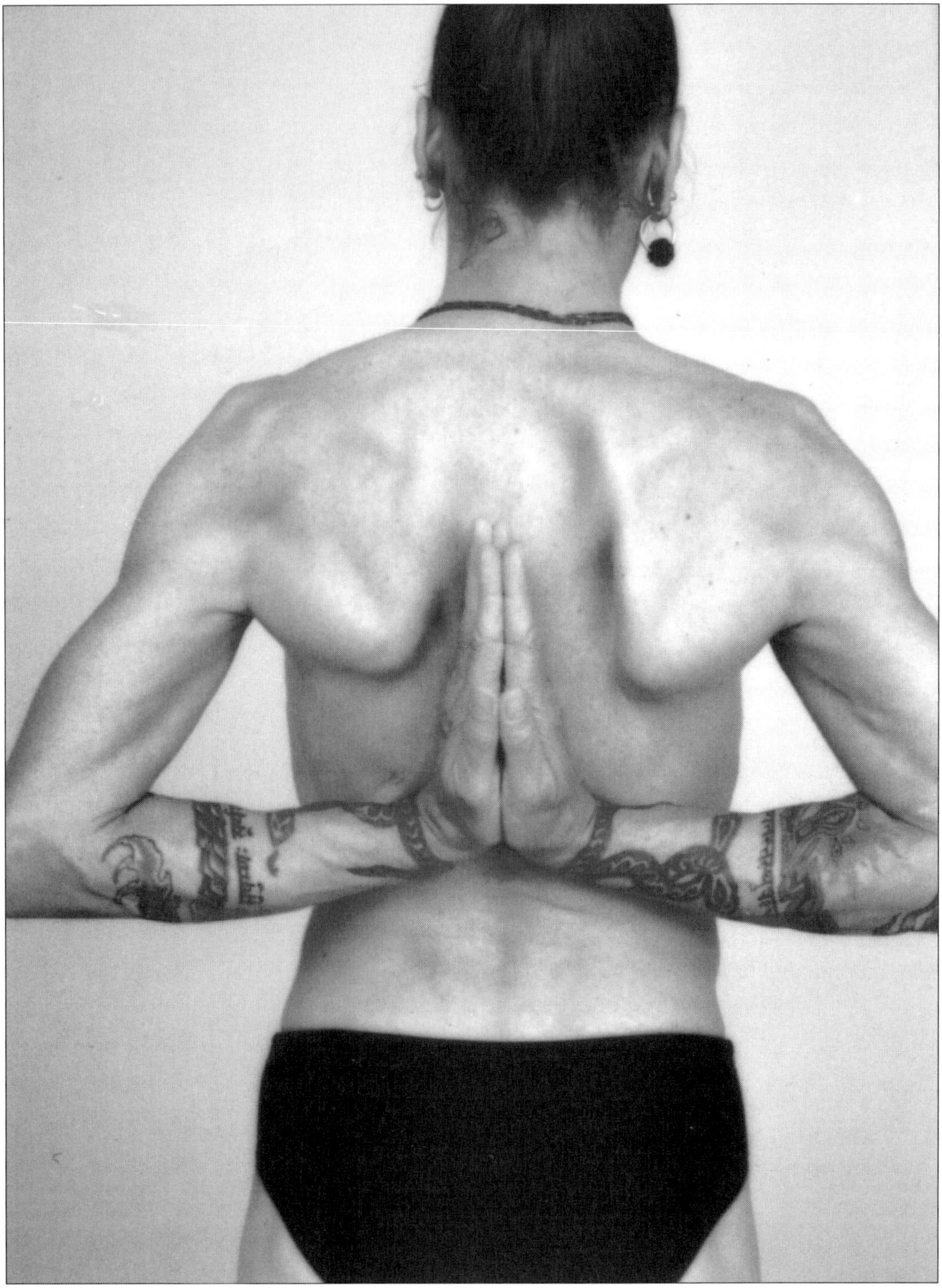

1

Jivamukti Yoga: Putting Yoga Together in the West

The jivanmukta is not transformed by pleasure or pain.
Joy does not exalt the mukta, nor is the mukta depressed by pain.
The jivanmukta no longer regards the world as real. . . .
The jivanmukta is pure like akasha. . . .
The jivanmukta is neither subject to attachment, nor to egoism.
The jivanmukta does not fear the world,
Nor does the world fear the jivanmukta
The jivanmukta is at peace with the ways of the world.
The mukta is free from worldly-mindedness . . .
Finally, the jivanmukta maintains a cool head.

—*Vidyaranya,* The Jivan-Mukti-Viveka

Jivamukti Yoga incorporates traditional yoga practices into a modern lifestyle without losing sight of the ancient, universal goal of liberation. We believe that liberation is possible even while living a modern urban lifestyle anywhere in the world. We believe that the ancient teachings and techniques of yoga, as laid out in Patanjali's *Yoga Sutras*, the *Bhagavad Gita*, and the

Hatha Yoga Pradipika, are as valid and exciting today as they were over five thousand years ago.

If you explore yoga yourself by reading the texts, chanting, practicing asanas, and meditating, you will begin to feel that it's not foreign or separate from you. It is not *not* of you or of your culture. You do not have to be Hindu to read the scriptures or practice yoga, although familiarity with Hinduism and the history of Indian philosophy is certainly helpful.

Hinduism is a religion, based on a way of life called *Sanatana Dharma*, or the Universal Way. It includes four pillars: (1) vegetarianism, (2) an acknowledgment of the law of karma (the law of cause and effect), (3) a belief in reincarnation, and (4) a belief in the possibility of *moksha*, or liberation from all forms of suffering. True Hinduism incorporates all religions, because it recognizes that if you have a way that works for you, it is valid—it comes under the umbrella of the Universal Way. Certainly there are many religious, racial, and class divisions in India, but what we came away with from our travels there was this essence of universality.

Yoga is not a religion; it is a school of practical philosophy. Yoga practices, however, are inextricably linked to the development of both Hinduism and the philosophical schools, including Yoga, Vedanta, Samkhya, Jainism, and Buddhism, which developed in ancient India. Their codevelopment in the modern era has commonality in language, myth, root teachings, practices, and beliefs.

When we began teaching yoga, we set ourselves this challenge: to relate the ancient teachings to modern experience without dumbing down the yoga practices or sacrificing their original aim, which was always and only to experience union with the Divine Self. We also asked ourselves: Is there anything in our own culture that could help us in our quest for enlightenment? Let's look at the lyrics in the Beatles' music; let's listen to what Van Morrison is singing about; let's be inspired by the fusion of Eastern and Western influences in the music of John Coltrane and Bill Laswell. What about the essential, idealist nature of the United States? Freedom, liberation through unity in diversity—that's what the Founding Fathers were all about. Teaching yoga based on ancient Indian scriptures to New Yorkers began to seem not only possible, but exciting.

Purusha [pure spirit] without Prakriti [nature] is lame, Prakriti without Purusha is blind.

—*Ishvarakrishna,* Samkhyakarika[1]

We had both been drawn to the East Village by our artistic pursuits. Along the way, we had inadvertently crossed paths with each other and with some of our greatest future influences.

In the late 1970s, a Seattle radio station broadcast a serial drama produced by Meatball Fulton called *The Fourth Tower of Inverness*, which used recordings of Bhagavan Das singing Sanskrit names for God. This singing captivated Sharon, who was at that time a busy dancer and musician with a strong interest in Indian philosophy. She had a feeling that she would meet Bhagavan Das some day.

David, meanwhile, was traveling around the country with his portfolio of drawings, trying on cities. As his old Chevy Suburban slid into Seattle he caught the last few minutes of *The Fourth Tower of Inverness*. Seattle didn't grab him, so he headed toward San Francisco. San Francisco, L.A., Palm Springs, Portland, Houston, Austin, New Orleans . . . eventually David limped back to Michigan with a broken trailer filled with soapstone and serpentine rock. A friend invited him to New York City. It didn't take long for him to see that it was the city he had been searching for.

David moved into a dilapidated storefront on 10th Street and Avenue B. The neighborhood's cheap rents were a by-product of rampant drug dealing. To cover holes in his walls, David wheat-pasted covers from old *Life* magazines over them. He opened the Life Café in 1980.

Back in Seattle, Sharon was dancing, reading poetry, and playing violin and singing for the band Audio Letter. At a sound check she slipped and fell hard on her lower spine. By the time the band left to perform at Life Café in New York, Sharon was in terrible pain.

A New York gig meant a lot, though, and the Life Café audience seemed to really enjoy the show. Afterward, Sharon sat near the piano with a cup of tea. She grimaced as pain shot through her back. Tara, a waitress, noticed and was concerned, so Sharon explained that she had fallen months before and was still in pain. Tara, who also taught a yoga class, said that maybe yoga could help. Sharon had always been curious about yoga; she had studied classical Indian dance and philosophy while earning her dance degree from the University of Washington.

David, meanwhile, was pleasantly surprised by Audio Letter. Sharon's lyrics, some in Sanskrit, were like mystical riddles: "Freedom is a psychokinetic skill." When Sharon and the guitar player, Sue Ann Harkey, moved to New York, David began playing with Audio Letter, too.

Soon neighborhood jazz musicians such as drummer Denis Charles and trumpeter Don Cherry began showing up to jam at Sharon and Sue Ann's apartment on East 7th Street. Charles and Cherry played on Audio Letter's 1988 album, *It Is This, It Is Not This.*

Sharon was still in a lot of pain though. When she went to a doctor, he diagnosed a broken vertebra and recommended surgery to fuse it. Tara gently urged Sharon to try yoga, explaining that yoga had helped her regain mobility after she had broken her pelvis in a car accident. Sharon was afraid at first, because the yoga postures were painful for her, but she trusted Tara, who was a very sensitive teacher.

Yoga's mysticism intrigued David, too, and, at thirty-four, he wanted to stave off the aches and pains of growing older. As he investigated yoga he realized that it was a physically challenging, deeply mystical practice with an intellectually advanced philosophical base.

Sharon and David tried different yoga teachers in New York but were frustrated with the focus on physical exercise and the exclusion of the spiritual and philosophical aspects of yoga. Meanwhile, they had begun incorporating asana, pranayama, and yogic teachings into dance and musical performances, which they performed everywhere, from vacant lots in the East Village to downtown clubs. They actually began teaching the audience Sanksrit chants and simple asanas.

David and Sharon performing, New York City, 1985.
Photographer: Sue Ann Harkey

Knowing that Sharon and David practiced yoga, friends in the audience began asking them to teach. Sharon and David brought the same elements from their performances into the yoga classes they began teaching: music, Sanskrit, yogic scriptures, and an open desire to connect with the sacred.

Feeling that they needed to learn more if they were really going to teach, Sharon and David decided to go to India.

We spent four months in India in 1986, earning teaching certificates the first month from the Sivananda organization. We were both excited about the ancient texts, like Patanjali's *Yoga Sutras*, which seemed to us to be vibrating with meaning for modern life.

After leaving the Sivananda program we traveled north on an overnight train to visit Swami Nirmalanda, "the Anarchist Swami." Sharon had been corresponding with him from New York. He and other amazing teachers we met in India encouraged us to pursue our vision of a modern yoga method based on the ancient traditions. Above all, they confirmed our growing sense that a yoga based on India's ancient scriptures could bring spiritual substance into the Western lifestyle of shallow materiality.

We opened the first Jivamukti Yoga Center in a creative hot spot, in Manhattan on 2nd Avenue and 9th Street (down the street from Saint Mark's Church, where great neighborhood poets like Allen Ginsberg read). We were inspired not only by our teachers in India but also by our friends, the tattooed, pierced, blue- and green-haired nonconformist artists, poets, and musicians who lived in our neighborhood. We remembered how the Beatles had come back from India and made the colors, sights, and sounds of India so hip that they had soaked into Western culture. We wanted to create a place that would turn everyone on like that to the richness of yoga.

During the 1970s, the writer Ken Kesey journeyed to Egypt. He reported back to America via installments in *Rolling Stone* magazine describing his trip and his investigation into the Egyptian mysteries. In the last installment, Kesey reported that the ancient Egyptian teachings were alive and well, due to the disinterest of modern Egyptians.

What didn't turn us on were the white walls and potted plants of the other yoga centers we visited in New York. So we painted the walls all kinds of beautiful colors, put up pictures of Indian deities, and rolled out huge Oriental rugs on the floor. We hung pictures of our inspirations and gurus over the altars, everyone from Swami Sivananda to our first teacher, Tara, to Saint Teresa of Avila and Glinda the Good Witch. And we played all kinds of spiritually uplifting music, from Bhagavan Das to Van Morrison to the Indian-jazz fusion of Bill Laswell.

Some people might consider it heresy to have Mother Mary share an altar with Hindu deities. Well, yoga was a heresy from the start because it put power into the hands of the people, not priests. Yoga philosophy says: You are the direct line to God. At Jivamukti we carry this idea further; we seek to diminish the divisions between religions by looking for their essential commonality. For example, you can find the essential nature of the Goddess in Mother Mary, Glinda the Good Witch, Isis, and the Hindu goddess Laxmi. They all represent her bountiful, merciful force.

When we started the Center we went to some meetings with other yoga teachers and, to be honest, they thought we were a little silly. They said things like, "Oh you're going to go bankrupt within a year. You can't put up those pictures from India. You can't paint the walls all those weird colors." And they warned us, above all, "You can't talk about God."

We saw, both in New York and in India, yoga teachers who were very concerned with keeping their students for financial and egocentric reasons, sometimes even prohibiting their students from studying elsewhere. In India we saw classes filled with small talk and gossip and tea breaks. We saw teachers of yoga classes for children beat their students with sticks. Few teachers based their classes on the yogic scriptures. In the States, the teachers either weren't aware of the scriptures or didn't find them relevant, and in India, many teachers considered them archaic.

We based our classes on the great ancient Indian scriptures—the *Upanishads*, the *Bhagavad Gita*, Patanjali's *Yoga Sutras*, and the *Hatha Yoga Pradipika*—because we found them genuinely exciting. We hosted many teachers and speakers from other schools of yoga and encouraged our students to educate themselves. We decided that we would teach for as long as people wanted to come.

To our surprise, within the year Jivamukti became a very popular yoga center. Teachers at other yoga centers were surprised, too, and became curious about us.

One teacher from another yoga center called to ask if we were going to close over the summer. We didn't have air-conditioning because we didn't have money to invest in a system, and India is very hot, after all. We told her that we weren't going to close. And she said, "Well, doesn't attendance drop during the hot months?" No, we said, actually July was our biggest month so far this year.

"Well," she said, "You must have some really expensive and up-to-date air-conditioning system over there. Could I ask what system?"

"We don't have air-conditioning," we told her.

There was a long pause and then she said, "Well, what do you do?"

And Sharon said, "Well, we start by chanting *Om*."

* * *

At the time, chanting Om to begin a yoga class was considered pretty far out. To divorce yoga practice from its original cultural, spiritual, and philosophical context, however, is like removing the motor from a jet and expecting flight. The jet may still look sharp, and it can certainly roll down the runway, but flying will not be possible. Yogi Sri Krishnaprem described all spiritual paths as the shadows on the earth of the ones who have learned to fly. And we do want to fly! So, at Jivamukti, we start by chanting Om.

We believe that yoga teachings should be based on the yogic scriptures. Yoga teachers should be able to draw meaning from the original texts and apply them to modern life. We're up against a lot of resistance, unfortunately, because many yoga teachers have never even opened these important texts. Many don't believe that it's necessary to have knowledge of the scriptures or for yoga practices to have a devotional aspect in the West—because we aren't Hindus here. They feel a yoga practice can be body-oriented and still be completely beneficial. We disagree, which is why we chant Om at the beginning of class.

Another reason we chant Om is that it means absolutely no-thing. It doesn't belong to any religion or sect. It is too primal for that. Om comprises the three most basic sounds that a human being can make: Ah, Oooh, Mmm. This takes it out of the realm of the intellect. It is beyond thought so it means no-thing. It is liberating to start a practice with the experiential acknowledgment that one can go beyond thought.

A Jivamukti Yoga class is physically challenging; it's about walking the razor's edge. Challenging your preconceptions about your abilities helps you push beyond the limitations imposed by your mind. In a Jivamukti Yoga class you will be encouraged to devote the fruits of this vigorous practice to God, in whatever form you feel comfortable acknowledging God.

The practices should be difficult enough to bring up resistances to your essential nature. Your essential nature is blissful, but when the teacher asks you to put your foot behind your head, you may resist your blissful nature in that moment and identify instead with the physical discomfort of tight hamstrings and your irritation with the request.

When such resistances are brought to light and observed with a detached mind, they are more easily shed. Most of us tend to identify with our problems. We identify with the struggles of the ego-personality, which has been convinced that happiness can be obtained from external sources. Yoga practices shift our identity away from the ego-personality and its struggles so that we can begin to reconnect with the essential nature of our being, which is bliss. We begin to understand that lasting happiness is inside us. We become independent: dependent inward.

If we practice the science of yoga, which is useful to the entire human community and which yields happiness both here and hereafter—if we practice it without fail, we will then attain physical, mental and spiritual happiness and our minds will flood toward the Self.

—*Shri K. Pattabhi Jois,* **Yoga Mala**[2]

In a Jivamukti Yoga class you will chant Om and sing Sanskrit prayers. You will be made aware of your breathing and learn pranayama techniques to control it. You may listen to the teacher read and discuss a passage from a yoga scripture. You will practice sequential asanas linked by breath and intention, and you will meditate. You will be encouraged to practice ahimsa (nonviolence), including vegetarianism. You will also be introduced to other inner and outer practices that may help you achieve the state of yoga, such as *satsang* (keeping good company), Kriya Yoga (purification practices), and Nada Yoga (the refinement of listening). And you'll hear some great music!

Although the emphasis in a Jivamukti class is on Hatha Yoga in its most elevated and esoteric form, five elements form the foundation of Jivamukti Yoga. These are:

1. Scripture

The sources for the teachings are ancient Sanskrit scriptures, notably:

- Patanjali's *Yoga Sutras* (the scripture that discusses how to overcome the mental obstacles to enlightenment).
- *Hatha Yoga Pradipika* (a technical manual on Hatha Yoga).
- *Bhagavad Gita* (Krishna's outline for the three paths to Yoga: Bhakti, devotion; Karma, service; Jnana, knowledge).
- *Upanishads* (the source scriptures that expound upon the nondualistic nature of God).

We also promote the study of the Sanskrit alphabet and grammar.

2. Bhakti (Devotion)

We recognize that God-realization is the goal of all yoga practices. To that end we:

- Encourage interreligious understanding and tolerance.

- Use altars, religious pictures, and iconography to create a devotional mood.
- Encourage the practice of *kirtan* (devotional chanting) and *japa* (repetition of the name of God).

3. Ahimsa (Nonviolence)

We recognize nonviolence as the primary ethic of yoga, so we promote:

- Ethical vegetarianism.
- Animal rights.
- Environmental and social activism.

4. Music

Nada Yoga is an essential component of Hatha Yoga. Music is used in a Jivamukti Yoga class to:

- Refine hearing through listening to uplifting, spiritually directed music during asana practice.
- Refine speech through kirtan (call-and-response singing).

5. Meditation

We encourage the practice and study of *meditation*. We feel strongly that without meditation, no attainment in yoga is possible. There is no point in practicing asana, for example, without also practicing meditation. It must be a part of every class or private practice session.

Our method differs from other approaches, in that we expect our students to include all these elements in every practice session and not, for instance, to practice asana separately from scriptural study, chanting, and meditation. We do this because the practice of asana creates biochemical changes that improve one's ability to reach a meditative state and gain insight into the scriptures. Just as it is important to move from alphabet recitation to sentence construction, so we hope our students move from attempting to stand on their heads to a liberating spiritual practice.

During one class we played "Across the Universe," a Beatles song in which the Sanskrit mantra *Jaya Gurudev* appears. After class an excited student ran into our office exclaiming, "Do you know that they are singing the same Sanskrit mantra that you taught us the other day?!"

She had been listening to that song for nearly thirty years and had never heard the mantra before. The class provided her with an experience conducive to a meditative state of receptivity in which she could hear things that were previously unavailable to her cognitive mind. In this way, art can fill the gap between the yogi in the Himalayan cave and the modern urban practitioner. There is no audience for this performance; there are only participants.

Originally, the shamanic role of the artist was to uplift people with authentic experiences of transcendence, to inspire them to move out of the mundane and toward the Divine. Today, however, we have become a mute audience: voyeurs rather than participants, consumers rather than creators. We collect, acquire, and hoard. With the growing popularity of yoga, it, too, could be reduced to a vacuous commodity. This is why we emphasize to our students that their practice must be grounded in humility and selflessness and a striving toward divinity.

I am often telling my artist friends that through my lectures I may reach a few hundred, a few thousand or a maximum of a hundred thousand people. But artists through music, painting or sculpture, whether it is a constructive message or destructive message, can reach millions. Therefore, artists can produce peace, love, compassion and harmony, which everybody wants, you see. Everybody is praying eagerly about that.

—His Holiness the Dalai Lama[3]

For us, creating Jivamukti Yoga was a natural continuation of our own artistic investigation into the mysteries of life. It was a way for us to share our findings with others who were also interested. At Jivamukti we use art, music, dance, and poetry, much as they were used during the "happenings" of the 1960s (minus the drugs!), to create an environment that inspires people to break out of their small selves and feel the Divine Self flowing through them. In this way, the world of appearances becomes a playground for deeper learning and a laboratory for the evolution of the immortal soul.

The *Upanishads* tell us that a liberated person views all with equanimity, seeing no difference between the mud puddle and the crystal lake, or the diamond and the dust. So, rather than reject our environment, we choose to view practicing yoga in New York City, with sirens blaring and people screaming, as the ultimate shortcut to liberation. This choice—to elevate the mundane toward the divine—is available to all of us wherever we live.

There are advantages to solitude, ashram life, and relating to nature, certainly, but we have never felt that New York City is not natural. After all, everything comes from Mother Nature. If you're attached to preferences—this is good, this is bad; this is natural, this is unnatural; this is clean, this is dirty—then you cannot know the truth. You're caught in the *chitta-vritti*, the fluctuations of the mind. That is what the mind is equipped to do: to separate this thing from that thing. Yoga practices teach us to go beyond the mind and perceive the cosmic consciousness that animates all beings.

Take from me all that is not free.
—Bhagavan Das, a chant to Kali Ma[4]

Most people fail to grasp that their own lives hold the keys to their happiness; instead, they tend to seek happiness elsewhere. There are many teachers in your life already, however, as this traditional chant to the guru, the remover of darkness, assures us:

Guru Brahma, Guru Vishnu, Guru Devo Maheshvara,
Guru Sakshat, Param Brahma, Tasmai Shri Guruvey Namaha

This chant is profound because it acknowledges that one's birth, present life situation, accidents, and illnesses are the keys to the doors of happiness. Let's look at it more closely.

> *Guru Brahma:* Brahma is the creator. Here, we appreciate and acknowledge our creation as a powerful Guru. Our birth and all its elements are potential aids for our enlightenment. The elements of our birth include our parents, the body they gave us and its genetic makeup, the conditions surrounding our delivery, and the procedures employed to assist our birth. The place we were born is also included: the country, the culture, the socioeconomic conditions, and so forth.
>
> By chanting Guru Brahma, we cover a lot of territory. For instance, how many of us are completely appreciative of our parents? Parental issues cause a lot of unhappiness. To appreciate and acknowledge truly the gift of life that came from our parents and our birth is a great step forward toward enlightenment.
>
> *Guru Vishnu:* Vishnu is the preserver. Vishnu represents the duration of our lives and all the experiences we accumulate as we live. Vishnu represents the present time, what we are going through right now. This includes our jobs,

our living situations and environments, and the people we live, work, and interact with each day. We appreciate and acknowledge our present lives as possessing the key to our enlightenment.

When you chant Guru Vishnu with sincerity, the way you view your everyday life will start to change. You will begin to perceive the magical qualities hidden in ordinary existence. You realize that everything and everyone can become your teacher, giving you clues to your blissful nature. It all begins by appreciating and acknowledging that this could happen. Even if your everyday experiences don't prove enlightening to you, is your ordinary life worse for the appreciation?

Guru Devo Maheshvara: Devo Maheshvara is another name for Shiva, the Destroyer. This is the transformational or revealing aspect of life, including all illnesses, tragedies, accidents, difficulties, and, ultimately, the death of the body. If you can appreciate and acknowledge Devo Maheshvara as Guru, then you are a very evolved soul. It takes spiritual maturity to embrace difficulties and to see within them potential for enlightenment. The greatest spiritual growth can come from appreciating difficult times in your life and facing them fully with an open heart.

Guru Sakshat: Sakshat means the guru that is nearby. Your teacher is your guru. How deep is your ability to appreciate and acknowledge your teacher? Ultimately, the Guru, the enlightening principle, is within ourselves. But until we can recognize that quality in another, we will never contact it within ourselves. The aim of yoga practices is to find a means to let the inner light of Self come through all the layers of personality and projection that confuse us. Having someone act as a mirror can help you see the divine Self within you. The outer teacher will help you to see where you are resisting your Self.

Param Brahma: This is the Guru that is indescribable and beyond all form.

Tasmai Shri Guruvey Namaha: This means "I offer all my efforts to the teacher." Without the effort of the student, no teaching can be obtained. I bow; I surrender all of my self to that Self. Not my will, but Thy will, be done. We surrender all of our efforts and practice, and the fruits of that practice, at the feet of our Guru.

All the gurus named in this chant are teachers always available to awaken you to who you really are—if you're willing to perceive them as such. This chant asks us to notice the people and situations in our own lives and appreciate them for giving us opportunities for Self-realization. You don't have to go anywhere or find anyone: it's all right there in your own life. Appreciating the modern relevance of this ancient Sanskrit chant is what Jivamukti Yoga is all about.

2

The Roots of Yoga . . . Back to the Source

If all the vast traditions of India's philosophies and literatures were to vanish and the Yoga-sutras of Patanjali alone were to be saved, each of those philosophies and literatures could in time be created again.

***—Pandit Usharbudh Arya,* Yoga Sutras of Patanjali**

The Sanskrit term yoga is found in the *Vedas*, the most ancient scripture known, prehistoric in origin. An Indian philosopher named Patanjali did not invent yoga, but he did write its manual, the *Yoga Sutras*, several thousand years ago.

Some Western proponents of yoga call it scientific, meaning that it is practical and systematic. Yoga swallows science, however, which is based on extension of the five senses only. The telescope and microscope are but extensions of the eye. Automobiles and rocket ships are extensions of the arms and legs. Computers are extensions of the brain. These scientific tools extend the reach of the senses, but are still restricted by the limitations of technology and materials, as well as by our ability to understand what we are shown.

Science helps us analyze the differences between things. Yoga, in contrast, seeks to join, not separate. The yoga practices are tools that enable us to have experiences beyond the limits of the five senses.

Yoga is the second most ancient of India's six philosophical systems, which are also referred to as *darshanas* or points of view and are considered complementary, rather than independent.

Grouped by their affinities, these six systems are Yoga and Samkhya (the oldest), Vaisesika and Nyaya, and Purva Mimamsa and Vedanta. Together with the highly refined philosophies of Buddhism and Jainism, these form the components of a complete Indian philosophy.

The founders of the six philosophical systems of India:

System	Exponent	Circa (Debatable)
Samkhya	Kapila	700–600? B.C.
Yoga	Patanjali	300? B.C.
Vedanta	Vyasa	200? B.C.
Nyaya	Gautama	150? B.C.
Vaisesika	Kanada	A.D. 200?
Purva Mimamsa	Jaimini	A.D. 200–250?

Yoga, Samkhya, and Vedanta deal primarily with the spiritual or metaphysical purpose of human existence. Purva Mimamsa is mostly limited to rituals that are considered preliminary means of ascending the spiritual ladder, and Vaisesika and Nyaya provide an analysis of the universe based mainly on empirical observations. Together, these six systems provide metaphysics, a religion, an explanation of ultimate and mundane reality, and a means of spiritual liberation. Yoga, because of its practical approach, links them together. The founders of all these systems were yogis.

Each founder codified his philosophical system in the form of succinct *sutras*, compact wisdom packages that students could learn by heart through an oral teaching tradition. The word sutra means "thread," and, like stitches in a garment, each sutra depends on the others.

Sutras are brief, seldom form a complete sentence, and are not ambiguous, yet the exactness of their meanings lies in layers. Here is an example from Patanjali's *Yoga Sutras*. (The notation YS I:23 means this is sutra number 23 from the *Yoga Sutras*, volume 1 of four volumes.)

Ishvara-pranidhanad-va. (YS I:23)
By giving your identity to God, you attain the identity of God.

A sutra like this has been expounded on in great detail over the years by various commentators seeking to extract its full meaning. According to Indian philosophy, the *Yoga Sutras*, like other yogic scriptures, were written by rishis. These were sages who, through yoga practices, entered the state of samadhi, or union with the Divine, and brought back information that formed the basis for Indian sciences and arts such as mathematics, astronomy, and poetry. Patanjali also wrote a work on the holistic medical science of *Ayurveda* and another on Sanskrit grammar.

Both Patanjali and the most prominent commentator on his *Yoga Sutras*, Vyasa, are considered rishis. Vyasa's commentaries are so dense that they, in turn, have generated their own commentaries.

Some scholars place Patanjali's birth around 300 B.C., but no one is really sure. He is thought to be an incarnation of the god Vishnu's vehicle Adisesha ("Endless"), the thousand-headed cobra who is the ruler of the serpent race said to guard the Earth's secret treasures.

According to legend, Vishnu, who is concerned with preservation, noticed that people on Earth were becoming too caught up in mundane things and were losing their ability to connect with the ecstatic. Vishnu is always concerned when people are unhappy, so he came up with an idea while resting on his couch, which happened to be the serpent Adisesha. Vishnu suggested that Adisesha incarnate as a sage and codify the method for attaining samadhi into a concise formula that people could use. The legend says that Patanjali is that sage. He codified the keys to happiness in the form of the *Yoga Sutras*, which were useful thousands of years ago and are being rediscovered in our present time.

As modern yogis, it's exciting to realize that we have access to the *Yoga Sutras*. But the *Yoga Sutras* will not tell you in words the meaning of life. All mystical writing is like musical notation: if you read the music and play it, you will experience the music. You have to play the notation to hear the music. In the same way, Patanjali doesn't describe samadhi; he gives you instructions. If they are followed, you will have an experience that could never be described in words.

Patanjali names five obstacles that prevent us from experiencing samadhi. These obstacles are the *kleshas*, and they hamper us today just as much (if not more) than they hampered Indians seeking enlightenment thousands of years ago:

1. *avidya:* ignorance or unreal cognition.
2. *asmita:* egoism.
3. *raga:* excessive attachment to pleasurable things.
4. *dvesa:* excessive aversion, hatred.
5. *abhinivesha:* fear of death.

Unreal cognition, Avidya, is the central foundation of all suffering.
***—Shri Brahmananda Sarasvati,* The Textbook of Yoga Psychology[1]**

All five kleshas stem from the first, avidya. We spend the first half of our lives developing a personality and the second half defending it because we worked so hard on it. ("Sure, I'm stubborn—I'm a Taurus!") As we become more attached to the personality we've created, we start to mistake it for our true identity. And it starts to shape our body and mind. This mistaking is avidya, ignorance of our true nature, which is the immortal, changeless Self.

If you cling to personality, you can be easily hurt if someone misunderstands you. "I thought you knew me!" you might exclaim. The personality, in turn, becomes more rigid and begins to limit our possibilities. The next time you catch yourself saying "I'm just not that kind of person," or "That's not really my thing," reflect that you do not *have* to behave in a fashion consistent with the personality you've constructed thus far. Loosen up (your identification with the body/mind, that is)!

To rid oneself of the kleshas, Patanjali recommends an eight-limbed system of yoga called Ashtanga, or Raja Yoga. Each limb of the tree of Raja Yoga represents a purifying yoga practice:

1. *yama:* restraint or abstinence.
2. *niyama:* observance.
3. *asana:* posture, seat.
4. *pranayama:* restraint or control of the life force.
5. *pratyahara:* withdrawal of the senses.
6. *dharana:* concentration.
7. *dhyana:* meditation.
8. *samadhi:* bliss, superconsciousness.

Through these yoga practices we seek to purify the body and mind so we can free ourselves of the kleshas and experience the incredible bliss and Self-knowledge of samadhi. Yoga practices like asana and pranayama stir up our fears, our ignorance, and our attachments. As we become conscious of them, we can begin to let them go.

The yoga practices are psychotherapeutic tools. Meditation enables us to watch the mind, observing our habits, preferences, and neuroses and gaining insights into the psyche, as well as the subconscious mind. The psychotherapeutic aspect of yoga comes from how it begins to integrate and purify the body, the emotions, and the mind by infusing them with spirit. Yet the science of psychology, too, falls short of yoga because it does not include enlightenment or liberation as a goal worthy of pursuit, or even consideration.

The so-called depth psychology and parapsychology are not deep enough to effect liberation. The repressions of childhood and their extirpation by psychoanalysis may enable a man to meet successfully the problems of life but he is still far from the reality of his psyche (soul). He is still a mortal and material being. There is no objective of spiritual release from the chain of relative existence.
***—Shri Brahmananda Sarasvati,* The Textbook of Yoga Psychology**[2]

The first duty of those who really want to do yoga is to eliminate from their consciousness, with all the might, all the sincerity, all the endurance of which they are capable, even the shadow of a fear. To walk on the path, one must be dauntless, and never indulge in that petty, small, feeble, nasty shrinking back upon oneself, which is fear.
***—The Mother,* The Sunlit Path: Passages from Conversations and Writings of the Mother**[3]

samadhi means "the same as the highest."
sam = same, connected with.
adhi = highest.
And the highest is One.

In the state of samadhi you realize that you are not alone, unique, one in a sea of many. You are One, who has taken many forms.

How to begin this investigation into your true nature? Begin with Patanjali's first sutra:

Atha yoganushasanam. (YS I:1)
Thus proceeds Yoga as I have observed it in the natural world.

This yoga sutra has always inspired us because it implies that everything we need to know to return to our natural state is laid out in front of us, if we would only allow ourselves to see. That's tremendously exciting. But how do we connect the seen with the unseen?

We can begin by observing ourselves during the practice of an asana. There is a yoga asana called Setu Bandhasana, literally, "the construction of a bridge." As you slowly raise your back off the floor until only the feet and the head touch the floor, you experience the linking of the near shore to the far. You do not stand and look at the opposite shore; you become the link. Bridges connect or bind one disconnected part to another. If disconnection is an illusion, then the bridge must be the illusion-buster.

Perhaps while you are practicing Setu Bandhasana you notice that your mind begins racing when your legs start to tire. Maybe you notice that when you deepen your breathing in an effort to bring strength into your legs, your mind begins to slow down. You begin to experience a subtle shift in consciousness. This is how the yogi learns to move into deeper states of consciousness and to gain control of the mind—by, as Patanjali suggests, observing how Yoga proceeds in the natural world.

In the second sutra, Patanjali defines Yoga.

Yogash chitta-vritti-nirodhah. (YS I:2)
Yoga is realized when identification with the fluctuations of the mind ceases.

Yogash: union with the Source of all.
Chitta-vritti: movement (from *vritti*: whirlings) of the mind-stuff, modifications of chittam, mind (from *cit*: to perceive).
Nirodhah: cessation, dissolution.

We have all been at the mercy of the fluctuations of our minds. Our thoughts can agitate us, please us, torture us—but they cannot lead us to the state of Yoga. To reach that state, Patanjali says we must allow our attention to disengage from the fluctuations of the mind so that we can go beyond thought, to a higher state of consciousness.

Our main duty is to go beyond thoughts.
—*Swami Nirmalananda,* The Silent Sage Speaks: Recorded Live at Viswa Shanthi Nikethan BR Hills, South India[4]

In Vedantic philosophy the Sanksrit word *Brahman* is used to refer to that which is real. According to Vedanta, Brahman alone is real. It is the supreme unchanging reality. Something is real only if it does not change, under any circumstance.

This concept raises some interesting questions:

Is your body real?
Is your mind real?
Is this world real?

According to Vedanta, they are not, because something is real only if it stays the same through all modes of time and space.

It's useful to have a foundation in Vedantic philosophy when discussing yoga, because Vedanta is a logical extension of Yoga. Yoga philosophy is dualistic: there is you and then there is God, although you can attain a state of Yoga, or union with God. Vedanta takes the idea of union with God further, into a nondualistic philosophy with the concept of Oneness at its core: you are God, and God is you.

The idea expressed in the *Chandogya Upanishad* scripture, "Tat Tvam Asi," or "Thou art That," is fundamental to Vedantic thought.

Brahman is God, the source of the entire universe: love itself; boundless, limitless joy. The *Taittiriya Upanishad* proclaims Love is the source of all. From Love all has come and unto Love all shall return.

Brahman projects itself as the physical universe through the power of *maya*, which in etymological terms means "measurement." Maya is usually translated as "illusion," because what you are trying to measure is eternity, or the infinite. In attempting to measure the infinite, humans created the concept of time, and where there is time, there is the relative universe. Maya, measurement, meter, matter, music—these are all related ideas existing in time and space.

Our whole notion of reality has actually been topsy-turvy. Instead of God being a vast imaginary projection, he turns out to be the only thing that is real, and the whole universe, despite its immensity and solidity, is a projection of God's nature.

—***Deepak Chopra,*** **How to Know God**[5]

Maya gave birth to this universe. Maya is the mother of the material universe, and she is strange, mysterious, and indescribable. Maya veils the true nature of Brahman, which is absolute and unconditional, and causes the One to appear as many.

Vedanta accords maya two powers:

The power to veil or conceal (the result of maya is known as avidya, which is also Patanjali's first klesha).

The power to manifest or project (also known as creation).

Maya demonstrates these powers through three qualities, called *gunas*. Qualities are limitations; when you remove them, the illusory appearance of a thing disappears. If you have a "real" building, made of walls, foundation, and roof, and you remove those qualities, you are left with nothing. The building disappears. Without the qualities of the building, the building cannot exist.

All aspects of material reality can be categorized according to the following three qualities or gunas:

Sattva: lightness, purity, tranquility, goodness, balance. *Sattva* binds with attachment to happiness or pleasure.

Rajas: activity, passion, growth, change, evolution. *Rajas* binds with attachment to activity.

Tamas: darkness, inertia, heaviness, resistance, involution. *Tamas* binds with attachment to delusion, ignorance.

The gunas may be compared to three robbers who waylay a man in the forest. Tamas, one of the robbers, wants to kill him and steal his money. Rajas, the second robber, persuades the group instead to tie him hand and foot to a tree and steal all his money and possessions. After some time, Sattva, the third robber, returns and unties the man and takes him gently out of the forest and sets him on the highway, which will lead him to his home. Then Sattva takes leave of the man because, being a robber, he doesn't dare accompany him for fear of the police.

Tamas wants to destroy the man; Rajas binds him to the world and robs him of his spiritual treasures; Sattva sets him on the path to freedom. Tamas has to be overcome by Rajas and Rajas by Sattva. But in the end, Sattva must also be overcome if the man is to seek total freedom. Truth lies beyond the three gunas.

It's good to become familiar with these three terms, because they are useful shorthand for describing people or things. Spiritual seekers, for example, can be described as:

sattvic: interested in truth, Self-confident.
rajasic: dependent, attached.
tamasic: desirous of power, manipulative.

Sattvic seekers demand nothing. Sattvic seekers are disciplined. That's why they are called disciples. Sattvic seekers use their teacher to connect with God. They are not concerned with getting attention from their teacher. They are interested only in truth.

There was a great teacher a long time ago said to be an incarnation of Shiva. His name was Dakshinamurti, the teacher who teaches in silence. He sat in deep meditation in a cave in search of the truth. He had three seekers who came to him for teachings. All he did was join his thumb and forefinger in chin mudra, and when they saw this they *knew*, they got it—they realized the Self! This is an example of both a sattvic teacher and very ripe sattvic seekers.

Rajasic seekers, in contrast, lack discipline; they preach more than they practice. Rajasic seekers are not disciples; they are followers who lack the perseverance to work hard to discover the inner essence. They can become passionately fanatical. They tend to imitate the outward appearance of their teachers. If a teacher's attitude toward them changes, they may be very affected emotionally.

The word attachment characterizes the nature of rajasic students. Their attachment is to the *look of a thing*. Remember, to be rajasic is to be attached to activity. They are not good at meditation or service. Rajas may simply be a phase you pass through when you begin your sadhana, or spiritual practice.

Tamasic seekers are uninterested in doing the disciplined work of sadhana. They are lazy. They will take the teachings and turn them upside down to suit their own bad habits and tendencies. They enjoy trying to make the teacher's life miserable. They like to take up the teacher's time just to see if they can get away with it. They may even try to seduce a teacher, using the pretense of interest in spiritual teachings. Usually they are after attention, time, or sex. Of course, they must have *some* interest in the subject of God-realization, but their tamasic tendency to stay the same usually predominates and causes them and the teacher problems.

As individual souls, or jivas, who are bound by maya, we are all mixes of the three gunas until liberation. Yoga is the means for liberating the jiva from the bondage imposed by maya. This liberation is called mukti; the jivanmukta is one liberated from bondage.

There are three types of jivas according to the gunas:

pravahi (tamas): Worldly; not interested in liberation or enlightenment; pretty busy with getting to know the world.

maryada (rajas): Interested in liberation; feels that there must be "a way." Maryada souls search for systems to study or follow. Worldly activities do not satisfy them; they wish to look behind the surface of appearances.

pushti (sattva): Pushti means "nourishment." These are grace-filled souls, nourished by the grace of God. They do not look for a way to obtain liberation; they leave it all to God's grace.

When a jiva finally realizes who he or she really is, the term jiva no longer applies. The realized soul becomes Atman. The Atman sees all; it is the indwelling witness. It is pure consciousness, in a state of absolute joy. It is unborn and deathless, not subject to growth and decay or the three gunas. It is unchangeable and eternal and is not destroyed when the body is destroyed. Atman is I-AM.

When jivas realize their true identity, they no longer identify with their minds or bodies. They have realized the immortal Atman and have become realized beings, or jivanmuktas.

> ***It is difficult to attain a human birth. To be born pure and with a desire for learning and spiritual attainment is even more rare and only comes after thousands of incarnations . . . Strive to find a genuine spiritual teacher, a guru, and by practice of yoga learn discrimination. Study the ancient spiritual writings, and by tranquility and purification try to gain knowledge of the Atman. . . . But among the means used for the search for liberation the foremost is devotion. . . . There is a means to cross the ocean of worldliness and reach the other shore. This is the means by which the yogis have crossed. The ancient writings have said that Shraddha (learning), Bhakti (love), Dhyana (meditation) and Yoga (self-discipline) will bring the results you require. These will release you from the bondage of reincarnation.***
>
> —***Sankaracharya,* The Viveka Chudamani (The Crest Jewel of Discrimination), *the clearest statement of Vedantic philosophy*[6]**

It is difficult to attain a human birth. It is as unlikely as a seal, swimming in the middle of the ocean, coming up for air and finding that it has stuck its nose through a life preserver that happens to be floating on top of the water in exactly that spot. We are blessed to have attained human birth, because as humans we are in a position to learn practices that have been passed down for thousands of years through an oral tradition from teacher to student. These ancient practices may reveal to us where we are resisting our natural state, which is happiness.

If you have an interest in liberation, you probably practiced yoga in previous lifetimes. You are not a complete beginner in this one, but are picking up where you left off.

To say that human birth is the most advantageous is not meant to discredit an animal's capacity for enlightenment. Animals are not less intelligent or less conscious than humans. It's just that, in this era, human beings are the dominant species—for better or for worse! The life choices available to even the poorest human being are more numerous than those available to most nonhuman animals—because humans control the fate of so many.

This has not always been the case. When Vishnu came to Earth in his earliest incarnation, for example, he chose to appear in the form of a fish, Matsya, because fish were the predominant species. As reptiles emerged from the sea, Vishnu chose his second incarnation, a turtle, Kurma. As mammals became more predominant, the avatar appeared as a boar, Varaha.

Whether you have the body of a human or a turtle, your body is a complex vehicle for progression toward enlightenment. As humans, we have available to us the yoga practices, which use the vehicle of body/mind. All the yoga practices are practices for purifying this body and mind, which is actually composed of five bodies: the physical, vital, emotional, intellectual, and bliss bodies.

Purification, from the yogic point of view, means to bring all five bodies of the self into a sattvic (balanced) state, in which neither tamas (inertia) nor rajas (activity) dominate.

The five bodies encase the true Self in a container called upadhi. *Upadhi* means vehicle. It's good to have a body because it is a vehicle for consciousness. The problem is that we mistake our vehicle for who we really are. Through yoga practices, however, we can purify the five bodies encasing the Self so that Absolute consciousness, Brahman, can shine through.

The Five Bodies
Artist: David Life

The five bodies fall into three categories: material, astral, and causal. The names of each of these bodies are made up of two Sanskrit terms. The first part identifies what makes up the body; the second part, *kosha*, means sheath or covering. Each body can be purified by specific yoga practices.

Material Body

1. **Annamaya kosha (physical body)**
   Annamaya=food; kosha=covering

   Practice: Because Annamaya kosha is made up of the food we eat, it can be purified by a vegetarian diet, asanas, and kriya (cleansing) practices.

Astral Bodies

2. **Pranamaya kosha (vital body)**
   Pranamaya=vitality; kosha=covering

Practice: Because Pranamaya kosha is composed of energy and vitality, it may be purified by pranayama (breathing practices) and kriya.

3. **Manomaya kosha (emotional body)**
   Manomaya=emotions; kosha=covering

   Practice: Because Manomaya kosha is made up of emotions, it may be purified by karma yoga (selfless service), bhakti (devotion to God), chanting, devotion, and yama and niyama practices.

4. **Vijnanamaya kosha (intellectual body)**
   Vijnanamaya=intellect; kosha=covering

   Practice: Because Vijnanamaya kosha is composed of thoughts and ideas, it may be purified by satsang, which is the practice of being in the company of other beings seeking liberation, or saints. It may also be purified by the study of scriptures, the study of Sanskrit, and meditation.

Causal (Seed) Body

5. **Anandamaya kosha (bliss body)**
   Anandamaya=bliss; kosha=covering

   Practice: Anandamaya kosha may be purified by ecstasy, samadhi.

All these bodies of the self permeate one another. They are all manifesting at the same time, and the condition of one body affects all the others. Your emotional state affects your health, for example; the food you eat affects your vitality. The bodies do not exist independently, save at death, when the material body separates from the astral and causal bodies. These more subtle bodies continue to exist and transmigrate into a new physical body for another incarnation.

You can begin to feel your own subtle bodies during asana practice when you become aware that you don't have to muscle through the more difficult postures. You might be struggling to balance in Bakasana (crow), for example, because your arms aren't quite strong enough, but if you tap into the vital body, suddenly your feet lift and there you are, flying. At that moment you can feel the vital body animating the physical body. Asana practice can help you develop a healthy physical body, but it's really about transcending the limits of the physical body. It's a method for experiencing the subtle bodies.

At any given moment, we are awake, dreaming, or in deep sleep. An unenlightened soul can experience no other state of consciousness. The yoga practices help reintegrate these three states and bring about a heightened state of awareness. The truth begins to shine through all our five bodies, preparing us to experience the first stage of samadhi.

While we remain unenlightened souls or jivas, however, we can experience only three states of consciousness:

> *jagrat* (waking state, objective reality): This is the reality we can all agree on while awake. In the waking state the soul identifies with the ego self, not with Atman. Time and space prevail. Maya deludes us.
>
> *swapna* (dream state, subjective reality): When you dream, it is *your* dream, not anyone else's. You exist in a state of subjective reality, in which the soul continues to identify with the ego self, not Atman. Time and space prevail, although they may become distorted. Maya continues to delude us.
>
> *sushupti* (deep sleep, unconsciousness): In this state there is no dreaming, no REM (rapid eye movement). The jiva is merged with Brahman. Time does not exist. The only way to know if you have experienced deep sleep is if you awake refreshed. The deep sleep state is essential for physical and mental health. A person deprived of deep sleep over time will go crazy and eventually die.

What motivates us to wake up and leave the Oneness state of deep sleep? Our undone deeds and our unresolved karmas. These motivate us to begin to dream again and then to wake up for another day.

As Swami Satchidananda says, "If you have a dirty and cracked mirror and you look into it you will see a dirty and cracked face. So you clean and fix the mirror and then you will see a clean and undistorted face. In the same way, if you clean the mind it will reflect the True Self, shining and bright."[7]

When that light begins to shine, we may experience a new consciousness called *turiya*. This word means "the fourth" or "beyond the other three." It is beyond time and space, and is the first stage of samadhi, superconsciousness. Turiya occurs when, after many lifetimes, the jiva finally wakes up and realizes that it is not the body and mind, it is Atman, the immortal divine soul.

We get a glimpse of this realization at the time of physical death.

There are two stages of samadhi. The first is *samprajnata,* or *sabija samadhi* (with seed). In this stage you still see others. You see their essence, their essential nature, their soul. You perceive that they are not separate from you, yet something draws you back into the world.

The second stage, *asamprajnata,* or *nirbija samadhi* (without seed), transcends all forms. Here there is no subject and no object; all are merged. Others do not exist. Time has no effect; the gunas have no effect. There is only complete merger, which does not separate again.

The highest level of asamprajnata is called dharma-megha-samadhi or kaivalyam. Kaivalyam means "alone," "only one." Here exists only one witness, one Atman—the entire universe is an expression of That, and you are That.

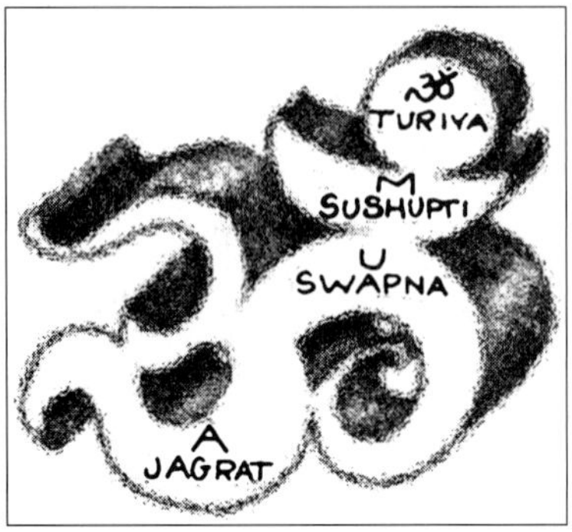

Om and the three states of consciousness
Artist: David Life

The soul leaves the physical body, looks back at it, and says, "Who is that?" The jiva realizes then that it is not the body, but it doesn't know fully who it is.

The Sanksrit word Om beautifully expresses the four states of consciousness—jagrat (waking), swapna (dreaming), sushupti (deep sleep), and turiya (samadhi)—both visually and in sound. Each part of the symbol for Om represents a different state of consciousness.

When we chant Om, we are really singing a three-part sound: AUM, Ah . . . Oooh . . . Mmm. Each part vibrates in a different part of the body and represents a different state of consciousness. The Ah blooms in the lower abdomen and represents jagrat, the waking state. Oooh vibrates in the solar plexus and heart and represents swapna, the dream state. Mmm occurs when we press our lips together, sending the vibrations into our skulls. With this sound we are calling to our awareness of sushupti, deep sleep. And finally, turiya exists in the continuing vibration, the resonating, unstruck sound of Om.

Om is the sound that is God's name. It is identical with God. "In the beginning was the word and the word was God," the Bible tells us. "That word is Om," the yogis added. When we chant Om, we are dedicating our practice to God in the most primal, abstract form. The ever practical Patanjali, however, suggests a more concrete way to connect with the infinite in his twenty-third sutra:

Ishvara-pranidhanad-va. (YS I:23)
By giving your life and identity to God you attain the identity of God.

Ishvara is the first, primal, willfully assumed dilution of Brahman. Ishvara manifests in form and so possesses the qualities of maya (illusion), but it is not bound by the gunas (qualities). Ishvara appears in the form of the trinity of:

Brahma the creator
Vishnu the preserver
Shiva the destroyer or transformer

Vishnu is always concerned with the welfare of all beings. In Hinduism, Jesus is considered one of Vishnu's incarnations and so is Buddha, as the life's purpose of both of these beings was to uplift consciousness and thereby alleviate suffering. Vishnu is sattvic; he is the sun god. Light is his predominant quality.

Brahma, on the other hand, creates, much like the Biblical God the Father of the Old Testament. Brahma is rajasic; he is continually creating, manifesting, birthing the universe over and over every moment. Without Brahma's creation, Vishnu and Shiva would simply stand in stagnant opposition without anything to shed light on or anything to tear apart.

Shiva is the tamasic power of change and upheaval, leveling that which has been created by Brahma and is trying to be preserved by Vishnu. Shiva is necessary for regeneration and evolution. In Christianity, the Holy Spirit, who came to the Virgin Mary with a message that was going to turn her whole life upside down, is analogous to Shiva.

We never really know what love is until we fall in love. We never really know what God is, until we can envision God in a form that we can relate to. It is difficult to relate to nothing. God has to assume a form that is somewhat like our own so that we can direct our love toward that form.

Patanjali says that devotion to the Lord is a necessary ingredient for yoga practice. This is why, at the beginning of a Jivamukti Yoga class, as the students are standing, ready to begin the first sun salutation, we often suggest they take a moment to devote their practice to God. God is love, and love is the tool that ultimately liberates.

We recommend this dedication because asana practice is very powerful. It can stir up a lot of energy, and the student may wonder, "What do I do with this energy I feel pulsing around in my body?" A teacher who is teaching yoga only as exercise—not as a physical, psychological, and spiritual system of purification—and responds "I don't know, do what you want with it," might as well take the student to the edge of an abyss and say "Go ahead, jump."

Students who are not taught to dedicate the energy released by asana practice to God tend to do one of two things. They may let all that power manifest in their bodies and personalities and become highly charged and very charismatic. If you look at their faces, however, you may see rage, as well as anger, jealousy, and selfishness. These are emotions that were stirred up by the practice but were never turned over to God. Or, the students may fall to pieces, destroyed emotionally and physically by the practice. These students will probably lose interest in yoga.

Neither of these outcomes will occur if you apply Patanjali's sound advice: Give it to God. Devote all effort toward God-realization.

Pranidhana means to offer up, to give up. Ishvara-pranidhanad-va, therefore, means to offer up yourself, your practice, and everything you bring to it, to God.

Brahma, Vishnu, and Shiva

Give it up. Devote the fruits of your practice to God and your practice will become full of grace.

There are two paths to the attainment of Yoga: the path of effort and the path of grace—maryada *marga* and pushti marga. Marga means path. Maryada describes the soul looking for a system to follow to gain enlightenment, and pushti describes the soul that simply surrenders everything to God.

The difference between maryada marga and pushti marga is illustrated by the old Indian tale of the baby monkey and the baby cat. When a baby monkey becomes separated from his mother, he will race around, swinging through trees looking for her. He is determined to find her. When he does finally find the mother, he grabs her body and holds on for dear life, and the two, united, go swinging through the trees. But when the kitten becomes separated from her mother she stays put. She does not run around looking for her mother. The kitten stays and cries out, "Meow Maaaaa." The kitten calls until the mother hears her. The mother comes to the kitten, picks her up by the scruff of the neck, and the two go off happily to snuggle.

The monkey is on maryada marga, the path of effort. The kitten trusts in the mother and by chanting her name continuously gets her to come to the rescue. The kitten is on pushti marga, the path of grace.

Patanjali's eight-limbed system is predominantly a maryada marga, an effortful path, but the last two limbs—dhyana (meditation) and samadhi (enlightenment)—cannot be attained through effort. They are the result of grace. Yet it is only through intense effort that we can prepare ourselves to receive such grace.

Ahhh. Samadhi.
Yoga is Samadhi.
God is One.
Yoga is One.
That's all.
—Shri K. Pattabhi Jois[8]

Hatha Yoga has come to mean "easy yoga" in the current vernacular, but the word hatha can be translated as "to forcefully bind to a stake." Hatha Yoga is a rigorous practice of purification leading to transcendental experience. This is a path of action, of directed movement toward God-realization. Through practices passed down through the ages we build a bridge between our individual experience and our Source, destroying the illusion of separateness.

You only need to take one step toward the Divine Mother and she will come across galaxies to your side.

3

Karma: What You Think, Say, and Do

The intense desire for God-realization is itself the way to it.
***—Shri Anandamayima,* Matri Darshan**

Our guru Swami Nirmalananda taught us a powerful mantra: *Lokah Samasta Sukhino Bhavantu*. "May all beings, everywhere, be happy and free. And may the thoughts and actions of my own life contribute, in some way, to that happiness and to that freedom for all." In doing so, he encouraged us to perform actions that benefit all beings, human and non-human. This is the essence of Karma Yoga. Karma Yoga is selfless service. This practical method for reducing suffering in the world is the foundation of all yoga practice. When we are suffering from self-pity and loneliness, a surefire cure is to care more for others and the reduction of their suffering. When we shift our thoughts away from our own suffering, it diminishes.

Whatever yoga practice you undertake, make it Karma Yoga by devoting the fruits of your practice to God, as Patanjali suggests in the *Yoga Sutras: Ishvara-pranidhanad-va*.

Karma Yoga should not be confused with the law of karma, which is that every action causes infinite effects. The law of karma is the law of cause and effect.

Karma Yoga, on the other hand, is a method for ensuring that the actions we take *cause* good karmic effects.

The law of karma is a universal doctrine, operating as surely as the law of gravity. You can observe it in the natural world, if you care to look. If you plant a seed in the ground, the karma of the seed is to grow. If you throw something up in the air, the karmic result is for it to come down.

Karma means action. It comes from the Sanskrit root *kr*, which means to act. It encompasses all movement, of the mind as well as the body. These movements can be conscious or unconscious; regardless, the karmic result is still ours.

The word karma is also used to refer to the accumulated results of past actions, present actions, and actions we will perform in the future. The karmas of the past, present, and future are of three types:

> *Sanchitta:* This is accumulated past actions or karmas waiting to come to fruition. Sanchitta is the storehouse of every action you have ever done, in all the lifetimes you have ever lived. These are all of the unresolved past actions waiting to reach resolution.

> *Parabda:* This is present action: what you are doing now, in this lifetime, and its result. You have taken from the storehouse, sanchitta karma, a certain amount of unresolved desires and ambitions, and will try to "work them out" in your present lifetime.

> *Agami:* Future actions that result from your present actions are called agami karma. As you attempt to resolve past karma, you unavoidably create new karmas that you may or may not be able to resolve in your present life. If you don't resolve them now, they will go into the storehouse to be resolved in a future life.

Every action creates a groove in the subtle atmosphere called a *samskara*. Samskaras represent your unfulfilled desires and ambitions, etched onto your soul by your actions. These must be fulfilled at some time, in this life or in another.

All karma results from ignorance of the true Self. Let's say you smoke a cigarette for the first time. You want to know what it tastes like, so you take a puff. You like it and say, "Oh, I'll take another," and soon you are tied to the cigarette. What is fascinating is that it is not the cigarette that makes you feel good; it is the fact that as you take a puff, you have no other desire for that moment. In that moment you experience your real Self, which is happiness, freedom from desire. But you mistakenly associate that happiness with the cigarette, not the Self, which is the true source of happiness. Instead of going to the Self directly, you go to the cigarette. You are bound in the karmic cycle of action and the resulting attachment.

The only way to be freed from having to resolve every desire is for the soul to realize the Self. Through enlightenment, no karmas can bind you. You are unbound, liberated.

When an action is selfless, it leads to future good karma and eventually to liberation. As yogis seeking liberation, therefore, we strive to perfect our actions. Most actions are preceded by a thought. To perfect an action, therefore, we must first perfect our thoughts. What is a perfect thought? A perfect thought is one devoid of selfish motive, free of anger, greed, hate, jealousy, and so on.

Most of us believe we can think any thought we like and be free of consequence, as long as we don't act on it. Yet how many times have you had something on your mind and a friend has looked at you and asked, "What's bothering you?" Our thoughts affect others and bear karmic consequences for ourselves. Our thoughts are significant even at the time of death, when a thought can propel us into the next lifetime—for better or worse.

Thought leads to action. The same action can be undertaken with a self*ish* intention or a self*less* intention. The act of sexual intercourse is a good example. When intended to control, manipulate, harm, or humiliate another person, it is called rape and is considered a crime. When it is motivated by the intention to love, honor, or uplift another, it is called making love.

The intention behind any action is always more important than the action itself. The intention contains the seed of the action's results. If you perform a good action but you have a negative intention, you will receive negative karma from that action.

A person who becomes a social worker to serve others, for example, will appreciate the people she serves because she recognizes that they are providing her with opportunities to perform selfless service. Her actions result in good karma for both her and them.

Another person might become a social worker to "help" people. This intention automatically sets up a superior/inferior duality. This social worker is more likely to become judgmental and aggravated by the people he encounters, and will find it difficult to evolve.

The underlying intention determines whether any act is liberating or binding. Even a yoga practice can perpetuate bondage if the underlying intention is selfish. The intention underlying a yoga practice should always be to serve the higher Self, not the small self.

When we commit ourselves to serving others, we work much harder and reap more benefit than when we act from selfish motives. If you need to eat and you are alone, you might just reach into the refrigerator and pull out a container of the least-aged contents and eat from it standing in the kitchen. But if you invite a good friend for dinner, you behave differently. You go out of your way to acquire the best ingredients for the meal. You clean the house. You spend hours preparing and cooking the meal. Finally, you serve your guest on your special china, making sure that he or she savors each bite. You might even find that you are no longer hungry. You have been satiated at the fountain of love and service.

According to the law of karma, your present situation is the result of your actions over this and previous lifetimes. It doesn't matter if you are a president, a pet cat, a pig in a factory farm, a tree, an accomplished musician, an acclaimed scientist, a homeless person, an orphaned child, a petty thief, or a crack addict. At some point you performed the actions that resulted in your present situation. It is a waste of precious energy to look on another's good fortune and be jealous, thinking that it landed in his or her lap. Luck does not figure into it.

"Oh, they have rich parents."

"She was born beautiful."

"With that kind of money I could afford to dress like that, too."

"Easy for you to say—you have a loving husband."

How often have you made such statements? They may be superficially accurate but do not reflect reality. Our suffering, as well as our happiness, is determined by our actions.

Please don't mistake the law of karma, however, for the judgmental Calvinist attitude that has infected the United States from its inception. The Calvinists, you might recall from eighth-grade history class, believed that rich people were rich because God loved them and poor people were poor because God did not love them. If you were rich, that was an external sign that you were a very spiritually evolved person. If you were poor, well, there wasn't much hope for your soul.

The Calvinists believed in predestination, not reincarnation. The Indian view of karma is much more complex. Results occur over many lifetimes and are not a form of punishment inflicted by a vengeful Lord. Your present situation is the solution, not the problem. Karma is God's gift to us, because it's an opportunity for us to learn, through experience, how it really feels to suffer from a particular experience. By suffering we learn compassion, which brings us closer to all beings.

The law of karma implies that the key to a happy life is actually pretty simple. The degree of happiness you will enjoy in your life is the result of how much you have contributed to the happiness of other beings, presently as well as in the past. The Judeo-Christian ideas of guilt and punishment do not figure into this. In the yogic model of karma, guilt is not spiritually productive or helpful. Guilt arises from the past. The past is something we cannot change. So why fret over it?

Act as if the future of the universe depends on what you do, while laughing at yourself for thinking that your actions make any difference.

—Buddhist advice

Being kind and cheerful to others is the most potent way to create good karma for yourself—and it's not so bad for the people with whom you interact, either! Unfortunately, we tend to treat other people and animals well in proportion to how useful they are to us. We look at objects the same way.

Try a simple experiment. Look around and rest your eyes on something—a chair, for instance. What do you see? You may see something to sit on. You may appreciate its beauty, if it pleases your aesthetic sense. If it is an antique, you may wonder if it is valuable.

Can you look at a chair and see its essential nature as something that has nothing to do with its usefulness to you? Can you look at a chair and see it as, in essence, the same as you? This takes great selflessness.

Look at how the majority of people view the state of Alaska: as an uninhabited wilderness available for development that would benefit humans. This is ridiculous; Alaska is not uninhabited. It has been inhabited by thousands of species for many years. What's more, these species have lived in harmony with one another and have kept Alaska in pristine condition.

We are taught from an early age to view people, animals, plants, and things with these questions in our hearts: "What can this do for me? How can I use this for my own purpose?" Our minds demand: "How can I dominate them? What can they do for me?"

Most of us never grow out of this immature behavior. Our society certainly doesn't encourage us to change. People who act selflessly, like the Dalai Lama and Mother Teresa, are viewed as pretty odd. Even when we admire them, we tend to think of them as inherently different—not as people like us.

There are basically three kinds of people. The first is the most numerous, the second is in the minority, and the third is very rare. The only difference among them is the intention underlying their actions.

Selfish people are the most common. They fall into two categories: very selfish and a little less selfish. Very selfish people feel that the world and everyone in it owes them a good life. They work only to fulfill their desires. They serve none but themselves. They cannot even serve their own families. They are so self-absorbed that they usually live in a constant state of fear. They fear losing—

property, time, or life itself. They worry about being robbed or violated in some way. Death is the ultimate outrage to these people and they fear it above all else.

People who are a little less selfish are able, once they've provided for themselves, to care for their family. They may work very hard and believe that they are sacrificing "everything" for their children, but this is actually a selfish act. They have produced their children, and their genes will survive through them. These people may put money into a trust for their children or spouse but they would never think of building a hospital or establishing a charity. Their vision is just not that wide. "Leave that to the rich people," they may say in their defense.

You may find selfish people practicing yoga. Their intention, though, is typically limited to using yoga practices to become more physically attractive, or less injury-prone, or better at their jobs. Dancers or actors who practice yoga to become better performers are an example. Such practitioners are hoping to improve their futures. But that future may not include the end of suffering for themselves or others.

More rare are charitable people, who work to improve the lives of others unrelated to themselves. They may not be without selfish motive, however, as they expect credit for their service. They first care for themselves and their loved ones, and then, if there is money left over, they may give the surplus to others. They may help build hospitals, cultural centers, or museums. They try to help, but they approach the situation on the symptomatic level only. Rarely do they help to stamp out the cause of suffering, which is ignorance of the Self. Seeing their names in a program or on a plaque gives them considerable satisfaction.

Scientists and religious leaders who are absorbed in investigating the workings of the cosmos can also make useful contributions to humanity. Often, however, pride contaminates their contribution. Here is another example of how a lack of humility can diminish the positive karmic results that could be incurred by a valuable contribution.

Do not give your alms before other men, to be seen of them: otherwise ye have no reward of your Father in heaven. Therefore when thou giveth alms, do not sound a trumpet before thee, that thou may receive glory from other men. Give your alms in secret and God will reward thee openly.

—*The Bible,* Matthew 6

Selfless people, on the other hand, are in service to the cosmic will and may help shift the consciousness of an entire age. This is the way of the jivanmukta. The selfless person works for the sake of the work, knowing that the Divine is the core of every being and thing. All work, all effort is without struggle or expectation of reward. These people offer themselves as instruments for Divine Will, realizing that God is the only doer. They allow the message from the Divine Source to come through them. The message of these beings is always joyous and reminds us all of our true nature.

Usually the effect of these people's work lasts long after their own physical bodies. Think of Jesus, the Buddha, and Lao-tsu. Their teachings are still raising consciousness thousands of years after their physical deaths. They caused acceleration in the evolution of consciousness. These are the truly famous people. Their fame vibrates all creation because they aligned themselves with the core of creation and forsook their individual gratification to uplift us all. Civilizations come and go, but God endures. Those who strive to serve God endure also.

For whatsoever a man soweth, that shall he also reap.
—*The Bible,* Galatians 6:7

The conditions that are most beneficial for the jiva's evolution have been determined by the soul's own past karmas or actions. These choices are continually being made, consciously or unconsciously, by the actions that we take daily.

Each soul is working out what it must on its road back to the Source. When you accept that you will never know the real story behind someone else's karma, you can stop envying or pitying others. You can start paying attention to your own karma, your own actions. You are the agent for your fate. You had everything to do with where you are now. What you did before matters. What you are doing now matters. What you are thinking now matters.

The yogi accepts a pleasant turn of events with equanimity, knowing that pleasure and pain never last forever. Yogis accept difficulties as opportunities to work out bad karma. It is wise to give thanks for everything that happens, knowing that the present situation can change in an instant.

Here is a story that illustrates the yogic mind, which has the capacity to be thankful for whatever happens:

> There once lived a farmer. He lived on a farm with his wife, his son, and one horse that the family had raised from a colt. The family planned to enter the horse in the annual county fair and hoped it would win prizes that could lead to breeding opportunities. This would ensure a nice future income for the farmer and his family.
>
> The night before the fair, a violent storm swept over the countryside. When the farmer and his family awoke early the next morning, they found that the fences had been blown down. Their prize stallion was nowhere to be found. The farmer's wife was beside herself with despair. The neighbors came and joined in the wife's grief.

"What terrible misfortune has befallen us!" cried the wife. "Yes, yes, this is most unfortunate," the neighbors agreed. But the farmer said, "Fortunate or unfortunate, I don't know, let's wait and see."

A week passed and the farmer and his family were sitting at the breakfast table. Looking out the kitchen window they saw a herd of horses galloping toward the farm. It was their faithful stallion, leading five horses and a little filly behind him. He had found a herd of wild mares, and now he was bringing them home. The farmer's family ran out to open the corral gate for the horses. The farmer's wife was overjoyed and exclaimed, "What a fortunate turn of events, this is unbelievable!" The neighbors rushed over, exclaiming, "How fortunate you are!" The farmer just said, "Fortunate or unfortunate, I don't know, let's wait and see."

Over the next weeks the farmer and his son were busy training the new horses. One day the son was thrown by one of the wild horses. He suffered a bad fall and broke many bones. The farmer's wife was very upset. Between her sobs she said, "We never should have let those wild horses in; this is a most unfortunate accident! My poor son." The neighbors came to commiserate with the wife about her misfortune. And the farmer said, "Fortunate or unfortunate, I don't know, let's wait and see."

Two days later the king's soldiers came by the little farm. The king had declared war on an adjacent country and the soldiers had orders to draft all able-bodied young men into the army. On seeing the farmer's son with both legs and both arms broken, not to mention several ribs fractured and numerous lacerations on his face and head, they left him home and continued on to the next family. The farmer's wife wept with relief, crying, "How lucky we are! This is most fortunate." The neighbors, most of whom had had sons taken off to war, said, "You are indeed most fortunate." The farmer said, "Fortunate or unfortunate, I don't know, let's wait and see."

Some months passed. The farmer's son was recovering nicely; he was able to walk, albeit with a cane. A messenger from the king's palace dropped by the farm to inquire about the health of the son. Seeing the son's improved condition he stated that by order of the king, the son must come at once to the palace to work in the gardens and stables. There was a shortage of workers at the palace due to the war. What could the family do but let their son go? The wife was bitterly angry and cursed the king for his unfairness. "How unfortunate we surely are! We have lost our only son and there will be no one to help us with the farm now." The neighbors came by to console the wife, murmuring, "What an unfortunate turn of events." The farmer just said, "Fortunate or unfortunate, I don't know, let's wait and see."

The king had a beautiful daughter. One day she looked out of her window and saw the handsome new gardener. She fell in love with him and went to her father and said, "Father, I have found the man I wish to marry. Please make it happen!"

The king, unable to resist a request from his lovely daughter replied, "Of course, it shall be done."

The next day a messenger was sent from the palace to the farm, bearing a wedding invitation for the farmer and his wife, as well as an invitation for them to come live permanently at the palace. Can you imagine the reaction of the farmer's wife? She was ecstatic and could hardly contain her joy. Jumping up and down she laughed, "This is incredible, how fortunate!" The neighbors exclaimed, "Indeed, *this* is a very fortunate turn of events!" And the farmer, as usual, said . . . !

The farmer was a yogi in his understanding of karma. He understood that it is best to stay detached and thankful for whatever happens. Life is all ups and downs. Change is the only thing we can be sure of, so why not accept it?

In whatever circumstances you may be placed, reflect thus: "It is all right, this was necessary for me; it is His way of drawing me close to His feet" and try to remain content. By Him alone should your heart be possessed.

—*Shri Anandamayima,* Matri Darshan[1]

To ensure good karma, give thanks to the Divine for whatever happens to you. The act of giving thanks itself creates good karma. How do you develop appreciation of even adverse circumstances? Through forgiveness of yourself and others. To forgive, you must realize that we all act according to our capacity. We act within our capacity at every moment that we act. But capacity can change. We could do something according to our capacity one moment, and then look back a moment later and see our action in a different light. Perhaps we should have, or could have, done something else. We must forgive ourselves, remembering that at that time we could not have done anything but what we did. If we realize that we are doing the best we can at any given moment, and that everyone else is also doing his or her best, then it is easier to forgive. Forgiveness frees us of negative binding karma.

Another good karma activity is to be happy when others are happy. Rejoice in their happiness for the sheer sake of happiness. This is easy when you approve of the source of someone's happiness. But what if you don't?

Geshe Michael Roach, a Buddhist teacher, describes a very practical way to incur good karma. It is called "rejoicing in the good karma of others." Each morning, before you get out of bed, reflect on at least five people whom you saw or heard about the day before who were engaged in performing good actions. Acknowledge each one of them and rejoice in their good actions. When you are happy about another's good karma you automatically share in that good karma. This good karma accumulates, creating its own magnetic field, which attracts more good karma.

Let's say your daughter is bringing her new boyfriend home to meet you. In your opinion, the boy does not deserve your daughter's love. In your mind you have a list of his unsavory qualities that justify your inability to share in your daughter's happiness.

You express your negative opinion of her boyfriend to your daughter. Because you *really* want her to understand how unhappy you are, you express your opinion with anger and frustration. This creates bad karma between you and your daughter that may or may not be resolved in this lifetime.

Consider, instead, setting aside your opinion about the cause of your daughter's happiness. Here is an opportunity to practice detachment. Simply rejoice in your daughter's happiness selflessly. Whenever selflessness occurs, good karma is not far behind.

This doesn't mean you don't have opinions about your daughter's boyfriend. Your opinions may be valid and could, if requested, help your daughter make decisions concerning her future karma with him. But do not allow unhappiness to guide your actions. Come into a state of happiness first, and then act accordingly. Your daughter will be more likely to hear your opinions if they are presented without anger and insult.

This is a radical approach. But as yogis, we are willing to try a new approach and see if it generates mental clarity and peace.

Activities that generate good karma:
Acceptance
Giving thanks
Forgiveness
Rejoicing in others' good deeds
Being happy when others are happy

By cultivation of feelings of friendship and fellowship toward those who are happy, by great compassion and love toward those who are unhappy and suffering, by joy and entertainment toward those who are meritorious and virtuous, by neutrality and indifference toward those who are demeritorious and evil-natured, a yogin should attain undisturbed peace and happiness of mindstuff, chittam.

—*Patanjali,* Yoga Sutras I:33[2]

This approach helps us develop equanimity of mind in all situations, which leads, in turn, to the understanding that running away from unpleasant situations will not lead to lasting happiness. Let's say you are unhappy with your job and wish to quit. Each day you go to work grudgingly, and throughout the day you tally up the reasons for your dissatisfaction. One day your frustration and anger reach a breaking point and you hand in your resignation. What are the possible karmic repercussions of this action?

When you find a new job, you may initially be elated, but it will probably only be a matter of time before frustration and anger take over again. You will find yourself upset and on the brink of quitting again. The way of karma is such that it will assure us of continued placement in "bad" situations until we transcend them.

Anger is never strong enough to transcend an unpleasant situation. Anger may feel good temporarily, as it seems to relieve frustration, but in the long run it causes harm because it disturbs your connection to the inner Self, which is joy. Anger mires us deeper in ignorance and pain.

The correct response, or rather, the response that would lead to evolution for the soul, would be to never leave a situation while you are in a state of anger, jealousy, or despair. If you wish to be permanently free of the unpleasant situation so that you do not have to repeat it, you must find a way to be thankful for it. You must leave while in a state of happiness. Don't wait to be happy until after you quit your job. Your job is not what is standing in the way of your happiness; your state of mind is.

Equanimity of mind leads to freedom from anxiety. This concept is illustrated beautifully in the *Bhagavad Gita*. The *Gita* opens with Arjuna, the warrior, and Krishna, his chariot driver and counselor, on the battlefield preparing to go into battle. Arjuna is filled with anxiety at the prospect of going into battle because he knows that many of the soldiers of the opposing army are his relatives and teachers.

Arjuna wants to turn back. He doesn't want to fight. Krishna urges him on and tells him that it is his job to fight. He is a soldier. He has been trained all his life to fight battles. He was born into this, as were his father and grandfather before him and their ancestors. It is the result of past karma.

Arjuna is overwrought with remorse, anger, and confusion; his mind has become unbalanced. Krishna advises him that now is not the time to decide to change jobs. Krishna tells Arjuna: You are in a state of anxiety and have lost all equanimity of mind. If you are serious about changing professions, first gain equanimity of mind, and then you can make decisions based on clarity and wisdom. You have spent lifetimes propelling this into motion and it is not so easily changed. The course of one's life can be changed, but for change to be lasting it must come from inner transformation.

In the rest of the *Bhagavad Gita*, Krishna teaches Arjuna yoga practices such as compassion toward others and devotion to God, which develop equanimity of mind.

Once there was a great yogi who lived in a small town. All day long he did practices like meditation, japa (chanting), *puja* (ritual worship), asana, and pranayama. One day a prostitute moved into the house across the street. All day long men came and went from the house. The yogi would see this out of his window and think, "What is going on over there? This is really horrible. I am a yogi. I should not have to live near such an impure, evil woman. This is not good, I do not deserve this."

The prostitute was very busy, but once in a while she would get a break and look out of her window and see the yogi. When she did, her heart filled with love and admiration for him. "Oh, what a wonderful man he is. All day long, he is so holy, thinking of God, worshiping God, oh what a great soul! Look how peaceful he is, his mind always on God."

After some time the prostitute and the yogi both died and went up to the gates of heaven. The angels and saints at the gate looked at the prostitute and said, "Oh, how wonderful to have you, we've been waiting for you! Please come in." They looked at the yogi and said, "You, back down you go!"

The yogi was very upset and protested: "This is unfair, there must be some mistake. All of my life I have been meditating and worshiping God." The gatekeeper said, "No, all day long you have been thinking about what could be going on in the prostitute's house, while all day long the prostitute was thinking of God. Even while looking at you, her mind was on God."

When did the first karma appear? The moment that jiva (the individual soul) attached itself to the upadhi (the body/mind) and identified with it. The moment jiva moved from "I-AM" consciousness to "I am my body/mind" consciousness.

What caused that to happen? No one knows. That is a transcendental question, and so it must have a transcendental answer. All we need to know is that it happened. What caused it to happen is irrelevant at this point.

When did it happen? It happened at the precise moment that it happened. The first line in the most ancient *Veda*, the *Rig Veda*, says, "Who knows this?" No one knows, because it is unknowable. The intellect can't grasp it. It happened in beginningless time. What propelled jiva into action was the desire to *know*, through the senses.

Yogis recognize, for example, that the act of eating food carries karmic consequences. It makes sense to eat a vegetarian diet, as it has minimal dire karmic results. The tragedy of a nonvegetarian lifestyle is that it causes needless, cruel victimization. We bear the karma not only of the animals' deaths, but also of the devastating environmental impact of meat eating: the pollution of water and air by slaughterhouses and farms and the razing of forests to create pastures. Due to the greed of the meat-eating majority, much of the world starves while the grains that could feed them are fed to cattle.

Don't fall into the trap of believing that your good life is separate from the suffering of animals who are abused or killed to maintain that good life. All of our karmas are interwoven. Your actions will either create future suffering or end future suffering not only for others, but for yourself as well.

What goes around comes around.
—popular saying

Let the small self with its petty, selfish desires get out of the way and allow the compassionate Self to come forth, guiding every thought and action. Karma affects those who think that *they* are the doer. Liberated beings know they never did anything, but are simply embodied out of a sense of compassion so they can serve others.

To develop a sense of universal responsibility—of the universal dimension of our every act and of the equal right of all others to happiness and not to suffer—is to develop an attitude of mind whereby, when we see an opportunity to benefit others, we will take it in preference to merely looking after our own narrow interests.
—*His Holiness the Dalai Lama,* Ethics for the New Millennium[3]

When good karmas accumulate, they will affect the very molecules of the physical body; the body will appear glowing and good. Generosity is the key to true beauty, a beauty that comes from inside.

The moksha (liberation) mantra describes this state of freedom from karma:

Om
Tryambakam Yajamahe
Sugamdhim Pushtivardhanam
Urvarukamiva Bandhanan
Mrityor Mukshiya Mamritat

In English, this sounds like a mysterious riddle:

Om
We worship the three-eyed one (Shiva)
Who is fragrant and who nourishes well all beings
May Shiva liberate us from death for the sake of immortality
Even as the cucumber is severed from its bondage to the creeper

We worship the three-eyed one (Shiva): Shiva is a name for our higher Self. Shiva has three eyes, because the Self can see both sides at the same time and perceives the oneness behind all duality. The eye in the center represents the transcendence of duality, of all pairs of opposites.

Who is fragrant and who nourishes well all beings: Shiva, the immortal Self, smells good! The sense of smell originates in the *muladhara chakra*, the root center at the base of the spine. This ability to smell and to be smelled has traveled into the highest level of perception: the *ajna chakra*, which is the abode of joy, of Shiva.

"THE STARFISH"
BY LOREN EISLEY

A young man was picking up objects off the beach and tossing them out into the sea. A second man approached him and saw that the objects were starfish.

Why in the world are you throwing starfish into the water?

If the starfish are still on the beach when the tide goes out and the sun rises high in the sky, they will die, replied the young man.

That is ridiculous. There are thousands of miles of beach and millions of starfish. You can't really believe that what you're doing could possibly make a difference!

The young man picked up another starfish, paused thoughtfully, and remarked as he tossed it out into the waves, It makes a difference to this one . . .

Shiva nourishes us with bliss, love, and joy. Keep in mind that Shiva is not some God living on a remote mythic mountaintop. This is our own inner Self, the very essence of our being.

May Shiva liberate us from death for the sake of immortality, even as the cucumber is severed from its bondage to the creeper: The mantra's last line is a poetic rendition of how enlightenment comes about. When cucumbers are picked unripe, as most cucumbers at the grocery store are, they have a little scar or stem indicating where the cucumber was attached to the vine. But a cucumber left to ripen and given nourishment from sun, soil, and water will become pushti, so fat that it falls gently off the vine. It will appear self-originating, whole and complete, like the enlightened soul that has gone through all the experiences of life and is now liberated, with the appearance that it was never in bondage at all.

The realization, which accompanies liberation, is that the soul was always liberated, that it was never born and will never die. It is whole and complete, and always was.

When the knot of ignorance breaks in their hearts,
all doubts vanish,
and witnessing Him,
all their actions from beginningless time are dissolved.
—Yoga Shikha Upanishad [4]

Photographer: Michael Lavine

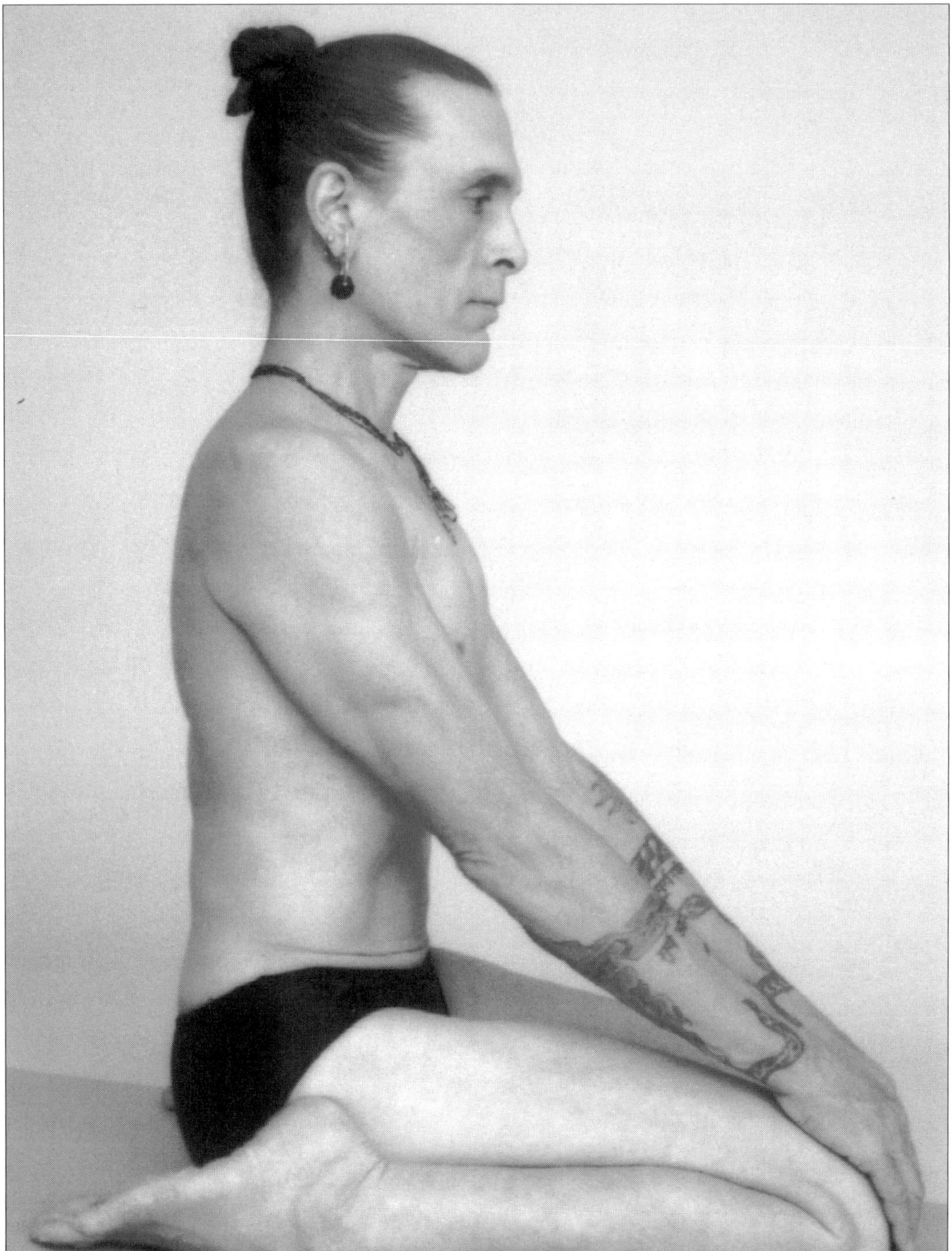

4

Ahimsa: Walking the Nonviolent Path

I've decided to stick with love; hate's too heavy a burden to bear.
—Dr. Martin Luther King, Jr.

A friend once told us that there's really not much difference between the hero and the coward: they both feel the same fears and anxieties. The hero acts in spite of these fears and anxieties, however, whereas the coward turns away from action. The cultural hero seeks to break the chains of his or her culture's particular illusions; the coward lives in denial.

We can break these chains. We make them up ourselves.
—False Prophets, "Baghdad Stomp"[1]

Throughout human history, cultural heroes like Dr. Martin Luther King Jr. and Mahatma Gandhi have chosen the path of nonviolence, or ahimsa. It is a challenging path to take, because it is rarely the path of the majority and because it takes more courage to meet violence with kindness and compassion than to meet violence with violence. Nonviolence also happens to be the ethical foundation of yoga, according to Patanjali's *Yoga Sutras*.

In the *Yoga Sutras*, Patanjali lays out an eight-limbed plan for liberation called Raja Yoga. The first step is called yama, which means restraint, and it includes five ethical restrictions. These five yamas are yoga's ethical backbone:

1. *ahimsa:* nonharming
2. *satya:* truthfulness
3. *asteya:* nonstealing
4. *brahmacharya:* continence
5. *aparigraha:* greedlessness

Ahimsa is a yama, a restraint. It is a recommendation for how you should restrain your behavior toward *others*, not toward yourself. The second limb of the Ashtanga system, niyama, consists of observances:

1. *shauca:* cleanliness
2. *santosha:* contentment
3. *tapas:* discipline
4. *svadhyaya:* study of Self
5. *ishvarapranidhana:* devotion to God

These are recommendations concerning your behavior toward yourself.

Nonetheless, some contemporary yoga teachers interpret ahimsa more as an observance than as a restraint, as a directive not to harm yourself. "Don't be aggressive in your asana practice, be kind to your body," they say, or "Don't restrict your diet with extremes like *vegetarianism*; it might harm you."

Not harming yourself is an aspect of ahimsa, certainly, but it is of less importance than the directive to avoid harming others. If you limit your practice of ahimsa to being kind to yourself, you will deny yourself the ultimate benefit of yoga practice, which is everlasting happiness. Everlasting happiness is achieved by putting the welfare of others before your own.

Ahimsa covers thought as well as action. Patanjali recommends that your yoga practice be based on the determination to avoid not just harmful actions, but even thoughts that could harm another being. Nonharming is essential to the yogi because it creates good karma—not only for the person or animal that is not harmed, but for the yogi who has refrained from causing harm. Good karma leads to eternal joy and happiness. The yogi, realizing this, tries to cause the least possible amount of harm and suffering to others.

Compassion is an essential ingredient of ahimsa. Through compassion you begin to see yourself in other beings. This helps you refrain from causing harm to them. Developing compassion does something else, however, which is of special interest to the yogi. It trains the mind to see past outer differences of form. You begin to catch glimpses of the inner essence of other beings, which is happiness. You begin to see that every single creature desires happiness. Every single being desires to know the Self, although this desire may not always be a conscious one.

If you seek enlightenment, or even if you seek happiness, go to the cause. Nothing exists without a cause. The root cause of happiness is compassion.
—His Holiness the Dalai Lama[2]

To develop compassion, examine the motives for your actions. Are they selfish or unselfish? Proclaiming that it is right to eat meat because it makes you healthier, for example, is *himsic*, or harmful, because it is an action stemming from a selfish motive. Using drugs or cosmetics that were cruelly and needlessly tested on animals is also himsic.

Your cultural upbringing may tell you that you need to eat meat to be strong and healthy, for example, but your yoga practice recommends that you practice ahimsa. Which path will you choose?

Cultural heroes risk their own happiness by defying what the culture tells them they must do to be happy. They choose instead to do what they believe is just.

Heroes can appear in any form. The Buddha first incarnated as a bull, laboring in an infernal realm. He was yoked with another bull and together they pulled heavy loads for their demon master. While straining to pull the cart, the Buddha felt compassion for the weaker animal joined with him and told the demon master that he would pull the load alone, thus allowing the other bull to rest. The demon became so enraged by the Buddha's selflessness that he struck him on the head with his trident, killing him on the spot. Thus the Buddha, by putting another being's welfare before his own, began his path toward enlightenment.

In truth, we all share consciousness, and harm inflicted on one being, whether animal or human, is felt by all, sooner or later. When you recognize that cows and chickens want happiness, just as you do, you recognize kindred souls. The distinction between you and other beings wears thin, as awareness begins to dawn.

There is so much suffering in the world because there is so much violence. There is suffering in your life because you have caused suffering in the lives of others—not necessarily in this lifetime, perhaps in previous lifetimes. We cannot

Ahimsa-pratisthayam tat-sanni-dhau vaira-tyagah. (Ys III: 35)

Pratisthayam: on confirmation of
Ahimsa: (mental waves of) non-injury, nonviolence
Sanni-dhau: presence
Tat: (in) his (such person's)
Vaira: hostility
Tyagah: (all living beings) give up

When mindstuff is firmly based in waves of ahimsa, noninjury, all living beings cease their enmity in the presence of such a person.

Injurious ways and malice kill the natural power of mindstuff, and waves of this injurious mind cause injury, knowingly or unknowingly. When these injurious waves are removed and mind is established in ways of noninjury, these waves radiate in all directions. Before such a yogi all living beings forget their hostilities. Himsa means harming: ahimsa means nonharming.

There are three classes of himsa, or harm:

1. Physical, by body and instruments, including war.
2. Vocal, by speaking against others, including psychological warfare.
3. Mental, by thinking against others.

Abstention from all types of injury is called ahimsa. This term is used without adjective; it includes every type of injury because it is used in a broad sense.

One cannot injure others without first injuring oneself because injury is the result of psychological planning. Vocal injury is more serious than physical, and mental injury is most serious. By physical injury one can destroy only physical forms. By vocal injury one can destroy both physical and mental forms. By mental injury one can destroy even the form of spirit. Consequently one will go to lower transmigration.

—Shri Brahmananda Sarasvati, *The Textbook of Yoga Psychology*[3]

Rabbits in stocks for cosmetic testing.
Photographer: PETA

change what we have done in the past and there is no point in feeling guilty about it. What we *can* do is start living compassionate lives right now.

Patanjali says that future suffering should be avoided, and he gives ahimsa as the method. Do not cause suffering to any being and the resulting benefit is that eventually you will be free from suffering. This benefit evolves, of course, after many years (and possibly lifetimes) of practicing ahimsa.

We may think that acts of compassion toward other beings benefit only the other, that we are sacrificing our happiness for another being to benefit. In the short term it might look like this, but this is because we do not understand the law of karma or what compassion really means. The law of karma states that what you do to others will be done to you. The practice of nonviolence benefits both parties *equally*.

Much cruel violence is perpetuated against animals in the name of medical research, for example, because it is thought to be a necessary evil. In using animals for medical research, we rationalize the cruelty involved by declaring that the results of the research may relieve suffering for many people. But no lasting benefit can ever come from causing harm to another. When we understand the law of karma, we realize that we cannot torture animals and receive any lasting benefit. Only the foolish would be deluded otherwise.

Nor can we use the law of karma to justify indifference to victims of cruelty with such phrases as "They deserve it, it's their karma." It is not your job to parcel out blame or judgment. Your job is to do all you can to relieve the suffering of all beings, no matter what they might have done in their pasts. Your job is to perfect your actions and act in the most selfless and compassionate way toward all beings. You must strive to see the Divine in all.

Being driven primarily by selfish motives mires us in the I-Me-Mine syndrome: What do I want? What's in it for me? That's mine. George Harrison's lyrics in the song "I Me Mine," from the *Let It Be* album, describe the condition of the person lost in self-centered motives, riding an emotional roller coaster of unsatisfied desires.

In Harrison's song there is a line that speaks of tears being shed for I, me, and mine. Those are the ego's tears, shed for self-centered reasons. How many people cry for God? How many cry because they are in an unenlightened state? How many cry because they knowingly caused harm to another? As Swami Satchidananda says, "Who will be the happiest person? The one who brings happiness to others."[4]

On the other hand, remember that ahimsa is a *practice*. You may not get it right from the start. Although perfection is the goal, the term "practice" implies the importance of the process. The fact that we are embodied spirits, living a physical existence, presupposes that we will cause harm to others to ensure our own livelihood. This realization should not be a pessimistic cloud settling over the yogi. On the contrary, it should give rise to humility and an awareness of the enormous harm human beings can cause. Simply strive to cause the least amount of harm you can.

Until we stop harming all other living beings, we are still savages.
—Thomas Edison[5]

Some people argue that vegetables have feelings, too, so what does it matter if we eat chickens or carrots? The answer is simple: the yogi strives to cause the least possible amount of harm, and it is clear that eating a vegetarian diet causes the least harm to the planet and all creatures.

The assumption made by some people that you can cause less harm by eating fish instead of cows, for example, is based on a false hierarchy. It is a false assumption to think that by eating fish you are causing less suffering than you would by eating cows. All animal beings—including fish and birds—possess five senses. Fish feel as much as humans or any other animal.

Plants also feel, but they do not possess five senses. By limiting your diet to

Jain nuns wearing gauze over their mouths to prevent them from accidentally inhaling and causing the death of insects.
Photographer: Sharon Gannon

plants, you limit not only the suffering you cause to other beings, but the amount of suffering you cause the planet as well. Eating meat takes an environmental toll that generations to come will be forced to pay. Take a look at these facts:[6]

- Raising animals for food causes more water pollution in the United States than any other industry because animals raised for food produce 130 times the excrement of the entire human population: 87,000 pounds per second! Much of the waste from factory farms and slaughterhouses flows into streams and rivers, contaminating water sources.

- Each vegetarian saves an acre of trees every year! More than 260 million acres of U.S. forest have been cleared to grow crops to feed animals raised for meat, and another acre of trees disappears every eight seconds. The tropical rain forests are also being destroyed to create grazing land for cattle. Fifty-five square feet of rain forest may be razed to produce just one quarter-pound burger.

- Of all raw materials and fossil fuels used in the United States, more than one-third is used to raise animals for food. Producing a single hamburger patty uses enough fossil fuel to drive a small car twenty miles and enough water for seventeen showers.

- Of all agricultural land in the United States, 87 percent is used to raise animals for food. That's 45 percent of the total land mass of the United States.

- More than half the water consumed in the United States is used to raise animals for food. It takes 2,500 gallons of water to produce a pound of meat, but only 25 gallons to produce a pound of wheat. A totally vegetarian diet requires 300 gallons of water per day, whereas a meat-eating diet requires more than 4,000 gallons of water per day.

- In the United States, animals raised for food are fed more than 80 percent of the corn we grow and more than 95 percent of the oats. The world's cattle alone consume a quantity of food equal to the caloric needs of 8.7 billion people—more than the earth's entire human population.

It's obvious that factory farming is shaking this planet's fragile ecosystem, but it is responsible for a great deal more harm than that. In these times of human overpopulation, agribusiness resorts to inhumane means to supply consumers with the animal products that the advertising agencies hired by the meat and dairy industries have convinced them they need to be healthy. The killing of billions of animals every year for human consumption is only part of the harm that is done. The real crime is that factory-farmed animals are forced to spend their lives in horrible conditions.

If people knew how badly animals are treated in today's factory farms, if people knew how completely confined and immobilized these creatures are for their entire lives, if people knew how severe and unrelenting is the cruelty these animals are forced to endure, there would be change. If people knew. But too many of us choose to look the other way, to keep the veil in place, to remain unconscious and caught in the cultural trance. That way we are more comfortable. That way is convenient. That way we don't have to risk too much. This is how we keep ourselves asleep.

—John Robbins[7]

Animals raised to produce food are treated monstrously. They are viewed as machines that pump out milk, eggs, hot dogs, steaks, pork chops, and more.

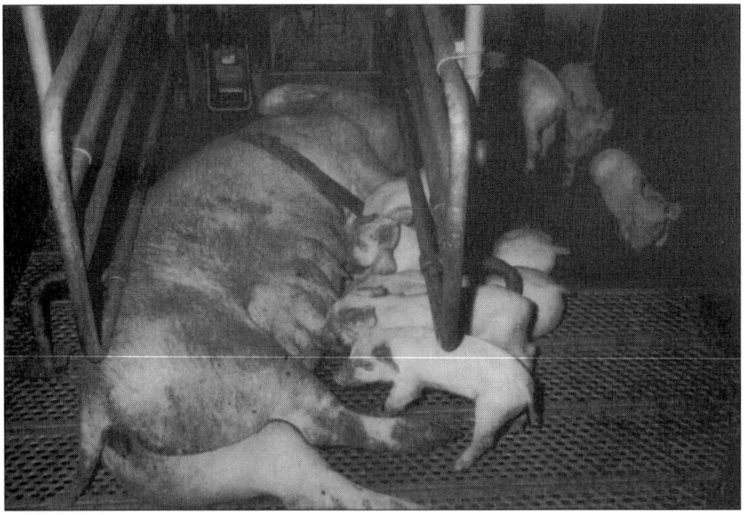

Mother pig with babies
Photographer: PETA

The image makers for the meat and dairy industries do not want consumers to know how the animals really live. If the public knew, industry profits would be jeopardized. But the time for sleeping in the bliss of ignorance is coming to an end for all of us who share this planet, as authors such as Karen Davis, John Robbins, and Ingrid Newkirk share their investigations.

The human commitment to harmony, justice, peace and love is ironic as long as we continue to support the suffering and shame of the slaughterhouse and its satellite operations.

—*Karen Davis,* **Poisoned Chickens, Poisoned Eggs**[8]

Did you know that there are more cows in the United States than there are people? This is surprising because we never see most of these cows. They are living horribly degraded lives and are dying cruel deaths by the millions. They are kept from our sight lest they disturb us. If we did see inside a factory farm or a slaughterhouse, we would probably swear off meat forever.

Some people misinterpret empathy for animals as weakness. Standing up against cruelty is actually an act of strength—especially when most people merely follow the crowd. We are the lucky ones—we are not standing day after day in a tiny space breathing the stench of our own waste, waiting only to be

slaughtered. Our actions can make a powerful public statement against the current treatment of animals.

—Why Vegan?[9]

Drinking milk and eating yogurt are also harmful to cows. Many misinformed people believe that we are doing cows a favor by milking them. This is not true. Dairy cows are forced to lactate continuously through artificial insemination and rarely get to nurse their babies, who are taken from them soon after birth and fed low-quality or synthetic milk. Humans then take the mothers' milk and profit from its sale. Eventually, every dairy cow stops producing milk. When that happens, she is slaughtered and becomes beef.

Women's liberation is a cherished ideal these days—liberation for human women, that is. Most feminists, male and female, probably have not thought about the cruelty and degradation inflicted on female animals, especially mothers. How many activists reflect on this as they crack their daily egg or pour a glass of mother's milk? Could the rising levels of breast and ovarian cancer in women have a karmic source in the inhumane treatment of the mothers of other species? The law of karma assures us: whatever we do to others will be done to us.

I do not believe any sensitive human being could see what is actually being done to cows, chickens, pigs, and turkeys in today's factory farms and slaughterhouses, and remain unmoved. We treat these animals, each one of them a sentient being, as if they were so much garbage. We subject them to conditions that frustrate every one of their natural instincts and urges, and that are a violation of the human-animal bond. In the name of cheap meat, poultry and dairy products, we are committing a crime against nature, against these animals, and against our own humanity. I cannot tell you how grateful I am that we are able to make food choices that do not collude and participate in this nightmare and that, at the same time, help improve our own health.

—John Robbins[10]

USDA statistics show that in 1940 cows averaged 2.3 tons of milk per year. Despite large milk surpluses, Bovine Growth Hormone (BGH) was approved in 1993 to further increase milk output. The 1996 average was 8.3 tons per year. Some BGH-treated cows have recently produced more than 30 tons of milk in a year.[11]

Chickens were the first animals to be factory-farmed. Male chicks are usually thrown into garbage bins; female chicks are stuffed into wire cages after their beaks are cut off with no anesthesia by a clipping machine. Many chickens die from shock during this procedure.

Hens in battery cages
Photographer: PETA

These egg-laying hens are crowded into cages so tight that their feet sometimes grow around the wire. The cages are stacked on top of each other, and excrement from chickens in one cage often falls on the chickens under them. They live like this for most of their short, stressed lives. When they can't lay any more eggs, they are slaughtered for meat.

Most people don't realize that American animal cruelty laws apply only to pets, not farm animals. A farm animal is an animal that can be tortured with impunity, although organizations like Farm Sanctuary and PETA are working to change this fact by urging the courts to prosecute farm animal abusers.

At least Americans don't eat cats and dogs . . . or do we? In actuality, millions of the cats and dogs that are euthanized every year by shelters and veterinarians end up in rendering plants. Most brands of commercial pet foods contain these rendered ingredients. So does livestock feed, which eventually becomes your hamburger.

The greatness of a nation and its moral progress can be judged by the way its animals are treated.

—Mahatma Gandhi[12]

Enlightenment is a lighting up of every bit of darkness. Most people aren't aware of the unpleasant facts in this chapter. Awareness is the first step toward choosing to walk a different path. If you are not aware of how meat and dairy products are produced, start reading. There are books, tapes, and videos listed in Appendix II: Recommended Resources that can enlighten you on this subject.

Once we become aware of the atrocities of *speciesism*, we can choose not to participate in this violence. Speciesism is the belief commonly held by humans that members of all other species exist only to benefit the human species. This prejudice allows us to believe that we have the right to treat other beings badly because they belong to another species. It's really no different from racism. Like racism, it has its roots in selfishness. We selfishly misperceive the true nature of other beings and focus only on how they could be useful to us. If you're unsure whether any particular situation represents a case of speciesism, just put a human being in the animal's place.

At a lecture given by the Dalai Lama, a person asked, "If you have a horse that has broken its leg, isn't it best to shoot the horse to relieve its suffering?"

His Holiness replied, "If your child broke his leg, would you shoot him?"

People often cite cruel behavior between animals to rationalize human cruelty against animals. But no other mammal, bird, reptile, or fish is capable of the mass annihilation of whole populations, or of the planet itself. Seen from this perspective, other animals are rather gentle creatures. Of all the creatures on this planet, human beings are the cruelest. No other animal has developed the killing force of humans.

Perhaps you have justified buying something that involves the suffering of an animal with rationalizations such as "I just needed to do something good for myself so I splurged and bought this leather coat" or "I just got a promotion. Let's celebrate with a steak dinner." But causing harm to another can never bring deep satisfaction. Wearing clothes or eating food that requires the torture and death of other beings cannot produce lasting happiness. To find joy in the pain and suffering of another can only lead one deeper into denial of the nature of the Self, which is connected to all beings.

Nothing comes from violence, and nothing ever could.
—Sting, "Fragile"[13]

Some people, many who profess to be yogis, argue that vegetarianism is not a healthful diet for everyone. We agree that vegetarianism is not for everybody; it is only for those who desire happiness and peace. It is definitely a must for those who are interested in enlightenment.

Collapsed dairy cow at slaughterhouse
Photographer: Farm Sanctuary

As long as we are the living graves of murdered animals, slaughtered to satisfy our appetites, how can we hope in this world to attain the peace we say we are so anxious for?

—*George Bernard Shaw,* **Living Graves**[14]

Yoga is not for everyone. Not everyone is dissatisfied with his or her present condition. Some people are not consciously seeking the source of their own being. But for those who are, the practice of ahimsa is of primary importance, due to its transformational effect on the mind and, consequently, the body. The body/mind consciousness, or personality, is purified through ethical vegetarianism and the practice of ahimsa.

Ahimsa is the touchstone of Patanjali's eight-limbed yoga system. A touchstone is a standard by which the purity of gold is judged: 10k, 14k, or 24k. To a yogi, the only true gold is universal consciousness, unconditional love. Ahimsa is the yogic touchstone that reveals how we are doing, how close we are to universal consciousness. The purity of our efforts to avoid causing harm reveals our spiritual evolution: Have we reached 10k, 24k, or just fool's gold?

In order to be kind, one must do. There is no point in thinking good thoughts and not acting on them. There is no currency in wishing things were better but not rolling up one's sleeves and helping to change them.

—*Ingrid Newkirk,* You Can Save the Animals[15]

Ways to cause less harm to others:

1. Eat a vegan (plant-based) diet with no animal products of any kind.
2. Eat a vegetarian diet that may include dairy products.
3. Eat a compassionate diet that is derived from organic sources.
4. Eat a moderate diet that is prepared in a sattvic atmosphere.
5. Do not harbor hateful thoughts about others, whether they are human, animal, plant, mineral, or elemental beings.
6. Refrain from speaking negatively to or about any being, even if just joking.
7. Do not sanction the abuse, torture, or killing of another being.
8. Do not physically abuse, hurt, or kill another being.

5

Guru: The Teacher You Can See and Feel

The guru said to the disciple:
"You have three jobs.
Your first was to find me.
Your second is to love me.
Your third is to leave me."
—Indian proverb

The aim of yoga is to realize that we are all connected. We share one heart, one consciousness, and one Divine Source. Yoga's method is to provide us with experiences that help us grasp this. To realize that we are all connected, it is helpful first to connect with one other person. In the yogic tradition this connection is experienced through a relationship with a *guru*, a teacher who facilitates the awakening of unitive consciousness. By acknowledging a guru, you connect to those who have trod the path before you. In doing so, humility dawns and awakening is possible.

The concept of guru is difficult for most Westerners to accept, because we like to think we are in charge. But the truth is that the predominant powers in our society control most people's lives. Big corporations and the advertising agencies that work for them decide what people think about and shape our society's values. Methods to gain genuine control over our lives are not taught in our schools; instead, working for material gain is emphasized. Most of us are at the mercy of our emotions, and when we can't handle them we use alcohol or other drugs, TV, shopping, eating, or sex to make ourselves feel happier. The idea that lasting happiness can be found inside, without having to buy, smoke, eat, watch, or drink anything, is foreign to us. We may need a translator. The guru is the translator.

For Westerners, guru is also a rather mysterious concept. Many students ask us, "How can I find my guru? Do I have to go to India? How will I recognize the guru?" We would like to take this opportunity to demystify the word "guru." Gurus do not necessarily have to be Indian, or enlightened. They may be married or not. They may have regular jobs and not head an *ashram*. A guru is a teacher who imparts to you insights or revelations about Yoga. A guru may also give you a method to practice so that you may realize for yourself the truth of those revelations.

For someone to be your guru, you must acknowledge him or her as such. A guru may not proclaim to you "I am your guru." That is for the student to proclaim. Once that acknowledgment and appreciation dawns, learning accelerates. Gurus do not require, as some in the West mistakenly believe, that blood oaths be taken or that all worldly possessions be turned over. If a guru demands something like that of you, you might consider running in the opposite direction!

We have a similar misunderstanding in the West of the word "swami," which in India merely designates a renunciate, someone who has taken vows of poverty and celibacy to further his or her spiritual practice. It does not mean, as Westerners often mistakenly believe, that the person is an enlightened being, although some enlightened beings are swamis.

You will be taught according to your capacity to learn. So to find your guru, become the perfect disciple. Become irresistible to the guru by becoming empty. When you come before any teacher, set aside "I know," so that you can be taught. If you are already filled up with knowledge, like a cup full of tea, and your teacher attempts to pour new tea into your cup, you will just overflow and no benefit will be obtained.

If you want lasting happiness, just be your-Self, which *is* lasting happiness. If you find that difficult, find someone who seems unwaveringly happy. Spend as much time as you can with him or her.

In this tradition knowledge passes from guru to disciple in a continuous, uninterrupted flow. The relationship of guru and student must have a particularly pure quality for the transmission to take place. Respect and love for the teacher must be understood as the same as respect and love for the Divine. This can be challenging, especially for westerners.

"What Americans need most is more humility. There is a lack of humility here," an Indian guru told us during one of his first visits to the States. "This will be very difficult," he continued, "because your culture does not support humility. In fact, humility is taken advantage of and overwhelmed in this society. In India humility is highly regarded."

We can cultivate humility by acknowledging that another person could shed some light to illuminate the darkness of our misunderstanding. Humility is like a magical elixir that cures arrogance. Arrogance will forever keep us separate from each other and from God. It will keep us from samadhi, because arrogance and ecstasy don't go together.

The guru tradition is based on humility and appreciation. The respect a student gives a teacher is not for the teacher's benefit; it benefits the student to acknowledge and bow to another because this opens the connection to the Self within the student.

It may be helpful to think of Guru as a force rather than a person. The yogi walks on the razor's edge, but sometimes the razor becomes dull. A guru can sharpen your practice by jarring you out of complacency and self-satisfaction so that new possibilities appear.

How should you choose a guru? The assessment should not be only intellectual. Your intuition, feelings, and experiences should guide your decision to devote yourself to a teacher.

Vidya, or universal truth, links all the gurus through time. The teachings of yoga are passed on via transmissional lineage. Much of this knowledge cannot be verbalized because it is beyond body and mind. Because of its subtle, secret, or even unspeakable nature, this knowledge is only imparted through relationship. Without direct transmission, from someone who has had direct transmission, no connection is established to the knowledge sought.

We've all had the experience of being either inspired or brought down by the people around us. Some people moan and groan about every little problem in their lives and after hanging out with them you find that you are all wrapped up in your small miseries, too. Some people are so upbeat, focused, and disciplined that they make you feel that anything is possible.

When in the company of a guru, this inspiring effect is especially noticeable. In his wonderfully comprehensive book, *The Yoga Tradition,* Georg Feuerstein writes: "In the company of a God-realized master,

"Gu" means darkness, ignorance, that which obscures beauty and Truth. "Ru" means "that which removes." So, the Guru removes ignorance.

Three necessary criteria for a good teacher are:

Lineage: The teacher should have had direct transmission of knowledge from his or her own teachers. The teacher also should have been blessed to teach by his or her teachers.
Practice: The teacher must have a regular daily practice.
Love: The teacher must love the students so much that he or she is willing to sacrifice anything to serve them.

the practitioner is continuously exposed to the realizer's spiritualized body-mind, and by way of 'contagion' his or her own physical and psychic being is gradually transformed. This can be understood in modern terms as a form of rhythm entrainment, where the guru's faster vibratory state gradually speeds up the disciple's vibration."[1]

This is the principle of satsang, which translates as "company of the True." It applies to hanging out not only with a guru but also with saints, devotees, fellow yoga students—with anyone who is making a sincere effort in spiritual practice to experience the Self. When people have an intense yearning for God, their mood is infectious. We get a contact high from their God intoxication.

Joining with others to reach for God is an emotional experience. It taps into one's heart, and the critical mind takes a backseat for a while. Satsang is different from ordinary social gatherings. Many of the rules of social engagement are suspended when the guest of honor is God. Small talk has no place at a satsang—only elevating speech and singing is heard here. God accepts all who are sincere.

Satsang is a very important yoga practice, yet Western yoga practitioners often neglect it, perhaps because we tend to glorify the accomplishments of the individual ("Wow, she can get her feet behind her head!") and downplay the potential of group effort. Also, when people get together socially in our culture there can be a lot of self-consciousness and jockeying for position. It's actually fairly rare for adults to get together in groups without consuming some alcohol, or other drugs, to try to get past self-consciousness and feel closer to one another.

The fastest sadhana, for sure, is to hang out with other people who love God.
—Shyam Das[2]

You may ask: "If all is one, what difference does it make whom I hang out with? If everywhere you look there is God, why does it matter?"

Well, it doesn't matter for the enlightened ones, who do see God in every person or situation. But until you are blessed with that vision, it is best to choose carefully the people and situations you expose yourself to. When a sapling is planted it is necessary to put a fence around it to protect it from animals that may trample or eat it or children who may break it. Once it has properly matured, however, that once-vulnerable sapling will be so strong that children can climb all over it without harming it and the cow can be tied to it for safety. Satsang is a safe environment for your spiritual maturation.

Once an individual attains enlightenment, society at large automatically becomes enriched. This principle was the heart of the Buddhist social revolution.
—*Robert Thurman,* **Inner Revolution**[3]

Sticking with a guru or staying in a satsang that challenges us to change for the better can be difficult. Sometimes it is initially uncomfortable to keep the company of people who inspire us to change. Also, in the West, because democracy and equality are stressed so highly, we tend to believe that the best teacher is the one who is most like us—like our personality self, that is. But the yoga tradition says that the best teacher may not be the person who is most like you. The guru should be capable of standing behind you with a stick, prodding you to investigate your full potential.

Yoga teachers must uphold the moral and ethical principles of yoga. Yoga practitioners must devote themselves to the God within the teacher; this is what Guru is. Ideally, your teacher is someone who has achieved that which is sought. Imagine having a violin teacher who did not play, but merely read about playing and decided to teach it.

What most qualifies one to teach yoga is the attainment of enlightenment. Very few teachers are enlightened, but a sattvic teacher will make the effort to become very familiar with the scriptures, which contain the direct words of saints and realized beings. If the guru has not attained enlightenment, he or she must rely on the traditional texts and the words of his or her own guru to impart knowledge to students. Sattvic gurus always turn to the traditional texts for both guidance and education. This is how lineage manifests.

When yoga teachers do not uphold the lineage, it deteriorates. In the West, as a result, most yoga teachers are thought of as personal trainers rather than spiritual guides. This is the fault of the teachers, not the students. The outer look of yoga remains without the subtle essence of Truth, which can be transmitted only through devotion to a guru. If the teacher has not had that experience, how can he or she transmit it to students?

You may not have enough experience to be able to assess a teacher's skill and the quality of his or her instruction. We recommend, therefore, that you begin your yoga practice with intense investigation: read the scriptures and take classes. You must also be willing to let trust develop between you and a teacher.

In our case, Guru revealed itself to us as a trinity of extraordinary teachers: Shri Brahmananda Sarasvati, Shri Swami Nirmalananda, and Shri K. Pattabhi Jois. They are our lineage, shining through everything we write, say, and do.

Enlightened anarchism is the need of the hour. For an unenlightened person, even when their heart tells them to do good, their mind may make them do evil. It is only through enlightenment that one is able to live as a free and intelligent person.

—*Swami Nirmalananda,* A Garland of Forest Flowers[4]

We found our first guru through the mail. In 1984 a mauni, or silent yogi, named Swami Nirmalananda wrote to the Libertarian Book Club of New York City seeking to correspond with anarchists. Our friend Peter Lamborn Wilson, anarchist, author, and a founder of Semiotext(e) Press, gave us the swami's address so we could write back to him.

In the early 1960s, Swami Nirmalananda, who was born in 1925 in Kerala, India, traveled through Asia, Turkey, Russia, England, Europe, and America for several years on a quest for truth and peace. He conferred with people such as Martin Buber, Alan Watts, and T. Z. Suzuki, and gave talks and taught yoga classes, mostly in church basements and community centers. Returning to India in 1964, Swamiji traveled in the subcontinent before retreating to the Himalayas. There he met his guru, Aryadev, a Jewish man from England.

After spending a short time with his guru, Nirmalananda moved into a small grass hut in the jungle of B.R. Hills. He fell in love with the jungle inhabitants: birds, trees, monkeys, flowers, tribal people, elephants, and tigers. He lived there in seclusion, and practiced *mauna* (refraining from speaking). He maintained contact with the world through correspondence.

Swami Nirmalananda was an avid letter writer, with correspondents all over the world. His principal interest was world peace. He wrote pleas for nonviolence to world leaders in fluent, precise English. When we first began corresponding with him he would send us essays he had written on the subject of *anarchy*. This brilliant man called himself "the Anarchist Swami."

In those days anarchy was a very popular, if vaguely defined, idea in underground culture. The general idea was that anarchy meant "We can do whatever we want. We don't follow any rules or laws imposed by government or corporate power." But Swami Nirmalananda interpreted the phrase "self-rule" differently from the punk rockers who were spray-painting the encircled A sign on urban walls.

The false self thinks—the true Self knows.
—*Swami Nirmalananda,* A Garland of Forest Flowers[5]

Swami Nirmalananda defined anarchy as Self-rule. To him, anarchy meant being ruled by the enlightened Self. To be true anarchists, Swamiji suggested, we must liberate ourselves from the "tyranny of the thinking mind, we must be able to go beyond thought."[6] We must become enlightened.

The color of our skin, caste, race, nationality, religion, belief, ideology, status, education, culture, tradition, etc. pertain only to the body and mind. But the core of our being is infinite, eternal, ever pure, without beginning or end. This core underlies all forms and all changes like an invisible thread in a garland full of various flowers, remaining unsullied and unaffected by these outer manifestations and differences which are the root cause of animosity and antagonism in society.

—*Swami Nirmalananda,* A Garland of Forest Flowers[7]

Sharon corresponded with Swamiji for several years, and in 1986 we traveled to meet him. Getting to his ashram in the Bilgiri Hills of southern Karnataka was a long, exhausting trip. First, we traveled overnight by train from Trivandrum at the southern tip of India north to Bangalore in the state of Karnataka. David was very sick with dysentery he had suffered from for weeks, with no relief.

From Bangalore, we climbed aboard a bus jammed with goats, chickens, children, and adults and headed for the hill station called B.R. Hills. For six hours we were bounced and jostled through the rural countryside in 120-degree weather.

The trip culminated with a climb straight up several thousand feet to the cliffs where Viswa Shantih Nikethan, Swami's ashram, overlooks an infinity of dusty, parched countryside. We arrived exhausted and sick, and were about to knock when we read the sign over the door: "Do not disturb between the hours of 2 and 4 P.M." Oh great! It was 2:30 P.M. We would just have to wait.

We turned to leave, hoping to find a shady tree to rest under until four, when we heard someone clear his throat. We turned around to see a demure little man wearing ochre robes and holding his long-fingered hands one over the other, just under his chin.

He bore a very strong resemblance to Klaus Kinski's Dracula. Our meeting was highly reminiscent of the scene in the film in which Dracula opens the door to greet the naïve Jonathan, enthusiastically inviting him into the castle. With his large eyes twinkling, Swami Nirmalananda beckoned us into his small house. He walked ahead, his hips swaying and his shoulders rounded toward the front and held high—a slight frame, not much over five feet. Because he was observing mauna and did not speak, he gestured with his hands and tilts of the head. He also communicated with very articulate grunts, groans, and sighs.

Swami gestured for us to sit and brought us fresh-baked whole wheat bread and chutney made with wild gooseberries from the jungle. He waited with slightly open lips for a response from us after each mouthful. He laughed like a child at our enjoyment of the holy food. After our meal he motioned to us to hand him a nearby pen and paper. He wrote a short note: "Go to the small house nearby and take rest. We shall come at five o'clock with tea." He ended this sentence with a lilting movement of his head from side to side and a big smile.

We stayed with Swami for a week. He cured us with sweet well water, fresh whole wheat bread and vegetables, and his illuminating presence.

Swami Nirmalananda, the Anarchist Swami
Photographer: Peggy Medani

Even though Swami Nirmalananda lived in a remote part of India and hadn't spoken to anyone in many years, he was more hip and up-to-date than most people. It was really funny to see a *Free your mind—smash the TV* sticker on his wall next to a picture of the saint Ramana Maharshi.

Swami enthusiastically directed the energy he saved from speaking into a daily writing discipline. In the silence of the forest one could often hear the relentless padding of his fingers on his old manual typewriter.

Each day he wrote letters to heads of state in the name of world peace. He also attended to numerous devotees through words of advice and spiritual teachings. Swami authored several beautiful books and small pamphlets, including *A Garland of Forest Flowers*, *Flowers from the Forest*, *Enlightened Anarchism*, *Zen, a Way of Life*, and *Music and Poetry in Life*.

We especially appreciated Swamiji's activism because in the United States yoga teachers and students sometimes erroneously interpret our constitutional separation of church and state to mean that anyone engaged in spiritual practice should be apolitical. He confirmed our developing sense that, actually, anyone engaged in spiritual practice *should* be politically active, too.

There is a world of difference between a bird sitting and singing in a tree and a bird singing in a cage. It is only when the mind is free that the person can be free, not otherwise. With a free and quiet mind, we are able to live with a song of life, a song of love, a song of joy in our heart! Yet our freedom should not be used as a reckless license to do anything we please. In true freedom and happiness we like whatever we do, but we do not always do whatever we like.

—*Swami Nirmalananda,* A Garland of Forest Flowers[8]

Swami Nirmalananda's activism included the shunning of all animal products, including dairy products. To refrain from consuming milk is almost unheard of for an Indian Brahmin, but Swami Nirmalananda was a *vegan* for ethical reasons. He understood the suffering endured by any being that is enslaved and exploited for its ability to produce a commodity. He realized that in modern India abuse of cows was rampant. He knew that it is not nutritionally necessary for humans to drink milk, even though it is portrayed as such by dairy industries and the *shastric* and *ayurvedic* traditions of India. In our time, this nutritional myth is pushed for profit.

Swamiji lived, like Saint Francis of Assisi, as a model of the virtuous saint practicing ahimsa, or nonviolence. He taught us a potent mantra:

Lokah Samasta Sukhino Bhavantu
May all beings, everywhere, be happy and free
and may the thoughts and actions of our lives
contribute to that happiness and to that freedom for all.

Swamiji lived this mantra. We continue to recite it every day as the core of our own spiritual practice. In doing so we feel his presence alive within us, even though he left his body in 1997.

Swamiji had perfected ahimsa to such an extent that all beings were gentle and kind in his presence. The animals of the forest were his devoted companions. Every day of his life he derived sheer joy from feeding the many wild birds that visited the ashram regularly.

We have come into this world to bring peace unto all beings. To achieve this goal it is necessary to adopt peaceful ways of harmless living and non-interference in all our endeavors.

—*Swami Nirmalananda,* A Garland of Forest Flowers[9]

Swami Nirmalananda lived the lone life of an ascetic in seclusion, deep in the forest. His sadhana consisted of vegetarian cooking, political activism, kindness to all beings, meditation, worship of the Divine, and the observance of silence. The atmosphere at the ashram was very calm and peaceful. Except for the songs of birds, there was a pindrop silence, and Swamiji was part of that silence.

Swami Nirmalananda initiates David Life into monkhood.
Photographer: Sharon Gannon

We returned to Swamiji's hilltop ashram for many visits over the years. David was initiated into *sanyaas*, or monkhood, there and given the name Swami Bodhananda by Swamiji. Since Swamiji's death in 1997, his devoted disciple Swami Brahmadev cares for the ashram.

The second guru we met, in contrast to Swami Nirmalananda, was a strong-voiced, lively family man. Shri K. Pattabhi Jois has taught yoga for more than sixty years since learning from his guru.

Pattabhi Jois's guru was T. Krishnamacharya; his guru's guru was Rama Mohan Brahmacharya. All three were householders with wives and families. Pattabhi Jois showed us that the yogi could walk in cities and towns, work in the world, have relationships and families, and yet be free of the comings and goings, the ups and downs, the good and bad. You don't have to move to India or become a Hindu to practice yoga. You don't have to move away from family and friends either. Yoga is freedom from chitchat, wherever you are—freedom from the fluctuations of the *chittam*, or mindstuff.

My Guru's Guru was Rama Mohan Brahmacharya. My Guru was going to school in Banares seventy or eighty years back. At that time, my Guru was quite a scholar in philosophy, religion, Ayurveda, Sanskrit, and Ashtanga Yoga of Patanjali. After searching many places, someone told him to go to the North, to a large jungle, and he would find a yogi living there. He did go and met Rama Mohan Brahmacharya, who was in an ashram, the father of eight children, and at that time a big and strong man who was 150 years old.

—Shri K. Pattabhi Jois[10]

Pattabhi Jois says we first came to be taught at his home in Mysore, India, in 1989. We can't dispute that because we don't write everything in a ledger book as he does: date of birth, age, mother's name, and fee paid.

We loved him from the start. He was demanding but gentle, as he drove us through the strenuous primary series of asana postures of Ashtanga Yoga. He laughed at our awkwardness one moment, then shouted admonishments the next. We had never had an Indian teacher who was a family man, not a sanyaas. He explained that renunciation is not the best platform for yogic attainment in this age; family life is. He and his wife, whom we called Amma, were an inspiring couple.

The method [of Rama Mohan Brahmacharya] involved teaching texts like the **Bhagavad Gita** ***together with yoga asanas, as one. This is the Ashtanga method: Yoga, philosophy, grammar, Ayurveda, and then the Yoga therapy portion of study. All these subjects were taught by one Guru.***

—Shri K. Pattabhi Jois[11]

Pattabhi Jois has tremendous charisma and pulsates with the aura of a true *siddha*, one who has acquired the unusual powers earned through dedication to

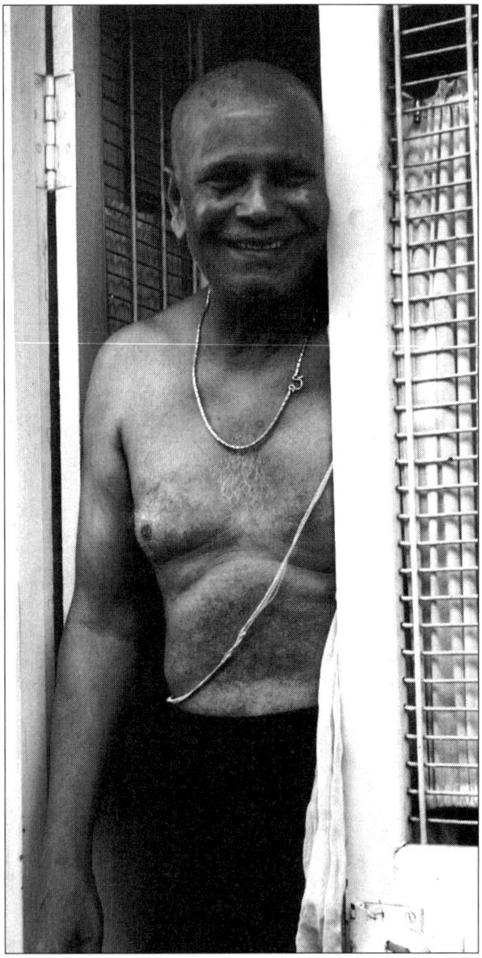

Shri K. Pattabhi Jois standing in the doorway of his yoga school in Mysore, India.
Photographer: Sharon Gannon

yoga practice and teaching for over six decades. Injuries that refuse to respond to any kind of therapy or bodywork disappear under his touch.

We visited Pattabhi Jois in India every year after our initial meeting, and in 1993 we hosted him in New York. He continues to travel, introducing many new practitioners to yoga by teaching them the vigorous asana practice known to the world as Ashtanga Yoga.

His wife, Amma, has left her body now, but even without her, Pattabhi Jois is still a family man. His son, daughter, and grandson assist him with teaching and touring.

Pattabhi Jois knows where all your buttons are located. With a few words he can make a devotee feel like a maharaja or a bad child. The work is subtle and psychological when one commits to a master. The asana practice becomes mere structure for the real work, which is transformation.

Pattabhi Jois transmits his knowledge primarily through touch and backs up everything with Sanskrit scripture. He is old school. That's partly what we like about him. He speaks and acts truthfully.

DAVID LIFE: Guruji, have you experienced samadhi?
PATTABHI JOIS: I am just a simple man.

Guess it takes an enlightened being to know an enlightened being.

Pattabhi Jois's classroom pulses with anticipation. In just a few minutes, all

David Life, Shri K. Pattabhi Jois, and Sharon Gannon
Photographer: Joel Sneed

the students will be dripping with sweat from the strenuous asana practice. Some start sweating just from being in the room, waiting for him to enter.

DAVID: What about people that sweat too much?
PATTABHI JOIS: Sweating is good, and the sweat should be massaged back into the skin. This creates lightness and removes toxins. Too much sweating is a weakness, and can be overcome in time.

Guruji moves around the room giving instructions and admonishments, evoking immediate corrections . . . and laughter. The man commands the respect that causes each of us to snap to attention. But then we have to laugh at ourselves along with him.

PATTABHI JOIS: Breath duration should not vary during practice.

During class Pattabhi Jois counts every breath. He teases with the breath count, mocks with the breath, and reprimands with the breath length. Part of the power of this teacher is his ability to make each of the hundreds of people in the room feel as if he is there for him or her alone. And he *is* there for each one, giving special instructions tailored to injuries, weaknesses, age, and temperament. The sophistication of his teaching is astounding in its seeming simplicity. He seems to look into each person's soul and teach to his or her highest potential.

Gurus demand total surrender from disciples. Disciples have an irrepressible need for the guru's approval. This is one subtle driving force of the relationship.

You may be in Navasana, boat pose, for the fifth time and dying. In the past your legs straightened, but now they won't. ("Why won't they straighten? They used to straighten. Will he see me cheating? Will he yell at me by name? I must try harder. I can't let him see me like this, a quaking mess. Got to concentrate on the breath.")

PATTABHI JOIS: Just one more.

("One more . . . sure. He always urges us on that way. Okay, I'll try it one more time for him.")

After each class there is a long receiving line with Guruji. You bow down to Guruji, touching his feet and then touching your hands to your head or heart.

One student said, "I want to go up to Guruji, but I've never bowed down to anybody before. I'm unsure of myself, but I feel drawn to do it."

"Don't bow down to just a man," we told him. "Instead, bow down to your highest Self that you recognize in him. Then bowing to him is no different from bowing before your own highest potential."

That student did bow down. He looked relieved afterward. That gesture is perhaps the most difficult of the entire program for many people. Gurus do that: they give us an opportunity to put aside our self-absorption and replace it with surrender and service.

What are the requirements for a good yoga teacher?
PATTABHI JOIS: A video. [laughter] Complete knowledge of the yoga method and patience with the students.
What are the requirements for the students?
PATTABHI JOIS: Some knowledge of Sanskrit and instruction in the yoga method from a qualified teacher.

Guruji is openly critical of meat consumption. He believes that for yoga practitioners there is no option other than a vegetarian diet.

Some yoga teachers say that a vegetarian diet is not necessary.
PATTABHI JOIS: [laughing] Oh . . . a new method!
Many Indians and Westerners eat meat.
PATTABHI JOIS: They are not practicing yoga. Meat eating makes you stiff.
What is the most important yogic practice in this time?
PATTABHI JOIS: Vegetarian diet is the most important practice for yoga.

Om Saha Navavatu
Saha Nau Bhunaktu
Saha Viryam Karavavahai
Tejasvi Navadhitam Astu
Ma Vidvisavahai
Om Shantih Shantih Shantih

Accept us both together
Protect us both together
May our knowledge and strength increase
May we not resent each other
Om peace peace peace

This is a traditional chant between student and teacher. The role of student and the role of teacher are *roles*, which can be interchanged. Nonetheless, they are essential. For any current to flow, you need a negative and a positive pole, a giver and a receiver.

Teachers can be classified by outer characteristics and tendencies, just as seekers were in Chapter 2, according to the three gunas: sattva (balance, light), rajas (passion, activity), and tamas (inertia, darkness).

Sattvic teachers are interested only in realizing the Truth and helping students to do so also. These teachers feel that serving the student is serving God. When both teacher and student are sattvic, they both learn and evolve because they are both interested only in *Atman jnana*, knowledge of the Self. Sattvic teachers treat all their students the same—but according to their needs and capacities.

Rajasic teachers don't want disciples, meaning self-disciplined students; they want followers. They are financially, emotionally, and spiritually dependent on their students. They take excessive care of their appearance to impress others, and may become depressed if a student doesn't like them. Their inner connection with the deeper spiritual truths is weak because they lack discipline. Instead of

The guru need not be a perfect enlightened being. The student's enlightenment does not depend on the teacher's attainment but on the student's sincere devotion to the Truth.

There was a guru with three disciples. The guru tells the first disciple: "You are not the body and mind. Jump off that cliff. You will not die." The disciple jumps off the cliff. The guru tells the second student: "You are the immortal Self. You could do anything. Go jump off that cliff." The student jumps off the cliff. The guru says to the third student: "You are the divine Atman, beyond death. Go jump off that cliff." The student jumps off the cliff. The guru tentatively walks to the edge of the cliff, thinking that he's going to see three dead students. He peers over the edge and is met with the sight of three happily smiling students jumping up and down and waving up at him. He becomes filled with pride. "Wow," he thinks, "I'm better than I thought I was." So he jumps off the cliff. And dies.

deepening their sadhana and maintaining humility, they become prideful and possessive.

Whereas sattvic teachers never have favorites and teach according to the specific needs of the students, a rajasic teacher keeps favorites who flatter him or her. Rajasic teachers may gossip about other teachers and forbid students to practice with other teachers out of insecurity, not out of genuine concern for the students' spiritual welfare. Rajasic teachers are overly concerned about payment, which determines the effort they put into teaching. A rajasic teacher is controlled by a need for praise and is more concerned with the students' approval than with God's.

You cannot help anyone—you can only serve.
—Swami Vivekananda[12]

Tamasic teachers cultivate blind followers who will do anything, including things that are immoral and unethical. They can go so far as to encourage drug taking, murder, and suicide. A tamasic teacher enjoys manipulating students to increase his or her power. Tamasic teachers will use any means to enhance their own ego-selves. Tamasic teachers use their charisma to manipulate others.

Always strive to develop sattvic qualities. If you are teaching, strive to be financially, emotionally, and spiritually independent of your students. Become dependent only on God. If you're a student, it won't matter what kind of teacher you have if your intentions are pure. You will benefit. Cultivate sattva in yourself and the teacher's faults need not affect you. Even a student with a tamasic teacher can obtain liberation.

A good teacher is interested only in your enlightenment. A good teacher wants you to become completely independent, meaning dependent-inward. The guru's job is removal of the false constructions within you that prevent you from perceiving your inner soul. The guru's job is to remind you that you are the divine Self.

As an old Indian proverb says: The devotee's job is to find the guru, love the guru, and finally leave the guru. When an inspirational guru leaves his or her body, this can be a dramatic time for devotees. The story of the life and death of our third guru, Shri Brahmananda Sarasvati, may shed more light on the complex relationship between teacher and student.

Back in 1979, a psychic told Sharon that she had a spiritual guide who was a doctor. Sharon asked if she would ever meet this man and was given the answer "Yes, but in the future. He says to be patient and keep working, as you are on the right path."

In May 1993 we went to the Pocono Mountains to participate in the Unity in Yoga Conference, which commemorated the centennial of yoga in America. The extraordinary lineup included Swami Satchidananda, Yogi Bhajan, Sant Khesavadas, Amrit Desai, Yogi Hari, Swami Dayananda, and Shri Brahmananda Sarasvati. Alongside these amazing Indian gurus were highly regarded American gurus, such as Lilias Folan, Ramajyoti Vernon, and Kali Ray.

There was something extra special about one of the presenters. He was a very animated man, wearing an orange beret and huge dark sunglasses. An enormous compass hung around his neck. Attendants and translators surrounded him. This man seemed to be speaking another language, but we learned that in 1983 he had had a severe stroke that had left his right side paralyzed and his speech impaired.

Shri Brahmananda Sarasvati had accepted this stroke as his "final enlightenment." His slurred speech demanded the presence of an "interpreter," but even in his disabled body his *shakti*, or life force, was extraordinary. Sparks literally shot out of his body when he talked. He was the most vibrant and enthusiastic speaker we had ever witnessed. He was passionate about his subject: enlightenment.

There was no doubt that this being was enlightened. His body and brain had undergone a debilitating and disfiguring stroke, but he was not in any way debilitated. He was free. His psychophysical condition could not impede his indefatigable energy and humor. The power of love shone through him with absolutely no inhibitions. We were riveted to our seats, utterly fascinated.

What was his lecture about? It didn't really matter *what* he said; it was how he said it. The amazing aspect of his lecture was the transmission of energy, the sparks that were shooting out of his being as though he were a high-voltage generator. The electricity in the room found its grounding in every body there. All we can remember clearly is the profound statement: "You are not the body and mind, although you have a body and mind. You are the Self. You are alive, feel the pulsation!" Wow!

We returned to New York City with renewed inspiration for the practice and teaching of yoga. A couple of months later, Sharon visited Ananda Ashram in Monroe, New York. The ashram was Shri Brahmananda's home. Many old photographs of him hung on the walls and, to her surprise, she recognized the man in them. Here was her spirit guide, the doctor she had known on the astral plane for so many years. Finally, through the grace of God and Guru, she had met him on

Shri Brahmananda Sarasvati
Photographer: Radha Devi

the physical plane. She felt a great relief, as if she had been reunited with a lost relative. A feeling of completeness that comes only from unconditional love enveloped her.

Shri Brahmananda Sarasvati was born into a Brahmin family as Ramamurti S. Mishra, in the North Indian state of Uttar Pradesh. His mother was a spiritual teacher with many disciples. His father was a high court judge and master of astrology and astronomy. Sanskrit was spoken in their home, and from early childhood Shri Brahmananda was immersed in meditation, yoga, and Sanskrit.

At age six, Ramamurti Mishra contracted a very serious illness and died. No vital signs or respiration were detected for thirty-six hours, so his family prepared to cremate him. As is customary, his father walked around the funeral pyre with a lit torch chanting *mantra*. He was about to light the pyre when the little boy sat upright. Frightened, the other people assembled ran away, thinking that a ghost had appeared. But the father moved closer and asked, "Who are you? Are you a ghost?" His son replied, "Father, it's me." Shri Brahmananda Sarasvati always considered this date, March 6, to be his real birthday.

At an early age Shri Brahmananda saw his life's plan and began preparations. He left home to pursue studies in Sanskrit and medicine and completed his first medical degrees in Ayurveda and Western medicine at Banaras Hindu University. In 1955, Dr. Mishra left India to continue his medical studies and practice in the West, specializing in ophthalmology, endocrinology, psychiatry, and neurosurgery. He served as a resident in neurosurgery at Bellevue Hospital in New York City.

Man needs to understand mind, the innermost center of his existence. Of all the wonders and mysteries of our universe, nothing is so wondrous as mind.
—*Shri Brahmananda Sarasvati*, The Textbook of Yoga Psychology[13]

In 1958, Dr. Mishra founded the Yoga Society of New York, Inc. In 1964 he founded Ananda Ashram, which became a very happening place, with gurus arriving from India and controversial American spiritual figures such as Timothy Leary and Richard Alpert (Ram Dass) visiting as well.

Dr. Mishra resigned from his medical career in 1966 to devote himself fully to helping sincere seekers remove the cause of human suffering. He was convinced that the cause of suffering was not within the realm of medical science, because it is lodged neither in the body nor the mind, but in ignorance of the true Self. Suffering would be eliminated by the discovery of one's spiritual identity, by answering the question: Who am I?

In 1972, Shri Brahmananda founded the Yoga Society of San Francisco, Brahmananda Ashram. Under his nurturing direction, Guruji's ashrams became lively centers of learning. Shri Brahmananda was enthusiastically devoted to uncovering the mysteries of the mind. He encouraged the investigation of science, art, philosophy, and metaphysics. He loved and supported all forms of sacred art. His disciples, with tireless dedication and creativity, continue to teach Sanskrit, the arts, Vedic studies and practices, and yoga at his ashrams.

Once a student asked Guruji, "How many enlightened beings are there?" Guruji replied zestfully, "One! Only One!" "And how many Gurus are there?" Again he replied, "One! Only One! The Self is One! Guru is your own Self."

Then Shri Brahmananda told the following story.

Once a group of disciples asked a Guru, "Sir, are you enlightened?"
The Guru replied, "I doubt it."
The disciples then asked, "Were Buddha, Moses, or Christ enlightened?"
The Guru gave the same reply, "I doubt it."
"Was anybody enlightened in the past?"
"I doubt it."
"Is anybody enlightened in the present?"
"I doubt it."
"Will anybody be enlightened in the future?"
"I doubt it."
Finally the disciples asked the Guru, "Who is enlightened?"
The Guru replied, "I-AM."

This kind of teaching defies logic and reason, the faculties of the thinking mind. Shri Brahmananda certainly knew how to use them, but he understood that to know the Self we must go beyond the intellect. The realization of the yogi is the realization of the eternal Self, which cannot even be imagined or contained by thoughts. It must be experienced to be known, and yet it is beyond experience.

Shri Brahmananda, like all great masters, taught meditation as the key to realization of the Self. Shri Brahmananda taught often from the *Mandukya Upanishad* scripture, the Frog Meditation. Frogs do not walk or crawl, they just jump, Shri Brahmananda would tell us. Meditation, he explained, is spontaneous and graceful. It allows you to jump from seeing to being. "Meditation is not step by step. Whatever we feel as step after step in meditation, it is only preparation of the house of the mind to receive the guest, God, who reveals Himself in a moment. When God will reveal Himself we do not know. He is our guest. In the Sanskrit language the word for guest is *atithi* (*a*=not+*tithi*=date): he whose date and time of arrival we do not know."[14]

Or, as the Bible says, "I come as a thief in the night."

Meditation is the frog jump from the known self into the eternal I-AM, the cosmic Self. The I-AM is beyond the body and mind, although it may have a body and mind. Our problems stem from avidya, or mistakenly thinking that we are the body and mind. Freedom from this ignorance is found through meditation, that state in which you stop identifying with your thoughts. "When you do not think, you are in the state of I-AM, and you are everywhere," Guruji often said.

Once we met Shri Brahmananda, we spent as much time as we could with him at Ananda Ashram until his death. He was a very powerful being, able to manifest miracles. What is a miracle? A miracle is a change in perception. Miracle workers help us see the true nature of being.

Sharon, Shri Brahmananda Sarasvati, and David Life (Swami Bodhananda) in the Blue Sky Theater at Ananda Ashram, 1993.
Photographer: Kimberly Flynn

Twice a day Shri Brahmananda held satsang, a gathering to which everyone was invited. The final day of his physical life he held evening satsang as usual. A disciple asked him, "If we are not the body and mind, then what are we doing here?" Shri Brahmananda replied, "We have knowledge that we are not the body and mind. Very good. Many people don't have that knowledge. But *feeling* is missing, therefore we are here."

You are not the Body and Mind, you are the Cosmic Self, the I-AM.
—Shri Brahmananda Sarasvati[15]

Shri Brahmananda left his physical body in mahasamadhi ("the great merger") at midnight on September 19, 1993, and became like the blue sky, present everywhere. He continues to love and guide us and remind us of who we really are.

After Shri Brahmananda died, close disciples instructed the funeral director, who had retrieved the body from the hospital, not to embalm it but to bring it to the ashram. The funeral director was very reluctant to do so. He warned them that the body would quickly bloat and decompose if it was not embalmed. The disciples had him bring the body to Ananda Ashram anyway, where they anointed it with ayurvedic oils and laid it out in state.

We arrived the next day, along with many devotees and admirers who had dropped everything when they heard the news to rush to be by his side. Soon the sounds of chanting, singing, and readings from Shri Brahmananda's texts filled the room. Devotees scattered flowers on the body. By the end of the three-day vigil Shri Brahmananda's body would be almost completely covered with a huge pile of flowers.

We stayed by the guru all that day, that night, and the next day. The anxious funeral director visited daily to check on the body's decomposition, but rather than decomposing, it became more and more beautiful. The deep lines of age disappeared from Shri Brahmananda's face and sweet smells arose from the body.

Late that night, after most of the mourners had come and gone, Sharon and a few other people were sitting in silent meditation with Shri Brahmananda's body. Overcome by a longing to be close to her beloved guru, Sharon walked over to the body, which was lying on a low bed. She reached out and put her hands on his hands, which were clasped on his navel. She was surprised to feel warmth and vibration. Sharon knelt by the body and rested her head on Shri Brahmananda's chest. To her amazement, she heard a profusion of sounds: whistling, a kind of humming, high-pitched frequencies, rumbling and clinking. The sound of rushing water, echoes. She sat up, wondering what was going on. Maybe these are the sounds of a decomposing body, she thought. But she heard nothing now that she was sitting up. And the body showed no signs of decomposition. She put her head back down and there they were again, those otherworldly sounds. She was staggered but kept the experience to herself.

A month later we returned to Ananda Ashram. After midnight, as Sharon was heading to her room to go to bed, she decided to meditate for a few minutes in the main room where Shri Brahmananda often sat to teach. His simple seat was still there, as he had left it. All the lights were out; just one candle was burning. Again, Sharon felt that longing to be close to her guru. She rested her head on his seat and once again, those mysterious sounds rushed in. She picked up her head, thinking perhaps she was hearing water running through the pipes in the house. She heard nothing. When she put her head down on the seat again, she heard exactly the same sounds that she had heard emanating from his body. Shri Brahmananda was once again giving her his timeless message that we are all beyond the body and mind; we are the vibration of the I-AM.

We close every Jivamukti Yoga class with this chant acknowledging the guru:

Om Bolo Sat Guru Bhagavan Ki Jai
Victory to God, the only real teacher.

God and Guru are the same. When we experience God in a teacher, the devotion we feel is transformational. Guru can remind us of God. We are thus reminded of our own divine nature.

Part 2

Outer Practices That May Lead to Yoga

Introduction

Sadhana: Conscious Spiritual Practice

Sadhana means conscious spiritual practice. In Part 1 we discussed some of the foundations of a conscious spiritual practice, such as a relationship with a guru, karma yoga (service), and ahimsa (nonharming). In Part 2 we explore four other yoga practices that can be used as sadhana: pranayama (freeing the life force), asana (perfecting the connection to the Earth), vinyasa krama (merging action and consciousness), and kriya (purification practices). All of these can be called "outer practices" because they use movements of the body and mind to effect the raising of consciousness. In Part 3 we will discuss various "inner practices," which still the body and mind.

Actually, each of these sadhanas has outward characteristics or outer forms and simultaneous inner forms. The outward aspect of asana practice, for example, might be a physically beneficial exercise program or "a good stretch." Although asana does provide these benefits, the inner, or esoteric, aspect of asana practice is that it is a technique for bringing about enlightenment.

Three factors contribute positively to sadhana:

1. Consistent practice over a long period of time.
2. An intention focused on God-realization.
3. Faith that enlightenment is possible.

Someone asked once if gardening could be a sadhana. It can be, if the intention is God-realization. If you garden to feed wild animals or as a service to a local charity or ashram, and you pledge your activity to a selfless intention and perform your duties with daily regularity, then your gardening can be a spiritual practice. If, on the other hand, you garden purely to obtain food or as a hobby, then your gardening is not sadhana. In the same way, an asana practice undergone just for exercise or as a hobby and performed in a lackadaisical manner is not sadhana.

All beings are working toward enlightenment, whether they are conscious of it or not. Nothing that happens in life is a waste of time. All experiences do not contribute to the evolution of the soul, however. Most people act unconsciously, with little understanding of karma or the habitual patterns that enslave them. When you decide to consciously work toward liberation, that's the first step toward developing a sadhana. Sadhana prepares you physically, energetically, emotionally, intellectually, and blissfully for enlightenment.

Running along the bottom of pages in the first three chapters of Part 2 are photographs of asana sequences that are used in classes presented in this book. Become acquainted with these sequences as you read the first two chapters. That way, by the time you reach the third chapter, "Vinyasa Krama: The Forgotten Language of Sequencing Postures," you will be ready to use them in the three complete yoga classes (simple, intermediate, and advanced) given in that chapter.

The number of breaths for which you hold an individual asana is optional and appears in parentheses. The other number appearing next to the photo indicates the degree of difficulty of the asana. You will find a more complete list of asanas ranked by difficulty in Appendix I.

When an asana sequence is new to you, it will take all your concentration to study and remember the sequence. Through repetition the sequences will become familiar to you and you will be able to concentrate more steadily on smooth transitions and unbroken concentration.

Photographer: Michael Lavine

6

Prana: Freeing the Life Force

From prana indeed all living forms are born and, having been born, they remain alive by prana. At the end they merge into prana once more.
—Kaushitaki Upanishad 3:2

The purpose of any sadhana is the awakening of cosmic consciousness. *Kundalini* is consciousness, sleeping like a coiled snake at the base of the spine, where the opening to *sushumna nadi*, the central energy channel, is located. When kundalini is awakened, she ascends up sushumna nadi through the levels of consciousness represented by the seven *chakras*, or energy centers. Kundalini's ascension to cosmic consciousness represents our evolution from self-absorption toward realization of the higher Self. To encourage kundalini to awaken and begin this ascent, the yogi must be able to channel *prana*, the life force, upward as well.

Where there is life, there is prana. In Sanskrit, *pra* means moving and *na* means always. Prana is like electricity, in that electricity exists in the natural world in wild and unpredictable forms. Lightning strikes here and there; you never know where it's going to hit. But if you capture that same electricity inside a wire, its movements become predictable and controllable. The electricity can be conducted via wire from point A to point B. The difference between electricity that will strike anywhere and electricity flowing through a wire is that the latter is useful for turning on lights.

Nadi is the Sanskrit term for the wires that conduct prana throughout the body. The difference between prana that flows randomly and prana that is consciously directed through the nadis is that the latter is illuminating.

As long as we live, we are prana conductors, but our wires may be bent, blocked, or broken. The yoga practices we discuss in Part 2—pranayama (control of the life force), asana (practicing postures), vinyasa krama (performing flowing sequences of asana postures), and kriya (purifications)—are designed to help us unclog the nadis so that prana can flow freely and we can learn to direct it toward enlightenment.

These yoga practices require conscious, controlled breathing. Breath is one of the yogi's most important tools, but control of the breath is not the ultimate goal of the yogi. Breath is the tool we use to work with prana. Control of the breath allows us to feel prana and direct this energy upward, through all seven chakras, so we can soar beyond the body/mind and reach a state of transcendental consciousness. Feel the blood pulsating. Feel the electrical pulsation of the nervous system. Feel the prana pulsing in the subtle body. Know that you are that pulsation beyond body and mind, Atman—the "I-AM."

Pranayama is one such practice for gaining control of prana through conscious breathing. Pranayama is really two words combined: prana and yama. Yama means "to restrain or control." Pranayama is the practice of restraining or controlling the normal movement of the breath to restrain or control prana. But

WARRIOR'S TRIANGLE—The yogic warrior's quest is threefold: truth, love, and beauty.

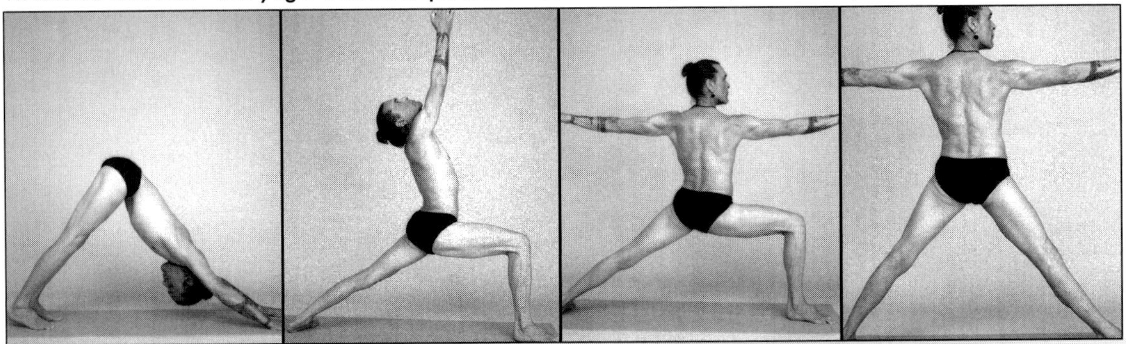

EXHALE	INHALE	EXHALE	INHALE
Downward-facing dog Adho Mukta Svanasana—1	Warrior 1 (hold 5 breaths) Virabhadrasana One—2	Warrior 2 (hold 5 breaths) Virabhadrasana Two—2	Standing Preparation—1

pranayama is also the combination of prana and *ayama*. Ayama means "unrestrained." The double meaning does not contradict itself. To set prana free, the yogi must first learn to restrain it and direct it into the sushumna nadi, or central energy channel, where it can then flow unrestrained toward Self-realization.

The nadis constitute the network that links the subtle body with the physical body and the bliss body. As you'll recall from Chapter 2, there are five coverings over the soul: the physical, vital, emotional, intellectual, and bliss bodies. The vital, emotional, and intellectual bodies comprise the subtle body. The nadis are the nervous system of the subtle body. The subtle body is said to have 72,000 nadis. The three principal nadis, which originate at the base of the spine, are the most important for the yogi:

The *sushumna nadi* moves straight up from the base of the spine to the top of the head. Sushumna is associated with spiritualized energy called *maha* prana, and the river Sarasvati.

The *pingala nadi* moves right, spiraling around sushumna nadi until it terminates at the right nostril. Pingala is associated with the sun (ha), fire, masculine energy (yang), the sacred river Yamuna, and the power of reason.

The *ida nadi* moves left, spiraling around sushumna nadi until it terminates at the left nostril. Ida is associated with the moon (tha), water, feminine energy (yin), the sacred river Ganga, and intuition.

EXHALE

Triangle (hold 8 breaths)
Utthita Trikonasana—2

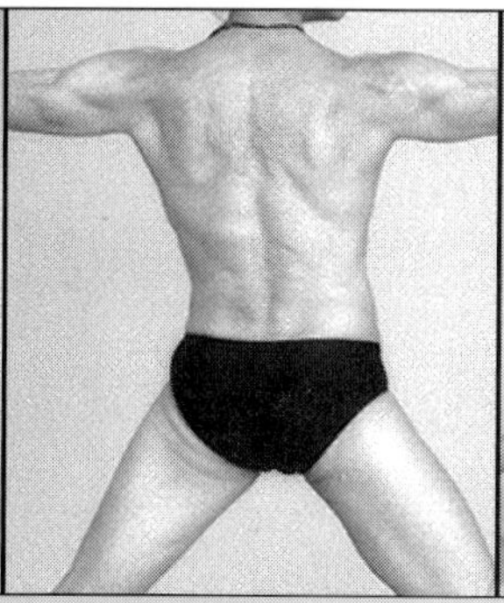

INHALE

Standing Preparation—1

EXHALE

Extended Angle—Utthita Parsvakonasana (hold 8 breaths)—2

INHALE

Standing Preparation—1

Stop here, go back to the start and change sides, or go to the next page.

When the prana is flowing freely in the nadis, all three sacred rivers join together at ajna chakra, the third-eye center. This is Hatha Yoga, the union of sun and moon.

When the nadis are clogged with avidya (ignorance), however, the third eye remains closed. Muscle tension is one example of how avidya manifests. Stretching the right side of the body in Trikonasana (Triangle pose), for example, can help us feel the movement of prana from the right foot to the right hand without interference or restriction. When we become aware of this subtle flow of prana, tension is eased and ignorance begins to disappear. Asana practice helps to open the nadis so that prana can flow freely.

Bahya-abhyantara-stambha-vrttir desha-kala-samkhyabhih
pari-dristo deergha suksmah. (YS II:50)
Modifications of pranayama are external, internal, and
total restraint. They are long and short and modified
according to space, time, and number.

Pranayama fine-tunes the prana, raising the frequency of its vibration. Patanjali defines pranayama as regulation of the inhalation, exhalation, and suspension of breath. The idea is to replace unconscious breathing patterns with conscious breathing patterns.

Bound Triangle—Physically bound to the earth, energetically bound to the heavens

INHALE — EXHALE — INHALE — EXHALE — INHALE

Standing Preparation—1

Extended Angle (hold 5 breaths)
Utthita Parsvakonasana var.—2

Extended Angle (hold 5 breaths)
Utthita Parsvakonasana var.—3

Extended Angle (hold 5 breaths)
Utthita Parsvakonasana var.—3

Normally, prana circulates in five directions in the body, performing different functions. These five winds of prana are called *vayus*.

Prana vayu moves from the diaphragm to the base of the throat. It is seated in the heart and regulates breathing, heart rate, circulation, and speech.

Apana vayu flows downward from the navel to the feet. It controls urination, defecation, giving birth, menstrual flow, ejaculation, and creative work.

Samana vayu occupies the space from the navel to the diaphragm. It flows back and forth like a pendulum there, regulating digestion and assimilation and balancing the prana and apana vayus.

Udana vayu flows from the base of the throat to the top of the head. It regulates coughing, choking, hiccupping, and swallowing.

Vyana vayu flows in all directions, carrying prana to each cell of the body.

During pranayama we change the direction of the normal movement of prana. We actively attempt to force apana vayu, which normally flows downward, to reverse direction and flow upward, so that we can use these energy sources to attain enlightenment. Conscious inhale turns prana vayu downward toward the earth and the opening of sushumna nadi at the base of the spine. Conscious

EXHALE INHALE EXHALE INHALE

Extended Angle
Utthita Parsvakonasana var.—3

Extended Angle
Utthita Parsvakonasana var.—2

Standing Preparation—1

Stop here, go back to the start and repeat to the other side.

contraction of the floor of the pelvis turns apana vayu upward, toward the opening of sushumna. When the diaphragm lifts up during exhale retention and the abdomen is hollowed out, prana, apana, and samana vayus join in sushumna. When the chest lifts up and the chin rests in the hollow between the collarbones, udana vayu is joined with the other three in sushumna nadi.

If you eat right before pranayama (or asana) practice, however, samana, apana, and vyana vayus will be busy digesting and will not be available to help with God-realization. Similarly, if you need to void the bladder because you are drinking water during practice, the apana will never turn upward. Perhaps you drink water out of habit because, unconsciously, you are a little afraid to succeed at reversing these powerful energy flows. The solution is simple: don't eat or drink right before practice and void the bowel and bladder.

If you are successful at reversing the flow of prana and forcing it to enter sushumna nadi, the mundane functions these vayus regulate may slow down, or even stop. This can adversely affect menstruation, which requires a downward flow of apana. Forcing apana upward during the first two to three days of menstruation can slow or even stop periods, and it may be difficult to get them going again. We suggest, therefore, that *yoginis* (female yogis) refrain from vigorous asana and pranayama for the first one to three days of the menstrual period. Women should use intuition to determine whether their body needs just one or two days or a full week off during menstruation. This is a good opportunity to focus on scriptural study, meditation, or service during those days.

Prana can be lost through any of the "gates" or openings in the body: nostrils,

Secret Prayer—The warrior for Love always keeps a secret prayer in a back pocket.

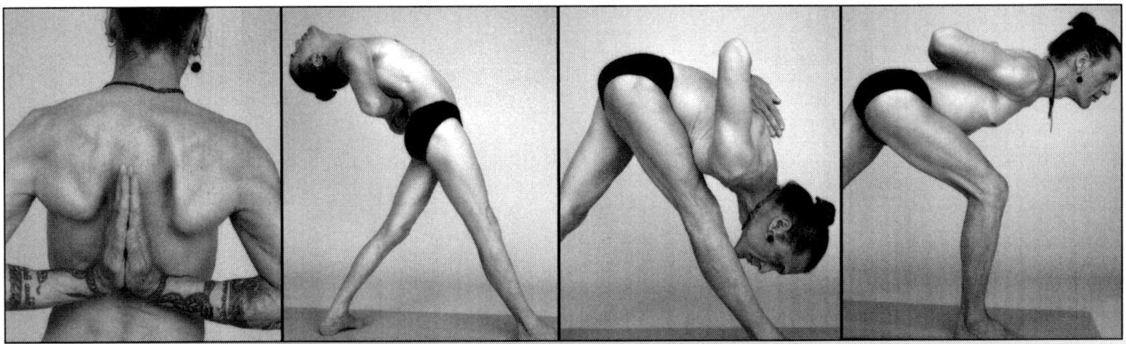

EXHALE — Mountain, Steady standing—Tadasana, Samastittihnamaste —1

INHALE — Preparation Parsvottanasana—2

EXHALE — Standing forward bend—Parsvottanasana (hold 8 breaths)—2

INHALE — Warrior 3—Virabhadrasana 3 namaste, preparation—2

EXHALE

ears, eyes, mouth, anus, urethra, vagina, and the mind. Looking, listening, touching, smelling, tasting: using the five senses encourages prana to flow out of the body. The gates are closed by consciously turning inward the energy that would normally flow out through the senses, the orifices, and the mind.

The first step toward pranayama is breath awareness. Relax on your back with your eyes closed and feel your breath going in and out. Don't regulate or modify the breath in any way. Experience the wonder of being breathed. Who is in control of this breathing? It happens twenty-four hours a day, every day for your whole life, without conscious effort. Unconscious breathing is regulated by the medulla oblongata, the primitive brain at the top of the spine that regulates heart rate, digestion, and all other autonomic workings of the body.

Now sit up in a comfortable position. Sit still and breathe awareness into your muscles. Don't let the breath get blocked anywhere along the way. Endeavor to make it like the mirror surface of a windless lake. The breath is the seat, the foundation for yoga practices like asana and meditation. A steady, unhindered breath seats both the mind and the body in an unwavering state.

Become very aware of the energy channels that run along the back of the body. See if you can sense their relationship to the energy channels running along the front of the body. Bring the chin parallel to the floor and open the chest, moving the shoulders back. Lifting the chest creates an uplifting and inspiring psychological effect. The chin is

PRANAYAMA

1. Pranayama is the practice of the conscious regulation of the breath combined with bandhas (locks) and *mudras* (seals), replacing unconscious energetic patterns with conscious energetic patterns.
2. When the breath is controlled, the fickleness of the mind is controlled.
3. Pranayama can be done with or without mantra.
4. The proper time for pranayama is just before sunrise, or sunset. It is also beneficial after asana and before meditation practice.

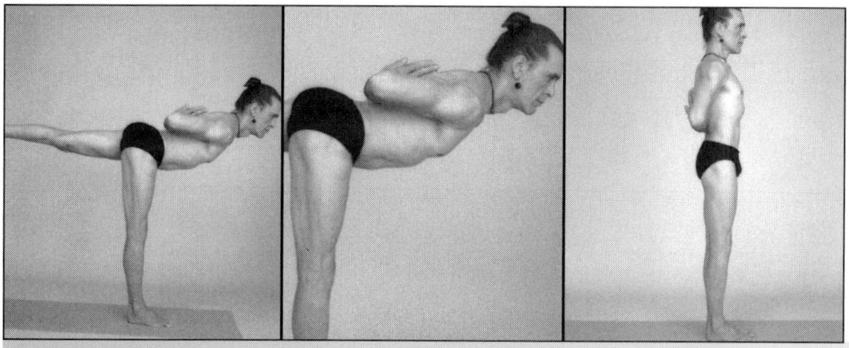

INHALE EXHALE INHALE EXHALE

Warrior 3—Virabhadrasana 3 may be done once for one breath or held steadily (hold 8 breaths)—3

Steady standing—Samastittih variation, back namaste—1

You could stop here and switch sides or continue to the next sequence.

directly connected to the sense of ego self, so lift the chest to the chin and allow the mind to subside into the heart.

By consciously controlling the breath, you have moved this function from the primitive medulla oblongata to the frontal lobes. You have made an unconscious activity conscious. This is pranayama: replacing unconscious breathing, and consequently energetic movement, with conscious breathing and the conscious movement of energy toward enlightenment.

The highest result of successful pranayama is samadhi, in which we find *kevala kumbhaka*, the spontaneous and effortless suspension of breath. This can also happen during meditation. When the thoughts cease, so does the breath—but prana continues moving. Kumbhaka means "retention." For yogis, the four parts of the breath are:

puraka: inhalation
antar-kumbhaka: holding the breath inside
rechaka: exhalation
bahya-kumbhaka: holding the breath outside

Please note: If you have high blood pressure, do not practice retention (kumbhaka). If you have low blood pressure, practice retention only after an inhale (antar-kumbhaka).

To use the four parts of the breath effectively in pranayama, you need some knowledge of the chakra system, a model for understand-

The breath shares some qualities with thoughts:

- Breath and thoughts cannot be *seen.* They are known only by their effects.
- Rapid uncontrolled breathing and rapid uncontrolled thoughts both usually reflect physical or mental stress. Conversely, slow deliberate breathing indicates concentration or steady thought.

Awkward Twist—In the most difficult of situations let the Divine Will become your own.

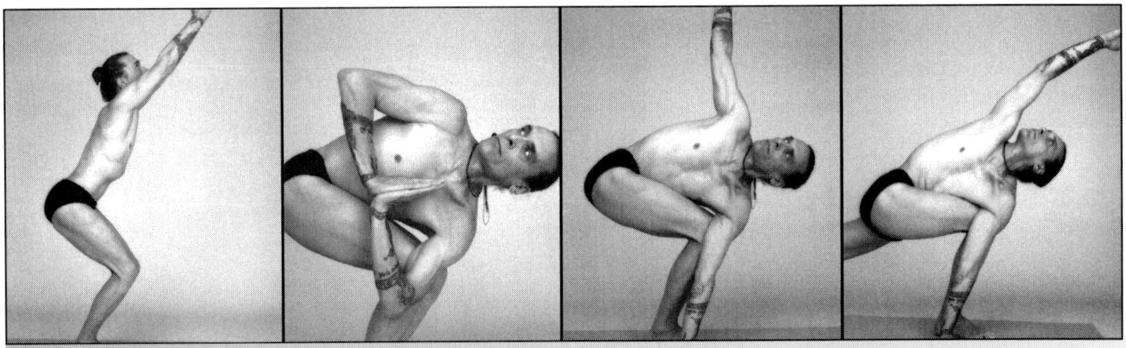

INHALE — EXHALE — INHALE — EXHALE — INHALE — EXHALE

Awkward Pose—Utkatasana—2

Rotated Awkward Pose—Parivritta Utkatasana (hold 8 breaths)—2

Rotated Awkward Pose—Parivritta Utkatasana arms open—2

Rotated side angle—Parivritta Parsvakonasana (hold 8 breaths)—3 ing levels of consciousness. Although chakras are not part of the physical body, physical reference points are given for each of these levels of consciousness. This is anatomy not of the physical body but of the subtle body, which includes chakras, nadis, and granthis (blocks to the flow of prana).

Associated Chakra	**Corresponding Location in Physical Body**	**Associated Glands/Sense**	**Element**
Muladhara (root place)	Base of the spine (root center)	Suprarenal/smell	Earth
Swadhisthana (her favorite standing place)	3 fingers below the navel (sexual center)	Gonads, prostate, testicles, ovaries/taste	Water
Manipura (jewel in the city)	Solar plexus (power center)	Pancreas, liver/sight	Fire
Anahata (unstruck)	Heart (compassion center)	Thymus/touch	Air
Vishuddha (poison-free place)	Throat (speech center)	Thyroid/hearing	Ether
Ajna (command place)	Between the eyebrows (third-eye center)	Pineal/intuition	Akasha (space)
Sahasrara (thousand-petaled lotus)	Top of head (universal consciousness)	Pituitary/I-AM	Akasha

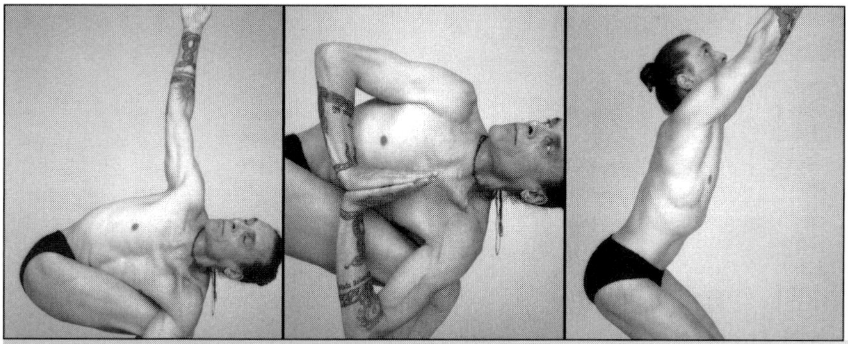

INHALE — Rotated Awkward Pose—Parivritta Utkatasana arms open—2

EXHALE — Rotated Awkward Pose—Parivritta Utkatasana namaste var.—2

INHALE — Awkward Pose—Utkatasana (hold 8 breaths)—2

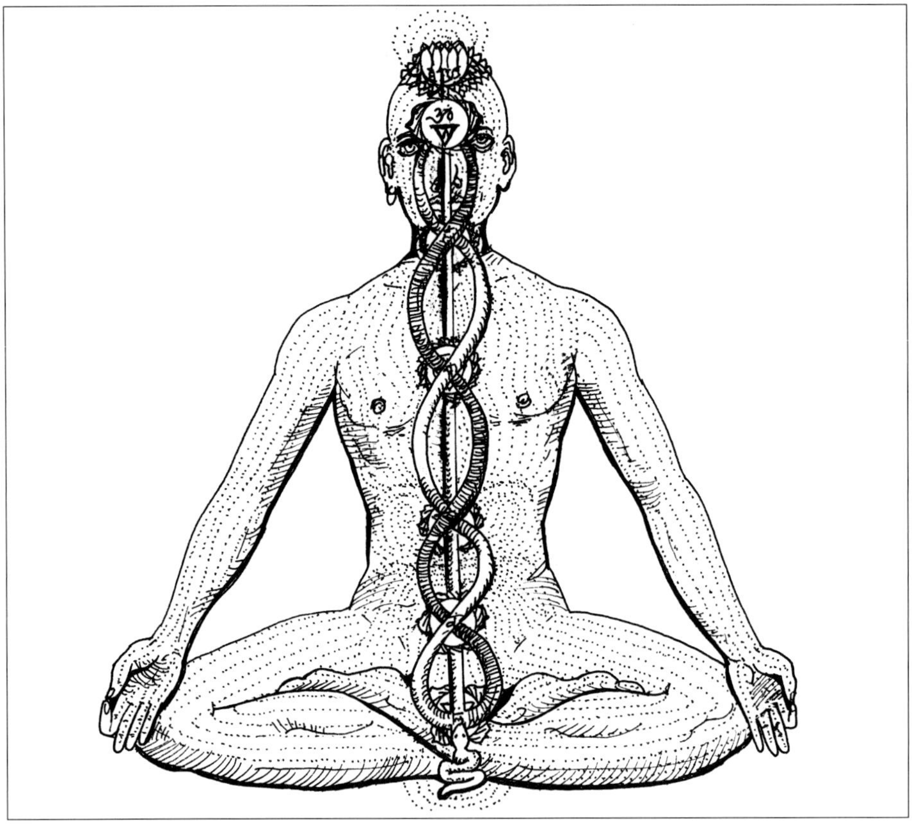

Illustration of the chakras, nadis, and prana vayus (dotted lines)
Artist: David Life

Kundalini's Descent—She waits coiled three and a half times at the base of the spine.

EXHALE INHALE EXHALE INHALE EXHALE

Downward-facing dog
Adho Mukha Svanasana—1

Lunge—1

Standing Split—Urdhva Prasarita
Ekapadasana preparation—2

Standing Split—Urdhva Prasarita
Ekapadasana (hold 8 breaths)—2

The external sun and moon divide each twenty-four hours into night and day, and the internal sun and moon, i.e., ida and pingala, are responsible for our perception of night and day; that is duality. Ida nadi predominates at night, the parasympathetic nervous system is active, there is a greater release of melatonin hormone within the brain and the subconscious mind is active. During the daylight hours pingala predominates, the sympathetic nervous system is more active and seratonin hormone is released within the brain which brings conscious functions to the fore and the subconscious mind submerges.

The two nadis, ida and pingala, and the nervous systems, pull the awareness from one extreme to the other, binding us to the duality of mundane circumstances because of the interrelationship with the external force of the sun and moon. The entire biological system is programmed to the movements of the sun and moon cycles. However, a yogi can develop control of the autonomic nervous system so that the body and mind are not swayed to the extremes. It means developing the voluntary and central nervous systems, activating sushumna nadi and ajna chakra. Such a person lives in a perfectly balanced state of being.

—Hatha Yoga Pradipika IV:17[1]

The last bit of yogic anatomy we'll get into before describing some breathing techniques is the three *granthis*, which are like knots that block the flow of prana and prevent kundalini from ascending toward enlightenment. These are:

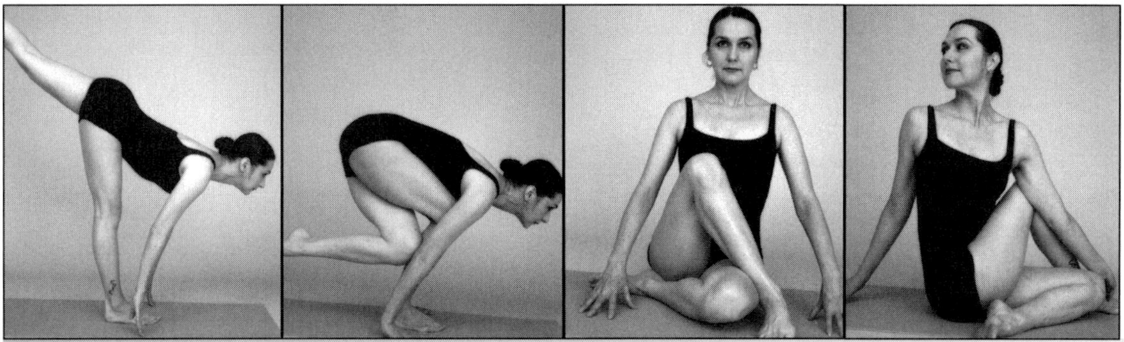

INHALE — Half Spinal Twist—Ardha Matsayendrasana preparation—2

EXHALE — Half Spinal Twist—Ardha Matsayendrasana preparation—2

INHALE — Seated Half Spinal Twist—Ardha Matsayendrasana preparation—2

EXHALE — Seated Half Spinal Twist—Ardha Matsayendrasana preparation (hold 8 breaths)—2

Stop here, go back to the start, and repeat to the other side.

Brahma Granthi: located at the base of the spine, where primitive brain functions, such as the "fight-or-flight reflex" exist. It prevents proper personality development and refinement.

Vishnu Granthi: located between manipura chakra, the seat of individual ego and power, and anahata chakra at the heart. Clinging to ego and personal power prevents us from ascending to the heart, where we could merge with compassion and selflessness.

Rudra Granthi: located between the heart and the third eye, representing the pull of the heart center and our fear of losing contact with others. When rudra granthi is pierced and energy moves to the ajna chakra, others (friends, family, etc.) disappear and Shiva or God is encountered directly.

To pierce the granthis, yogis use *bandhas*, or energy locks. Bandha means "tied" or "bound." When a chakra is activated by application of a bandha, prana is forced to flow correctly through that chakra, toward the third eye.

The bandhas really represent the correct application of consciousness. There are five bandhas, listed in ascending order:

Physical benefits of bandhas:

- Have a direct effect on the endocrine system.
- Lower respiration rate.
- Induce calmness and relaxation.
- Regulate blood pressure and heart rate.
- Tone and massage the digestive system.
- Establish urogenital harmony.

Psychospiritual benefits of bandhas:

- Establish flow of prana through nadis.
- Pierce the granthis.
- Can lead to samadhi.

SEAT OF ISIS—**The Goddess requests your attention to Her Earth with each step you take.**

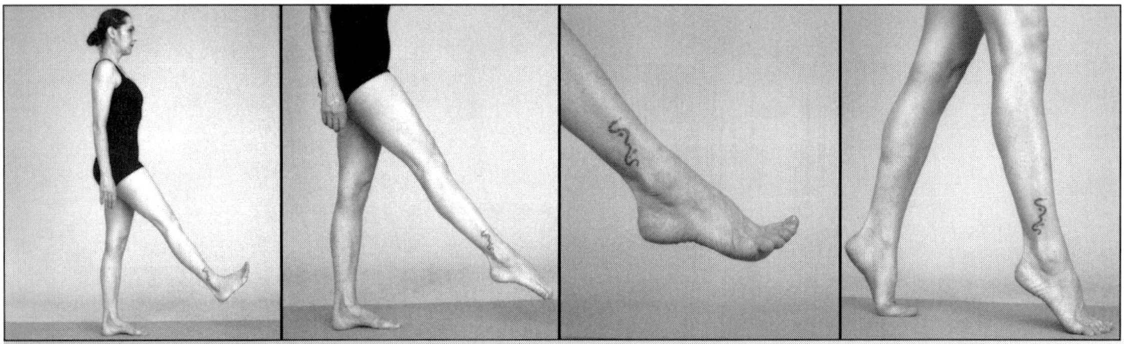

EXHALE INHALE EXHALE INHALE

One leg balances—Eka Pada Samastittih; two variations, may be done once with one breath each or repeated alternately pointing and flexing (repeat 5 times)—1

One leg balance—Eka Pada Samastittih ball of the foot extends, toes pull back—1

Tip Toe balance—Step forward onto the ball of the front foot—2

Mula Bandha, Root Lock: a contraction of the perineum for men and the vaginal walls for women that results in a lift from pubic bone to navel; can be applied anytime.

Uddiyana Bandha, Flying-up Lock: the whole abdomen is drawn in and up; can be practiced only on exhale retention.

Jalandhara Bandha, Cloud-catching Lock or Net Lock (named for the network of nadis in the neck): protects the small nadis in the throat; can be engaged after inhale or exhale by bringing chest to chin.

Maha Bandha: the combination of all three of the above bandhas.

Brahma Bandha: fixing one's consciousness on the all-pervading Source.

Mula Bandha, the Root Lock

Mula bandha is the most important bandha. In Sanskrit, *mula* means root. Mula bandha contains and channels the energy associated with the muladhara chakra, located at the base of the spine. Muladhara chakra represents the stage of consciousness where basic survival needs dominate. The root concerns of any species are eating, sleeping, and staying alive.

On a physical level, mula bandha is a contraction of the floor of the pelvis. The floor of the pelvis consists of muscle fibers and fascia. For our purposes, there are three muscular levels, which intersect and overlap in the pelvic floor. They can be detected and, to some extent, isolated.

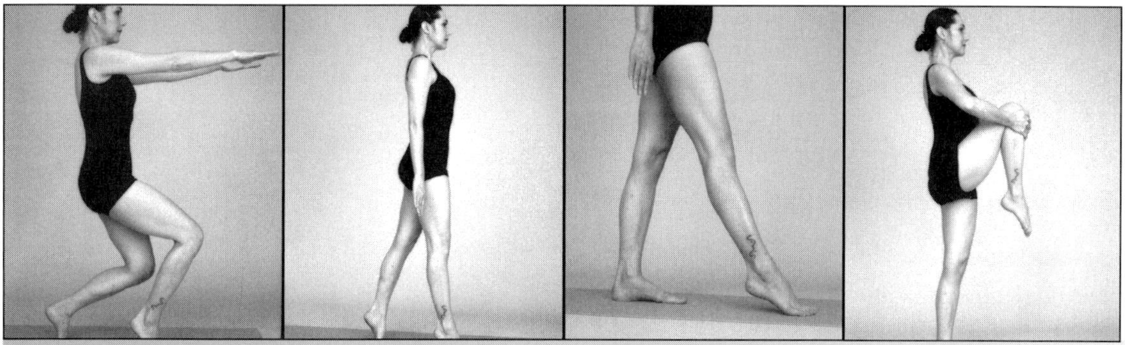

EXHALE INHALE EXHALE INHALE EXHALE

Seat of Isis and Tip-Toe Posture may be done once with one breath each or repeated, alternately raising the arms and bending knees in the Seat of Isis, or lowering the arms and straightening the legs in a Tip-Toe balance (repeat 5 times)—1

Steady Standing—Samastittih preparation by lowering the back heel to floor—1

One leg balance—Eka Pada Samastittih, squeezing the knee—1

The most superficial contraction of mula bandha corresponds to the instruction "Contract your anus." The anal sphincter does connect via ligaments to the tip of the spine and, hence, to muladhara chakra.

Our own introduction to mula bandha was pretty funny. We had been practicing yoga for some years before we heard of it. Then we visited Shri K. Pattabhi Jois in Mysore, India, for the first time.

We were sweating profusely and had come to the end of our asana practice for that day. In full lotus, we planted our palms alongside our thighs and pushed down. We lifted our seats off the floor in mock levitation. "Lift your knees!" he shouted as we strained to stay aloft.

"Contact Uranus, contact Uranus!" he shouted in his heavy Indian accent.

Contact Uranus?

We don't know how long it took us to realize that he was saying "Contract your anus, contract your anus." It was his way of telling us that we should be doing something in the floor of the pelvis to help us lift up.

Contacting Uranus is not a bad metaphor for mula bandha. Contracting your anus with awareness is the first step to understanding mula bandha, which is the launching pad for excursions into more cosmic realms.

In actuality, the anal sphincter contraction is not mula bandha but a cousin, called *ashwini mudra*, which is named after a habit that horses have of pursing the anal sphincter like lips. To feel the difference, place a finger in or on the anal opening and feel it squeeze shut and protrude outward. With mula bandha applied correctly, the anus should soften and lift into the body, not push out. The

EAGLE'S FLIGHT—The more we reach out to others, the greater is the strength we feel within.

INHALE EXHALE INHALE EXHALE INHALE

One leg balance—Eka Pada Samastittih; variations can be done once with one breath each, or repeated alternating straight and bent repeat 5 breathes—2

One leg balance—Eka Pada Samastittih variation (hold 5 breaths)—3

Warrior 3—Virabhadrasana 3 preparation—1

contraction of the anal sphincter is, however, a doorway to deeper layers of mula bandha.

With some experience you will find that you can refine mula bandha by isolating the perineum, thereby moving deeper into the pelvis. The intermediate contraction of mula bandha involves the isolation of the perineum (the external portion) and the perineal body (the internal portion). This refinement carries the contraction inward and upward.

To feel the perineum, press a finger into the space between the anus and scrotum or labia. Or sit on a tennis ball or place the heel of your foot in the space between the anus and genitals. You should learn to feel the difference among three contractions: anal plus perineal contraction; perineal contraction only; and anal contraction only.

The deepest contraction of mula bandha corresponds on the physical level to instructions such as "Interrupt the urine flow" and "Squeeze the vaginal walls." It includes a lift of the pelvic diaphragm. The pelvic diaphragm is the innermost layer of the pelvic floor. It comprises the levator ani and the puborectalis muscles, including the perineal body. In Latin, *levitas* means light, and lifting the levator ani lightens the body. (The levator ani levitates!) These muscles form a sling that extends from the pubis to the coccyx and supports the upper half of the vagina, the uterus, the bladder, the prostate, and the rectum. The pelvic diaphragm also regulates the bowel.

This contraction does not involve the external anal sphincter or the external surface of the perineum. It is similar to Kegel exercises used to prevent urinary

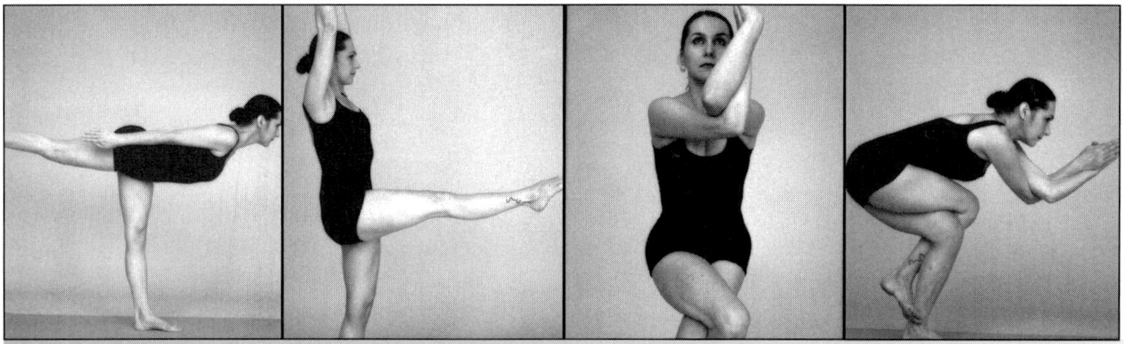

EXHALE — INHALE — EXHALE — INHALE — EXHALE

Warrior 3—Virabhadrasana 3 variation (hold 5 breaths)—3

One leg balance—Eka Pada Samastitih var.—3

Eagle—Garudasana preparation—2

Eagle—Garudasana (hold 5 breaths)—2

Change sides or go to next page.

incontinence and strengthen the vaginal walls after childbirth. Practicing the interruption of urine flow can produce an awareness of mula bandha. The isolated contraction of the muscles that control the flow of urine is actually vajroli or sahajoli mudra, however. In combination with a few other muscles, it comprises mula bandha.

You will discover that it is possible to lift the floor of the pelvis deep inside, without contracting the anus or the exterior layers of the perineum. Apply mula bandha and feel the lift under the bladder, vagina/uterus or prostate, and rectum. Now relax the surface muscles and feel this contraction inside, at the base of the abdomen—in the pelvic diaphragm. Put one finger on the very tip of the tailbone and see if you can feel it being drawn inward and upward when you contract mula bandha.

Mula bandha turns normally downward-flowing apana upward. This increases the volume of the breath, organizes the body and the mind, and organizes the intention behind the practice. Please remember, however, that ultimately, mula bandha is not a muscular contraction, it is an intense and continuous desire for God-realization—to such an extent that prana begins to move upward toward the Divine. Don't confuse the method for the goal.

Mula bandha leads to the following benefits:

- Mula bandha pierces brahma granthi, the first energetic knot that interferes with our journey toward enlightenment.
- Mula bandha contracts the supportive musculature of the pelvis, increasing the stability of the pelvis. The pelvis is the seat of the spine.

PICKING UP THE STEP—External difficulties will never disturb the heart of a yogini.

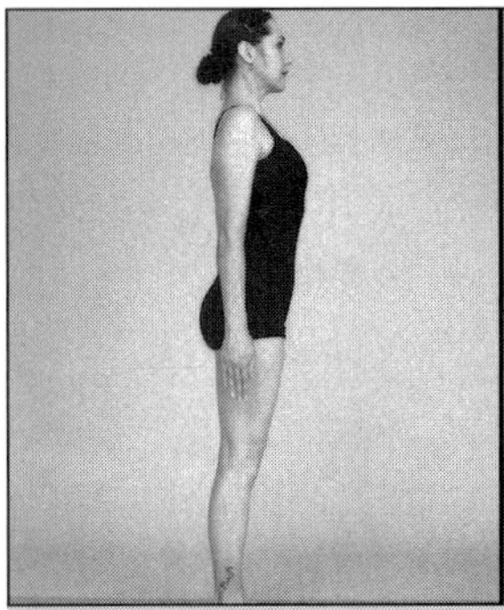

INHALE

Mountain, Steady standing—Tadasana, Samastittih—1

EXHALE

Standing forward bend—Uttanasana—2

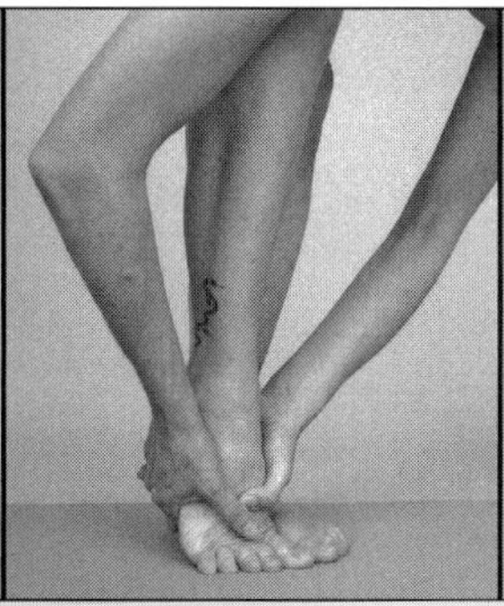

INHALE EXHALE

One leg balance—Eka Pada Samastittih preparation—2

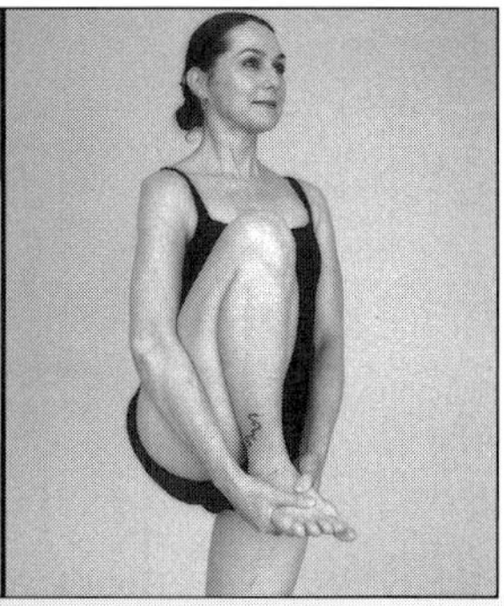

INHALE EXHALE

One leg balance—Eka Pada Samastittih variation—2

- Mula bandha lifts and compresses the bowel and lower abdominal region. When mula bandha is properly applied, the body is less earthbound and more mobile.
- Through gradual refinement, mula bandha becomes less muscular and more subtle. This movement from mundane to subtle is uplifting.
- Mula bandha can be practiced by itself or combined with practices like asana, meditation, kriya, and pranayama. Whenever it is used, it focuses the mind on God.

Uddiyana Bandha, the Flying-up Lock

Uddiyana bandha is activated only on an exhale retention. The entire abdomen is drawn inward and upward toward the chest cavity, hence the name "Flying-up Lock." Unlike mula bandha, uddiyana is used only during pranayama or *shat karma* kriya cleansing exercises.

Uddiyana bandha is not an abdominal contraction, but, because of the vacuum created by the movement of the diaphragm into the chest cavity, it draws the abdomen muscles upward. If applied correctly, the diaphragm will lift high enough to embrace the physical heart. Potentially, this bandha could be a heart stopper. The diaphragm and heart make intimate contact, which is why this stimulation to the heart muscle increases circulation and enhances the yogi's ability to control heart rate and blood pressure.

Uddiyana is said to be the lion that conquers the elephant Death. It stimulates metabolic processes in the abdomen by literally squeezing the organs. On a psychospiritual level, uddiyana bandha gives the ego over to the heart. On a

INHALE

One leg balance—Uttita Hasta Padangusthasana preparation—3

EXHALE

One leg balance—Uttita Hasta Padangusthasana (hold 5 breaths)—3

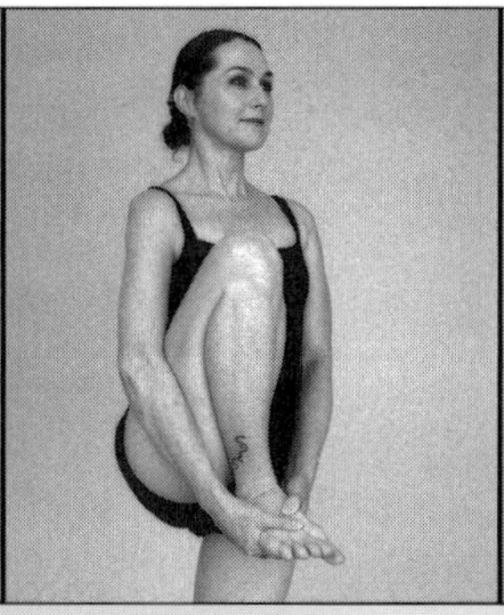

INHALE

One leg balance—Samastitih preparation—2

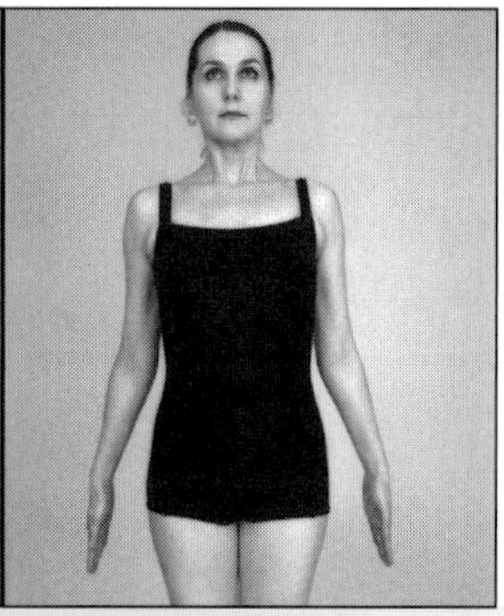

EXHALE

Steady standing—Samastitih—2

INHALE

Change sides.

pranic level, uddiyana bandha joins apana, prana, and samana in sushumna to pierce the vishnu granthi, allowing prana to flow from the *manipura chakra* (in the solar plexus region) to anahata chakra, the heart.

Most people do not move beyond the first three levels of consciousness represented by the first three chakras: survival (muladhara chakra), sex and creativity *(swadhisthana chakra)*, and power (manipura chakra). The first step toward the heart *(anahata chakra)* is the renunciation of I, Me, Mine. The thinning of the waist in uddiyana is like the thin waist of the renunciate who forgoes comforts to relieve the suffering of others. To enter the heart is to discover compassion and to feel universal love.

Uddiyana is usually applied after mula bandha has been applied, and before the third lock, jalandhara bandha.

Jalandhara Bandha, the Cloud-catching Lock or Net Lock

The third lock, jalandhara bandha, protects the small nadis in the neck region. If the prana surging up the sushumna nadi channel were to break into the fine network of subtle nerves in the neck, the nadis would be injured. This lock joins apana, prana, and samana with udana vayu in sushumna to pierce rudra granthi. It completes the movement of energy from microcosmic physiology to macrocosmic consciousness. Physically, it consists of lifting the chest so that the chin rests in the depression between the collarbones. Do not shorten the lower back and collapse the chin onto the chest. Keep a straight spine by lifting the chest.

This lock can be applied after inhale or exhale retention. You can think of it as capping a bottle that you have either just filled or emptied. This lock stimulates

MOONRISE—The Moon rises and brazenly displays a new garment for each new phase.

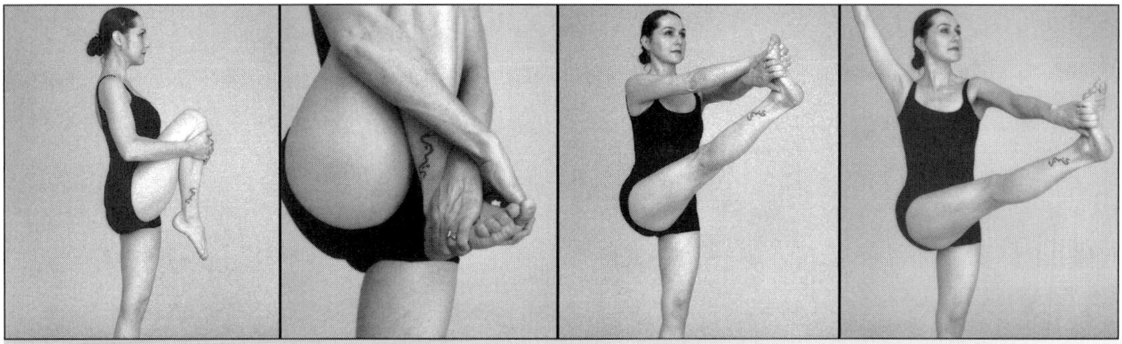

INHALE — One leg balance—Eka Pada Samastittih variation—2

EXHALE — One leg balance—Eka Pada Samastittih variation—2

INHALE EXHALE — One leg balance—Uttita Hasta Padangusthasana variation—2

INHALE — Dusk—Parivritta Uttita Hasta Padangusthasana preparation—3 the thyroid and parathyroid glands by squeezing them. The stimulation of vishuddha chakra at the throat has a purifying effect on thoughts and actions.

Jalandhara bandha inspires the mind to subside into the heart. The head drops toward the chest and the heart/mind is born. The subsidence of the mind into the heart allows all the pairs of opposites to merge into Oneness as the third eye (ajna chakra) opens.

Maha Bandha

When all three locks—mula, uddiyana, and jalandhara—are applied simultaneously, this is called maha bandha. Usually, the bandhas are combined with a physical posture called a mudra. The classic mudra for maha bandha is performed by sitting on the floor with the left heel pressed into the perineum and the right leg extended straight out, with the right big toe clasped with the first two fingers of both hands. The mudra is then repeated on the other side.

Maha bandha corrects energy flow and stimulates the endocrine system. It is energizing and healthful. Because kundalini may be awakened by the application of this bandha, it may lead to visions or emotions for which it is best to be under the instruction of a teacher.

Brahma Bandha

As with any yoga practice, the most exalted application of any bandha is to devote it to enlightenment. This is brahma bandha, which means locking your mind on God. Any bandha can become brahma bandha if the faculty of attention is steadfast and locked on God.

EXHALE

Moonrise—Parivritta Uttita Hasta Padangusthasana (hold 5 breaths)—3

INHALE

Dawn—Parivritta Uttita Hasta Padangusthasana variation—3

EXHALE

One leg balance—Samastittih preparation—3

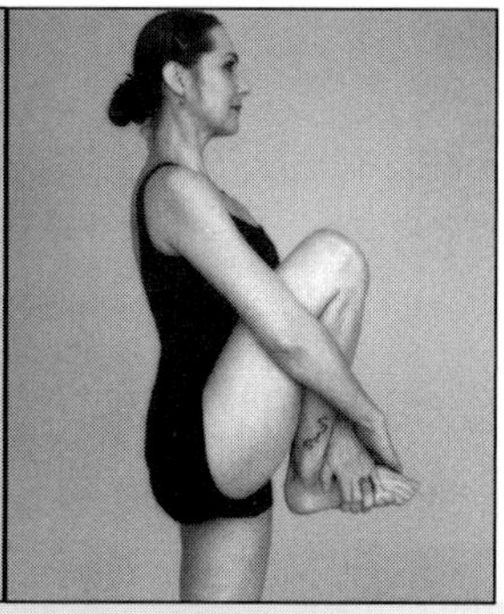

INHALE

Steady standing—Samastittih release—2

Stop here, go back to the start, and repeat to the other side.

Now we're going to get into specific physical instructions for pranayama. Although it may appear that these practices are done on a physical level only, this is a superficial application. The practices affect the deeper energetic levels of being.

Pranayama is a sitting practice that emphasizes breath retention and bandhas. The instructions for the techniques described below use a ratio system. The ratio represents the duration of the breath or of the retention. For instance, if you take a 4-count inhale and a 4-count exhale, the ratio is 1:1. If you take a 4-count inhale, hold the breath for 16 counts, and exhale for 8 counts, the ratio is 1:4:2. This duration can be timed with a clock, metronome, or mantra, or counted. There are hundreds of pranayama techniques with infinite variations of ratios.

The first time you try to follow the instructions for the breathing practices in this chapter, you might get frustrated. Or you might run out of air and feel panicky. Yoga practices such as pranayama are methods for creating circumstances that are potentially frustrating—even frightening. These are challenging practices for a reason. To do them, you will have to shift your attention away from the body's struggle and the mind's compulsive chatter and work backward through your actions, thoughts, and feelings until you reach prana: pure energy.

Samavritti Pranayama

The easiest pranayama technique is called *samavritti*, or equal breathing. It can be performed while seated. It can also be used without retention while you are performing asana sequences.

STANDING SPINAL TWIST—**Yearning for a perfection that is only slightly beyond reach**

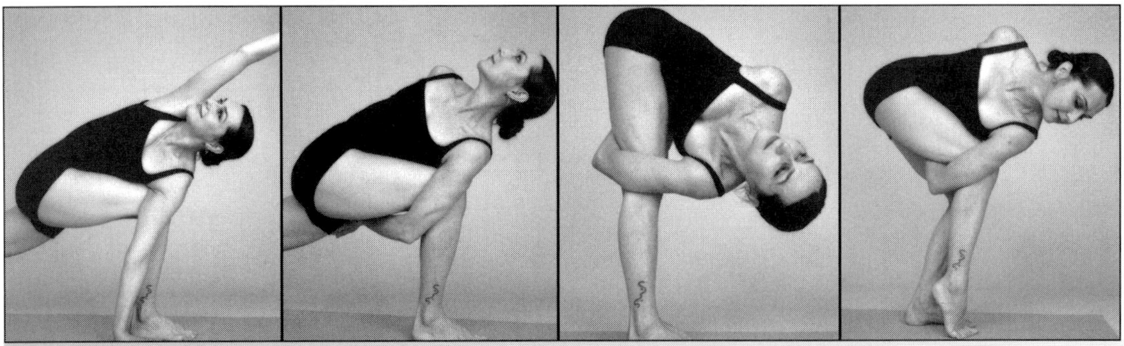

INHALE EXHALE INHALE EXHALE INHALE EXHALE

Extended Spinal Twist—Parivritta Uttitha Parsvakonasana (5 breaths)—2

Extended Spinal Twist—Parivritta Parsvakonasana wrist grab—2

Hanging Spinal Twist (hold 5 breaths)—4

Standing Spinal Twist preparation—2

1. Initially, samavritti is practiced with only inhalations and exhalations, each of equal duration without unevenness or irregularity. The ratio is 1:1.

2. After smooth regular inhales and exhales have been established, you can add an inhale retention. The transition from retention to breathing should be smooth, with no gasping or fluctuation. Use the ratio 1:1:1.

3. Finally, you can also retain the breath after exhaling, applying samavritti to all four parts of the breath (inhale, retain, exhale, retain). Use the ratio 1:1:1:1. When retention is used, pranayama should be done only as a seated practice, with mula bandha, uddiyana bandha, and jalandhara bandha applied.

One form of samavritti pranayama is *ujjayi*. Without retention, ujjayi is the best form of breathing for asana practice. As a seated pranayama practice, ujjayi is done with retention.

1. Sit in padmasana (lotus), siddhasana (adept's pose), or virasana (hero's pose).

2. Place fingers in chin mudra on knees by touching the tips of the index fingers and thumbs together.

3. Close the eyes. Gaze toward ajna chakra (turn eyes upward and focus on the third eye, between the eyebrows).

4. Exhale to begin the practice and apply mula bandha.

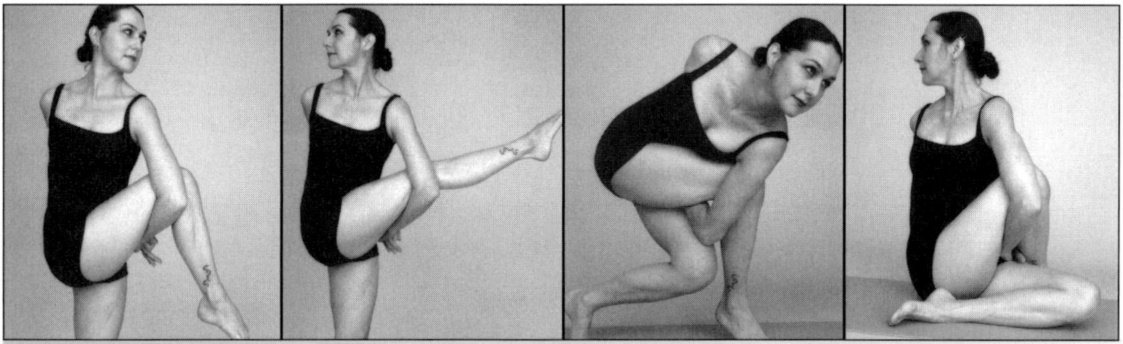

INHALE — Standing Spinal Twist preparation—3

EXHALE — Standing Spinal Twist (hold 5 breaths)—4

INHALE EXHALE — Half Spinal Twist—Ardha Matsayendrasana preparation—2

INHALE EXHALE — Seated Half Spinal Twist—Ardha Matsayendrasana (hold 8 breaths)—2

Stop here, go back to the start, and repeat to the other side.

5. Inhale (puraka) through both nostrils for 4 counts with the breath making a whispered aaaaaahhhhhhhh sound. Apply jalandhara bandha.

6. Retain (antara-kumbhaka) for 4 counts. Then release jalandhara bandha. Maintain mula bandha.

7. Exhale (rechaka) through the nose for 4 counts with the same whispered aaaaahhhhh. Apply uddiyana bandha and then jalandhara bandha.

8. Retain the breath out (bahya-kumbhaka) for 4 counts. Then release uddiyana bandha, then jalandhara bandha. Then breathe in, still applying mula bandha.

This completes one round of ujjayi pranayama. Build up slowly, gradually increasing the amount of time you practice.

Visamavritti Pranayama

Visamavritti means "unequal breathing." This pranayama technique brings conscious awareness to the breathing by creating challenging irregular and interrupted rhythms.

One form of visamavritti pranayama is nadi shodhana. Nadi shodhana alternates nostrils and inhales and exhales with breath retention in a ratio of 1:4:2:3. This ratio could be interpreted as, for example, a 4-count inhalation, followed by a 16-count retention, an 8-count exhalation, and a 12-count retention.

RISHI TWIST—The sages and wise ones know that the yoga knowledge is in all creation.

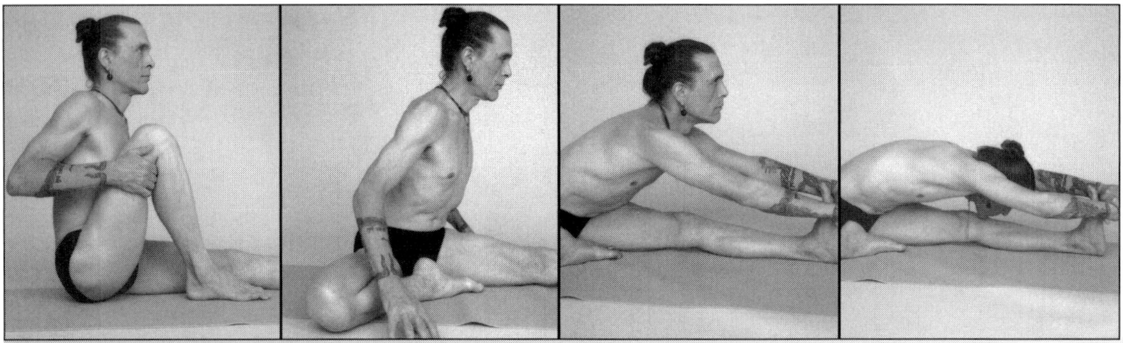

INHALE	EXHALE	INHALE	EXHALE
Knee Lift—Janu Sirsasana preparation—1	Torso Rotation—Janu Sirsasana preparation—2	Head of knee down—Janu Sirsasana preparation—2	Head of knee down—Janu Sirsasana (hold 8 breaths)—2

Nadi shodhana is good preparation for meditation. It should be done only in a seated position, with all the bandhas applied, as described below.

1. Sit in padmasana, siddhasana, or virasana.
2. Close the eyes. Gaze toward ajna chakra.
3. Place left hand on left knee in chin mudra (index finger and thumb touching, palm up or down).
4. Apply vishnu mudra by pressing the index and second finger of the right hand into the right palm.
5. Exhale through both nostrils, then apply mula bandha, maintaining it throughout the exercise.
6. Block the right nostril with the right thumb and inhale through the left nostril for 4 counts. Apply jalandhara bandha by lifting the chest and locking it to the chin.
7. Close both nostrils and retain the breath for 16 counts. Then release jalandhara bandha.
8. Lift the right thumb and exhale out the right nostril for 8 counts. Apply uddiyana bandha and jalandhara bandha.
9. Close the right nostril; retain the breath out for 12 counts. Then release uddiyana and jalandhara bandha.
10. Open the right nostril; breathe in for 4 counts. Then apply jalandhara bandha.

INHALE

Rishi Twist—Marichyasana C preparation—2

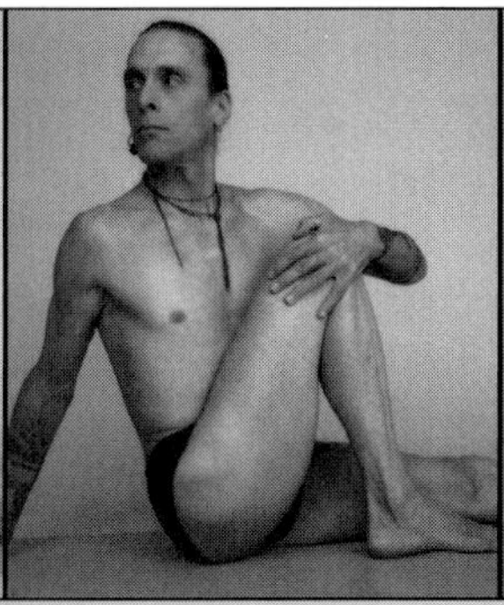

EXHALE INHALE

Rishi Twist—Marichyasana C preparation—2

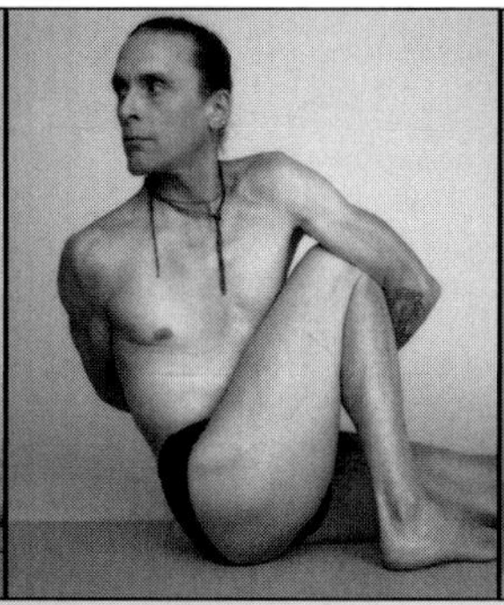

EXHALE

Rishi Twist—Marichyasana C (hold 8 breaths)—3

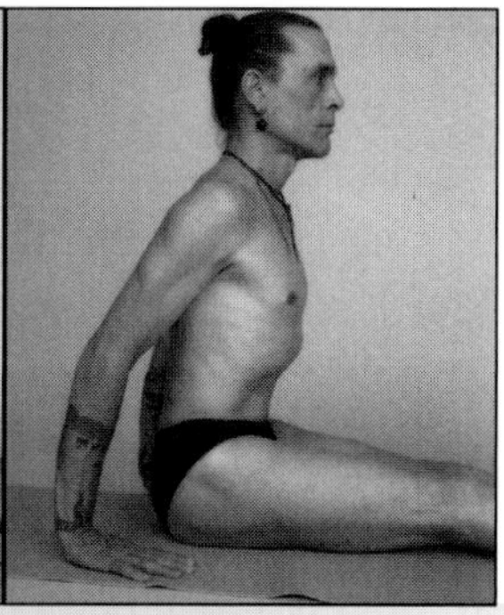

INHALE

Staff pose—Dandasana—1

Stop here, go back to the start, and change sides.

11. Close the right nostril; retain the breath in for 16 counts. Then release jalandhara bandha.

12. Open the left nostril; exhale for 8 counts. Apply uddiyana bandha and jalandhara bandha.

13. Close the left nostril; retain the breath out for 12 counts. Then release mula bandha, uddiyana bandha, and jalandhara bandha (in that order). Then breathe in and resume normal breathing.

This is one round of nadi shodhana. Do at least two rounds, increasing slowly up to twenty minutes. Always start and end exhaling through the left nostril.

The primal energy is omnipresent and omnipotent. All types of energy have one common factor: they vibrate.

—Shri Brahmananda Sarasvati, **Nada Yoga**[2]

Our actions are generated by our thoughts or unconscious reflexes, which in turn are modified by our emotions. As prana is transformed into emotion, it acquires qualities such as anger or love. It has been colored by the gunas at work in us (the illusory qualities of sattva, tamas, rajas). By the time feelings affect thoughts, prana has been transformed from its original pristine state. Our thoughts or unconscious reflexes become actions, with all kinds of karmic repercussions.

COBBLER'S TABLE—The cobbler engages in humble repetitious work with the presence of a yogi.

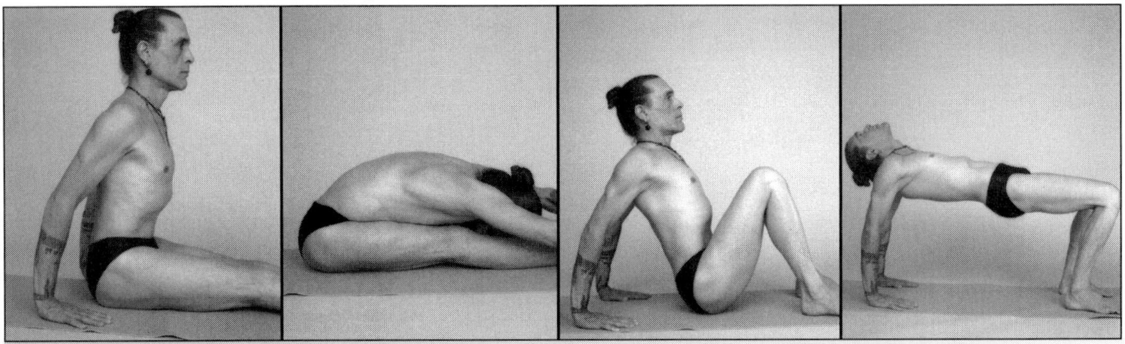

INHALE — EXHALE — INHALE — EXHALE — INHALE

Staff pose—Dandasana—1

Seated forward bend—Paschimottanasana (hold 8 breaths)—2

Tabletop preparation—1

Tabletop (hold 8 breaths)—2

Through the regular practice of pranayama, however, we learn how to tap into the quality-less form of prana, beyond the three gunas. When we connect with that prana, it will carry us to back to *satchitananda*: Truth (sat), Knowledge (chit), and Bliss (ananda).

This movement from action to pure energy, from unconscious to conscious, from lower to higher is symbolized by the lotus flower growing out of the muck and mire and ascending toward the Light. The sahasrara chakra, the crown chakra, is called the thousand-petaled lotus. Like the lotus opening to the sun, it opens to the Light of cosmic consciousness.

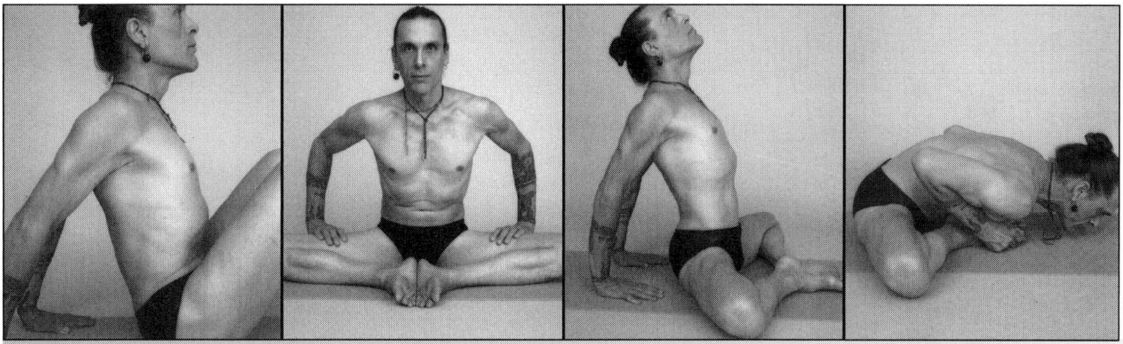

EXHALE INHALE EXHALE INHALE EXHALE INHALE

Cobbler's pose—Baddha Konasana preparation—1

Cobbler's pose—Baddha Konasana preparation—2

Cobbler's pose—Baddha Konasana preparation (hold for 5 breaths)—2

Cobbler's pose—Baddha Konasana (hold 8 breaths)—3

Stop here, or continue to page 126.

7

Asana: Giving Structure to the Desire for Yoga

It looks like I'm moving but I'm standing still.
—Alan Watts

Sit down! Just sit down and hold still! Sounds simple, but it's not so easy when you have a mind filled with thoughts moving this way and that.

The Sanskrit word asana is most commonly known as the name for the yogic practice of assuming various physical contortions, but it actually means "seat." By taking a seat, you establish a connection to the Earth. So asana, or the establishment of the seat, means the practice of connecting to the Earth. By Earth we mean all things, all manifestations of reality. Earth not only means the ground we walk on, the air we breathe, or the water we drink, but also all the beings—animals, plants, and minerals—that we come into contact with daily. Through asana practice we consciously connect to a touchable, tangible, sense-able level of reality.

According to Patanjali, the seat that you establish should be steady and joyful, in body as well as mind. The word asana, therefore, also describes the goal of this yoga practice, which is to consciously relate to all beings with steadiness and joy.

Sthira-sukham asanam. (YS II:46)
The connection to the earth should be steady and joyful.

sthira: steady, stable.
sukham: easy, joyful, comfortable.
asanam: seat, posture, connection to the Earth.

Once you have established a seat, you are grounded and can begin to play with prana, the life force. The form of cosmic energy that moves a muscle is electrical. Electrical energy moves through nerves to the muscles, causing them to respond in a certain way. Your ability to articulate the muscles depends on your ability to control these electrical impulses inside the body. You could define life as the gradual transformation of energy into matter. Likewise, death can be defined as the gradual transformation of matter back into energy. Yogis are interested in how matter changes into energy and how subtle energy changes into matter. They harness energy to direct it toward God-realization, or enlightenment.

Asana practice is a method for learning to direct prana, instead of just unconsciously letting it flow indiscriminately. The effortful practice of asana can prepare us for the final graceful, effortless realization of samadhi. To prepare for such a leap, you must first establish firm footing on the ground. The practice of asana gives structure to the desire for Yoga, or union with the Divine Self, which is by nature an unstructured event.

HIPPIE TWIST—The earth and water elements combine for fertile ground for the lotus flower.

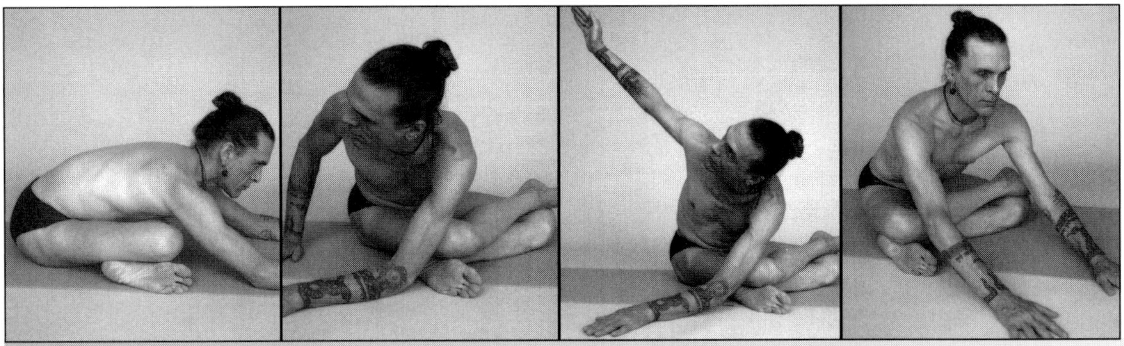

EXHALE INHALE EXHALE INHALE EXHALE INHALE EXHALE

Ankle to Knee (hold 8 breaths)—2

Ankle to Knee rotated preparation—2

Ankle to Knee rotated variation (hold 5 breaths)—3

Ankle to Knee preparation—2

Know that which has form to be unreal and the formless to be permanent. Through this spiritual instruction you will escape the possibility of rebirth.

—Ashtavakra Samhita, *I:18*[1]

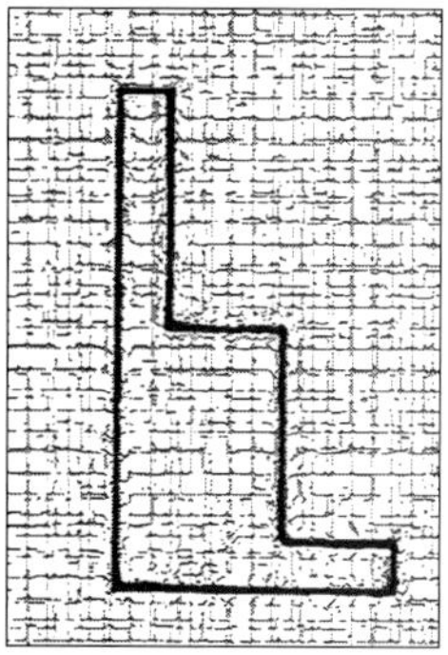

Isis glyph
Artist: Sharon Gannon

Interestingly, the Egyptian hieroglyph for Isis, the Divine Mother Goddess, looks like a chair. Her hieroglyph looks like a seat and its phonetic sound is *st*, like the Sanskrit sound *sthit*, which represents stability (the English word "steady" is related).

Obviously, the Egyptians did not mean that Isis should be referred to as "Your Chairness." They were worshiping a quality of connectedness and relationship to the Earth that is inherent in the power aspect of the goddess.

To the ancient Egyptians the Goddess Isis was the divine personification of the perfection that comes through the ability to connect perfectly. It was Isis, after all, who, through the power of her love, reintegrated the dismembered body of her brother/husband, Osiris. She knew how to put it all back together because she held the key that connects: love.

Ram Dass put a chair on the cover of his classic 1971 book *Be Here Now*. Not a symbolic chair like the Egyptian hieroglyph for Isis, but an Early American ladder-back, rattan seat chair, entangled in a network of interconnected lines that forms a wheel.

How appropriate for such an innovative book, one of the first books on yoga

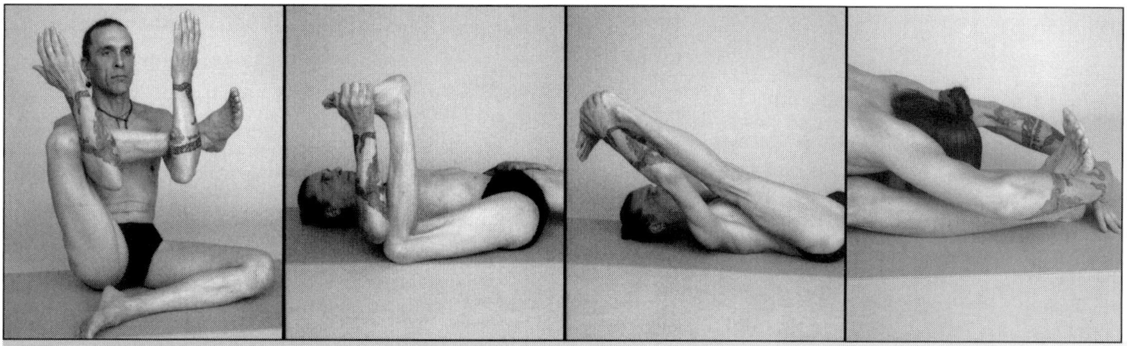

INHALE EXHALE INHALE EXHALE INHALE EXHALE

Cradled Leg—Supta Trivikramasana preparation (hold 5 breaths)—2

Hip opening—Supta Trivikramasana prep (hold 5 breaths)—2

Reclining leg stretch—Supta Trivikramasana prep (hold 8 breaths)—3

Seated forward bend—Paschimottanasana (hold 8 breaths)—2

TADASANA
MOUNTAIN SEAT

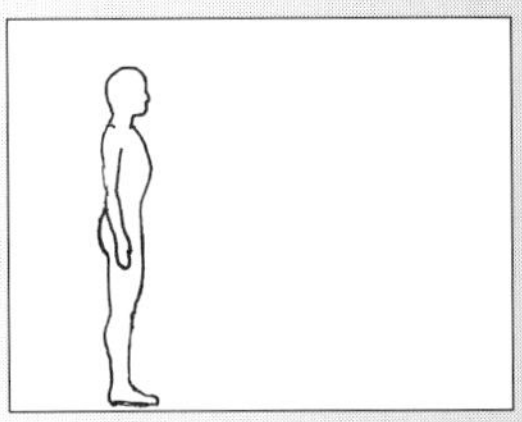

The mountain is the meeting place of the terrestrial and celestial forces. It is the youngest child of heaven and earth. The mountain base is anchored to the earth.

Volcanoes are so connected to the core of the earth that they spew out the fire of that core. Yet the peak of the mountain stretches toward the blue sky. The mountain conducts the energy of the heavens into the earth, and the earth energy toward the heavens. In India the mountains are the abode of the gods or even God itSelf.

The spine is very important to yogis; it is considered the tree of life. Vitality of the spine is said to represent the vitality of the whole being. It could be compared to the steady mind, upright and becalmed through yogic techniques. The upright spine represents a being thriving in the realm of gravity, not being pulled down by it.

Cover of Ram Dass's book *Be Here Now*
Artist unknown

written by an American to reveal that yoga is about so much more than physical exercise. Yoga is about being kind and good and connected to the whole world. When you are, the earth will support you in her chair. When you are *really* good, she will give you her throne.

The Goddess loves those who help themselves and are not greedy. Selflessness is the key to living right and being happy in the world. It is the key to successful asana practice. It is the way of the jivanmukta, the liberated being. A yogi can walk in peace upon the earth, giving back more than he or she takes.

The root of every asana is this steady connection to the earth. When your connection to the earth is stable, you feel ease in body and mind. How did we become so estranged from our blissful source

BLOSSOMING LOTUS—The lotus blooms serenely and courageously despite the obstacles.

EXHALE INHALE EXHALE INHALE EXHALE

Cobbler's pose—Buddha Konasana preparation—2

Blossoming Lotus—Parivritta Vikasitakamalasana preparation—3

Twisting Blossoming Lotus—Parivritta Vikasitakamalasana prep—2

Twisting Blossoming Lotus—Parivritta Vikasitakamalasana (hold 5 breaths)—2 and become the fearful, paranoid people we are today? The Agganna-Suttanta of the *Digha-Nikaya,* an ancient Buddhist text originally written in the Pali language, gives an explanation of our descent into darkness and fear in the form of a profound myth:

> In the past we were mind-created spiritual beings nourished by joy. We soared through space, self-luminous and in imperishable beauty. We thus remained for long periods of time.
>
> After the passage of infinite times, the sweet-tasting earth rose from the waters. It had color, scent, and taste. We began to form it into lumps and to eat it. But while we ate from it our luminosity disappeared. And when it had disappeared, sun, moon, stars and constellations, day and night, weeks and months, seasons and years made their appearance.
>
> We enjoyed the sweet-tasting earth, relished it and were nourished by it, and thus we lived for a long time. But with the coarsening of the food the bodies of beings became more and more material and differentiated, and hereupon the division of sexes came into existence, together with sensuality and attachment. But when evil, immoral customs arose among us, the sweet-tasting earth disappeared, and when it had lost its pleasant taste, outcroppings appeared on the ground, endowed with scent, color, and taste.
>
> Due to evil practices and further coarsening of the nature of living beings, even those outcroppings disappeared, and other self-originated plants deteriorated to such an extent that finally nothing eatable grew by itself and food had to be produced by strenuous work. Thus the earth was divided into fields, and boundaries were made,

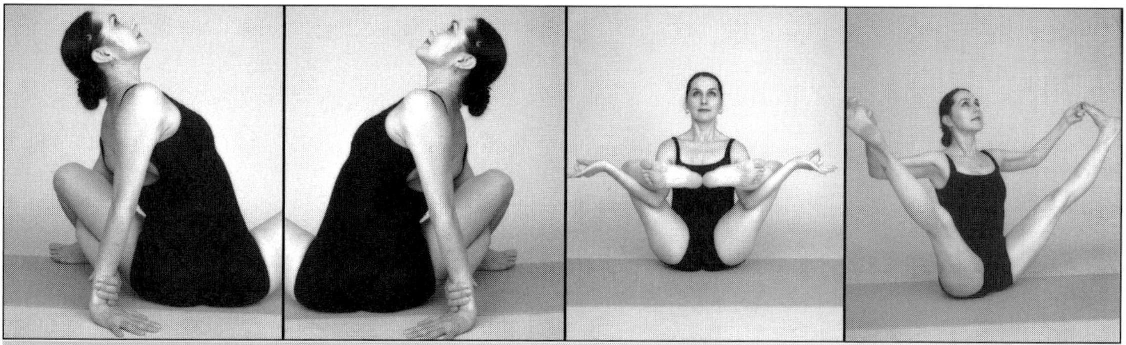

INHALE EXHALE INHALE EXHALE INHALE EXHALE INHALE EXHALE

Twisting Blossoming Lotus—*Parivritta Vikasitakamalasana*; should be held for 8 breaths to the right, then repeat the sequence to the left—2

Blossoming Lotus—*Vikasitakamalasana* (hold 5 breaths)—2

Extended Blossoming Lotus—*Utthita Vikasitakamalasana* (5 breaths)—2

Stop here, or continue to the next page.

HASTA UTTANASANA
SUN REACH, EXTREME FRONT STRETCH

Hatha Yoga is the method of joining the sun and moon. The sun and the moon represent all pairs of opposites in the world: up and down, left and right, male and female. *Ha* means sun and *tha* means moon. Sun energy is equated with chit or intellect, the right nostril, and the subtle nerve channel running down the body called the pingala nadi. It channels yang energy. Surya is the sun in its fullness. This asana represents abundance and fullness. It represents fullness that must return to emptiness. The sun is the source of all growth and development on earth. We are made of light. Sunlight nourishes us through the food we eat.

whereby the idea of "I" and "mine," "own" and "other" was created, and with it possessions, envy, greed, and enslavement to material things.[2]

We practice asana and other yogic techniques to reverse the process of dense unconscious materialism described in this myth. The road taken on this journey to cosmic consciousness is *through* the forms of the material world, not away from the material realm. As yogis, we are trying to find our way back to our Source, which is limitless and boundless joy. To liberate ourselves, we must begin by becoming conscious of our material nature and of the nature of the Earth, our world.

To practice asana means to practice perfecting one's relationships with all aspects of the Earth and all beings that inhabit the Earth. The Earth is another way of saying the Divine Mother. Mother Earth is the Goddess. An ancient Sanskrit mantra says:

Sarva Mangala Mangalye Sive Sarvatha
Sadhike Tryambake Gauri
Narayani Namosthute, Narayani Namosthute

I salute the three-eyed Divine Mother, Narayani, who brings total auspiciousness and who fulfills the desire for liberation. Realization arises with her blessing. She is the world itself. Only through the experiences of life can the soul be perfected.
Honor this gift, your life.

BALANCING COMPASS—The direction of our attention is always toward the Divine.

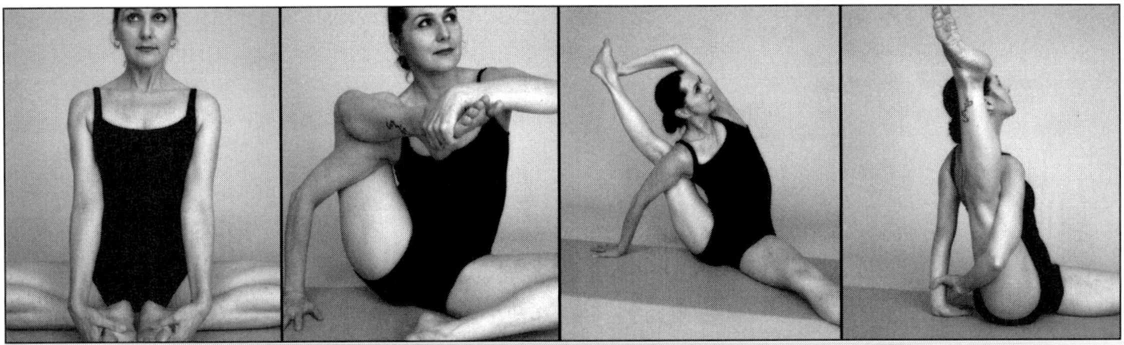

EXHALE INHALE EXHALE INHALE EXHALE

Cobbler's pose—Baddha Konasana preparation—2

Leg Lift—Konasana preparation—1

Compass pose—Konasana (hold 5 breaths)—3

Compass pose—Konasana wrist grab (hold 5 breaths)—3

Our relationship to the Earth, however, has become like a chair with two short legs and two long ones—very unsteady. How can it be otherwise when imprisonment of the mothers of many species to make money from their eggs, milk, children, and flesh is considered normal, and ethical vegetarianism is considered offbeat? When resources are depleted without replenishment, and the water, air, and land are polluted with the toxic residues of greed? Humans have abdicated their responsibility to the Earth because they have come to feel that what they do does not matter. They sit, therefore, in a very rocky seat. It is becoming clear, however, that what we do *does* matter. We cannot continue to ravage the Earth without dire consequences.

To honor the Earth is the essential component of the practice of asana. Asana is a form of goddess worship. We must learn to treasure the Divine with each step on her mantle, with each perfect action, with each passing breath. Enlightenment is not a denial of the world. It is the experience of seeing deeply into the nature of existence.

Don't try to get out of the World, get into it.
***—Bhagavan Das,* What Is Yoga?**[3]

The yogic scriptures refer to a limited number of asana postures. The truth is, probably just about any movement that you could possibly dream up has been attempted over the ages. The list of postures is

UTTANASANA
STANDING FORWARD BEND

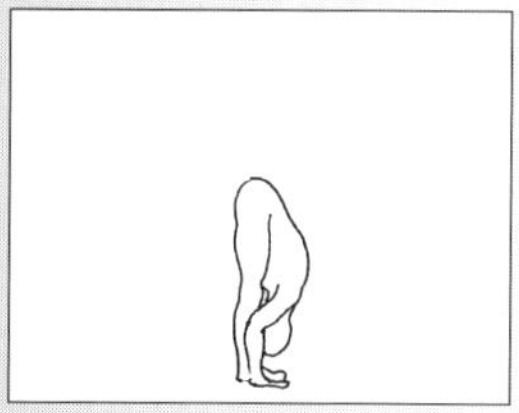

This gesture of bowing down brings consciousness into our relationship with the earth. The highest joins the lowest as the heart is elevated over the brain. The seat of the ego at the solar plexus is empty and levitates as the palms of the hands and feet gravitate. This is a simple gesture of our desire for balance and a perfected relationship to the earth. Presently, our relationship to the earth is out of balance: air, water, and soil are degraded and depleted by human greed and disregard. Our relationship to the earth and all earthly beings is a complex web of existence in which the degradation of one part affects the whole. Through acknowledgment and gratitude, however, all the ills of modern times can be healed and the earth returned to a peaceful balanced state.

INHALE — Compass pose—Konasana balance (hold 5 breaths)—2

EXHALE — Balancing Compass release—2

INHALE — Extended Compass—Visvamitrasana (hold 5 breaths)—3

EXHALE — Extended Compass—Visvamitrasana release—1

Stop here, go back to the start, and repeat to the other side.

Traditionally, the asana is thought of as a cushion-type platform for a person to sit on, above the cold and dust of the ground or floor. A yogi's asana is sometimes described as kusa, or sacred grass, covered with the hide of a dead animal. The earliest known depictions of a yogi, however, which are found on the mysterious "seals" from India's Harappa River Valley, depict the yogi seated with various animals surrounding him, not sitting on the dead skin of one.

Pashupati, the Lord of the Animals depicted on the seal, would be known in later times as Shiva. In the Bible the Lord gives humans dominion over the animals, instructing human and animal alike to eat plants. The Shaivite ideal is very similar. Some people, however, interpret dominion as license to abuse, torture, kill, and eat animals, rather than simply care for them. This delusion is a product of ignorance, speciesism, and greed, and it makes our relationship to the earth very unstable.

as long as the list of different manifestations of energy into matter: geometric shapes, trees, mountains, saints and sages, gods and goddesses, snakes, birds, turtles, fish, camels, horses, even a baby in the womb.

Asana practice is both invigorating and exorcising. The veil of unhappiness is lifted for a moment and we glimpse our original Self beneath it. Once, two women came together to a beginner yoga class. About a third of the way into the class they could not stop giggling and rolling on the floor. When we asked them why, they said that they were sisters and had grown up together. At night when they were very young, they would perform asanas, unknowingly, under the covers for their own amusement. In class they had been transported back to those happy days of childhood, which they had completely covered over with a veil of struggle and confusion in their adult lives.

Jesus said, "Become as children again to enter the kingdom of heaven." If you observe young children, especially newborns, you quickly sense that they are very near the source from which we all emerge as babies. If you have any doubt that a baby emerges from bliss into confusion, watch how preferences quickly arise, like "I prefer to be held by Mother" and "I prefer dry diapers to wet diapers." Observe how attachment to these preferences causes pain and suffering.

Of course, that baby's initial contact with bliss was devoid of conscious awareness. The yogi aspires to the same connection *with* consciousness. Asana encourages a balance of acting and being and movement within stillness that helps us strip away our layers of opinion,

MOON DANCE—**The moonbird feeds on the moonbeams.**

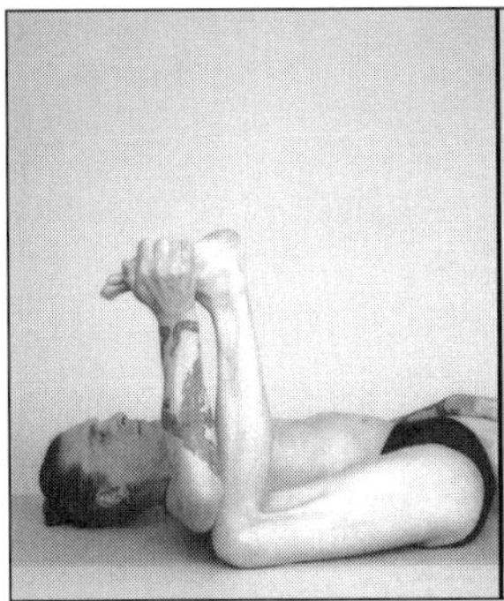

EXHALE

Hip opening preparation (hold 8 breaths)—2

INHALE EXHALE

One foot behind the head reclining—Bhairavasana (hold 5 breaths)—4

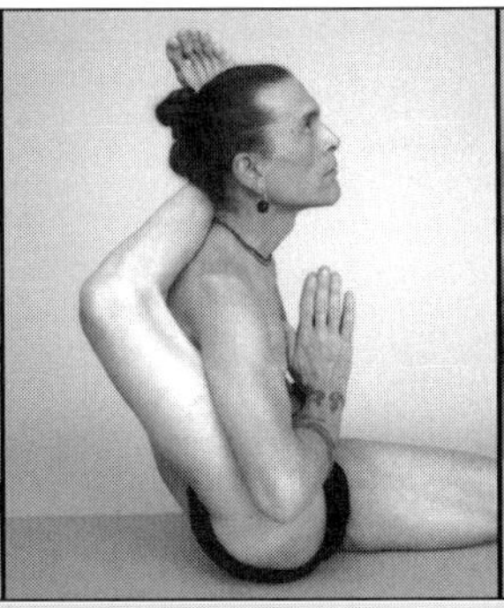

INHALE

One foot behind the head seated—Eka Pada Sirsasana (hold 5 breaths)—4

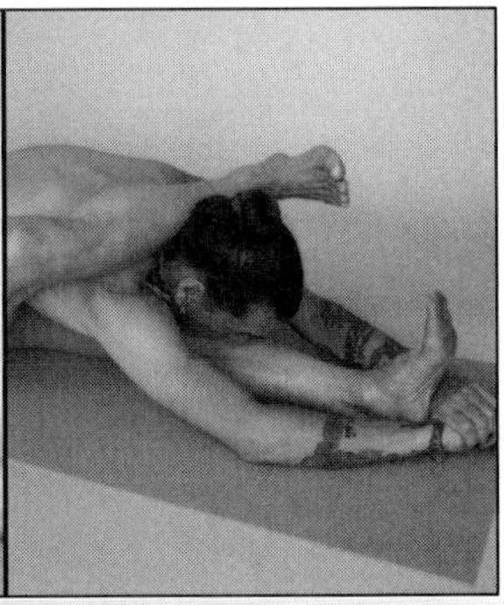

EXHALE

One foot behind the head, forward bend—Skandasana (hold 5 breaths)—4 preference, attitude, and prejudice to reveal an unstained consciousness in touch with its source: Bliss.

Usually people come to class with certain ideas about what they are capable of achieving. For example, they may feel that a handstand is something for kids. Maybe they did such stunts when they were young—twenty, thirty, forty, or fifty (or more) years ago—but believe they could never do them now. In some cases, this attitude prevents them from even attempting a challenging asana like handstand, or at least causes them to fail in their attempts. With regular practice over a long period of time, however, one day they find themselves in handstand. In this way, asana undermines the hold that our beliefs about our limitations have on us, and we gradually see that they are not necessarily true. When we find that the old dog *can* be taught new tricks, we feel reborn.

There are asanas for bending forward, bending backward, sitting, standing, bending sideways, balancing, twisting, inverting—even asanas for practicing being a corpse. By far the most potent asanas are the inverted practices. In an inversion, the head is placed below the heart. The Downward-facing Dog, Adho Mukha Svanasana, is one of the simplest inversions. The profound nature of the inverted poses is due to their dramatic effect on both the physiology and psychology of the practitioner.

Physiologically, inverted postures reverse the internal dynamic pressures that affect blood flow, endocrine function, bone formation,

CHANDRASANA VARIATION, LUNGE

Chandra means moon. The moon is yin, the feminine, the subtle nerve channel running down the body called ida nadi, extending from the left nostril to the base of the spine. The crescent moon teaches that what you don't see is just as important as what you do see. Stability comes from the equalization of opposing forces: light and dark, sun and moon, ha and tha. Sunlight merges with moonlight and forms moonbeams. The feminine expresses itself in diverse creation. Through asana, we begin to see the importance of balancing the force of nature, intuition, with the forces of intelligence, reasoning and logic. This is true for every system, whether an individual body, a government, a culture, a society, or the relationship of all beings to the earth herself.

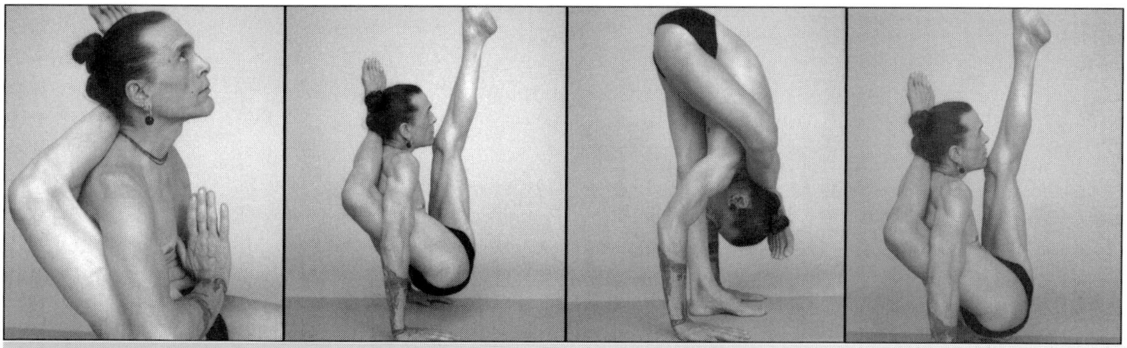

INHALE — Sit, foot behind the head—Eka Pada Sirsasana (transition—1 breath)—4

EXHALE / INHALE — Moonbird, Chakorasana (hold 5 breaths)—4

EXHALE — Standing forward bend, foot behind head—Ruchikasana (hold 5 breaths)—4

INHALE — Moonbird—Chakorasana (1 breath—then release)—4

Stop here, go back to the start, and repeat to the other side.

muscle tone, connective tissue, waste removal, and organ function, including brain chemistry. The effect of gravity is reversed, and to compensate for that reversal, the body must make dramatic internal changes.

Psychologically, inverted yogic practices make us feel "My whole world was turned upside-down today." If we could get used to that feeling, it would not be such a drama when our lives are overturned. If we turn things upside down, voluntarily and regularly, it's less of a shock when that happens without warning. Inversions also give us a fresh perspective, such as a painter obtains when he or she turns a work upside down to view it with more detachment. When we look at things from a completely different point of view, they may appear in a more honest light.

Shoulderstand should be held for a minimum of five minutes so that certain chemical secretions can be released from the glands. (If you have a neck injury, ask a teacher to show you how to modify the pose so that you can hold it for five minutes.) Master glands such as the pituitary, pineal, and thyroid will be stimulated, and you'll feel wholeness. Wholeness is the opposite of separateness, which causes all kinds of suffering. The Sanskrit name for shoulderstand is Salamba Sarvangasana, all-parts position. It's a wholesome asana.

Whether you are in handstand or mountain pose, your breath should remain the same: even and steady. If it fluctuates, you've let your thoughts take over. Any thought besides "I am the immortal Self, breathing in and breathing out" interferes with smooth, easy breath-

ADHO MUKHA SVANASANA, DOWNWARD-FACING DOG

The Downward-facing Dog is one of the most basic inversions. The base of the triangular figure from hands to feet represents the relationship to the earth: other beings, matter, and gravity. The three sides of the triangle represent the creative force (Brahma), the sustaining force (Vishnu), and the force of change (Shiva). The concavity of the lower abdomen represents the levitational forces: the celestial or divine realm, spirit. This asana represents the pivotal point at which the forces of entropy and evolution are in perfect balance and harmony. Birth is followed by life, which is followed by decay and death, which is followed by life again. Full awareness within each aspect of this cycle is part of the yogic quest.

Life can be defined as the gradual transformation of energy into matter, just as death can be defined as the gradual transformation of matter into energy.

TORTOISE SQUAT—The whole universe rests on the back of the tortoise.

INHALE — Prayer squat (hold 5 breaths)—1

EXHALE — Bound, rotated squat (hold 5 breaths)—2

INHALE EXHALE — Bound, twisted, hanging squat—2

INHALE — One leg tortoise staff—Eka pada jurma dandha prep—2 ing. Thoughts like "I can't do this" or "I'm doing this so well!" will distract you from your breathing.

During asana practice, thoughts about problems in your love life, work life, or family life may begin to flood your mind and demand your attention. When you realize this is happening, shift your attention back to your breath. Asana practice is not the time to chew on your thoughts. Focus your precious attention only on your Divine Nature, that which is ecstatically blissful and fully conscious, and which in the long run really does have the capacity to solve your problems.

It may help to chant a mantra internally throughout your asana practice. You could try the mantra "hamsa," for example. Hamsa is the swan; it represents the migrating bird flying south, only to fly north again, just as the breath moves in and moves out again, and life comes and goes. Breathe in "ham" (pronounced hum) and breathe out "sa" (pronounced sah), letting the mantra fully inhabit your mind. Another suggestion is the simple mantra "Let Go," internally chanting "Let" on every inhale and "Go" on every exhale. If your thoughts begin to wander, gently bring your attention back to the mantra that you have tied to the breath.

When you're in any asana and feel limitation, don't focus your attention on the limitation. That directs your energy toward the tendency that created the limitation. Whatever we give our energy or attention to gets stronger. If we focus on our difficulties, they gain power from that focus. Instead, let energy flow through your body and mind

These transformations have a beginning, middle, and end just as your asana has a beginning, middle, and end. At the end of each transformation, a new cycle begins. Each nuance of action can have infinite effects. The entire cosmos reverberates with the accumulated actions of all its inhabitants—from outer space to inner space.

What matters in your life is the quality of your actions and their resulting effects. These accumulated actions (karmas) and their infinite repercussions are what propel us into the next life. In Downward-facing Dog, we are poised at the tenuous balance point between opposing gravitational and levitational forces, in a position of dynamic harmony.

EXHALE

One leg tortoise staff—Eka pada kurma dandha (hold 5 breaths)—3

INHALE

One leg tortoise staff—Eka pada kurma dandha release—2

EXHALE

Bound rotated squat—2

INHALE

Prayer squat—1

Stop here, go back to the start, and repeat to the other side.

PLANK, PUSHING UPWARD POSE

The forces of growth move through wood from its roots to its tips, and from the tips to the roots. The movement of wood is upward from the earth. The movement of sunlight is through the leaves into the roots. The gravitational energy of the earth travels through the hands, feet, arms, and legs toward the navel. From the navel, the force of will sends consciousness toward the head, legs, and arms.

unimpeded. Focus not on the outer form, but on the essence, which interpenetrates the vessel and is unlimited in brilliance and capacity. Then bodily tension and restriction can subside.

The physiological benefits of asana practice are far-ranging. The daily stimulation of the endocrine system causes the level of hormones to be equalized and sustained. Your muscles are toned and alignment corrected. The psychotherapeutic benefits are life changing. Yet all these benefits pale by comparison to the possibility of Yoga—enlightenment.

In advanced practitioners, limberness and tone remain even when asana practice is discontinued, because the source of tightness, which was the identification with limitation, has vanished. The main thing that holds the body tight is the rigid grasping of ego identity. That grasping-and-holding-for-fear-of-losing results in locked organs, nerves, ligaments, muscles, and joints.

The shape of your body is a result of your thoughts, unconsciously and habitually appearing in the form of ego identification, reasserting themselves each moment in the flesh, nerves, blood, organs, bones, connective tissue, and musculature. Mistaking the body/mind for your true identity is the main obstacle to freedom.

Where does the Truth lie? The Truth lies in all things. All things lie apart from the Truth, all things lie a part of the Truth.

—Audio Letter, untitled song[4]

FLYING CROW—If we expect to fly, we must first take ourselves lightly.

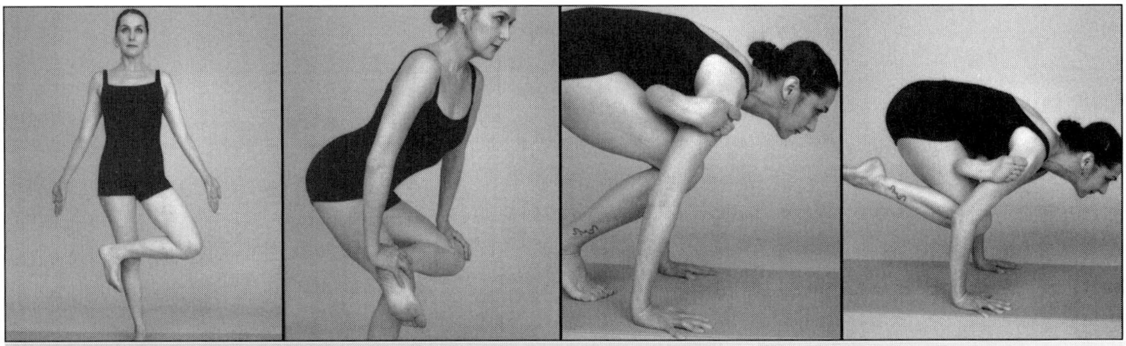

INHALE EXHALE INHALE EXHALE INHALE EXHALE

Ankle cross—Eka Pada Galavasana preparation—1

Bend knee—Eka Pada Galavasana preparation—1

Ground hands—Eka Pada Galavasana preparation—1

Lift foot—Eka Pada Galavasana preparation—2

Things do not last forever. Change is the inherent nature of material existence. Even your body will let you down in the end. It will grow old and die. When we expect life to proceed unchanged, change—when it does come—leaves us surprised and hurt.

When we resist change and cling to yesterday, disappointment is quick to appear. In our desperate search for stability, we look in all the wrong places. When babies grow up, when gray hair and wrinkles abound, we cry for the immortality that we thought meant this wouldn't happen. Much of what we experience as aging in the body is the result of resistance to change. As the ego tries to hold the body to a narrow expression of itself, it tightens and withdraws in fear.

Asana practice reveals how the body changes on a daily, weekly, or monthly cycle, or throughout a lifetime. A youthful body is capable of more rapid development and repair: the middle-aged or elderly body must proceed more slowly and heals more gradually. Through asana practice, we discover the importance of embracing change in the realm of body/mind and we discover stability in the soul realm. Surrender to change. In fact, allow it to happen to you. Don't resist it. To allow the great forces to move through you without resistance creates freedom. Embracing change creates ease in the world.

Follow certain instructions, then you will understand certain things that cannot be described. And that, of course, is what yoga is all about. All mystical writing really is instructions. It is not an attempt

ASHTANGA NAMASKARA, EIGHT PROSTRATIONS

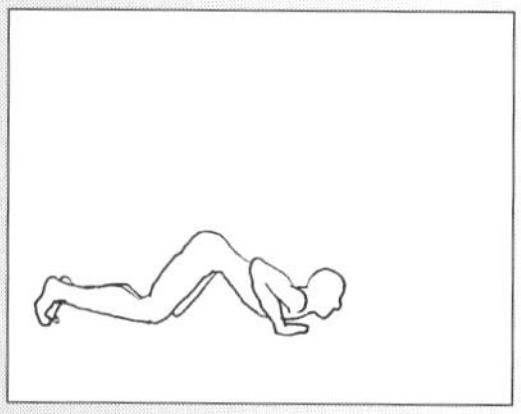

The undulating form gathers inward to project outward. Like the winding of a clock, it is a coalescence of energy for future movement. To throw or kick a ball very far or with accuracy, we must first pull back our arm or leg in preparation for projecting outward. In the same way, to project our presence on the earth with balance, refinement, and integrity, we must first draw inside and experience a Divine identity with infinite possibilities. Then we can project ourselves into the world with true creativity and originality.

INHALE

Flying Crow—Eka Pada Galavasana (hold 5 breaths)—3

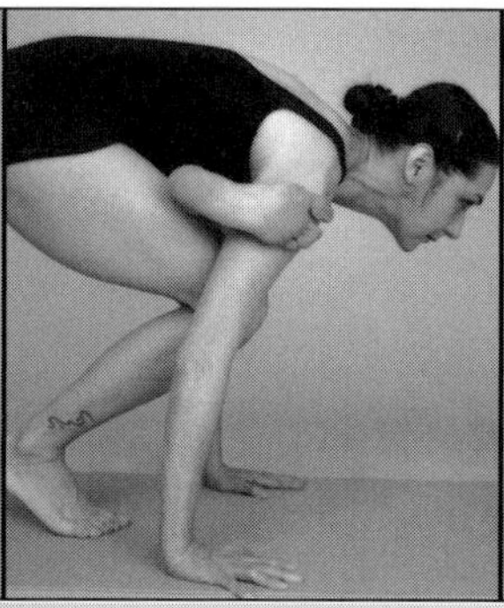

EXHALE

Release your foot to the ground—2

INHALE

Prepare—2

EXHALE

Standing half lotus forward bend—Ardha Baddha Padmottanasana—2

Stop here, go back to the start, and repeat to the other side.

BHUJANGASANA, COBRA

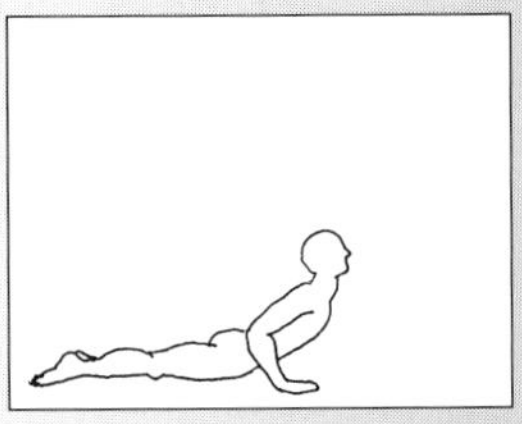

The cobra is an important mythopoetic icon in yoga. Cobras are said to be attracted to beings of high attainment. Like us, they are invigorated in the presence of the wise ones. Snakes hold the knowledge of the earth, where they live, and of the heavens, from which they came. Shiva wears snakes about his body, and kundalini (individual consciousness) is represented as a snake. Patanjali, the compiler of the *Yoga Sutras,* was said to be the embodiment of Adisesha, the endless snake. When kundalini is awakened, she is attracted upward toward her celestial lover, who resides at the third eye. This is the abode of Shiva, or undifferentiated consciousness. This ascent is the movement of consciousness from ignorance to bliss.

to describe the universe, to describe God, or to describe other realities. Every mystic knows that cannot possibly be done. The word mysticism, from the Greek muo, *means silence, mum's the word, shut up. (I should talk . . .) That's Yoga.* Shut up . . . shut up and listen.

—*Alan Watts*[5]

Sometimes he [God] is felt with ecstasy, but just as often there can be pain, anguish, and confusion. This mixture of feelings reminds us that two entities are coming into conjunction. One is spirit, the other is body. The body can perceive spirit only through the nervous system. As the intensity of God increases, the nervous system is overwhelmed by it.

—*Deepak Chopra,* How to Know God[6]

In asana practice, each part of the body becomes an expression of the desire to realize God. The hands, fingers, feet, toes, and all the body parts express this yearning for the Divine. The eyes are no exception.

Did you ever play a childhood game called Hide the Thimble? The goal in Hide the Thimble is to hide this tiny object in plain sight—not out of view. This game reveals how we search when we think something is hidden from us. We look in obscure and hidden places, ignoring the most obvious locations.

The yoga practices are methods for searching for something that has become difficult to see or experience. That something could be

THE SNAKE AND THE DOG—Forms come and forms go, but One remains the same.

EXHALE — Downward-facing Dog—Adho Mukha Svanasana (hold 8 breaths)—1

INHALE — Walking Snake—Plank pose—1

EXHALE — Crawling Snake—Knees, chest, and chin—1

INHALE — Praying Snake—Clasp hands over head (hold 5 breaths)—1

EXHALE

called happiness. We have a habit of looking in all the wrong places for it. We need to develop a special gaze to see it.

You search, babe, at any cost, but how long, babe, will you search for what's not lost?

—Bob Dylan, "I'll Keep It with Mine"[7]

Drishti, which is the technique of gazing during practice, is often misunderstood. Specific gazing points—such as up, down, left, right, tip of the nose, navel, third eye, toes, fingers, or thumbs—are recommended for certain asanas. Actually, these points are not directly looked at, but rather are gazed beyond and used as a sort of aiming mechanism. Gazing should be a naturally evolving method that helps you concentrate on the goal of the practice: union with God.

The proper gazing point for any particular asana is the one that most benefits the energetic movement of the asana. In Warrior One (Virabhadrasana I), for example, the gazing point is your thumbnails because this point requires the arms to move into their correct alignment for the posture. You won't be able to see your thumbnails if your arms are behind your ears. You won't be able to lift your chest and open your heart, either.

If you find yourself closing your eyes and spacing out during practice, open them and use the gazing point that appears obvious for the shape of the asana you are practicing.

Once God was frustrated with the constant nagging of people unsatisfied with their lot in life and complaining to God to change things to suit them. Heal this person, give wealth to that one, find a husband for this one, grant these two a child. There was always some request. He needed a break, but wherever He hid, they found him and started asking for things again. So He called together a council of the other gods and goddesses at Mount Meru, to try to solve this problem.

Shiva told him to hide on the moon; they would never find him there. Somehow, God felt they would find him there very quickly. Vishnu suggested that he hide at the bottom of the deepest ocean. No one would look there! God knew that hiding place would never last. Finally, Sarasvati, laughing, said the answer was obvious. "Just hide right inside their own hearts. They will never think to look there!"

In temples in North India, you sometimes see people using a very creative gazing technique. The worshiper makes his or her fist into a tube and gazes through it toward the deity, using the fist like a little telescope. In this way, the worshiper cuts out extraneous vision and has a private experience of viewing the deity.

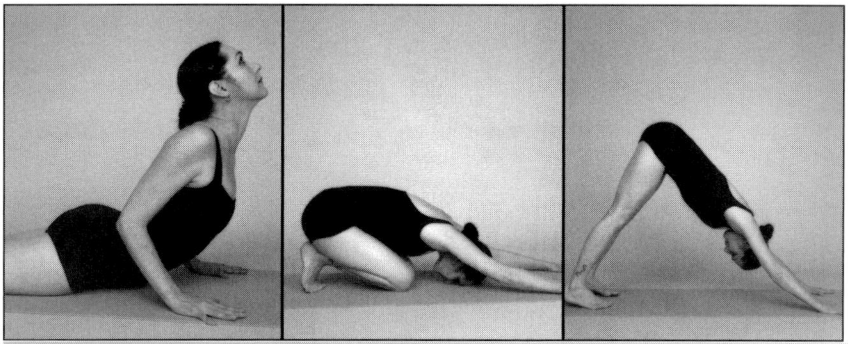

INHALE — EXHALE — INHALE — EXHALE

Cobra—Bhujangasana (hold 5 breaths)—2

Bheki—Child Pose—1

Downward-facing Dog—Adho Mukha Svanasana—1

Gazing is not the same as looking. Looking implies that the object of the vision is in the same dimensional reality as the looker. The act of looking is fixed in duality. There's a looker and an object being looked at. Gazing, in contrast, is a method for looking beyond mundane objects. One gazes toward that hazy realm of perception beyond the clearly focused. The devoted practitioner yearns for a vision of God beyond the limits of eyes.

Although pointed outward, correct gazing is fixed inward also. Space is curved, so if you had a telescope that was strong enough, you could gaze through it and see the back of your own head in the lens. Indeed, if this telescope were also capable of special X-ray vision, you could see right through the back of your own head into vision itself.

Gazing is a fascinating, helpful method for intensifying concentration. Like other yoga methods, such as restricting the breath in order to expand it (pranayama), gazing is a method for confining vision in order to expand it beyond object orientation.

Normal vision is linear and objective. Yogic vision is multidimensional and beyond subject/object dichotomy. Normal vision sees edges that separate the beginning of one thing from the end of the next thing. Gazing expands vision beyond the separation of one thing from another to the underlying causal sameness.

By maintaining the appropriate gazes during asana practice and breathing steadily, you will develop the ability to detach from your efforts and from the fluctuations of the mind and the body that occur as you practice. This same detachment helps you develop the ability to be generous and not attach importance to

HERO MONKEY—The monkey mind is tamed with the quest of the heroine.

INHALE — EXHALE — INHALE — EXHALE — INHALE

Hero—Virasana—2

Reclining Hero—Supta Virasana (hold 5 breaths)—2

Hero—Virasana—2

Hands and Knees—Adho Mukha Svanasana preparation—1

your anger, your fear, to any emotions that would prevent you from becoming sweeter and sweeter.

Asana practice clears the subtle pathways through which prana flows. As we become aware of the movement of prana, we become aware of our expansive potential. We realize that we are not limited to one unchanging static form. This is expressed in Surya Namaskar, or Salute to the Sun. There are many versions of Surya Namaskar; the one here is based on the asanas illustrated in this chapter's sidebars.

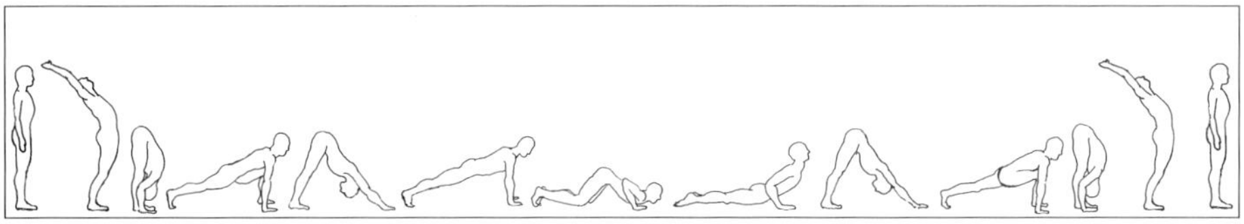

Surya Namaskar, sun salute
Artist: David Life

Asana encourages awareness of prana by giving us an opportunity to put ourselves into the various shapes and patterns of existence and experience the dynamic force that animates all form. In the Celtic myth of Camelot, Merlin teaches the young Arthur how to become a good king. The wizard transforms the boy into various life-forms: animals, plants, and minerals. As Arthur experiences the perspectives of those over whom he has lordship, he is better prepared to rule with compassion. This is Yoga, the experience of the vitality of life in all forms of life.

EXHALE — INHALE — EXHALE — INHALE — EXHALE

Dog pose—Adho Mukta Svanasana—1

Split —Hanumanasana—3

Split—Hanumanasana arm variation (hold 5 breaths)—3

Dog pose—Adho Mukha Svanasana—1

Stop here, go back to the start, and repeat to the other side.

8

Vinyasa Krama: The Forgotten Language of Sequencing Postures

The newborn baby is not able to walk like a young child; it gives constant suggestion to its body through the mind and after one or two years of the practice of suggestion, the baby walks. Any knowledge that we are acquiring at present, or that which we expect to acquire in the future, will come to us through the power of suggestion. If there is evil suggestion this will result in an unhappy life, good suggestion will result in a happy life.

—*Shri Brahmananda Sarasvati,* The Textbook of Yoga Psychology

Many books illustrate asanas as static postures. Learning only static postures does not reveal the incredible potential of asana, however. When individual asanas are linked together correctly in a sequence, the result is a physiological mantram, a fleshy vortex of intersecting rivers of everything.

The word vinyasa means "a joining or linking mechanism." Krama means "the process"; it refers to the succession of changes that occurs from moment to moment. Vinyasa krama means the succession of changes undertaken with a single pointed intention, free from fluctuation.

Most people are not conscious of their intention from moment to moment.

Details fill their lives, but the causal thread of the vinyasa remains elusive. They may often find themselves in situations wondering, "How did I get into this one?" When we establish a conscious intention and teach ourselves how to remain aligned with that intention, no matter how much we are dissuaded or distracted by the external world, the process unfolds as it should.

The vinyasa is the element that sews together the various moments in a sequence of changes. It is like the string on which pearls are strung for a necklace. The linking strand may be of two types: conscious or unconscious. Change is always occurring, but usually a sequence of changes is linked by *un*consciousness; in other words, the conscious mind fails to perceive it. The yogi, having escaped from the illusion of duality, is able to perceive the moment-to-moment sequence of changes: past, present, and future. When one perceives clearly both the instigation and the outcome of moment-to-moment changes, one can choose to undertake a sequence of actions that has a conscious endpoint and will have a particular effect.

When you practice a sequence of asanas, you link them with conscious breathing. The real vinyasa, or link, however, is the intention with which you practice the asanas. It is the intention that links the postures with consciousness instead of unconsciousness. The breath is merely a metaphor for that intention. If your intention is to practice asana to realize the Self, every breath you take will help break down your sense of separation from others. You will realize that the atmosphere is filled with atoms of air that once filled the lungs of everyone who ever lived. We are breathing each other. From this realization, it's not hard to leap to the realization that we are all sharing consciousness in the same way

AWAKENING SNAKE—**When the energies of Cosmic intelligence and life converge . . .**

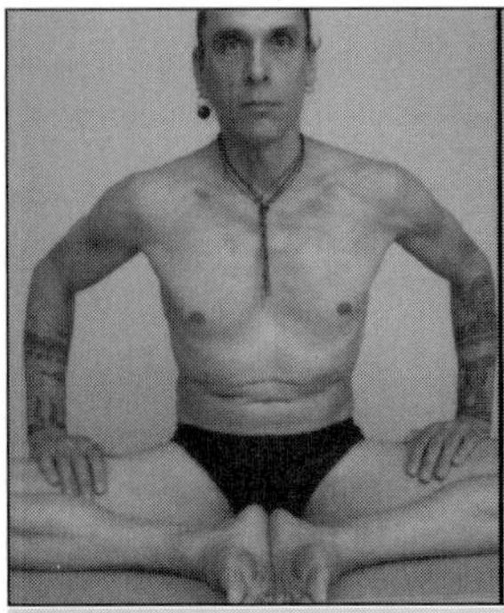

INHALE

Cobbler's pose—Baddha Konasana preparation—1

EXHALE

Goddess pose—Reclining Baddha Konasana (hold 20 breaths)—1

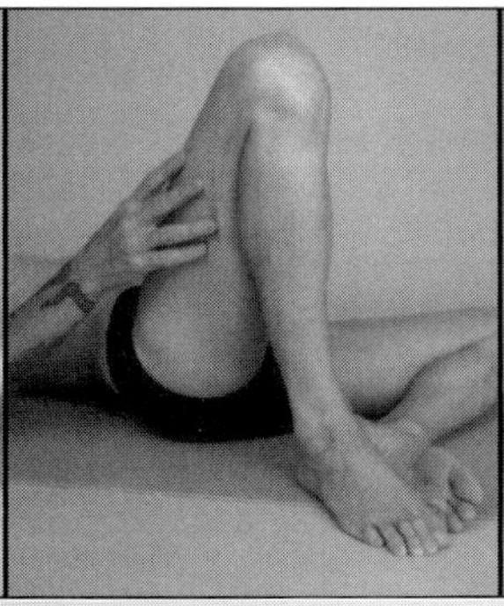

INHALE

Lift knees—Ardha Urdhva Dhanurasana preparation—1

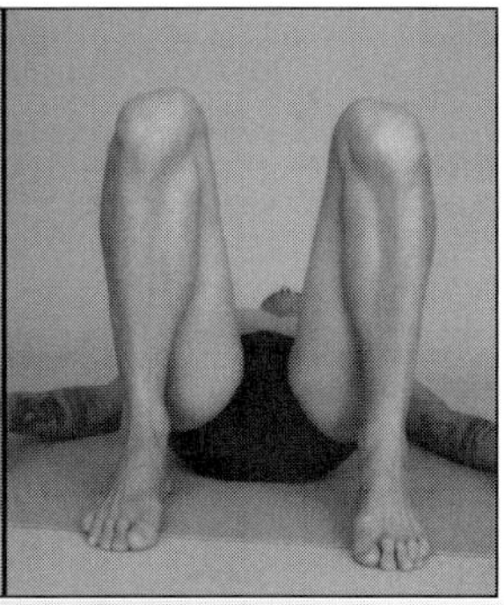

EXHALE

Ground feet—Ardha Urdhva Dhanurasana preparation—1

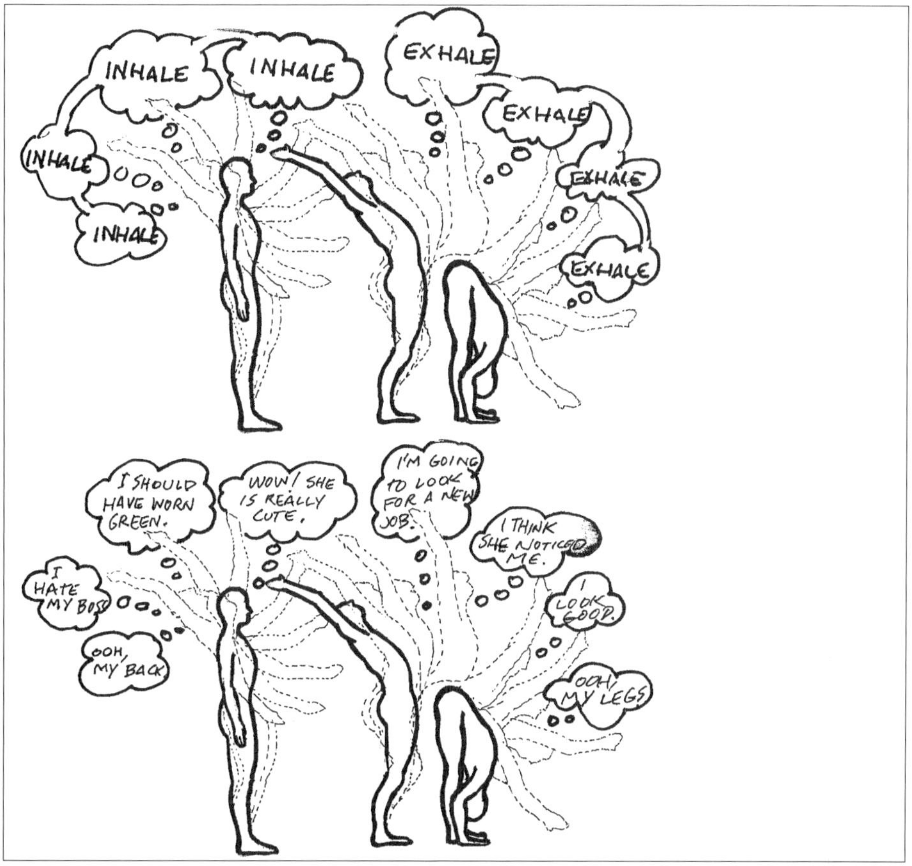

(top) Vinyasa with focus on breath (bottom) Vinyasa with focus on thoughts
Artist: David Life

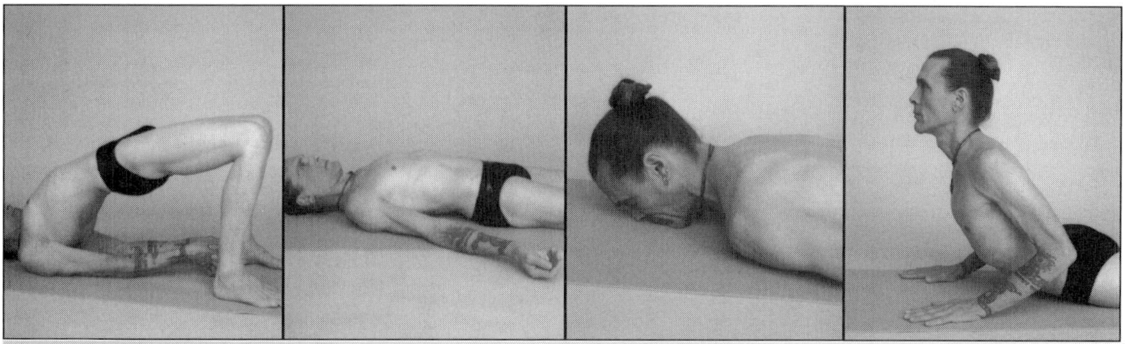

INHALE — EXHALE — INHALE — EXHALE — INHALE — EXHALE

$^1/_2$ Wheel—Ardha Urdhva Dhanurasana (hold 10 breaths)—2

Corpse—Savasana—1

Roll over to abdomen—Bhujangasana preparation—1

Cobra—Bhujangasana (hold 10 breaths)—2

Stop here, or continue to the next page.

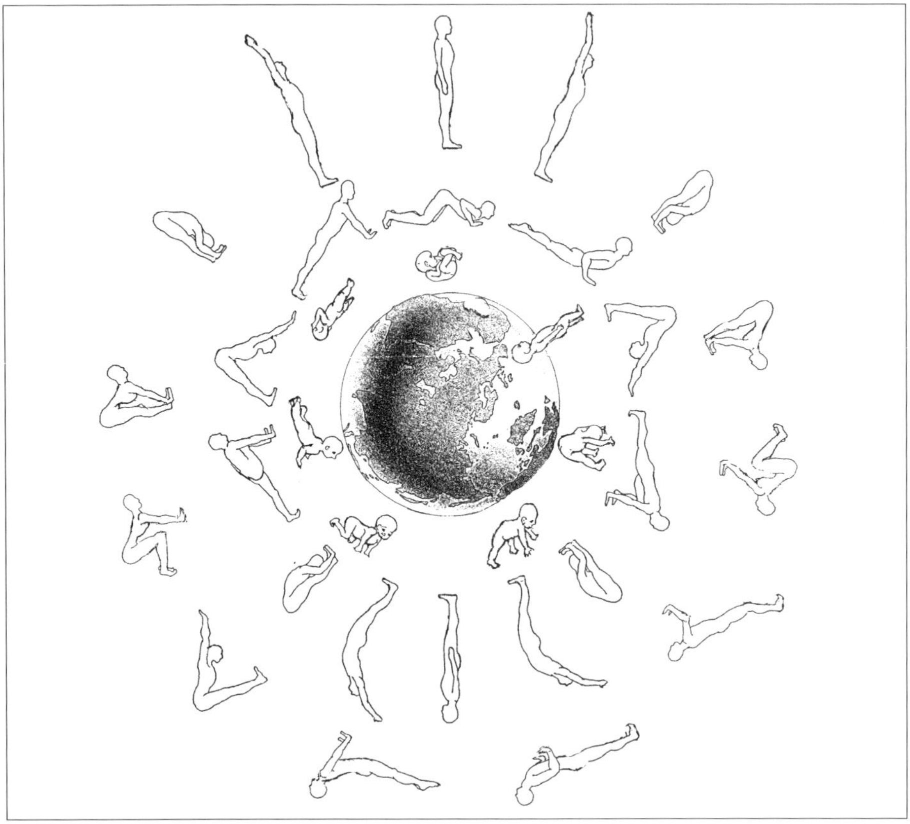

Surya Namaskar (Sun Salute) mandala
Artist: David Life

THE LOCUST AND THE CAMEL—Resistance to change is felt as dis-ease in the body.

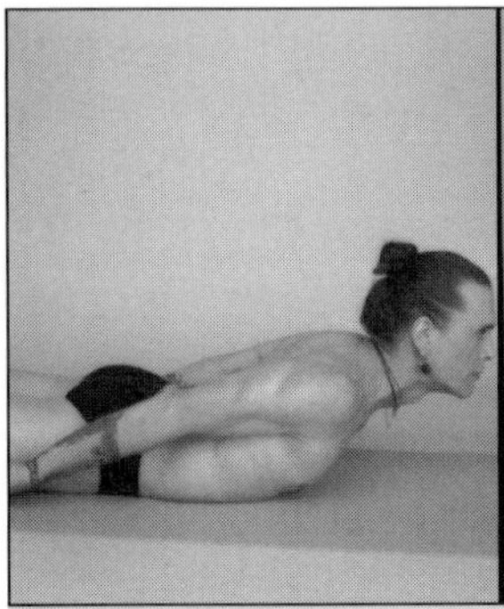

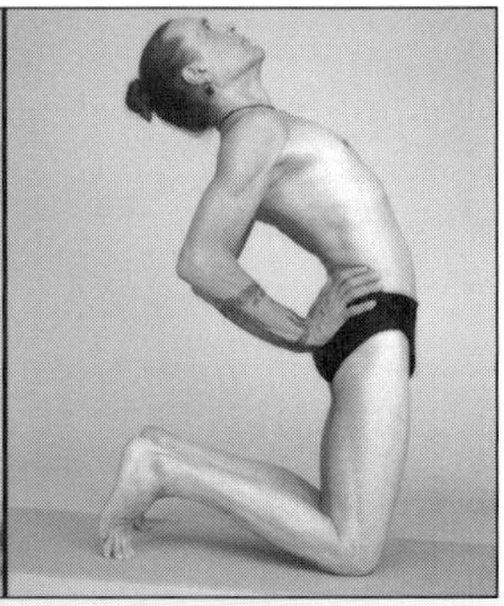

INHALE EXHALE INHALE EXHALE INHALE EXHALE

Shalabhasana—Locust (hold 8 breaths)—1

Bow—Dhanurasana (hold 8 breaths)—2

Downward-facing Dog—Adho Mukha Svanasana—1

Stand on knees—Ustrasana preparation (hold 5 breaths)—2

that we share the air we breathe. The awakening of consciousness will benefit all others, because we all share in the consciousness and its awakening.

The vinyasa krama with which most yoga students are familiar is Surya Namaskar. A classic Sun Salute was presented in the previous chapter. There are many variations, one of which is the jumping version also shown in the illustration on page 146. (If you are not familiar with some form of Sun Salute, or any of the other asanas mentioned in this book, please seek out the guidance of a good teacher before attempting the classes given in this chapter.) Many schools of yoga use Surya Namaskar as the "warm-up" for a yoga class. The natural development of a child from fetal position to standing is duplicated in reverse in Surya Namaskar, where we move from standing to crawling. This echoes yoga's journey, which is to move from matter into spirit:

1. The child is in a fetal or forward bending position in the womb.
2. The child learns to stretch out on a flat surface.
3. The child lies on the abdomen in an upward-facing dog position.
4. The child pushes back on hands and knees.
5. The child presses to a downward-facing dog pose.
6. The child walks feet toward hands in Uttanasana.
7. The child stands in a wobbly Samastittih.

A Sun Salute, Surya Namaskar

Exhale, steady standing, Samastittih.
Inhale, lock thumbs, arch back.
Exhale, bend forward, Uttanasana.
Inhale, step right foot back to lunge, Chandrasana variation.
Exhale, step to downward-facing dog, Adho Mukha Svanasana.
Inhale, Plank posture.
Exhale, knees, chest and chin to the floor, Ashtanga Namaskar.
Inhale, Cobra, Bhujangasana.
Exhale, seat to heels, then downward-facing dog, Adho Mukha Svanasana.
Inhale, step right foot forward.
Exhale, bend forward, Uttanasana.
Inhale, bend knees, lock thumbs, reach up as you straighten legs and arch back.
Exhale, steady standing, Uttanasana.
Repeat for at least 5 minutes.

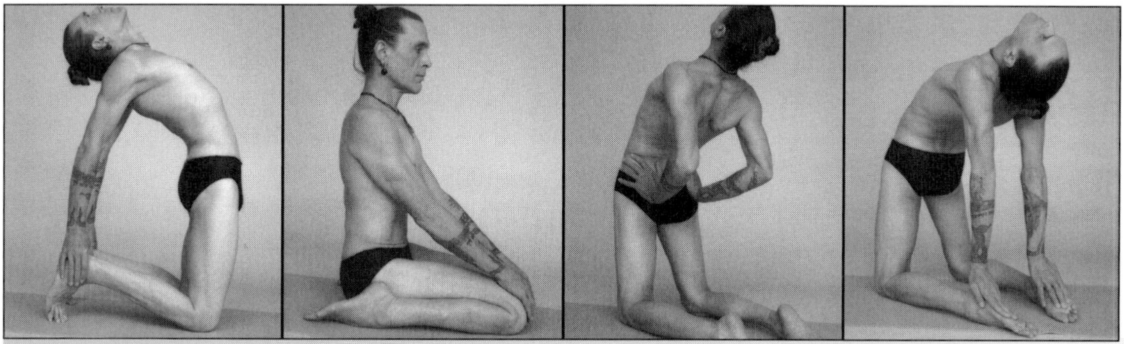

INHALE EXHALE INHALE EXHALE INHALE EXHALE

Rabbit—Ustrasana variation (hold 8 breaths)—3

Hero—Virasana (hold 5 breaths)—2

Stand on knees—Ustrasana preparation (hold 5 breaths)—2

Camel—Ustrasana (hold 8 breaths)—3

Stop here, or continue to the next page.

The breath is the outer vinyasa, or connecting element; the intention is the inner vinyasa. Controlling the breath will help you control the thoughts. Try to eliminate extra breaths. There should be only one inhale or exhale per movement while moving. The durations of inhale and exhale should be equal and the breath should last from the time a movement begins until slightly after it is completed. When we perfect the ability to invest each of the positions with the same steady, even breath, we may perceive the ever-present consciousness inhabiting all worldly forms.

As yogis, we start with the wobbly Samastittih and reverse the order of these movements. Surya Namaskar explores, in a microcosmic way, these early childhood activities. As we change from form to form—from dog to warrior to stick to mountain—one thing stays the same: the breath and our sense of "I-AM." As a baby we struggled to crawl, stand, walk, and run, but inside, our experience of "I-AM" never changed.

There are many styles of Surya Namaskar and each is helpful when performed with proper attention to the vinyasa. The performance of a Surya Namaskar vinyasa establishes intention for your entire practice because it is akin to bowing in a temple in prayer. It is bowing down in respectful prayer to the heavens, the Earth, and all earthly beings. We experience the continuity in everything that is passing. We join with that continuity.

Asana sequences are a powerful way to explore both the concept and the practical aspects of vinyasa krama, because they *are* a sequence of changes undertaken in a controlled situation, with Self-realization as the conscious intention.

As we observe from a detached point of view the way that our habits, fears, and tendencies determine our participation in or denial of the changes we are experiencing as we practice asana, we learn about our unconsciousness and about the nature of mind.

In the beginning, we use the breath, the intention, the bandhas, and the gaze to train our minds to guide the senses rather than let them

TRAVELING FROG—The frog leaps to the goal directly.

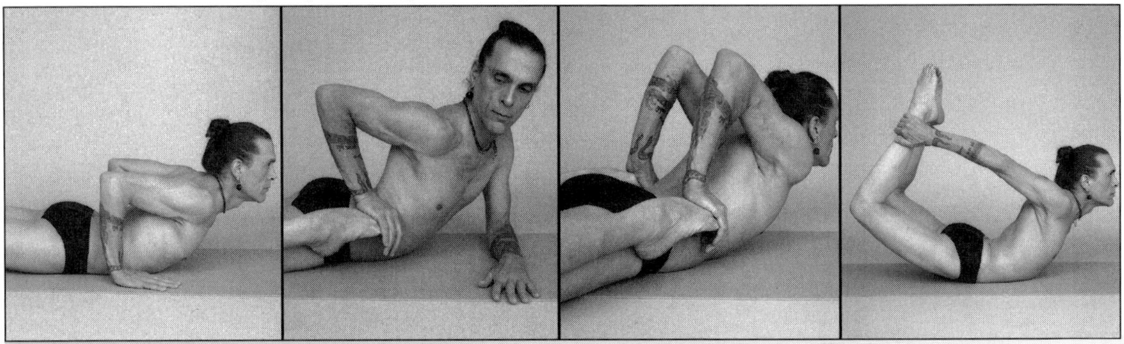

INHALE — EXHALE — INHALE — EXHALE — INHALE — EXHALE

Shalabhasana—Locust (hold 5 breaths)—1

½ Frog—Ardha Bhekasana (hold 5 breaths per side)—1

Frog—Bhekasana (hold 5 breaths)—2

Bow—Dhanurasana (hold 5 breaths, repeat 3 times)—2

go in any direction they please. It is the nature of the mind to be pulled by the senses as they flit from sensation to sensation. By focusing on the breath and then placing the seamless execution of asanas in the way of that concentration, however, we learn to focus the attention single-pointedly. When we've learned to focus the mind uninterruptedly for long periods of time, this focus is called dharana. Dharana will eventually lead spontaneously to the meditative state, dhyana.

Vinyasa krama is the sequential arrangement of asana for specific results. Some sequences are invigorating, some are very refined, some involve balance, some are therapeutic, some are dance-like, some are martial, some tell stories, and all may lead to samadhi: enlightenment! Sequencing adds prayerful potency, elements of physical challenge, artistic refinement, and therapeutic effect to the asana practice.

Each asana has a discrete vibrational essence, much like the individual phonetic sounds that make up the alphabet of a language. When asanas are linked properly, they form invocations that yield results according to the nature of the intention and the content of the invocation. Sequences should be developed slowly and carefully, therefore, with awareness.

A vinyasa may be continuous for a portion of a class, or even for an entire class. Consciousness is the ultimate linking mechanism, so while we move through the postures we use the breath as a training tool for the attention, thereby awakening consciousness. To use the breath for the vinyasa means to account for each breath and tie each breath to the appropriate movement into or out of a posture. The breath illuminates and fills the asana.

During vinyasa, the breath should always be flowing in or flowing out; breath retention is never correct. When you feel yourself holding the breath, reflect on

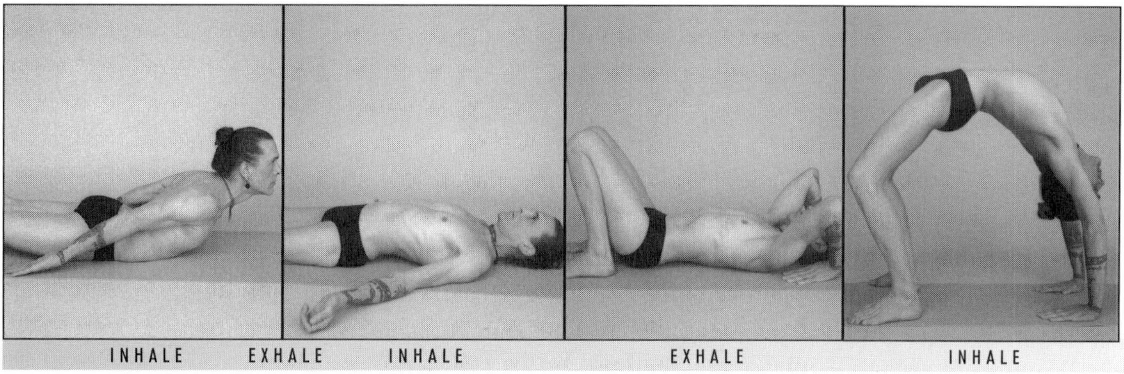

Shalabhasana—Locust
(hold 5 breaths, repeat 3 times)—1

Roll over—Savasana—1

Ground hands and feet—Urdhva Dhanurasana preparation—1

Upward-facing bow—
Urdhva Dhanurasana
(hold 5 breaths, repeat 3 times)—3

Stop this sequence here.

The following aids are extremely helpful for creating an underlying elevated intention that will function without interruption throughout an asana practice. When you notice your mind wandering, use these aids to regain your concentration. With experience, you will determine which works best for you.

1. Pictures of deities or of inspiring saints who dedicated their lives to the uplifting of consciousness.
2. Inspiring, devotional music that is uplifting and reminds us of our goal, Yoga.
3. Chanting of mantra internally, coordinating it with the inhale and the exhale.

the underlying mental impressions that led to your holding on to the breath. You might even receive an insight into the way these underlying mental tendencies cause you to hesitate during other important moments in your life.

Here are some important breathing guidelines for the practice of vinyasa:

1. Inhales and exhales should be only through the nose, of equal duration, and move the same volume of air. Ujjayi breathing makes the breath audible and easier to regulate. If you aren't familiar with Ujjayi breathing, please see a yoga teacher for instruction. Some instruction is also available in Chapter 6 under pranayama techniques.

2. Typically, the breath is inhaled during ascending movements and movements that open the front of the body.

3. Typically, the breath is exhaled during descending movements and movements that open the back of the body.

4. No movement is undertaken without being intimately connected to either an inhale or an exhale.

5. The quality of the breath reflects the quality of the mind in any posture. If the breath has an unaffected quality, free from attachment to pleasure or aversion to pain, the mind will have that same quality.

6. The least possible number of breaths and movements are used to enter into, transition between, and exit from one position to another. No fussing, fidgeting, adjusting, daydreaming, or complaining.

FISH PLAY—The swimming fish plays unhindered by ups and downs.

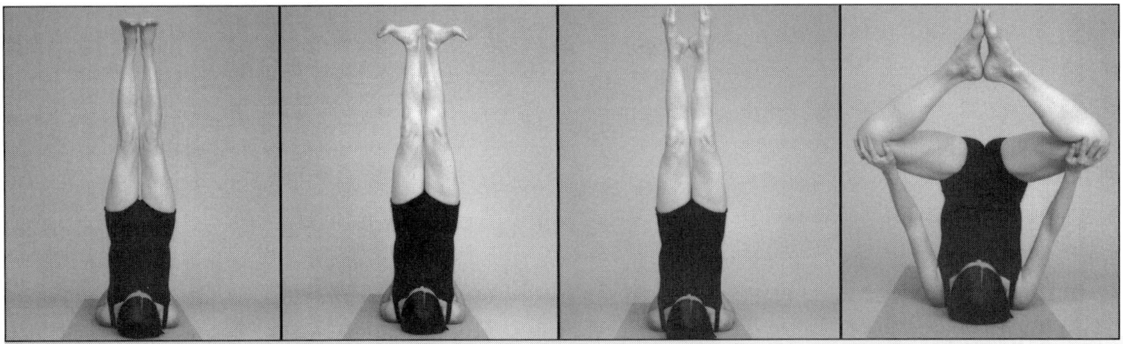

INHALE — Shoulderstand—Salamba Sarvangasana (hold 100 breaths)—2

EXHALE — Turn out and flex ankles—Salamba Sarvangasana variation—2

INHALE — Point toes—Salamba Sarvangasana variation—2

EXHALE INHALE — Rest knees in palms—Niralamba Sarvangasana var. (hold 10 breaths)—2

Ksana-pratiyogi parinamaparanta-nirgrahyah kramah. (YS IV:33)
Krama, the process, is the succession of changes that occur from moment to moment, which becomes apprehensible at the final end of the transformation of the three gunas.

In this sutra, Patanjali tells us that when the three gunas (the qualities of illusory existence) are transcended, the process, or krama, is revealed. An asana practice dominated by tamas includes sleepiness, yawning, and even visions of power and control. An asana practice dominated by rajas is competitive, frantic, erratic, and aggressive. To avoid these tendencies, cultivate a sattvic practice, characterized by steadiness (sthira) and joy (sukham).

Cultivate a consistent, conscious practice that is not affected by your daily irregularities. The classes given in this book are a good basic starting point for establishing a program of asana practice. After you have worked with some of these class sequences, you'll get the hang of it and begin to understand the elements that make up a class. Then, you'll be able to improvise and modify by including more sequences and adding or excluding asanas. This inclusion or exclusion should not be based on whim or fancy from day to day, however. It should be based on experiential knowledge of the eventual outcome of a sequence and mastery of the technique of the proper balancing and sequencing of a whole class.

In the back of this book we provide an appendix that lists asanas

- Counterpose: a pose that moves energy in the opposite direction of the previous one. A counterpose is needed after holding one pose for a long time. For example:

  Pose: Salamba Sarvangasana (Shoulderstand)
  Counterpose: Matsayasana (Fish)

- Neutralizing pose: a pose that moves energy to a neutral position, allowing you to either move in a different direction or continue moving in the same direction with more intensity.
  - Neutralizing postures, such as tabletop and Adho Mukha Svanasana (Downward-facing Dog) are used between asanas, as well as between sequences before the practitioner moves on to the next, higher level of difficulty.
  - A particular pose may be a counterpose or a neutralizer, depending on the context in which it is used. Tabletop, for example, is a neutralizing pose, yet it can also be considered a counterpose when used after forward-bending poses.

EXHALE INHALE EXHALE INHALE EXHALE INHALE

Toes to head—Halasana variation (hold 5 breaths)—2

Plow—Halasana (hold 10 breaths)—2

Tranquility—Niralamba Sarvangasana II var. (hold 10 breaths)—2

Fish—Matsyasana (hold 10 breaths)—2

Stop here, or continue to the next sequence.

you can use to create your own asana sequences. In Appendix I, the asanas are ranked by difficulty to help you order a sequence from least difficult to most difficult asana.

Daily dedication to your asana practice will allow you to transcend like and dislike, attraction and aversion, and feel the full potency of the subtle structure of each sequence as a method to achieve that transcendence. The ideal situation is to repeat a sequence unchanging until you've mastered it. To put it simply: repetition forces the magic to rise.

To transcend the three gunas, focus first on bringing your practice into a sattvic balance. Once that is accomplished, the transcendence of which Patanjali spoke tends to occur effortlessly.

Your daily practice should:

- Focus attention toward a spiritual goal.
- Cleanse the nadis (the subtle nerve channels) and promote pranic flow.
- Maintain overall endocrine stimulation and regulation.
- Gradually increase strength, flexibility, and happiness.

During any section of an asana session, each successive sequence of poses should increase in intensity to the capacity of the practitioner and then decrease in intensity using neutralizers or less intense asanas. We move from the more general to the specific and back to the general, from the less difficult to the more difficult, and eventually back to the less difficult.

The chart below illustrates how the practice should move forward in increas-

CHASING KRISHNA—The world is His playground, the sky His path.

Bheki—Child Pose (hold 5 breaths)—1

Headstand—Salamba Sirsasana preparation—1

Headstand—Salamba Sirsasana preparation—2

Headstand—Salamba Sirsasana (hold 50 breaths)—3

ing waves of difficulty, with the body moving into neutralizing postures before each new wave. The numbers 1 through 4 indicate the degree of difficulty of the asana. The thick black line represents an advanced practice, the thin black line an intermediate practice, and the dotted line a beginner practice. Across the bottom are the names of the focus of that section of the class. A complete practice might flow something like this, with the addition of side bends, twists, and neutralizing postures.

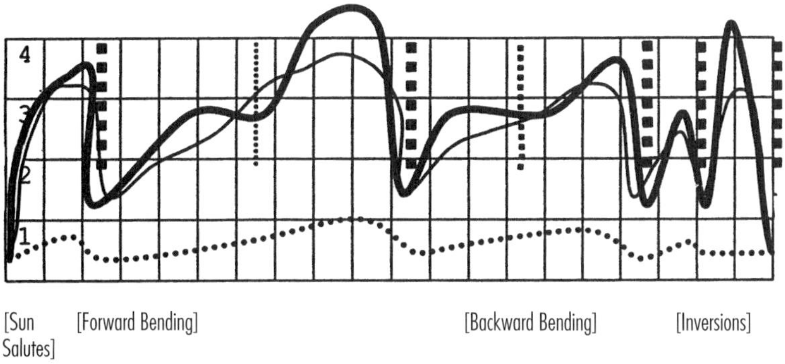

The vertical light dash lines represent where neutralizing asanas can be placed. The vertical heavy dash lines represent where counterposes can be placed. Here you can see the structure of using neutralizing postures where necessary and increasing the intensity of the practice in waves.

Here are some general rules for your asana practice:

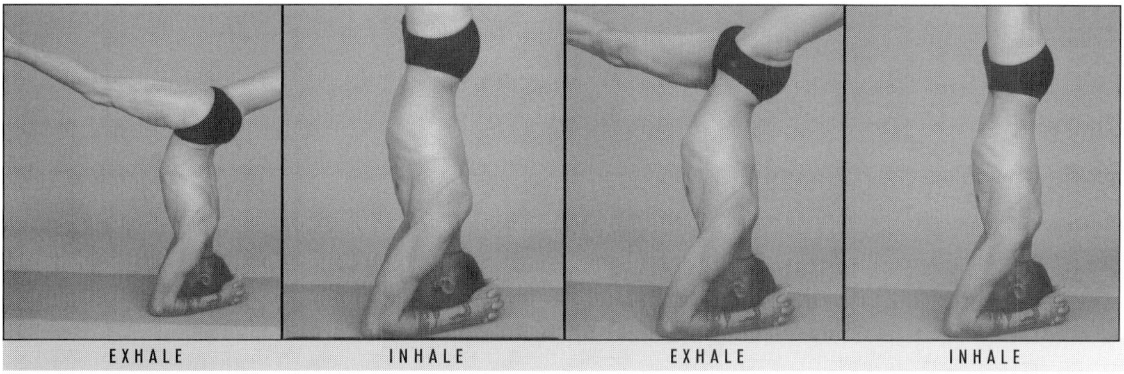

Headstand—Salamba Sirsasana variation, walking legs forward and back alternately with each breath, coming to the center after each step (repeat 10 times)—3

Headstand—Salamba Sirsasana—3

Stop, then release to Child Pose for 5 breaths.

1. Always begin with an invocation, prayer, or dedication.

2. Use breath awareness exercises that shift attention to the breath. Examples: *kapalbhati* kriya (described on page 188) or ujjayi (described on page 119)

3. Warm up with 5 to 15 minutes of Surya Namaskar (Sun Salute) Vinyasa.

4. Postures can be held for any length of time, but most usually are held only 5 to 20 breaths. The exception is inversions, which may be held for several minutes depending on the practitioner's capacity.

5. Standing poses should usually precede forward bends, back bends, or inversions. They seat the body through the feet to the earth, bringing stability, strength, and awareness to the legs.

6. Twisting should not be neglected, either in the beginning of practice, where it affects the internal organs and enhances movement of the spine, or throughout the practice, where it can be used to neutralize.

7. Never alternate back bends and forward bends in the same sequence without careful and continuous vinyasa of the breath. In Surya Namaskar, which by nature alternates back bending and forward bending, you are protected from injury through adhering to a strict vinyasa, in which every breath is consciously counted.

8. When holding asanas you should group forward bends only with other forward bends, backward bends only with backward bends, side bending only with side bending.

9. If you choose to focus on a particular aspect of the asana practice in one class session, choose only one (e.g., forward bending or backward bending), not both. You may choose to alternate the emphasis every day or every few days. Focus on back bending on Monday, Tuesday, and Wednesday, and forward bending on Thursday, Friday, Saturday, and Sunday, for example.

10. Do not counter a forward bend series in midstream with a back bend, or vice versa. Neutralize instead, by twisting, for example.

11. In any practice session, always start with the less difficult postures and transition into more difficult postures.

12. Do not extend a sequence for more postures on one side than you can remember to repeat on the other side.

13. Insert neutralizing asanas such as Adho Mukha Svanasana (Downward-facing Dog) or Bheki (Child's Pose) periodically.

14. Use complementary counterposes after finishing a section of

TRANSITIONS

One of the more challenging aspects of sequencing is figuring out how to move into or out of a particular asana. Here are some general rules that should help:

1. No movement should be undertaken without a corresponding breath.
2. Superfluous movements or embellishments should not be added.
3. When in doubt, move out of one asana completely and realign the body with a neutralizing asana before moving to the next asana.

same-category poses. Use neutralizing poses at regular intervals during and between sections. A forward-bending series can be countered with Tabletop or Inclined Plane, for example, and then neutralized with a Twist right and a Twist left.

15. Relax in Shavasana (Corpse Pose) for 10 to 15 minutes at the end of practice.

16. Meditate for at least 5 minutes (for instruction on how to meditate, please see Chapter 10).

Think of vinyasa krama as a language of asana. The meaning is in the rhythm of movement and the careful choice among the infinite possibility of combinations.

We all know that the shape of an antenna determines the kind of signal that it sends or receives. That's why an FM antenna is shaped differently from a color TV antenna or a satellite dish. When we shape the body differently by assuming the various asanas, we, too, vibrate at a particular frequency and are able to receive a particular frequency.

Each asana is a unique vibrational expression of an aspect of manifestation. In each vinyasa krama, you experience the flowing river of life as you become cat-cow-cobra-dog. When we place ourselves in an asana, we express both the vibrational essence of its Sanskrit name and the vibrational essence of the life-form that the asana embodies. For example, while performing eagle pose, you might begin to feel what it is like to fold up your wings and gaze down a long beak as you perch on the branch of a tree.

We can use these vibrational signatures to compose words, sentences, stories, and mythologies. The combination of vibrations becomes an invocation to cosmic consciousness.

Here are some sample classes for beginner, intermediate, and advanced practitioners. We list the name we have given to each asana sequence, followed by the page the sequence is pictured on. We also name individual asanas and the degree of difficulty of the sequence or individual asana. Neutralizing asanas, such as Bheki (Child's Pose), are marked with an asterisk.

To learn each sequence, go to its pages and study the strip of photos along the bottom. Once you have memorized all the sequences for a class, you will be ready to do it. After each class instruction, we have provided a visual reference chart that contains all the sequences in the order in which they are practiced for that class. Ideally, however, you will rely on your memory of the class, not the chart, so that you can flow freely through the sequences. Once you have an understanding of these basic classes, you can begin to create your own. Use our sample classes and what you have learned in this chapter about combining poses, counterposes, and neutralizers to begin to develop your own sequences.

TIPS FOR USING THE ASANA SEQUENCES

Note: These sequences are best learned under the guidance of a certified Jivamukti teacher.

1. Scan the sequence to familiarize yourself with it, reading the instructions beneath it.

2. Place the sequence in the context of a class. We offer simple, intermediate/advanced classes in this chapter.

3. When the correct place for the sequence arrives, repeat it, alternating sides, until you learn it. (Once you know it, you need perform it only once on each side.)

4. For asanas that are one-sided, do the right side first, then repeat to the left.

5. Pay special attention to the breath instructions at the bottom of each picture.

6. Put on some inspiring music, and have fun!

Here is an example of a simple class. The numbers in the right-hand column indicate the degree of difficulty of the asana.

Simple Class 1

1. Offer all of your efforts to God and Guru with this chant:

Guru Brahma, Guru Vishnu, Guru Devo Maheshvara, Guru Sakshat, Param Brahma, Tasmai Shri Guruvey Namaha (Refer to pages 17–19 for chant translation.)

Pledge your actions to the end of suffering and the freedom and happiness of all beings:

Lokah Samasta Sukhino Bhavantu (Refer to page 78 for translation.)

2. While standing or sitting, spend a few moments bringing awareness to your breathing. Equalize the duration and volume of your inhale and exhale.

3. Practice Surya Namaskar for at least 5 minutes (see page 147 for review). Then move into the following asana sequences. Intermittently, individual asanas that are not part of the photographed sequences are given, along with the breath count for which they should be held. Where page numbers are not given, simply perform the asana named (Bheki, or Child's Pose, in this example). The numbers in the far right column simply indicate the difficulty level of each asana or sequence of asanas.

Warrior's Triangle	pages 100–101	1–2
Kundalini's Descent	pages 108–109	1–2
Cobbler's Table	pages 122 123	1–3
Awakening Snake	pages 144–145	1–2
*Bheki (Child's Pose, hold for 10 breaths)		1
Fish Play	pages 150–151	2

4. Lie down in Shavasana (Corpse Pose) for at least 10 minutes. 1
   - Sit up and meditate in silence for at least 5–10 minutes.
   - Put your hands together in prayer, bow your head toward the heart, and chant *Om*.

Simple Class 1

Sun Salute

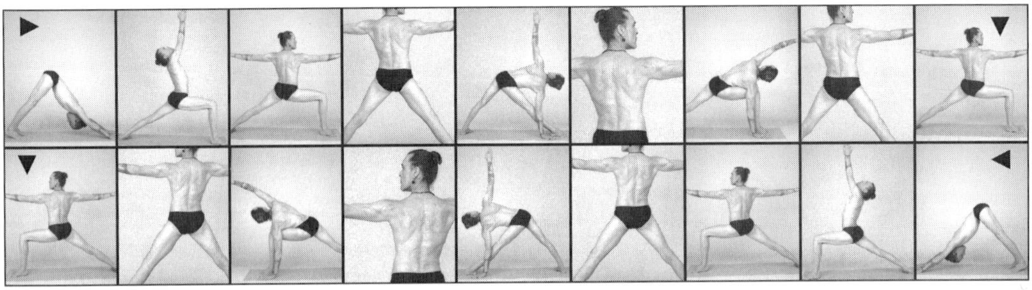

Warrior's Triangle

Kundalini's Descent

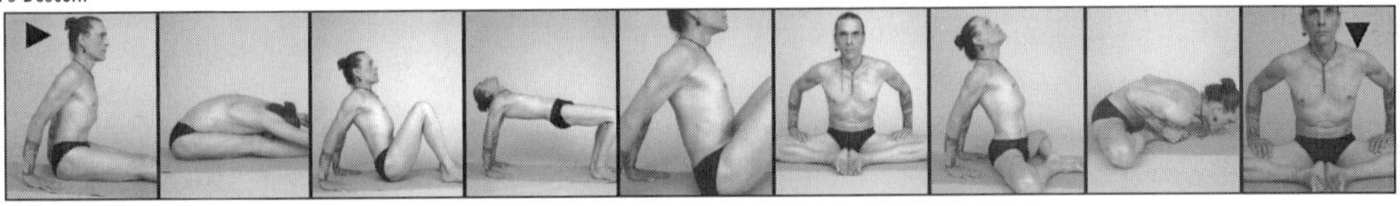

Cobbler's Table

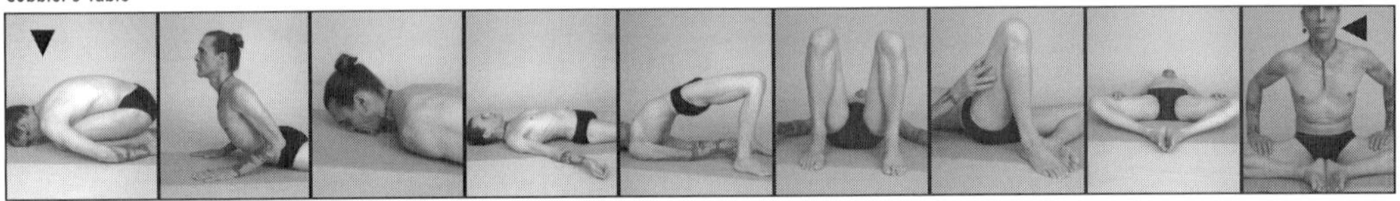

Child's Pose

Awakening Snake

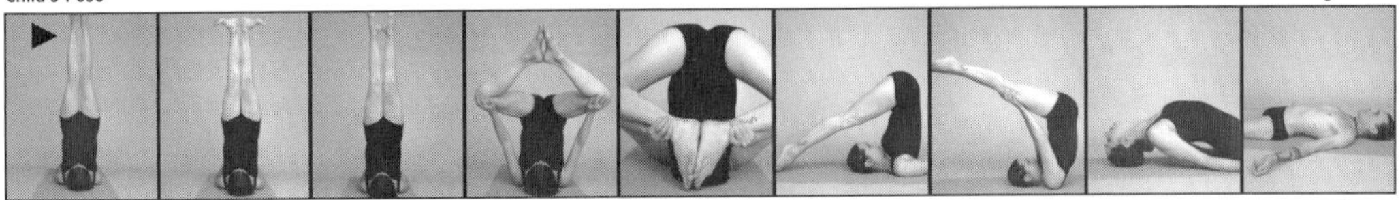

Fish Play

Corpse

Simple Class 2

1. Offer all of your efforts to God and Guru with this chant:

Guru Brahma, Guru Vishnu, Guru Devo Maheshvara, Guru Sakshat, Param Brahma, Tasmai Shri Guruvey Namaha

Pledge your actions to the end of suffering and the freedom and happiness of all beings:

Lokah Samasta Sukhino Bhavantu

2. In a standing or seated position, spend a few minutes bringing awareness to your breathing. Equalize the duration and volume of your inhale and exhale.
3. After practicing Surya Namaskar for at least 5 minutes, perform the following sequences and individual asanas.

Seat of Isis	pages 110–111	1–2
Awkward Twist	pages 106–107	2–3
Warrior's Triangle	pages 100–101	1–2
Cobbler's Table	pages 122–123	1–3
The Snake and the Dog	pages 138–139	1–2
Seated forward bend, Paschimottanasana (hold for at least 10 breaths)		2
Fish Play	pages 150–151	2

4. Lie down in Shavanasa for at least 10 minutes. 1
   - Sit up and meditate in silence for at least 5 to 10 minutes.
   - Put your hands together in a prayer mudra, bow your head toward the heart, and chant *Om*.

SIMPLE CLASS 2

Sun Salute

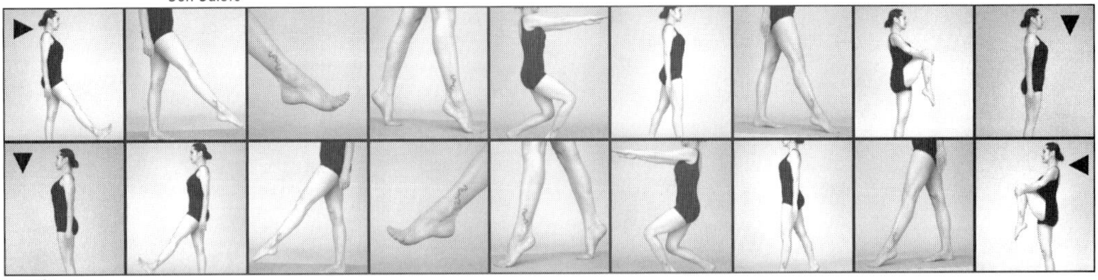

Seat of Isis

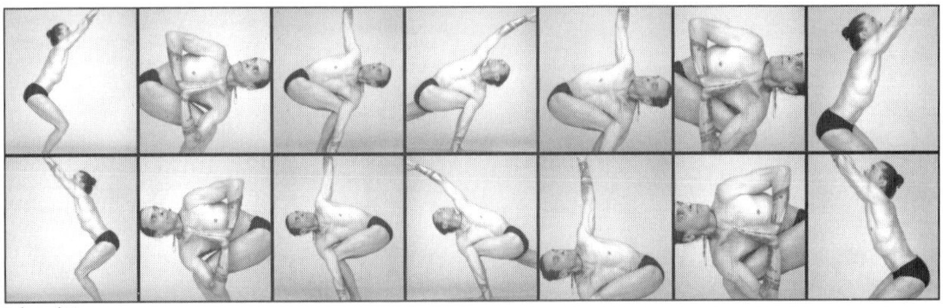

Awkward Twist

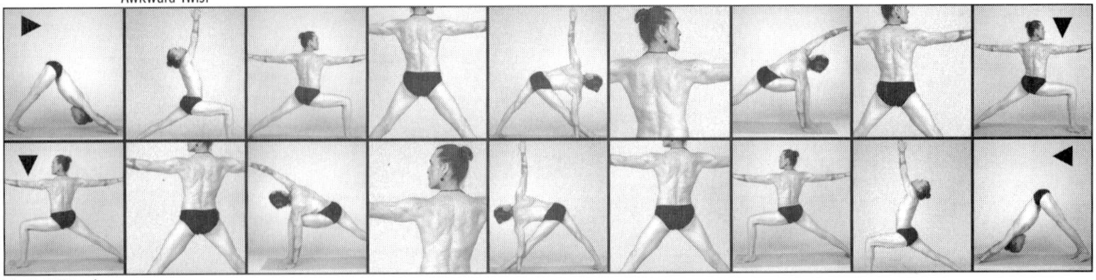

Warrior's Triangle

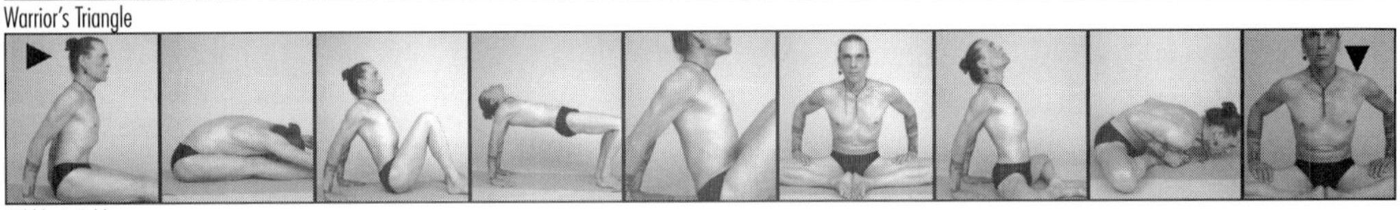

Cobbler's Table

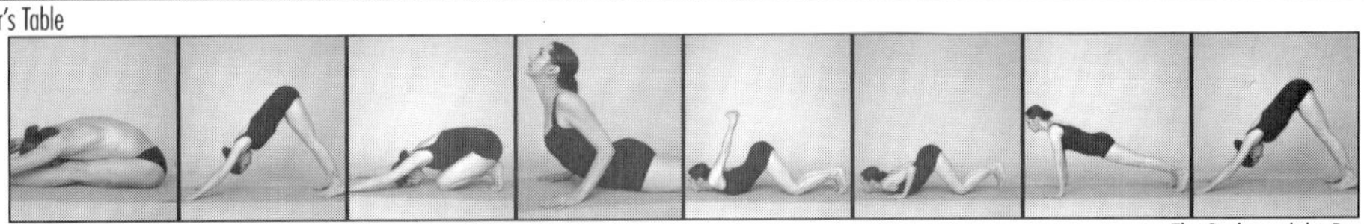

Seated Forward Bend

The Snake and the Dog

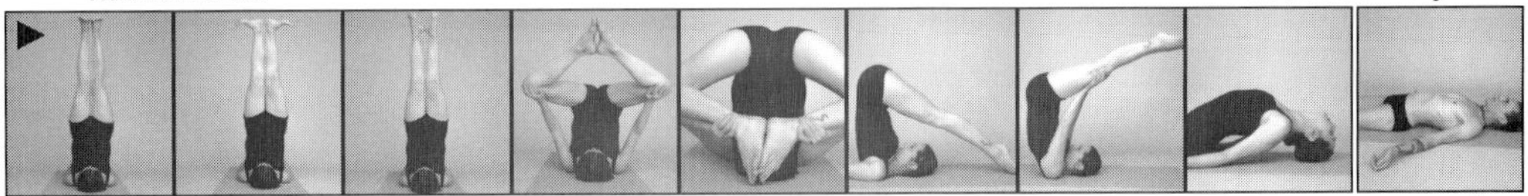

Fish Play

Corpse

Simple Class 3: Emphasizing Hip Opening

1. Offer all of your efforts to God and Guru with this chant:

Guru Brahma, Guru Vishnu, Guru Devo Maheshvara, Guru Sakshat, Param Brahma, Tasmai Shri Guruvey Namaha

Pledge your actions to the end of suffering and the freedom and happiness of all beings:

Lokah Samasta Sukhino Bhavantu

2. In a standing or seated position, spend a few moments bringing awareness to your breathing. Equalize the duration and volume of your inhale and exhale.

3. After practicing Surya Namaskar for at least 5 minutes:

Warrior's Triangle	pages 100–101	1–2
Kundalini's Descent	pages 108–109	1–2
Cobbler's Table	pages 122–123	1–3
Hippie Twist	pages 126–127	2–3
Blossoming Lotus	pages 128–129	2–3
Tortoise Squat	pages 134–135	1–3
Crow, Bakasana (hold for 5 breaths)		2
Awakening Snake	pages 114–115	1–2
Traveling Frog	pages 148–149	1–3
*Uttanasana (hold for at least 15 breaths)		2
Fish Play	pages 150–151	2

4. *Lie down in Shavasana for at least 10 minutes. 1
   - Sit up and meditate in silence for at least 5 to 10 minutes.
   - Put your hands together in a prayer mudra, bow your head toward the heart, and chant *Om*.

SIMPLE CLASS 3

Sun Salute

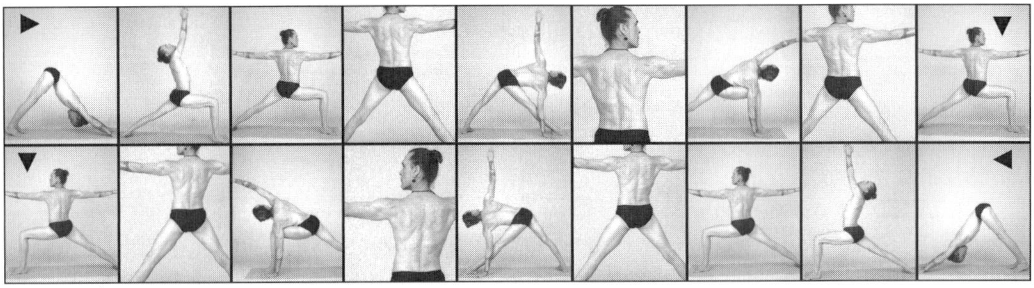

Warrior's Triangle

Kundalini's Descent

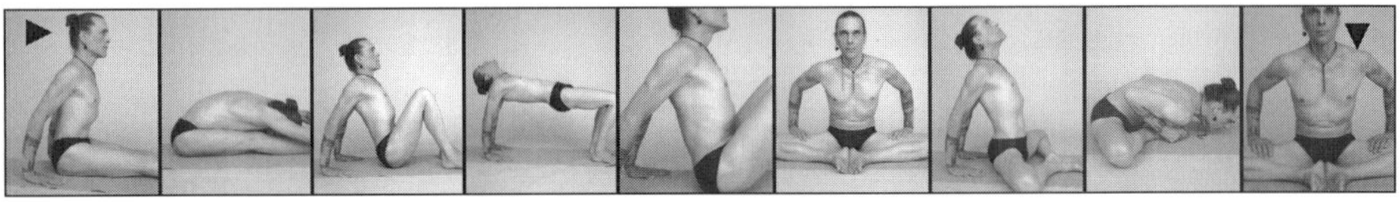

Cobbler's Table

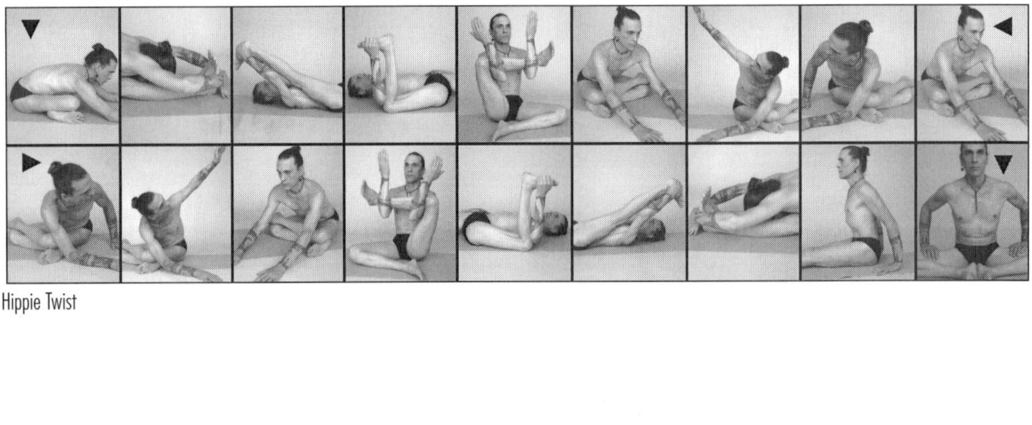

Hippie Twist

Blossoming Lotus

Tortoise Squat

Awakening Snake

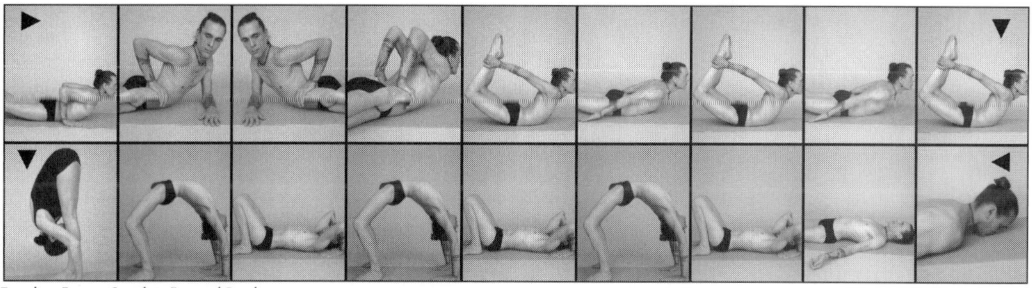

Traveling Frog—Standing Forward Bend

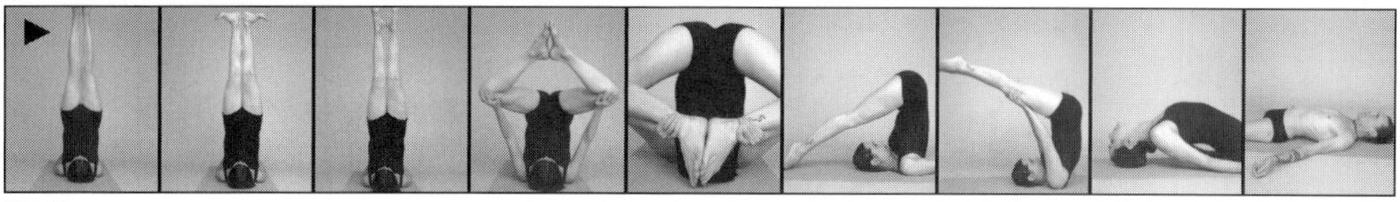

Fish Play

Corpse

Intermediate/Advanced Class 1: Emphasizing Forward Bending

1. Offer all of your efforts to God and Guru with this chant:

Guru Brahma, Guru Vishnu, Guru Devo Maheshvara, Guru Sakshat, Param Brahma, Tasmai Shri Guruvey Namaha

Pledge your actions to the end of suffering and the freedom and happiness of all beings:

Lokah Samasta Sukhino Bhavantu

2. While in a standing or seated position, bring awareness to your breathing. Equalize the duration and volume of your inhale and exhale, using ujjayi breathing (see page 119 for review).

3. After practicing Surya Namaskar for at least 5 minutes:

Warrior's Triangle	pages 100–101	1–2
Bound Triangle	pages 102–103	1–3
Secret Prayer	pages 104–105	1–3
Awkward Twist	pages 106–107	1–3
Kundalini's Descent	pages 108–109	1–2
Seated forward bend, Paschimottanasana (hold for at least 15 breaths)		2
Rishi Twist	pages 120–121	1–3
Cobbler's Table	pages 122–123	1–3
Blossoming Lotus	pages 128–129	2
Balancing Compass	pages 130–131	1–4
Moon Dance	pages 132–133	1–4
Handstand, Adho Mukha Vrksasana (hold for 10 to 20 breaths)		4
Hero Monkey	pages 140–141	1–3
The Locust and the Camel	pages 146–147	1–2
Traveling Frog	pages 148–149	1–3
*Standing forward bend, Uttanasana (hold for 15 breaths)		1
Fish Play	pages 150–151	2
Chasing Krishna	pages 152–153	1–3
*Bheki (Child's Pose)		1

4. *Lie down in Shavasana for at least 10 minutes. 1
   - Sit up and meditate in silence for at least 5 to 10 minutes.
   - Put your hands together in a prayer mudra, bow your head toward the heart, and chant *Om*.

INTERMEDIATE/ADVANCED CLASS 1

Sun Salute

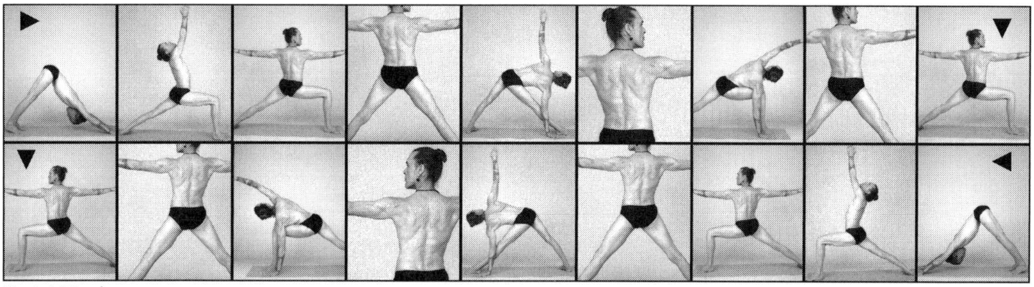

Warrior's Triangle

Bound Triangle

Secret Prayer

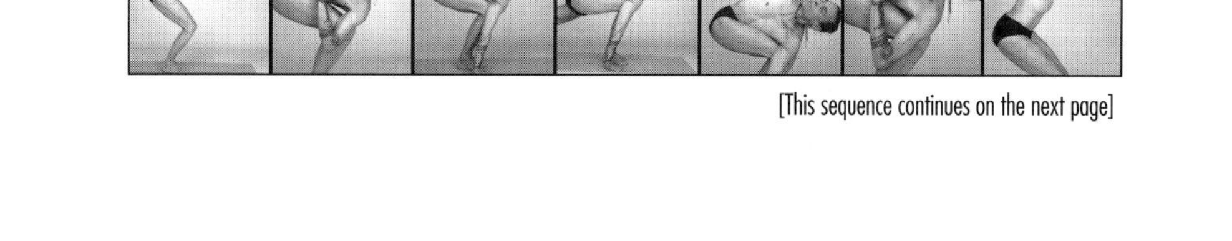

[This sequence continues on the next page]

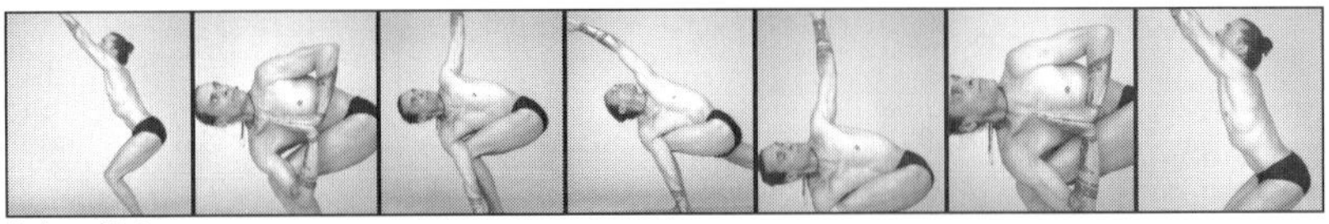

Awkward Twist

Kundalini's Descent

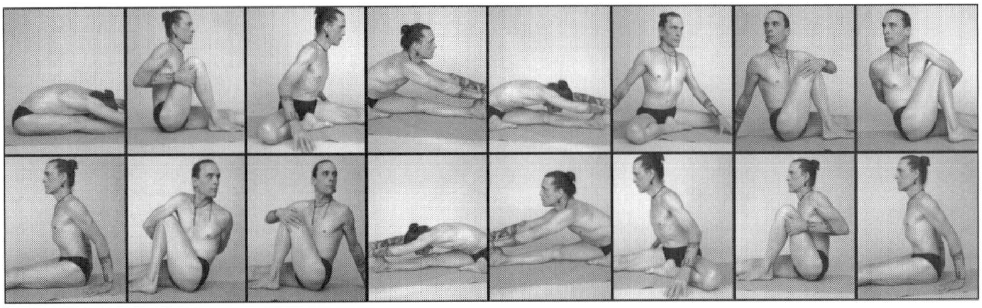

Seated Forward Bend—Rishi Twist

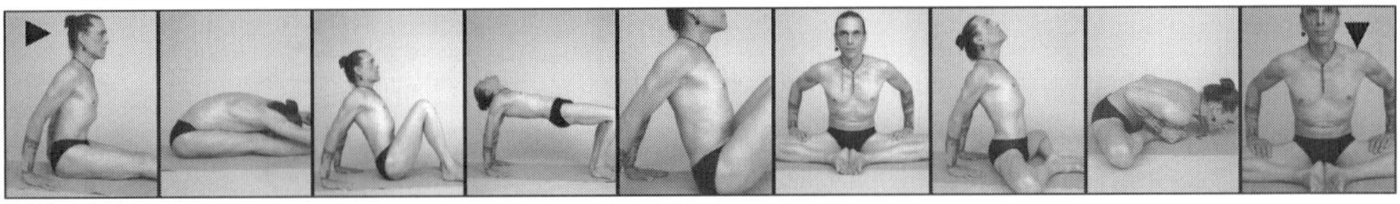

Cobbler's Table

Blossoming Lotus

Balancing Compass

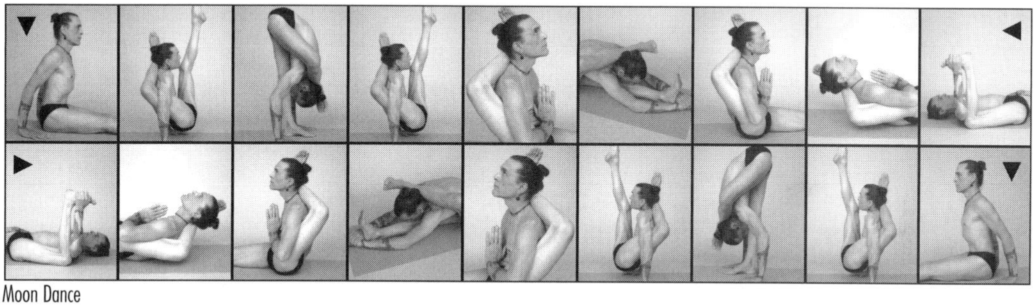

Moon Dance

Handstand—Hero Monkey

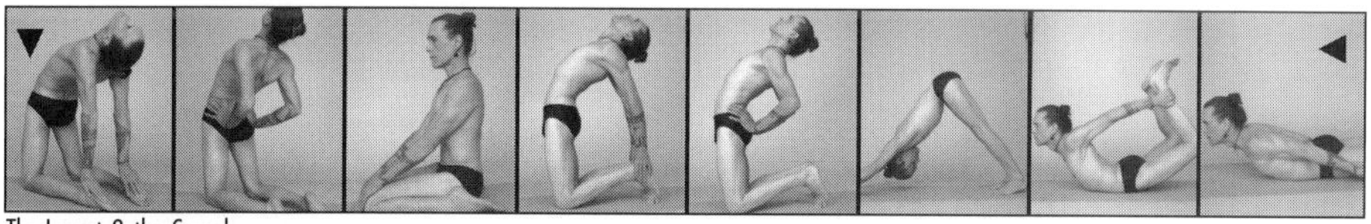

The Locust & the Camel

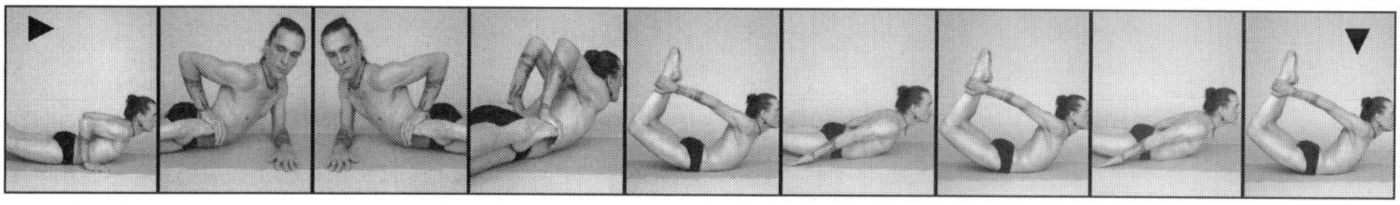

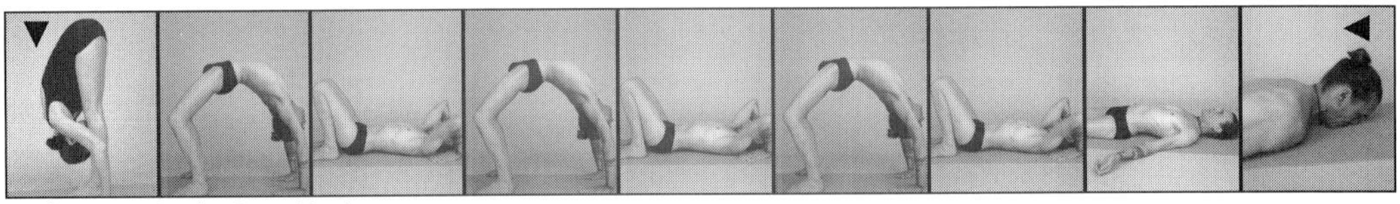

Traveling Frog—Standing Forward Bend

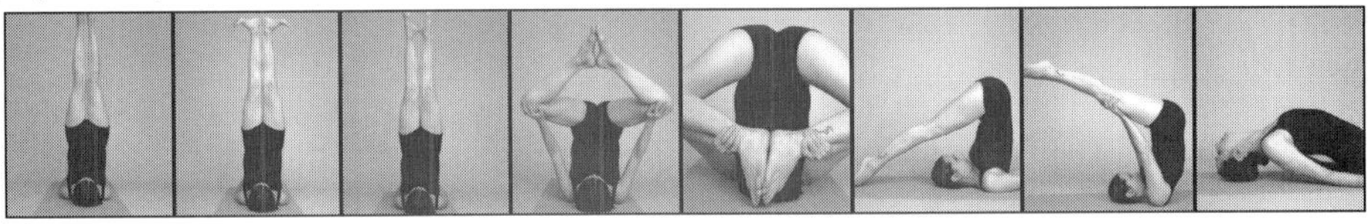

Fish Play

Chasing Krishna

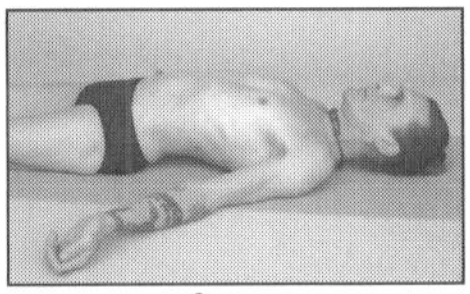

Corpse

Intermediate/Advanced Class 2: Emphasizing Backbending

1. Offer all of your efforts to God and Guru with this chant:

Guru Brahma, Guru Vishnu, Guru Devo Maheshvara, Guru Sakshat, Param Brahma, Tasmai Shri Guruvey Namaha

Pledge your actions to the end of suffering and the freedom and happiness of all beings:

Lokah Samasta Sukhino Bhavantu

2. In a standing or seated position, bring awareness to your breathing. Equalize the duration and volume of your inhale and exhale, using ujjayi breathing (see page 119 for review).

3. After practicing Surya Namaskar for at least 5 minutes:

Warrior's Triangle	pages 100–101	1–2
Bound Triangle	pages 102–103	1–3
Standing Spinal Twist	pages 118–119	1–4
Secret Prayer	pages 104–105	1–3
Handstand, Adho Mukha Vrksasana (hold 10 to 20 breaths)		4
Hero Monkey	pages 140–141	2–3
The Locust and the Camel	pages 146–147	1–3
Traveling Frog	pages 148–149	1–3
*Standing forward bend, Uttanasana (hold 15 breaths)		1
Hippie Twist	pages 126–127	2–3
Rishi Twist	pages 120–121	1–2
Cobbler's Table	pages 122–123	2–3
Fish Play	pages 150–151	2
Chasing Krishna	pages 152–153	1–3
*Bheki (Child's Pose)		1

4. *Lie down in Shavasana (Corpse Pose) for at least 10 minutes.
   - Sit up and meditate in silence for at least 5 to 10 minutes.
   - Put your hands together in a prayer mudra, bow your head toward the heart, and chant *Om*.

INTERMEDIATE/ADVANCED CLASS 2

Sun Salute

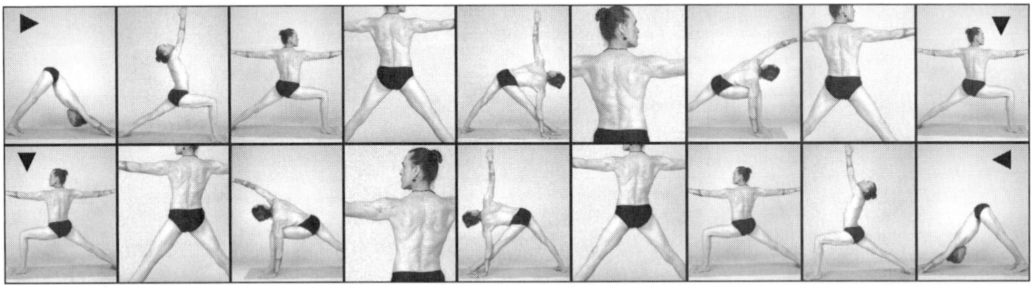

Warrior's Triangle

Bound Triangle

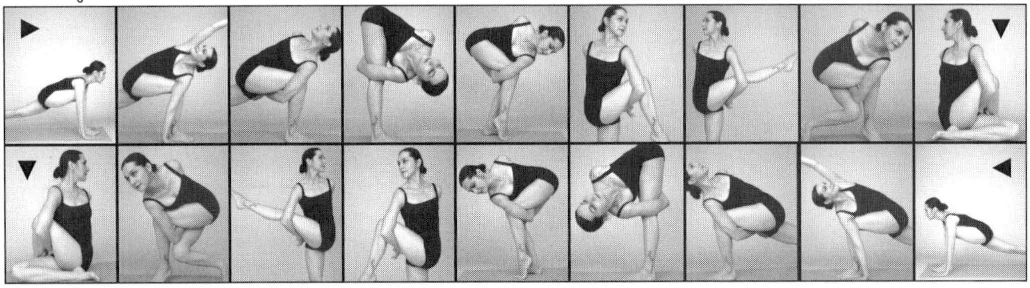

Standing Spinal Twist

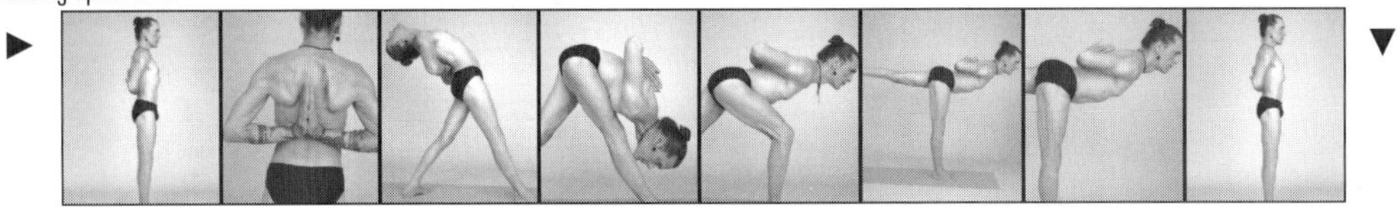

[This sequence continues on the next page]

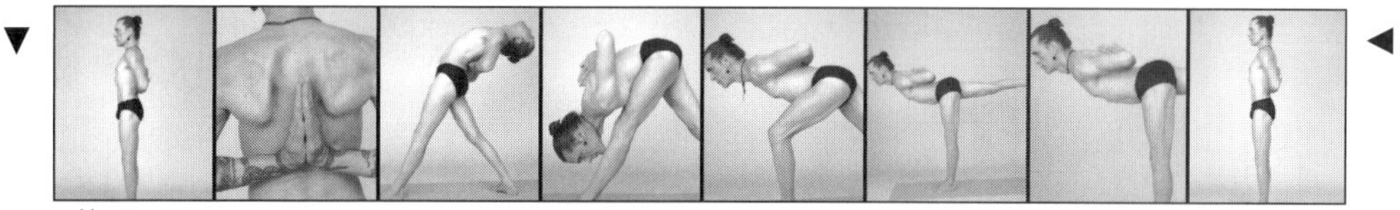

Hidden Prayer

Handstand—Hero Monkey

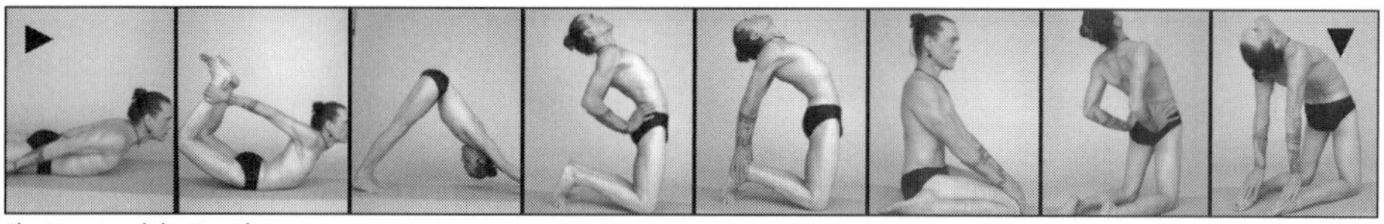

The Locust and the Camel

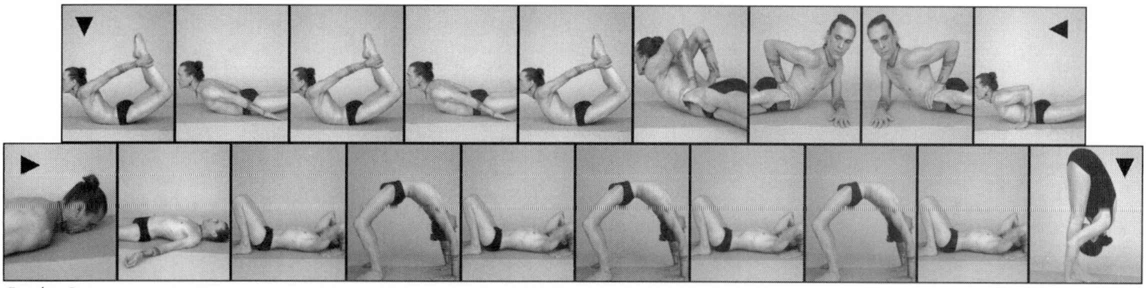

Traveling Frog

Standing Forward Bend

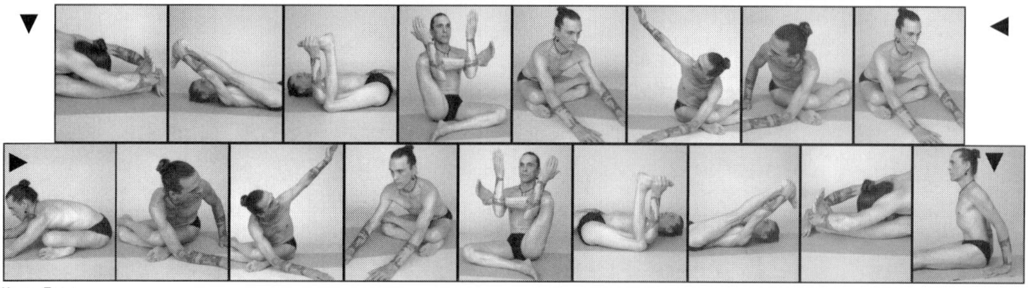

Hippie Twist

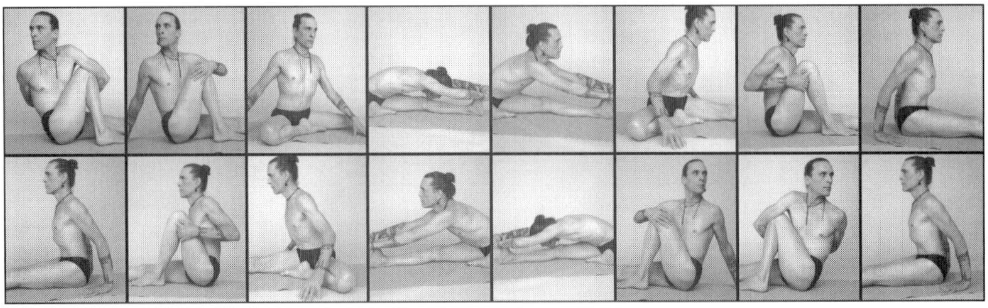

Rishi Twist

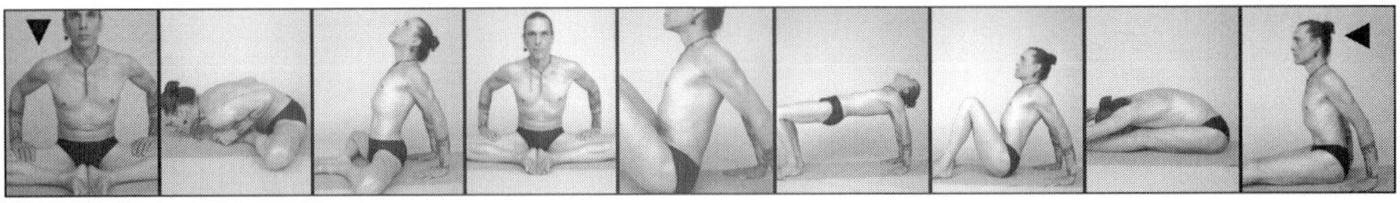

Cobbler's Table

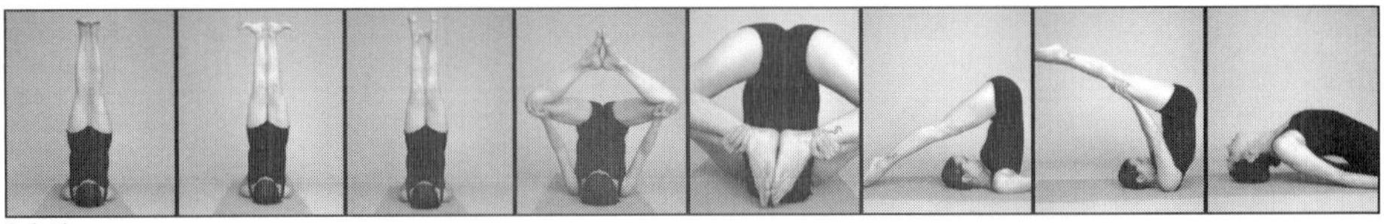

Fish Play

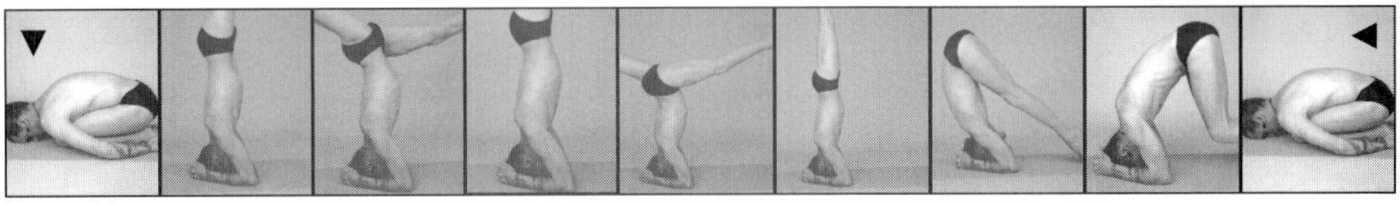

Chasing Krishna

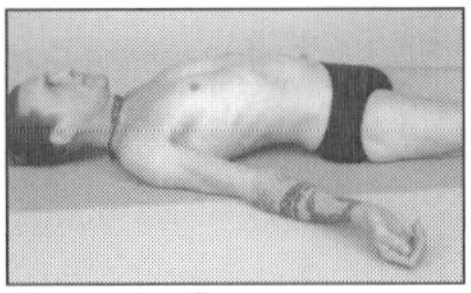

Corpse

Intermediate/Advanced Class 3: Emphasizing Standing Balances

1. Offer all of your efforts to God and Guru with this chant:

Guru Brahma, Guru Vishnu, Guru Devo Maheshvara, Guru Sakshat, Param Brahma, Tasmai Shri Guruvey Namaha

Pledge your actions to the end of suffering and the freedom and happiness of all beings:

Lokah Samasta Sukhino Bhavantu

2. In a standing or seated position, bring awareness to your breathing. Equalize the duration and volume of your inhale and exhale, using ujjayi breathing (see page 119 for review).

3. After practicing Surya Namaskar for at least 5 minutes:

Warrior's Triangle	pages 100–101	1–2
Bound Triangle	pages 102–103	1–3
Kundalini's Descent	pages 108–109	1–2
Seat of Isis	pages 110–111	1–2
Eagle's Flight	pages 112–113	1–3
Picking Up the Step	pages 114–115	1–3
Moonrise	pages 116–117	2–3
Tortoise Squat	pages 134–135	1–2
Flying Crow	pages 136–137	1–3
*Standing forward bend, Uttanasana (hold 15 breaths)		1
Seated forward bend, Paschimottanasana (hold 15 breaths)		2
Rishi Twist	pages 120–121	1–3
Cobbler's Table	pages 122–123	1–3
Awakening Snake	pages 144–145	1–2
Hero Monkey	pages 140–141	1–3
The Locust and The Camel	pages 146–147	1–3
Traveling Frog	pages 148–149	1–3
*Star, Tarasana (hold 10 breaths)		1
Fish Play	pages 150–151	2
Chasing Krishna	pages 152–153	1–3
*Bheki (Child's Pose)		1

4. *Lie down in Shavasana (Corpse Pose) for at least 10 minutes.
   - Sit up and meditate in silence for at least 5 to 10 minutes.
   - Put your hands together in a prayer mudra, bow your head toward the heart, and chant *Om*.

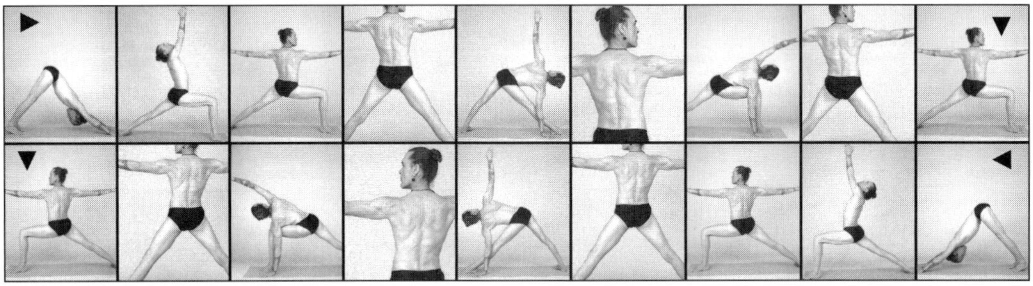

Warrior's Triangle

Bound Triangle

Kundalini's Descent

[This sequence continues on the next page]

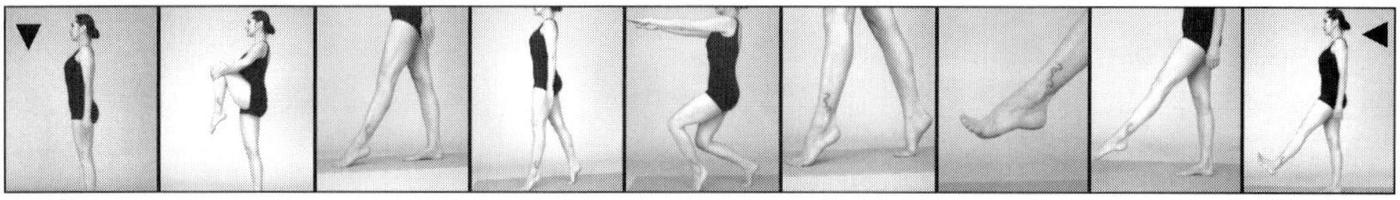

Seat of Isis

Eagle's Flight

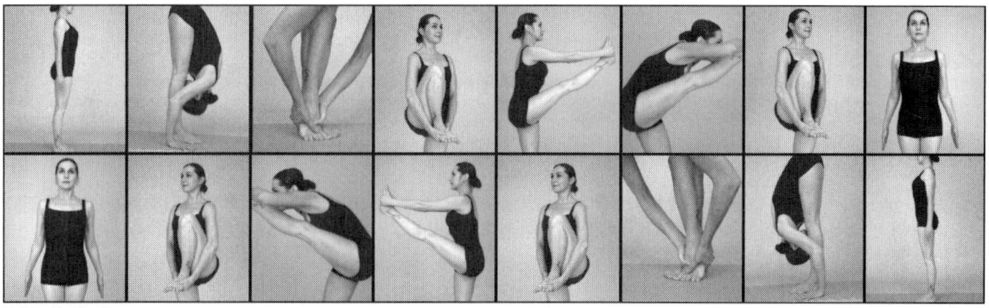

Picking Up the Step

Moonrise

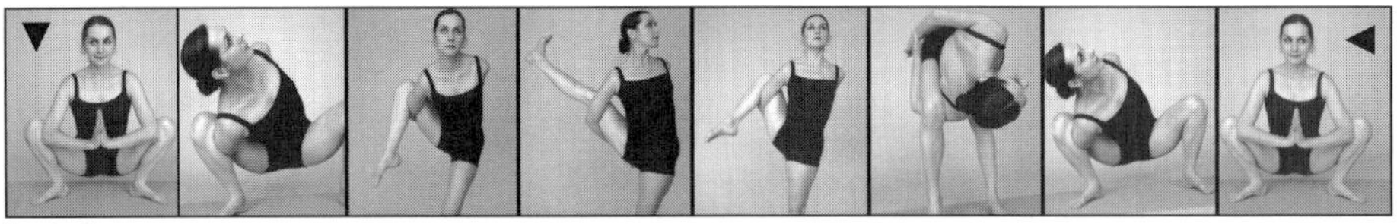

Tortoise Squat

Flying Crow

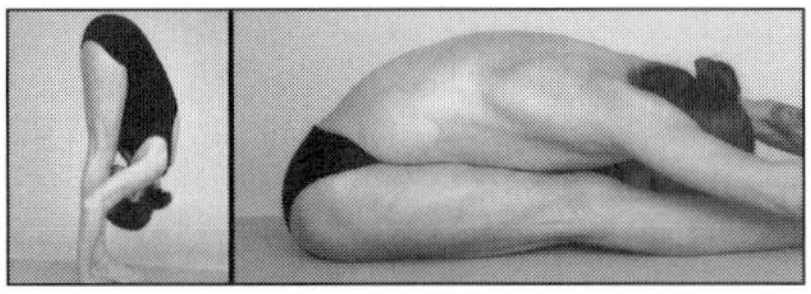

Standing Forward Bend—Seated Forward Bend

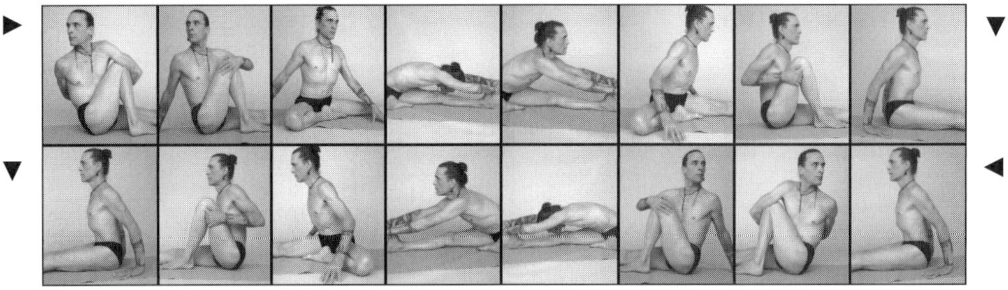

Rishi Twist

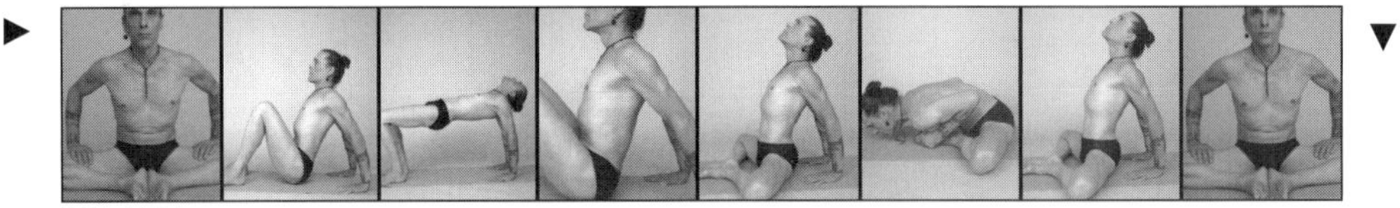

Cobbler's Table

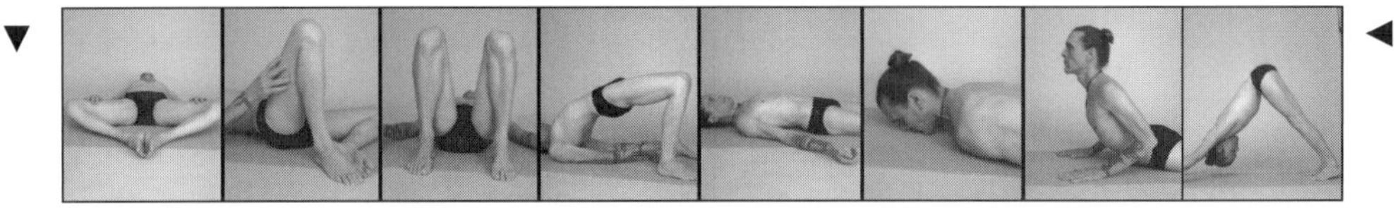

Awakening Snake

Hero Monkey

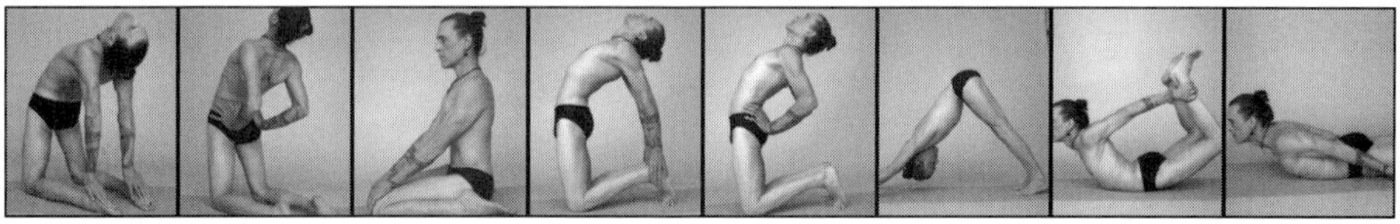

The Locust and the Camel

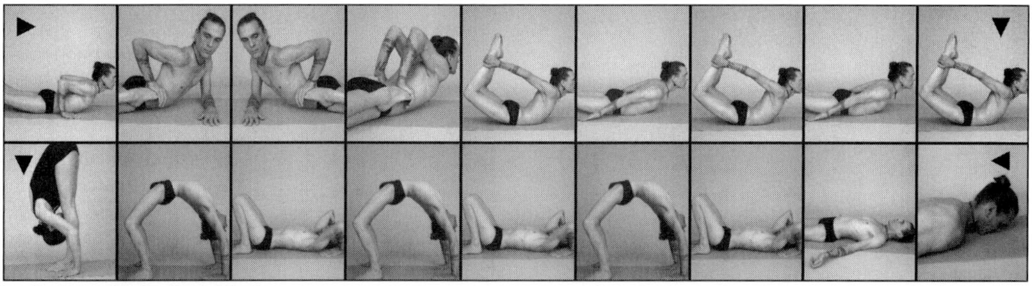

Traveling Frog—Standing Forward Bend

Fish Play

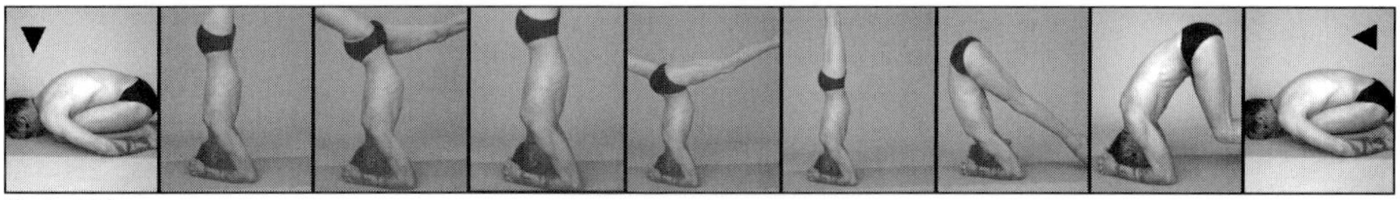

Chasing Krishna

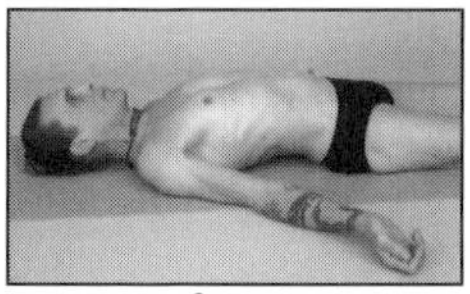

Corpse

Daily asana practice, like nightly deep sleep, serves to reconnect us with our true nature. And like deep sleep, asana practice is very refreshing. It can also be very challenging because it puts us right up against our limitations. Most of us stubbornly hold on to self-centered thoughts, focused on I, me, and mine. The rigidity that we feel during asana practice is the mind's reaction to a false identification with the limitation of form.

People can react very strongly when feeling their limitations. In asana practice, some students crumple to the floor in sobbing heaps and give up; others become enraged and force their way past their limitations, injuring themselves; still others cower in fear and never do make peace with limitation because they don't allow themselves to get near it.

The solution is simple: Do not identify with the limitations you come across while practicing asana, or in your daily life. The yogi on the bed of nails feels every nail, but the look of serenity on his face shows that he identifies not with this limitation, but with his immortal limitless Self. Simply expose yourself to the various changing asana shapes, which are methodically introduced limitations, and use the breath to work through the tendency to react negatively.

If you catch yourself thinking "I can't do this," "I hate this!" or "I'm such a loser—everyone else does this posture better than I do," or even "Wow, I do this asana really well," just witness these self-centered thoughts and bring your focus back to the breath. Rededicate your practice to realization of the Divine Self, which is beyond thought, and to the service of the higher consciousness in all beings.

In a 1979 lecture, Ram Dass told a great story about not getting caught up in preferences, based on a teaching from the Third Chinese Patriarch:

> *The great way is not difficult for those who have no preferences.*
>
> Just look at your life and think how many preferences you have. You prefer pleasure over pain? Life over death? Friends over aloneness? Freedom over imprisonment? Love over hate? Where are your attachments? Where are your clingings? Are you stuck in polarities? That is what the Third Patriarch is asking. "Make the slightest distinction, and heaven and earth are set infinitely apart," he says. Make the slightest distinction, and you've created hell. "If you wish to see the truth, then hold no opinions for or against anything. To set up what you like against what you dislike is the dis-ease of the mind." Are you ready to live like that? Do you realize how spacious you have to be, to live by that kind of philosophy?
>
> That's the fiercest kind of philosophy I know. But I like to have that kind of fierce friend to hang out with me, to keep reminding me how much I "hold opinions." This should be like this, and that should be like that, and I want everybody

to be thus and so, and wouldn't it be better if . . . ? Instead of just being spacious with it, we're full of opinions. Not to "hold opinions" doesn't mean we don't have them—it means we are not *attached* to them. It doesn't mean we don't have preferences, it means we're not attached to our preferences. I can prefer blue over green, and decide that when there's a choice, I'll pick the blue over the green, but if I end up with green, ah, so.

"Ah, so"—remember the "Ah, So" story? There was a monk who lived in the monastery up on the hill. The local girl down in the village got pregnant by the fisherman. She didn't want to cause problems for him in the village, so she said, "It was the monk up in the monastery." When the baby was born, the townspeople carried it up the hill to the monastery. They knocked on the gate, and the monk opened the door; they said to the monk, "This is your baby—you raise it." And the monk said, "Ah, so." And he took the baby, and he closed the gate. I mean, the guy's whole life changed just like that, in that moment, and his only reaction is, "Ah, so."

Nine years later the girl was dying. She didn't want to die without admitting what had happened, so she said to the people, "Look, I lied. It really wasn't the monk, it was the fisherman."

The villagers were horrified! They went up to the monastery and they knocked on the door. The monk opened the gate, and there standing next to him was this nine-year-old child. The villagers said, "We've made a terrible mistake. This isn't your child after all. We'll take him back down to the village to raise him, and you're free to go back to your monastic life." And the monk said, "Ah, so." He was so much right *here* that whatever new change arose, "Ah, so."[1]

If you practice yoga for small, selfish reasons, you will remain the same, bound by your beliefs about what you can and cannot do. Let go and offer all your effort to limitless potential. Dedicate yourself to the happiness of all beings.

Keep your attention fixed on seamless, economic breathing, integrated with movement. Keep your mind fixed on God. If you can do this during asana practice, you will create a vinyasa of happiness and contentment that will be unshakable in the face of life's ups and downs.

You might like forward bending and dislike backward bending, or vice versa. But when you choose to perform both with equal zest, you will attain some freedom from the tyranny of thoughts. When you can experience your likes and dislikes from an amicable distance and transcend their usual hold on you, Yoga is possible. Ah, so.

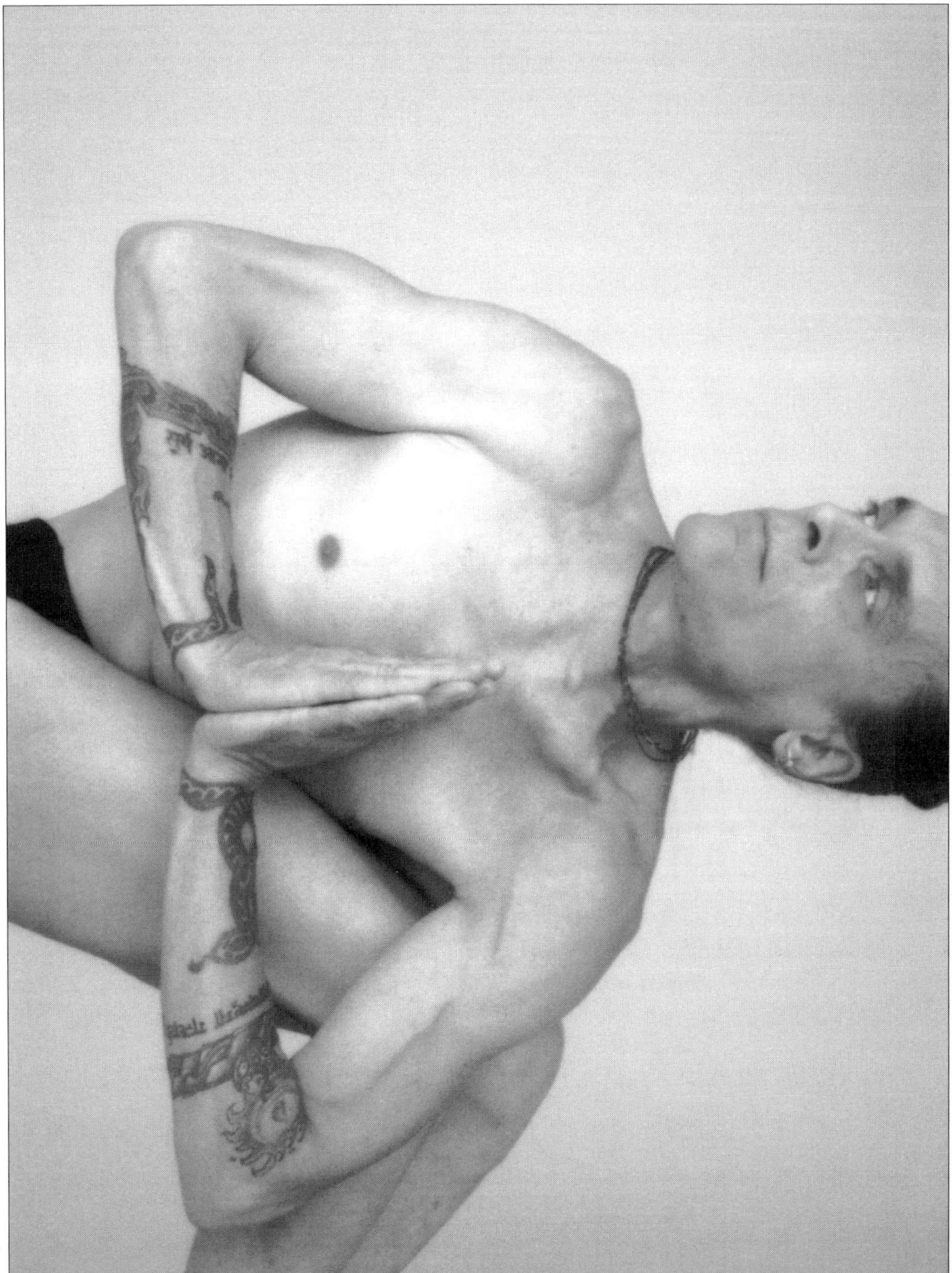

9

Kriya: Discipline, Study, and Devotion

You carry with you, around you, in you, the atmosphere created by your actions, and if what you do is beautiful, good and harmonious your atmosphere is beautiful, good and harmonious.

—*The Mother,* **The Sunlit Path**

Although yoga practices like pranayama, asana, and vinyasa krama are exciting to learn, it can be tempting to get so excited about accumulating exotic methods that we forget why we began a spiritual practice in the first place. Patanjali saw the danger of presenting too many methods, or outer practices, without reminding readers that, basically, this is a very simple process. All we really have to do is work hard and be devoted to the goal of knowing God. This is why Patanjali began his chapter on practice with a simple three-step plan for the attainment of enlightenment called Kriya Yoga.

Like the word karma, kriya is derived from the Sanksrit root *kr*, which means action. Karma means any action, whereas kriya means action taken specifically for purification purposes. Kriyas are cleansing actions taken to purify your life and set you on the path to God-realization.

Tapah-svadhyaya-Ishvara-pranidhanani kriya yogah. (YS II:1)
A burning desire for Self-realization, Self-study, and
surrender to God constitute the yoga of action.

Patanjali's three-step plan is very straightforward. He simply states, in this sutra, that the hard physical work of spiritual practice must be combined with scriptural study and motivated by devotion. Patanjali tells us in this yoga sutra that the perfect action is one that meets three criteria: tapah (a burning desire manifesting in spiritual discipline), svadhyaya (study of the Self), and Ishvara pranidhana (surrender to God).

tapah: to burn.
svadhyaya: study of the higher Self.
ishvara pranidhana: to devote or give up all the actions—thought, word, and deed—of your life to God.

How can you infuse your sadhana (spiritual practice) with these three elements? In India, some practitioners take extreme measures to make their sadhana fiery, or tapasic. Standing on one leg for years, or holding an arm straight up in the air until it withers are forms of tapas that yogis in India have practiced for millennia. Standing in cold water up to the chin all day, or sitting in the middle of a circle of fire with a firepot on the head in the blazing sun are also classic yogic tapas. You do not have to go to such extreme measures to make your practice tapasic, although if you feel so inclined, far be it from us to discourage you!

Patanjali says that our spiritual practices should transform us in the flames of their difficulty and light a fire within us that burns away selfishness. This is the internalization of the sacrificial fire of Vedic India. The fire element in the body is used to burn impurities. Of course, the main impurity is avidya, or ignorance of the higher Self. What is offered into the fire is the ego, or lower self.

Your sadhana—pranayama, asana, meditation, or whatever it might be—is tapasic when you practice consistently over a long period of time. These practices are tapasic because they go against the grain of modern life. It's much easier to become complacent and determined to stay the same, but this apathy won't generate much transformative heat in your life.

The principal method of svadhyaya—study of the higher Self—is the reading of scriptures. These scriptures provide guidelines for ethical, righteous, yogic action in the world. Reading about the lives of Self-realized, enlightened beings is also a form of Self-study. Their lives are examples of the joining of perfect intentions to perfect acts. The saints are role models for your own spiritual evolution.

Chanting the names of God is another form of svadhyaya. Sanskrit chants are said to contain the vibrational essence of the form of God being invoked. When we chant the sound over and over, our cells begin to resonate at the same vibrational level as the Sanskrit. Repetition of the names of God in Sanskrit builds the actual deity form within us.

The third component of kriya yoga, after tapas (purification) and svadhyaya (study of the higher Self), is Ishvara pranidhana (devotion to God). Ishvara is the Lord: God in a form that can be visualized and to which you can offer your devotion. Pran is vitality, or life energy. Dhana means to give or direct energy. Without this devotion, yoga practices become self-serving and binding. Patanjali recommends that you offer each thought, word, and deed to God.

Once, a student told us that he had been undertaking an arduous asana practice but he wasn't sure if it was good for him. During practice he felt good, but later, strong feelings of anger would overwhelm him and he would find himself getting into arguments with friends and workmates. Should he give up his yoga practice? he asked.

We told him that Patanjali had a recommendation for just this problem: Ishvara pranidhana. The student needed to create a noble and uplifting focus for the energy unleashed by his asana practice. We suggested that he choose someone or something that could represent this noble and uplifting intention to him and direct all energy released by his practice toward that focus.

The yoga practices amplify and direct the pranic flow. If we do not consciously aim that flow upward, it will flow to whatever tendencies might be passing through the mind. If anger is in the mind, anger will be amplified by the yogic practices. If the mind is focused on devotion to God, devotion will be amplified.

The psychotherapeutic power of the yoga practices lies in their ability to bring unconscious feelings to the surface. This can be overwhelming, unless the practice is steadfastly dedicated to God. When that unleashed energy is directed toward God-realization rather than toward expressing unconscious selfish emotions, it becomes liberating rather than binding.

For a yoga practice to be purifying, it must satisfy all three criteria from the Kriya Yoga sutra. A challenging asana class might be tapasic, for example. You might sweat profusely and find that in the heat of the class you can go beyond what you thought your body's physical limitations were. You might even feel that you are purifying your body in the heat of the practice. But if you become obsessed during the class with a fight you had with a coworker, or comparing your abilities to those of other people in the class, you have forgotten a key component of purifying action: Ishvara pranidhana, devotion to God, which means relinquishing selfish motives.

And, if you are looking around the room to see which other students managed to get into an asana, you are not involved, in that moment, in svadhyaya, or study of the higher Self. You are pretty much at the mercy of the obsessions of the small self.

Study of the Self involves determining where need ends and greed begins. We can make that determination only by experimenting with our body and mind until we figure out how to remove clutter and confusion.

Perhaps you have met people who obsessively accumulate anything from newspapers to old clothes. We wonder how they could possibly live with no space in their home. Yet we all have the same sort of clutter inside our head. From the moment we arrived in our body, we have been accumulating habits, attitudes, prejudices, likes and dislikes, affectations and characteristics.

People who accumulate things in their house get used to the clutter. It seems normal to them to have nowhere left to sit, sleep, eat, or live. We all get used to the clutter inside us, too. We even call it by name: "This clutter is called Frank, the Irish Catholic, Taurus plumber who lives on the Upper West Side." We live in fear of losing any small scrap of it.

Without space, creation cannot take place. When you purchase a house, you purchase the space, which is surrounded by the walls. The more space, the more valuable the house. You cannot think anything if you have no space within your mind. You cannot welcome any guest in your house if you have no space within your house. You cannot receive any thought from outside if you have no space within your mind.

The outer space is the first and eldest of all the elements, without which creation cannot take place. In the same way, inner space is the first and eldest of the inner elements, without which no thinking can take place in your mind.

What is the reason that many people are very creative? They have space in their minds. What is the reason that many people are fools? They have no space in their minds. Their minds are always congested with all sorts of thoughts, like a warehouse with furniture.

Nobody is a fool and nobody is wise. It is the space that makes you foolish or wise. If you have space within your mind, then you become wise, and if you have no space in your mind, then you become "other-wise." If you have no space in your mind, then you cannot understand God or "I-Am," and vice versa, if you have space within your mind, then you can grasp the operation of "I-Am" or God in you, according to space, qualitatively and quantitatively.

—*Shri Brahmananda Sarasvati,*
Terrestrial and Celestial Magnetism[1]

Patanjali called this clutter chitta-vritti, or mind fluctuations. The mind, misguided by the senses, assumes that all that is seen is real and all that is unseen is unreal. The pursuit of pleasure and retreat from pain is a result of this misapprehension of the world. The kleshas all stem from the primary klesha, which is avidya, commonly translated as "ignorance." But ignorance implies that one is unaware of something, whereas avidya really means that what you think you know as true is actually false. "Ignorance of the Self," "misknowing," or "delusion" are better translations of avidya.

Avidya leads to the other kleshas: asmita, which is excessive ego identification or pride; raga, excessive attachment (likes); dvesa, excessive aversion (dislikes); and abinivesha, fear of death (insecurity). Kriya Yoga is Patanjali's suggested program for clearing the kleshas and removing the clutter from our minds and bodies, making room for the possibility that grace may enter.

Avidya comes about because we are used to believing the evidence of our senses. If you can see, hear, feel, touch, and taste it, it must be true! In the realm of the senses, truth is relative. My truth may not be your truth. Time falls forward or springs back, yesterday's truth is today's myth, buildings (and bodies) deteriorate no matter how well made they are.

In the yogic vocabulary, however, "true" means universally true—never changing. If we are mired in the realm of the senses, we mistakenly believe that the senses will lead us to truth. In pursuit of it, we seek pleasure and run away from pain. But no matter how hard we pursue pleasure, we can never get enough, because the happiness it provides is temporary. No matter how fast we run from pain, it will catch us around the next corner. In the pursuit of truth, attachment and aversion are disappointing dead ends.

Svadhyaya means Self-study. "Adhyaya" means to study and "sva" means Self. Svadhyaya is scriptural study, including recitation of scriptures and mantra repetition. Svadhyaya can also take the form of satsang with an enlightened master (either by reading a book by the master or actually meeting him or her). To find universal Truth we can study the words and actions of people who have attained the Self and transcended suffering. As we study, chant, and seek the company of enlightened beings, we lose identification with body/mind. As we associate with the True Self, identity with the false self subsides. As identification with the false self subsides, knowledge of immortality arises.

This loosens the grip of abinivesha, the fear of death. The truth of the immortal soul revealed by svadhyaya becomes your foundation. Fear of death haunts us because we mistake bodily death for our death. Ironically, when we can let go of this fear and observe the body/mind container with detachment, we begin to live much more fully. We can play our parts in the drama of life much more freely.

Sat-Sangatve Nissangatvam
Nissangatve Nirmohatvam
Nirmohatve Nishchala-Tattvam
Nischala Tattve Jivan-Muktih
Bhaja Govindam Bhaja Govindam
Bhaja Govindam Mudha-Mate

Good and virtuous company gives rise to nonattachment. From nonattachment comes freedom from delusion. With freedom from delusion, one feels the changeless reality. Experiencing that changeless reality, one attains liberation in this life. I-Am is the ocean of awareness. Realizing this, one feels, "I am not the body and mind, although I have a body and mind." Realize Govinda, realize Govinda, realize Govinda in your heart, O wise one (chant from *Shankaracharya,* translated by Shri Brahmananda Sarasvati).

Giving up attachment to the ego and to the world perceived by the five senses is not a negation of the ego or the world; it is an effort to end the suffering caused by ignorance. This is the true pursuit of happiness.

Giving up attachment to the ego and the world of the senses is tapasic, and thus purifying. Exposing ourselves to experiences to which we may have an aversion in order to become more wise and resilient is tapasic. Study of the higher Self provides us with opportunities to grasp the truth of the immortal soul—but we need daily reminders to keep it in our sights. These daily reminders are our yoga practices: asana, pranayama, ethical vegetarianism, whatever sadhana we have committed to practicing daily in order to know God.

Patanjali realized that his three-step plan for Kriya Yoga, although true, was difficult and did not offer the practical methods that some people might need to reach enlightenment. That's why he also included a more detailed, eight-step plan in the *Yoga Sutras* called Ashtanga or Raja Yoga (which is really a sixteen-step plan—read the fine print!).

THE EIGHT-STEP PLAN OF ASHTANGA YOGA

1. Yama

Restrain your actions toward others (through nonharming, truthfulness, nonstealing, sexual continence, and nonhoarding).

2. Niyama

Observe the yogic guidelines concerning the actions you take in relation to your own body and mind. These are cleanliness, contentment, hard work, Self-study, devotion to God.

3. Asana

Develop a steady and comfortable relationship with the Earth and all beings.

4. Pranayama

Learn to direct energy, so that you can contain the life force and set it free.

5. Pratyahara

Redirect the senses inward toward their source.

6. Dharana

Develop the ability to concentrate the mind, by directing your attention to one object.

7. Dhyana

Meditative absorption.

8. Samadhi
Superconsciousness, ecstasy.

Over the centuries, other yogic texts set down more specific instructions for the Hatha Yoga practices that form part of Patanjali's eight-step plan. Between the sixth and fifteenth centuries A.D. there was a renaissance in Hatha Yoga. During that time, the most prominent texts on Hatha Yoga were refined from preexisting knowledge in India. Texts such as *Goraksha Samhita* by Yogi Gorakhnath, *Gherand Samhita* by the sage Gherand, and *Hatharatnavali* by Srinivasabhatta Mahayogindra set down the ancient wisdom in an organized way. In the fourteenth century, a detailed manual for Hatha Yoga was written by Swatmarama called the *Hatha Yoga Pradipika*. The English translation of this scripture's title is *Light on Hatha Yoga*.

One principal feature of the *Hatha Yoga Pradipika* is shat karma kriya. Shat means "six," and karma means "action." Kriyas are actions that remove the obstacles that prevent us from perceiving our true nature. Poor health can be one such obscuration, whereas good health supports a robust spiritual practice.

Ayurveda was designed by the Rishis especially for those individuals who want to enjoy the world healthy. Its daily and seasonal routines, dietary guidance, therapeutics and doctrine of antidotes for the side effects of addictions can keep you hale, hearty and having a high time well into your senescence if you can restrict yourself sufficiently to follow these precepts strictly. You must consciously choose how much you wish to indulge, which determines how healthy you will be. There is no free lunch.

—***Robert E. Svoboda,*** **Prakruti: Your Ayurvedic Constitution**[2]

Shat karma kriyas are the "six actions" said to bring balance to the doshas that, in the ayurvedic view, constitute the body. Ayurveda means "the science of life," and it is the ancient Indian system of medicine and healing. Ayurveda defines the doshas as:

vata: wind
pitta: bile
kapha: phlegm

When these doshas are out of balance, the body is susceptible to disease.

Although centuries old, the concept of individual constitution is a new concept for the Western mind, a new way for all of us to understand our "relationship" with Nature. Ayurveda is above all meant for all people who by harmonizing themselves seek to act as a harmonizing force in the universe.

—*Robert E. Svoboda,* Prakruti: Your Ayurvedic Constitution[3]

Please seek direct instruction from a teacher before attempting any of these six cleansing practices:

1. *dhauti:* cleansing with water and scrubbing. This includes brushing the teeth, scraping the tongue, throat clearing, flushing the ears, blowing and washing the interior of the nose, washing the stomach, intestines, internal organs, and anus.
2. *basti:* cleansing with colon irrigation. You can easily learn to administer enemas to yourself, when necessary. During fasting, daily enemas or occasional colonics are required.
3. *neti:* nasal cleansing. This includes cleaning the nasal cavity with a probe or catheter or with saline solution. Water is poured into one side of the nose and drips out the other. Or a rubber catheter or string is threaded through the nose and out of the mouth. Moving the catheter back and forth stimulates the back of the nasal cavity.
4. *trataka:* eye cleansing. This involves staring without blinking, until tears wash the eyes. Use a candle or a yantra, which is a geometrical device for invocation of a deity or beneficial quality.
5. *nauli:* digestive stimulation and intestinal cleansing. This includes a dynamic massage of the intestines, colon, and internal organs that is created by using the abdominal muscles and diaphragm. On an exhale retention the abdomen is lifted in and up, isolating the central portion, which is moved side to side, rotated, or undulated up and down.
6. *kapalabhati:* skull shining. This practice shines the skull by lifting energy upward. In the process, the air passages are cleaned. First, breathe deeply in and out a few times; then, inhale to a comfortable level and begin a series of 25 to 50 sharp, strong exhalations, allowing the diaphragm to move in and up with each exhale. Use the same action you would use to blow your nose. Emphasize the exhalation only, and allow a small inhalation simply to happen in response to each exhale.

By consciously moving the energy upward with each exhale, this kriya eliminates stale gases and foreign particles from the lungs. Rubbing with the breath aligns the electrons in the lining of the air passage, polarizing the electrical charge of the mucous membrane. This creates an upward flow of electrical energy: the electrical charge of the trachea. As you emphasize that upward moving breath on a physiological level, you begin to feel uplifted emotionally, psychologically, and even spiritually.

Your first impression may be that the shat karma kriyas will affect only the physical body. They actually purify the entire being: the physical, vital, emotional, intellectual, and bliss bodies. They are really methods for studying the Self by clearing away clutter. When the clutter is removed, the Self remains.

We begin to realize that we can free ourselves from avidya by becoming clearer and cleaner. Ignorance is the real dirt that the shat karma kriyas remove.

We aren't what we eat. We are what we don't shit.
—Hugh Romney[4]

Another interesting by-product of practicing shat karma kriyas is that as we erase the mystery about the function and structure of our internal organs and systems, we erase our attachment to them. When we witness the true nature of the physical body and the impossibility of keeping it clean or young forever, we loosen our attachment to it. We do the best we can to keep it healthy because it is our instrument, but we give up attempts to keep the body looking the same forever.

Through the practice of the kriyas, we develop *viveka*, the ability to discriminate between what is passing and what is everlasting, and *vairagya*, which is dispassion or detachment. In the case of our guru Swami Nirmalananda, his practice of shat karma kriya strengthened his ability to see his body as a passing phenomenon and know his soul as everlasting. He chose, therefore, to take *prayopavesha*, a conscious and willful death, on January 10, 1997. He was seventy-three, Self-realized, and in perfect health.

It is said that a person dies as he or she has lived. Swami Nirmalananda lived an enlightened life and died in the state of enlightenment, free and happy.

Swami sent us an announcement from his ashram in India, as he did to many, informing us of his pending death. It was strangely like receiving an invitation to someone's wedding or college graduation. He wrote: "It is almost time to take leave of you all. It has been a joy and a privilege to have known you and received your love and affection. . . . My so-called end is endless, as there is no end and beginning for life. Feel the infinite state of our Being and feel the limitless expansion of the heart."

The announcement informed us that he would leave his body on a certain date and that if we wished to visit him before he died, we should come before that date. He chose this way to die because, he told us, "I do not want to die in the state of *roga* [disease] but in the state of yoga [ease]." He said that he had finished his work and it was time to leave his body.

As soon as we received the news, we went to India to see him. We begged him not to die. We suggested, instead, that he come back to New York City with us. We promised to do all we could to secure him speaking engagements. We felt pretty confident that we could help to arrange something at the United Nations for him. He answered, in his humorous way, that he would rather die than come to New York City. Then we tried crying and imploring him. He said that if we cried, we would make him sad. He did not want to be sad. During those last days he was the happiest we had ever known him to be.

A person who is in relatively good health and decides to die in a good and sound state of mind and body assists the process of prayopavesha by not eating or drinking, and by practicing various kriyas, including basti (enemas). In preparation for prayopavesha, Swamiji stopped eating solid food and then took only barley water (the water that is left after soaking barley grains) and pure water for one month. After this he took nothing, not even water. After a period of five days without water, the great and gentle swami allowed his physical body to fall away.

Swami Nirmalananda's conscious death was a logical extension of his entire life, throughout which he gradually let go of more and more attachments. First he was a vegetarian, for example, and then he gave up dairy products and became a vegan.

Veganism was a tapasic practice for Swami Nirmalananda because he was raised a Brahmin, and Brahmins typically lean heavily on dairy products in their diet. In our culture, vegetarianism and veganism are also tapasic because they are difficult practices to sustain while living in a culture that promotes the degradation of animals. Not everyone can stand on his or her head all day, meditate in silence for three years, or chant the name of God continuously, but everyone usually eats every day. If you do nothing else, make eating your spiritual practice. Consciously choose to eat food that has been obtained by causing the least amount of harm to others. Be sure to eat that food with appreciation, respect, and gratitude for the sacrifice it made to become part of you. And let your own sacrifices of preference and taste be a method for keeping the fire in your practice.

If you want to progress on a spiritual path, you must challenge your actions—including what you eat—as to whether they are authentic expressions of the love and spirit within you. You must ask whether what you are doing bespeaks compassion or indifference to the suffering of others. As long as you act—and eat—without compassion, you remain mired in the realm of separation, loneliness, and frustration, because you have not yet given voice, with your life, to the great heart within you.

—John Robbins[5]

Dietary restriction in the form of vegetarianism, veganism, fasting, and so forth can also be forms of svadhyaya, because they can help you acquire knowledge about the higher Self. One example of a traditional food tapas is to restrict the intake of food according to the moon phase. During the first day of the new moon, eat no food. The following day, eat one tablespoon of food only. Each day the ration of food increases by one tablespoon until at full moon you may eat fifteen tablespoons of food. The ration then decreases to fourteen, thirteen, twelve, eleven tablespoons and so on for successive days, until you are fasting again during the new moon.

A restrictive food tapas like this is not undertaken by a yogi to affect his or her health but as an investigation into the nature of Self. After all, our body is made of the food we eat and our mind is affected by the food we eat. Even the thoughts in our mind are made out of energy obtained from the food we eat.

Interesting lessons about how the body and mind operate can be learned from experimenting with how food affects them. You probably already know that the quality of your thoughts can be affected by the food you eat. Don't make the mistake of thinking that you can put anything inside your body and escape the results of that action. If you are interested in purifying the body and the mind, then the food you eat and the way you eat it must be charged with good intention. Your cells absorb all the actions taken to bring that food to your table. The growing of food, its harvesting, storing, and preparation, together with the act of eating, are all opportunities to invest that food with beneficial qualities.

Our overweening, arrogant passion for self-indulgence has poisoned our world. If we hope to continue living on this planet, we must now reverse the damage, both in ourselves and in our environment, so that we can calm Nature's ire and return ourselves to health. . . . Everyone should have a real home, a haven they can always go home to, inside and outside themselves. All of us have a Mother in Nature, and only she can lead us home.

***—Robert E. Svoboda,* Prakruti: Your Ayurvedic Constitution**[6]

Shauca is the Sanskrit word for cleanliness, but it means more than physical cleanliness. Shaucha means cleanliness of body, mind, and spirit. We can use shat karma kriyas to clean the body, but how do we clean the mind?

The easiest way to clean the mind is to be careful about what we expose it to. The mind is like a clear crystal. The crystal takes on the color of whatever is near to it. When it is resting on a red cloth, it appears red. In the same way, the mind is colored by what you bring near to it. If you watch television or movies or read books of a disturbing, gratuitously sexual or violent nature, your mind will be tinted by those images and your life will be negatively affected. If you practice svadhyaya by reading inspirational books and watching inspirational videos, TV, and movies, you begin to purify the mind. And you become inspired. Making an effort to see the Self in others—even in animals, plants, and minerals—is also svadhyaya.

Kriya Yoga is a method for eliminating obscurations to your happiness. If you want peace, joy, and happiness, perform actions that bring about peace, joy, and happiness for all. When we arduously devote all of our daily activities (eating, washing, studying, spiritual practice, hanging out, etc.) toward harmony, we are performing Kriya Yoga—the yoga of actions that lead to unconditional love.

Part 3

Inner Practices That May Lead to Yoga

Introduction

Pratyahara: Turning Inward . . . Toward Independence

Is this a bridge, exactly? Then what is it connecting to what?
—*Audio Letter,* "Is This a Bridge Exactly?"

The yoga practices we have discussed so far, such as pranayama, asana, vinyasa krama, and kriya, help purify and strengthen the physical and subtle bodies for the hard work of superconsciousness. The natural evolution of a yoga practice is from these outer practices toward more refined and subtle inner practices such as concentration and meditation. Pratyahara provides the bridge from outer to inner practices.

In the *Bhagavad Gita*, Arjuna begs Krishna to reveal to him the totality of his image. Krishna refuses, saying that Arjuna's limited eyes and senses would not be capable of enduring this vision. Arjuna implores him, so Krishna gives him special "god sunglasses." The vision is still too much for Arjuna to process, and he cries to have it stopped. After Krishna says "I told you so," he advises Arjuna that he must expand his perceptual capacity beyond the five senses. He teaches him pratyahara, the practice of withdrawing the senses and directing them inward. And he teaches him yoga practices such as meditation, Bhakti Yoga (devotion), and Nada Yoga (listening for the sound of God, inside).

These inner practices help us develop a new subtle sensibility with which to perceive reality. Normally, we experience the universe through our five senses. Their ability to give us a complete picture is limited by their physical construction. Our physical nervous system is really more of a filtering instrument than a provider of the complete picture. The narrow band of visible light is a fraction of the range of light that exists. The range of sound vibration, also, is much larger than the portion that our physical ears detect. The same is true for the other senses.

"Senses" is a good name for them, because that is what they do for us: they make sense out of an overwhelming universe of possibilities. If we saw the full light spectrum or heard the entire range of sounds, we might go mad.

The senses provide an objectively agreed-upon reality that is seen, felt, heard, touched, and tasted. Even though we know that we are experiencing only a very narrow slice of the pie, most of us are quite content with our slice. Unfortunately, we get so used to this small slice, and its verifiability and usefulness, that we forget about the rest of the universe. What's more, each of the senses uses our energy to sustain its perception of the universe. When you watch television, for example, you may feel you're receiving something—entertainment, information, or pleasure—but the truth is that the act of looking draws energy away from other possible actions you could take.

The same is true of all the senses: they are thieves of the life force. Vairagya (detachment) and viveka (discrimination), in contrast, are like the two wings that allow kundalini to fly up toward superconsciousness.

At some point in our life we become disappointed in the degree of happiness that the unrestrained five senses can provide, and we yearn for the Truth. Through pratyahara we can journey from outward fixation to inward revelation. If you are able to withdraw your senses inward all the way to their Source, you will perceive the Truth. The outer senses reveal only a portion of the Truth. By withdrawing our energy from that partial truth and concentrating it on inner refinement, a larger portion of the Truth is made perceivable.

Pratyahara also means "flowing toward the center." When our vitality is no longer continuously flowing outward and we devote it toward inner practices, we will be able to cross the bridge that we have built.

Photographer: Michael Lavine

10

Meditation: Sitting in the Seat of the Soul

Our main duty is to go beyond thoughts.
***—Swami Nirmalananda,* The Silent Sage Speaks**

Meditation is the practice of watching your mind think.

Why would you want to watch your mind think?

Well, when you can watch something, you know that you are not that something. You cannot watch and be what you are watching at the same time.

The yogi is striving to shift his or her identification with body and mind to identification with the Divine Self. If a yogini can watch the mind, she begins to realize that she must not *be* the mind. That's a good start.

This shift in identification is the first step toward God. To know God you must become God. You must step away from identification with the body, the mind, and the thoughts generated by the mind.

Meditation is not the same as prayer or contemplation. Prayer often means asking for something from someone other than yourself. Contemplation means to dwell on thoughts or concepts. Meditation means to listen within. To listen, you must stop talking. Trusting that everything is exactly the way it should be, the meditator rests in the timeless.

Meditation is not exclusively a Hindu or Buddhist practice. It is older than any doctrine preached by any organized religion. Those individuals willing to bypass thought and intellect to reach an indefinable experience of being have practiced it for countless centuries by simply, as the Quakers say, "listening to the still voice within."

To understand what happens during meditation, we must first have some understanding of consciousness, which is the knowing principle. A being can be in a high state of consciousness or a low state, depending on the degree of avidya (misknowing or ignorance). Avidya can cloud consciousness, so that it is as if we are trying to see who we are in a dirty mirror, and mistake the dirt for our face.

The practices of yoga are psychotherapeutic methods for cleaning the mirror of consciousness. They are designed to free the practitioner of despair and depression and from dependence on external substances or external conditions for happiness.

Lay it down, drop it, let go, sing out, throw it out. Going all the way is holy but alas some linger on the path to see and smell the pretty sunflower or hold hands with eternity or practice ecstasy, bliss or circulate the light or reach neither perception nor non-perception but lingering anywhere you might. Move! Move! Move!

—Bhagavan Das[1]

All yoga practices, including meditation, are designed to reveal the existing happiness in every cell and tissue of the body and every thought wave of the mind. Through these practices, the yogi seeks to clear the mind of all thoughts that cloud the truth of the psyche: that the inner soul, or Self, exists eternally in a state of happiness. To truly be happy we must bring the mind into a condition of clear perception. With clear perception the mind reflects the Self, like a clean mirror.

In the first chapter of the *Yoga Sutras*, Patanjali answers the question: What is Yoga?

Yogash chitta-vritti-nirodhah. (YS I:2)
Yoga is the cessation of the fluctuations,
or whirlings of the mind.

When you stop identifying with your thoughts, the fluctuations of mind, then there is Yoga, which is identification with the Self, samadhi, happiness, bliss, and ecstasy! Almost the entire first chapter of the *Yoga Sutras* is devoted to the practice and benefits of this reduction in the fluctuations of the mind and the resulting state of samadhi or superconsciousness. In the second chapter of the *Yoga Sutras*, Patanjali includes a method for doing this: meditation. It appears as dhyana, one of the eight limbs of Raja or Ashtanga Yoga.

To practice meditation we must first practice pratyahara, drawing the five senses inward. Once we can sit down and draw inward without being distracted by the senses, we are prepared for meditation, which may happen spontaneously and naturally when the ability to concentrate the faculty of attention on one object and hold it there for some time has been mastered. We cannot make ourselves meditate. We can only make ourselves concentrate.

To develop our ability to concentrate, we have to learn to not allow our faculty of attention to become distracted by every thought that passes through the mind. It is the nature of the mind to think. Thinking is a form of talking. The mind is usually chattering on and on, and we are engaged in constant dialogue with this chatter. To interrupt it, Patanjali recommends that we concentrate on something else—the flow of the breath, for example. Let the mind go on talking to itself, but you disengage. This concentration is called dharana.

The various schools of meditation differ from one another primarily in the object chosen for concentration. This object may be elaborate or simple visualizations, a mantra, a candle flame, a mandala, or the movement of the breath. Only through prolonged concentration can the experience of meditation begin to dawn. You cannot *make* yourself meditate, just as you cannot make yourself fall asleep. If you want to fall asleep, it is helpful to create a situation that invites that shift into another state of consciousness. You brush your teeth, wash your face, put on your pajamas, lie down in a comfortable bed, turn out the lights, close your eyes, and within a few minutes you are asleep . . . maybe.

Meditation is similar. It is an effortless state that can arise only after you have trained yourself to sit still and concentrate on one object without distraction. Even with all that preparation you may not be able to shift into the meditative, thought-free state. But through practice you do get closer and closer. You don't give up on sleep if you have a sleepless night. The next night you try again. The same is true for meditation. Don't give up—try again.

Your concentration may be interrupted many times during one

The Last Four Steps of Patanjali's Ashtanga Yoga

Step 5, Pratyahara: Sense withdrawal. The first step toward the inner practices is to surrender the infatuation with the world of the senses.

Step 6, Dharana: Concentration. The meditator may lose his or her concentration now and then and become distracted, but is able to bring the attention back to the object of focus each time the attention wanders.

Step 7, Dhyana: Meditation. When the concentration on the chosen object of focus becomes one-pointed, steady, and uninterrupted for some duration, meditation occurs.

Step 8, Samadhi: Superconsciousness. This is Yoga. The meditator, through intense concentration (dharana), has allowed the state of meditation (dhyana) to occur, and the mind has receded into its Source, which is the same source of all creation. Thus, this experience is the realization of the Oneness of existence and is synonymous with ecstasy or boundless joy.

sitting practice. It doesn't matter. What matters is that you are diligent. When you become aware that you have lost your concentration, bring it back to the focus. With practice, your concentration will become so strong that it is no longer easily seduced away from its focus. Then it moves into the next stage: uninterrupted concentration, or dhyana.

The ancient teachings describe these two stages metaphorically like this:

> Dharana (concentration that is interrupted) is like pouring water into a pot. Water does not pour in a steady stream, but as separate drops.

> Dhyana (meditation, uninterrupted absorption) is like pouring oil into a pot. It pours as an uninterrupted stream toward its goal, the pot.

After a period of not engaging with the thoughts, they begin to quiet down. Space between the thoughts becomes apparent. The silence out of which thoughts originate is continuous. This is another level of vinyasa in action. Your state of consciousness begins to shift, from a condition of fragmentation to one of concentration. This shift in consciousness is typified by a peaceful feeling, which affects both body and mind. This peacefulness is the result of identifying with the infinite rather than the finite, which we experience as thoughts.

There are three normal states of consciousness. Or, rather, normal consciousness appears to manifest in three states. In Sanskrit these normal states of consciousness are called:

jagrat: waking state
swapna: dream state
sushupti: deep dreamless sleep

These three states are experienced by all living beings, usually within a twenty-four-hour period.

During the waking state, consciousness is governed by thoughts, which consist of memories of the past and ideas about the future. Very rarely does the mind gain awareness of the present moment while awake. In this state, we perceive reality from a level of consciousness that respects the physical laws governing the objective universe of time and space.

The dream state draws from the waking state for its images. You can't dream of anything that you have not already seen or experienced somehow in the waking state in this or previous lives. But in dreams, the physical laws governing the universe may be suspended. In dreams we may be able to fly, walk through walls, and interact with people who we know have died.

Deeply buried images from the subconscious may surface in dreams. Most of the characters that appear in our dreams are really aspects of ourselves. These subconscious personae may appear in disguised form and confront our "normal" waking consciousness. Dreaming has the potential to help us resolve unfinished actions from the past. It can free us to live with less confusion by integrating the subconscious with the conscious.

In both the waking and the dream state, we identify with the ego-personality, not with the Divine Self—except perhaps in rare, momentary flashes of pure happiness. During a dream, all seems "real." Only on awakening does the unreality of the dream become obvious to us. The waking state is no more substantial than that of the dream state, but because of its objective nature we regard it as real. On awakening to our true nature, the waking state also appears as a dream: insubstantial and transient.

In deep sleep, the ego-personality self rests by merging with its Source, the Divine Self. This is not a state of Divine realization because the ego-personality self is completely unconscious. On waking, it will remember nothing of its merger with God and will return to the misknowing of avidya, identification with body and mind.

Even so, the soul maintains surveillance while we are in deep sleep. If someone calls out while we are in deep sleep, we will wake up. The witness part of consciousness listens.

The aim of meditation is to experience something similar to the deep sleep merger with the Source—but while awake. This state is called turiya ("the fourth" state), or samadhi. It is known only to enlightened beings, whose consciousness, through effort and grace over countless lifetimes, has been allowed to fully manifest. They have attained such control of the mind that they are able to direct it inward, toward its Divine Source. You may have experienced such a state in a brief flash of bliss during a moment when your thinking mind relaxed its grip on your attention.

We like to use the image of a wheel to describe the process involved in meditation practice. For most of us, our attention is usually whirling about attached to thoughts, to the rim of the wheel.

As the wheel rolls along we go with it, one thought at a time, a continuous stream of thoughts all day long. At the end of the day we are so exhausted that we fall asleep. While asleep, we continue to roll along with our thoughts in the form of dreams. The dreaming state

Daily Meditation Instruction

1. Choose a seat. Select a comfortable seated position in which the spine is perpendicular to the Earth. If you are sitting on the floor, elevate the seat by sitting on a pillow or folded blanket to make it easier to bring the spine fully erect. You must be able to hold the position still for the duration of the meditation practice. Choose a position for your hands that you can maintain comfortably for the duration: folded in your lap, perhaps, or resting on your knees.

2. Be still. Don't move the body, so that you can experience stillness. Your body will become still when you eliminate any reason to move it.

3. Focus on the breath. Don't follow the breath into the body. Feel it at the tip of the nose or in the rise and fall of the abdomen. Do not control the breath; just notice when it is going in and when it is going out. Keep the attention on the movement of the breath. Let it come and let it go. Like life itself, the breath comes and goes.

   Allow the thoughts to align themselves with the movement of the breath. Don't hold your breath and don't hold on to a thought and begin thinking it. Instead, let the breath come, let a thought come. Let that breath go as you let that thought go. Don't breathe; instead, let the breath breathe your body while you watch. Don't think; instead, let the thoughts flow through the mind, while you watch. Become the nonjudgmental witness, the *sakshi*. Let go.

continues until we move into deep sleep. In deep sleep there are no dreams, no thoughts, no images. The mind has receded back to the Source, beyond thought. We are at the still, unmoving center of the wheel—but we are not aware that we are there.

The center of a wheel is called *sukha* in Sanskrit, when the axle rides smoothly. Sukha also means "happiness." A happy axle is one that is turning smoothly at the very center of the wheel. To dwell in the sukha is to dwell in the eternal happiness of the soul.

Bicycle wheel
Artist: David Life

By practicing concentration, we attempt to move *consciously* away from riding on the rim of the wheel, turning with every thought, to concentrating on one object. When this concentration is uninterrupted, attention will slide down one spoke to reach the center. At the center, the wheel continues to turn, but we do not turn with each movement, with each thought.

The nature of the Self is bliss, ecstasy, and boundless happiness. You become blissful automatically when you stop identifying with the endlessly rolling wheel and reside in the sukha, the good center, where nothing is changing and everything is real. The source of all that moves is that which is unmoving.

Time is suspended and the truth is revealed. The truth is One. The truth is changeless and eternal; it is unconditional love, the source of all being.

The form of meditation that is right for you is the one that *works* for you. Teachers teach techniques that have proved helpful to them. There is no right or wrong technique. The right technique is the one that works. Choose a method and start practicing. To get results, be patient and practice regularly for a long time.

Although an advanced meditator may be able to meditate sitting in a subway or waiting in an airport, for most of us it is helpful to set aside meditation space in our homes. Choose a quiet place, preferably a room with a door that you can close.

It can help to have an altar, where you can put a candle or a picture of a saint or Divine being, or perhaps just flowers. Your altar may start out very simple and grow as your spiritual practice grows. Or it may start out very elaborate and become simpler as you refine your practice. An altar acts as a mirror. It is an externalization of the clutter or the desired clarity of mind. It can serve to help you see your own soul.

Your meditation space is a h-OM-e base you can return to every day. But if a special space is not available, you need not give up meditation practice. Even your bed can serve as your meditation space. Sometimes it is the most private space available, especially if you share a home with others or are traveling.

If possible, use a timer while meditating, so that you can concentrate without having to check a clock or glance at your watch. When you are just starting a practice, do not spend too much time meditating. The important thing is to do it every day. If you are overly ambitious and try to force yourself to sit for one hour every day, you will probably give up after the first or second day. Start with a reasonable amount of time that you will be able to stick to with regularity.

We always suggest that beginners start by sitting for five minutes each day at the same time of the day. If you can stick to this for two months without missing a day, then begin to increase your time by five minutes. Practice for ten minutes each day for two months, and then increase that to twenty. After you establish a daily practice of twenty minutes for two months, increase that time as your schedule allows. Meditation practice can be a separate practice or it can be combined with other yoga practices in a daily regimen.

Meditation will become something you enjoy doing, but let this evolve naturally. On the other hand, your practice will not evolve if you are unable to adhere to some kind of discipline.

Once you have a meditation space, choose your seat. Meditation should be practiced with the spine in a position perpendicular to the Earth. A reclining position renders the mind dull and unconscious.

A perpendicular spine can act like an antenna. Shri Brahmananda Sarasvati often described the body/mind as a television or radio capable of picking up the cosmic station transmitting from the Divine Source. The nervous system and all faculties of attention are available for tuning in to the Divine.

Sthira-sukham asanam (YS II:46)
The connection to the earth should be steady and joyful.

This yoga sutra, which is often limited to asana, also applies to meditation practice. Sthira means steady. For there to be physical steadiness, a sense of awareness or alertness must be expressed throughout the body. This is most likely to happen if the meditator

These components promote a good meditation practice:

1. Same place. A meditation space should be a place you can come back to each day to meditate.
2. Same time. Try to establish a regular time to practice every day.
3. Use a timer to free yourself to concentrate without having to keep track of the time.

KEEP A MEDITATION JOURNAL.

1. Every day, use a small date book to record the time of day and the amount of time you practiced.
2. Note any insights or disturbances that arose. This can help you observe patterns, habits, and breakthroughs in your practice.

consciously places the body in a chosen position. In doing so, the meditator invests the body with the mind's intention. When there is a strong mental intention, the body will rise to meet it.

Sukham means comfortable. It means the same as sukha, happiness or joy. So to begin your sitting practice, choose a position for the body in which it can be both alert and comfortable. Don't try to force the body into positions it may not be ready to handle. If it is extremely difficult to cross your legs in padmasana, lotus pose, for example, don't choose it as your meditation seat. Practice padmasana another time. Choose a seated position that is comfortable for you. That feeling of comfort may change as the minutes tick by, but at least give yourself a fair chance by beginning in the most comfortable position you can find.

An attitude of sincerity and humility is the first prerequisite on the spiritual path. We've got to know that we don't know. We've got to know that there's nothing to know, that there's only being. The best attitude is to be very grateful and thankful and constantly generous.

—*Bhagavan Das,* It's Here Now (Are You?)[2]

Seated Positions for Meditation Practice

The following are positions that may be conducive to a seated meditation practice. They are listed in order of difficulty, with the easiest first.

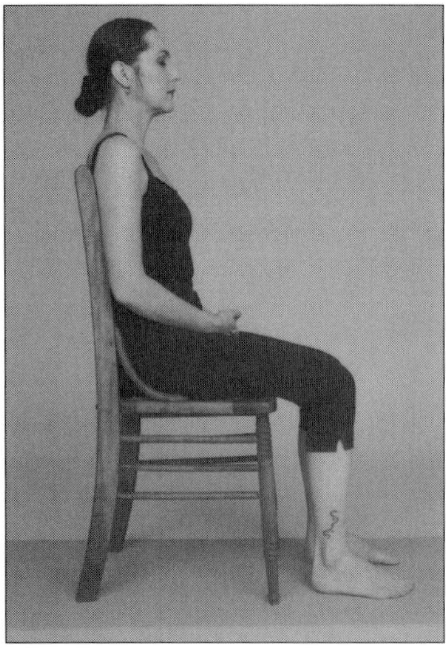

Sitting in a chair

1. Sit in a chair

Choose a chair that is not too soft and has a straight back and, if possible, no arms. When you sit, put both feet on the floor. If your feet do not touch the floor, place a box, block of wood, or telephone book under your feet. The bottoms of your feet should feel grounded. Legs should be parallel to each other. When beginning, go ahead and lean against the back of the chair. Eventually, sit forward so that your spine is extended upward and is not supported by the back of the chair.

Hands can rest lightly on thighs with palms facing down or up. Elbows should be slightly bent, shoulders relaxed.

2. Easy cross-legged seat

Spread a blanket or rug under your buttocks and feet to provide a padded surface to rest on. Cross your legs at the ankles. Place a cushion or folded blanket under your buttocks to raise your seat so that your hips are higher than or at least even with your knees. If your knees feel as though they are hanging in midair, place folded blankets or towels under each knee for support. The knees should feel as though they are dropping into the blankets or towels. Gradually, through sitting cross-legged, your hips will become more open and your knees will drop closer to the floor. Until then, don't force your knees to the floor.

Cross-legged

If it is very difficult to sit upright, lean against a wall for support. Eventually you should wean yourself away from the support of the wall and experience the support of your own spinal column.

3. Supported Virasana

Kneeling, bend both knees so that the tops of the feet rest on the floor and the inside edges of the feet rest against the thighs. Place a folded blanket or a pillow under the buttocks, lifting the seat as high as necessary so that you have no pain in the knees. If the feet hurt from the pressure of the floor, first spread a blanket or a rug under you from the knees all the way back to underneath the feet and beyond the toes. The spine should extend upward. Don't allow the lumbar area to sway.

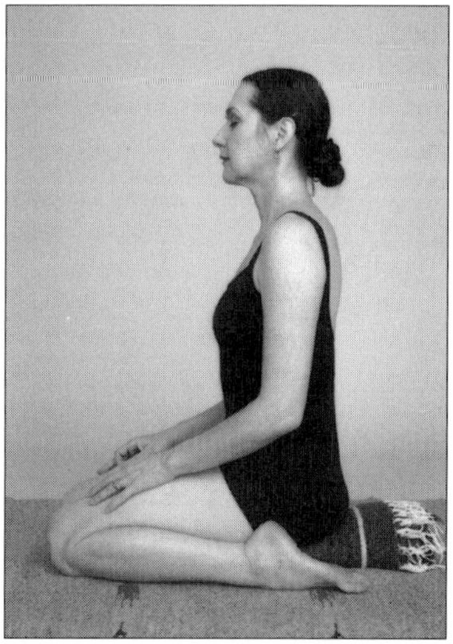
Supported Virasana

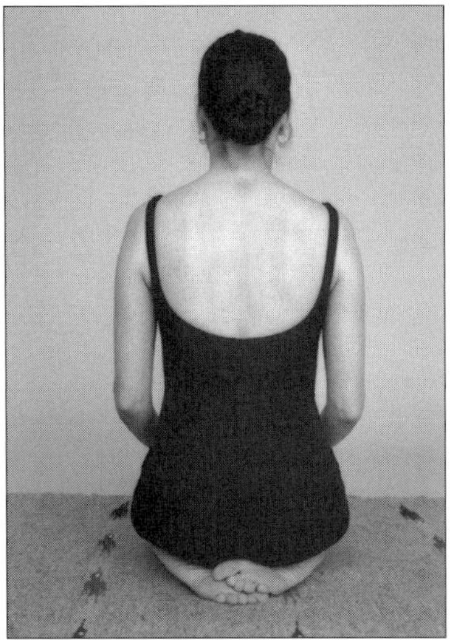

Vajrasana

4. Vajrasana (thunderbolt pose)

Kneeling, sit on the inside of your feet, placing the heels on the outside of the buttocks. Bring the big toes together. Allow the right big toe to rest on top of the left.

5. Half Lotus

Sit cross-legged, placing the right foot on top of the left thigh. The soles of both feet should turn upward. Sit on a pillow or folded blanket so that your knees drop closer to the floor.

6. Preparation for Siddhasana

Sitting cross-legged, draw your left foot close toward the pelvis and place the right foot on top, tucking the right toes between the calf and thigh of the left leg. The right heel should rest on top of the left heel. The soles of both feet should turn upward.

7. Siddhasana (the pose of perfection)

Sit so that the left heel presses against the perineum or vaginal opening and the left toes are tucked between the calf and thigh of the right leg. Place the right heel on top of the left heel and tuck the right toes between the calf and thigh of the left leg.

Half Lotus

8. Padmasana (Lotus pose)

Place the right foot on top of the left thigh, as close to the pelvis as possible, then lift the left foot and place it on top of the right thigh, as close to the pelvis as possible. The soles of both feet should turn upward.

Hand Positions for Meditation Practice

Our hands are instruments through which we express the feelings in our hearts. Hands can be tense, constantly clenching or grabbing, or they can be graceful and generous. The nature of the spiritual heart is joyous and compassionate. How well the spiritual heart is able to manifest through the layers of body and mind depends on how open the energy channels (nadis) are. If the nadis are blocked, the actions of the hands are also blocked and cannot freely express joy and compassion.

The energy channels that emanate from the fourth or heart chakra (the anahata chakra) radiate from the area of the physical heart through the arms and into the hands. Through the use of hand positions called mudras, we can help purify these energy channels during meditation practice. The mudras help circulate prana throughout the physical and subtle bodies.

Siddhasana

The following is a list of hand mudras that can be used during meditation practice. They may be used with any of the seated postures already described:

1. Hands resting on thighs, palms up or palms down

The fingers should be relaxed and allowed to fall slightly apart from each other; elbows slightly bent, with shoulders open and relaxed.

2. Chin mudra

Join the tip of the thumb with the tip of the first finger of each hand; the other three fingers of each hand are separated, palms up or palms down.

3. *Bhairavi mudra*

Place the hands in the lap, palms facing up. Left-handed people should rest the left hand on top of the right, as this renders the active hand more passive. Similarly, right-handed people should rest the right hand on top of the left.

Padmasana

Practicing Meditation

Once you have chosen your seat and your mudra, scan the body for tension and make any necessary adjustments. Begin with your feet. Consciously relax and place the feet in the most comfortable position possible. Then move upward, into the legs and buttocks. When you reach the buttocks, feel that they are moving downward into the earth. Consciously give in to this downward-moving force; it is the force of gravity. Sit *down*.

If you can sincerely surrender to gravity, the terrestrial force, then you will spontaneously feel the force of levitation, the celestial force. This force will be felt as an uplifting movement in the spinal column. The joints of your body will feel spacious, as energy begins to circulate more freely. Feel your physical body form a bridge between the terrestrial and the celestial.

Relax your hands, arms, and shoulders. Allow the abdomen and chest to be placed in a way that allows the most freedom for breathing. Soften the sides, back, and front of the neck. Place the head on top of the spinal column with the chin parallel to the ground. Make sure that the chin does not jut out too far forward and cause tension in the neck. Relax all the facial muscles, especially in and around the mouth. Allow the tongue to rest in the mouth. When the tongue is quiet, the mind can begin to quiet down. The tongue may rest against the roof of the mouth. Close your eyes gently, so that you do not strain the muscles surrounding the eyes. Allow the area between the eyebrows to widen and soften. Let the forehead relax as you allow the frontal part of the brain to slip back slightly into the skull.

Now you are ready to sit still.

Having taken the time to place your body in the most comfortable seated position, the next step is to be still. Do not doubt the position that you have chosen. Do not allow a change of position to be an option. Sit it out. The next time you sit, you may want to try something different, if your last choice proved very uncomfortable after a few minutes. If you have tried nearly every option and they are all equally uncomfortable, give up! By surrendering your struggle to find the right position, it may reveal itself to you.

Most of us never stop moving, day or night. To place the body in one position and hold it in a state of repose, to watch the breath move through the body and watch the thoughts move through the mind is a very precious and rare opportunity. It is an experience beyond what is thought of as "normal." This is an opportunity to transcend the mundane.

Do not allow any moving of the outer form. Let the breath move in and move out. Let the thoughts move in and move out. Until you can sit still and let the mind think without becoming involved with the thoughts, you will never be able to control your mind. Be free of thoughts by watching the thoughts pass through the mind.

In the instructions that Jesus gave for meditation, he said, "Be still and know that I Am." When we move we are responding to a thought. The thought may be an unconscious one that has become so deeply ingrained that we are unaware of why we move. Most of us are so uncomfortable with ourselves that it is difficult for us to simply be still.

The Dalai Lama once commented, "Most Westerners lack Self-confidence." You see this very clearly if you watch a group of Western people waiting in line for something, or if you watch a group of beginning yoga students waiting for class to start. They can't sit still; they fidget constantly because they are uneasy with themselves.

True Self-confidence comes from a connection to the Source, to the Self, to that which is at peace. Attaching to the movements of the mind results in lack of Self-confidence. False confidence is based in pride and arrogance, which are rooted in fear, not in the happiness of the soul. A changeable mind can never bring calmness and stability.

What happens if, while you are trying to meditate, the urge to scratch or move a certain body part becomes so overwhelming that you give in and scratch or move? What usually happens is that you will have relieved that particular annoyance, but pretty soon another area of your body will begin to bother you, and the whole scenario will repeat itself. The result? You spend your meditation time running away from annoying sensations.

Seeking pleasure and avoiding pain is what most of us normally do in life. This strategy may occasionally result in happiness, but this happiness is short-lived because it is dependent on people and situations—and those are all likely to change, diminishing our happiness. This strategy rarely leads to lasting happiness.

If we wish to become truly independent and truly happy, we must try another strategy. Sitting still is an opportunity to break the habitual cycle that has us continually running away from the slightest discomfort and seeking pleasure outside of ourselves. To sit still, no matter what, is not how we usually react to an uncomfortable situation. Yet if we try it, we venture deeper into ourselves, exploring our potential. We will come closer to the source of happiness.

Be assured that no one has ever died from a foot falling asleep. The circulation will return as soon as you move around. Next time you sit to meditate, just choose a more comfortable and well-supported position so that the foot is less likely to fall sleep.

Physical discomforts will naturally arise when you begin the practice of seated meditation. There are deep tensions held in our body. When we allow the body to be stilled, these repressed tensions may surface in the form of painful sensations. If you want to be free of these painful tensions, maintain your chosen focus. Tension and pain are simply forms of thought. If you allow them to move, they will. But if you hold on and identify with them, they will remain with you.

We have built a personality from all of our preferences. We get stuck in our likes and dislikes and in our short-lived pleasures and disappointments. We carry them with us in the very way we move and hold our body. Meditation practice allows these patterns to surface so that we can let them go, allowing for a transformation of personality. Letting go of old ways of reacting to situations and things allows us to become open and flexible and not hold on to a rigid sense of self.

When we are able to remain still in the outer body, the inner work of transforming the mind can take place. We can begin to concentrate.

What happens when you sit down to meditate is usually not meditation but an attempt to work on dharana, the ability to concentrate. In other words, you give your mind something to do, then you watch while it tries to do it.

The breath is a practical focus for concentration, as it is readily available. Even when a mantra is used, the inner repetition of the mantra is coordinated with the movement of the breath.

To practice dharana, become aware of the breath. Fix your attention on a place where you are most likely to feel the action of breathing. The two areas most commonly used for this purpose are the tip of the nose, about a quarter of an inch in front of the nostrils, or the area in the abdomen where the diaphragm muscle gently rises with each exhale and falls with each inhale.

If you choose to focus on the entrance and exit of the breath at the tip of the nose, then stay there as if you were a doorman at the entrance to a grand hotel. The doorman doesn't follow each resident into the building and into the elevator and on up to his or her room. Instead, he simply stands and opens the door for the entrance and exit of each person. The doorman views each person with equanimity. A good doorman never falls asleep on the job.

Watch the breath as the doorman watches the people who come in and out of the hotel. Allow and acknowledge each breath as it comes into the body and then exits again through the nose. Do not follow the breath up into the sinuses, down the trachea, and into the soft tissue of the lungs. No, just stay put at the entrance, about a quarter of an inch in front of the nostrils, and pay attention.

If you choose to place your attention in the abdomen, then let it rest lightly inside, on top of the diaphragm muscle. The diaphragm muscle is shaped somewhat like an umbrella. The center moves up with the exhale and drops down with the inhale. Allow your attention to rest gently on this dome. Let it be moved up and down.

Once you have established attention and can feel the breath, don't breathe. Instead, allow the breath to breathe your body while you watch. Make your body an open conduit for the breath to move through.

Watch every breath. Breathing in and breathing out. You may wish to silently say to yourself: "Breathing in and breathing out." Listen to the breath. To listen, you have to be in a state of receptivity.

Don't miss a breath: breathing in, breathing out, acknowledging each time the breath moves in and moves out of the body. Don't try to manipulate the breath. Just let breathing happen while you watch. Concentrate on watching each breath without changing the breath. This is how you develop the art of witnessing.

Let go of any judgmental attachment to the breath. Be the impartial observer. After a short time, the thoughts will begin to align themselves with the movement of the breath. Allow this to happen and keep your attention on the breath, witnessing the breathing. Don't try to stop thinking or block out thoughts. Instead, let each thought come, and let each thought go. Don't hold your breath and don't hold on to a thought. Let there be a continuous movement of breath through the body and thought through the mind.

Your only task is to encourage the process of letting go. Don't let the breath get stuck and don't get stuck on a thought and begin thinking it. Let go of any tendency to ride a thought into the thinking process. Breathe in and breathe out. The movement of the breath is essential for the practice of letting go, which is essential to the practice of yoga. Let it come, let it go, whatever it is. If difficulty arises, acknowledge, appreciate, and let it go. When pleasure arises, acknowledge, appreciate, and let it go. Each inhale, each exhale, move it on through. Let it go.

Mantra can help you keep the attention focused on allowing the breath to come and go. The silent repetition of a mantra, coordinated with the inhale and the exhale, will help to ensure that the breath does not get stuck.

The Sanskrit word mantra is composed of two sounds, *man* and *tra*. Man means the mind or the thinking instrument, and tra means to bridge or to cross over. Tra is the root of the English words travel and traverse. A mantra allows you to travel beyond thought.

A mantra can provide protection for the mind. It protects the mind from negative or distracting thoughts. What you think becomes your reality. If you are silently repeating the name of God, then that vibration is slowly reconstructing your thought patterns into something divine. To know God is to merge with God, to become God. You cannot know something, really, without becoming it.

The mantra is the name of our lover. That's His or Her name, whatever name of God touches our heart. It is very intimate, deeply passionate. It has to be an erotic love affair that keeps us engaged so that we're all excited when God calls. This is the real Romance.

—*Bhagavan Das,* It's Here Now (Are You?)[3]

Mantras can also be in the form of encouraging phrases that direct the mind. *Not my will, but Thy will, be done* and *Lord, have mercy* are helpful mantras of this type.

Let Go is a very powerful mantra for encouraging purification. With each inhale, silently say *Let*, and with each exhale say *Go*. In doing so you are letting go of the resistances that are blocking the Divine Self from manifesting through your being. You are opening up to the power of love that is your own soul. You are letting go of all your resistances to Yoga. When you let go, you automatically let God.

It always comes back to just letting go with love. Just put love in it, whatever it is, and if you can't put love in it, don't do it.

—*Bhagavan Das,* It's Here Now (Are You?)[4]

During the practice you will lose your concentration and wander off with a thought. When you become aware that this has occurred, gently bring your attention back to concentrating on letting each breath and each thought go. You never know what a powerful hold your thoughts have over you until you practice letting them come and go.

With each letting go, the mind begins to recede back into its source, the same source that our consciousness retreats to during deep sleep. But unlike the sleeper, the meditator is awake and is conscious of this process. He or she is witnessing it.

By identifying with the sakshi, the witness, you let go of all that has within its nature the ability to go. What will remain is that which you are seeking; that which has been there all along: the Self.

The Self is beyond thought. It is changeless and eternal. It is the "I Am" of the Vedas, the real you: the same you that was once five years old; the you that was at your high school graduation; and the you that is here now, reading this book. The outer form of your body has certainly changed. Your mind has changed billions of times, but your inner essence has not changed. You are still here. So, be here now. Meditate!

By letting it go, it all gets done.
—Tao Te Ching

11

Nadam: Listening for the Unstruck Sound

Tasya vachakah pranavah.
Always chant OM; God is OM, supreme music.
—Patanjali's Yoga Sutra I:27

The *Hatha Yoga Pradipika* declares that samadhi is achieved when the *anahata nadam*, the unstruck sound, can be heard. The aim of Hatha Yoga is to hear this soundless sound, which is Om, the beginning and end of all sound and the music of the spheres. To do this, the yogi must first perfect the ability to listen. The fruit of meditation practice is the ability to listen, to be receptive enough to perceive the subtlest sounds emanating from within each of us.

A teacher who wanted to show his students the transformational value of deep listening took them to a cremation ground. There, he picked out three skulls. Taking the first skull, he put a stick through the hole where the ear once was, and it came out through the other side of the skull. The teacher said, "This is a person who heard the Truth with one ear, but was too lazy to contemplate what he had heard. Instead, he let it go out the other ear."

The teacher picked up the next skull and put a stick into the ear hole. The stick got stuck in the middle of the skull and moved upward. "This person," the teacher said, "not only heard the Truth, but contemplated it."

When the teacher put the stick into the third skull, it entered the ear, moved upward toward the brain, and then came down toward the heart. "This is the skull of a person who not only heard the Truth and contemplated it, but also let it permeate the heart. This person cultivated the type of deep listening that leads to God-realization."

Sound is the essence of all energy. The first vibration, the Nadam, is "unstruck," meaning that it is self-originating; it occurs without striking two things together. That first very subtle vibration is still resonating through each and every vibration that has arisen since the beginning.

In the beginning was the Word and the Word was with God and the Word was God.

—Bible, John 1:1

Nada Yoga is the yoga of deep inner listening. Nada is a Sanskrit word meaning sound; the related word nadi means river or stream. It also means rushing or sounding. Nadis are the subtle channels through which consciousness flows.

We find many references to Nada Yoga in the *Hatha Yoga Pradipika*. The fourth chapter deals with samadhi, and much of this chapter is devoted to Nada Yoga.

The essence of all beings is earth,
The essence of earth is water,
The essence of water is plants,
The essence of plants is man,
The essence of man is speech,
The essence of speech is sacred knowledge,
The essence of sacred knowledge is word and sound,
The essence of word and sound is Om.
—*Chandogya Upanishad*[1]

Namah Sivaya Gurave
Nada-Bindu-Kalatmane,
Niranjna-Padam Yati
Nityam Yatra Prayanah.
—Hatha Yoga Pradipika IV:1

Shri Brahmananda Sarasvati interpreted this verse as:

> Salutations to the Nadam, which is the inner guide and the inner life, the dispenser of happiness to all! It is the inner guru appearing as nada (sound), bindu (the point of immortality), and kala (time). One who is devoted to the inner guru, the nada, the inner music, obtains the highest bliss.[2]

To begin the practice of Nada Yoga, the yogi first practices pratyahara by drawing the senses inward and forcefully shutting out as many external sights and sounds as possible. The first stage of pratyahara is to become still and quiet and allow an inner tranquility to permeate the senses.

This is not easy to do, so a prerequisite might be to refine your ability to really listen to the sounds around you. Once you refine your external listening, you can turn your ability to listen inward.

To listen is to be receptive. Receptivity is very important to the yogi, because enlightenment is not something you can capture. It is something that is received. Samadhi cannot be gained through effort. It is a spontaneous gift that occurs when the soul is ready to receive.

To become receptive is to become like a baby, as babies must receive care. It is interesting to note that the physical ear resembles a fetus. The tissue of the outer ear is remarkable in other ways, too. No other organ in the body contains all three cell types present during the gestation of the human embryo:

The ectoderm, which contributes to the brain and nervous system.
The endoderm, which make up the organs of digestion.
The mesoderm, which grows into the bones, muscles, and circulatory system.

This is one reason why the ear is an ideal acupuncture site.

Who hath ears, let him hear.
—Bible, Matthew 11:15

Vision is linear and easily fooled. The ears hear sound from all directions, with exceptional perception of details, such as small differences in tone and harmonics. The ear perceives finer differences than does the eye, which is absorbed in gross details and linear perception.

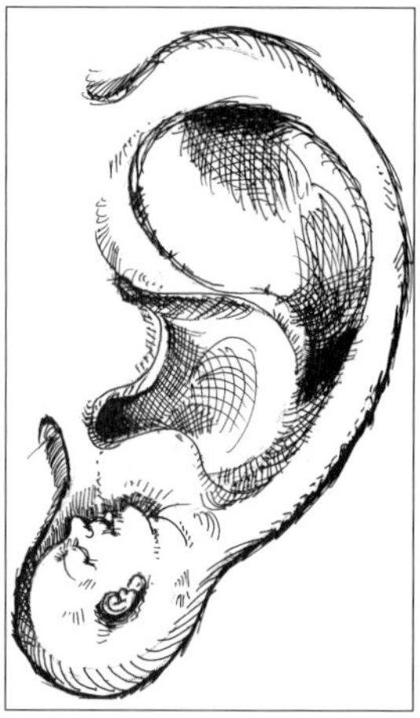

Ear resembling a fetus
Artist: David Life

According to Joachim-Ernst Brent, author of *The World Is Sound, Nada Brahma*, "We all know the expression *optical illusion*. There are dozens of such illusions. You can find descriptions of them in any textbook on physiology. The parallel expression *acoustical illusion*, however, does not exist. This is so because, in fact, there are only very few acoustical illusions, that is, because our ear informs us more correctly about reality."[3]

The eyes rove and are constantly on the lookout for something to grasp. God cannot be grasped, however, because God is already present. God can be heard, if we listen.

Most of us use our eyes far more than we use our ears. Bhagavan Shree Rajneesh calls this obsession with seeing "Kodakomania." He says: "Eighty percent of your energy is devoted to the eyes. The other senses suffer very much, because there is only twenty percent left for them. The eyes have become an Adolf Hitler. You have lost the democracy of your senses. Don't get too interested in pictures, otherwise you will lose more and more the ability to perceive reality."[4]

We can close our eyes, and we do, but we cannot close our ears. We hear before we are born and we continue to hear after death. When we are dying, the sense of smell goes first; then taste, then sight, and then touch. But hearing remains long after death. This is why it is very important that the people surrounding a dead person continue to speak to their dearly departed one.

The ancient Tibetans knew this truth. *The Tibetan Book of the Dead* was originally entitled *Bardo Thodol*, which means *Liberation by Hearing in the In-between State.* Professor of Indo-Tibetan-Buddhist studies at Columbia University Robert Thurman notes, "To use the phrase 'liberation by hearing' is not quite accurate and may give the wrong idea about the original meaning. A closer word would be learning rather than hearing. Closer still would be the Sanskrit word *shravana*, but unfortunately we don't have a close translation in English."[5]

Shravana is hearing in which the listener has not merely heard but has fully comprehended what was heard, so that learning, or knowing, is the result. It's like when you say, "I hear you!" meaning "I really know what you mean. I got it. I fully understand."

Hearing begins with listening and listening begins with being quiet. Without quiet there can be no space to receive. Let go of the constant urge to grasp and give meaning to every thought, sight, or sound. In doing so, quietness begins to creep in like the dawn or the dusk.

One who desires complete dominion of yoga should thus explore the nada with an attentive mind and abandon all thoughts.

—Hatha Yoga Pradipika IV:93[6]

To refine your ability to listen, start by appreciating good music. Put energy into the development of your ears rather than your eyes. Turn off the TV. Put on the headphones and turn on the stereo. Modern music contains the same universal teachings that have awakened the heart via music through all ages—if you allow yourself to feel the music.

Feeling music rather than trying to analyze it intellectually is one way to bypass the thinking mind and move closer to the heart. But be choosy about what you allow to enter your being through your ears. Although the essence of all sound is Om, it is helpful to choose music that induces an inner state of well-being.

When a man surrenders to the sound of music and lets its sweet, soft, mournful strains . . . be funneled into his soul through his ears, and gives up all his time to the glamorous moanings of song, the effect at first on his energy and initiative of mind, if he has any, is to soften it as iron is softened in a furnace, and made workable: but if he persists and does not break the enchantment, the next stage is that it melts and runs till the spirit has quite run out of him and his mental sinews (if I may so put it) are cut, and he has become what Homer calls "a feeble fighter."

—***Plato,*** **Republic**[7]

Music can make you feel happy, jealous, aggressive, calm, depressed, or elevated. The ancient musicians of India understood this well. By playing certain ragas, they could make the clouds rain or flowers bloom. They knew which combination of sounds caused which emotional responses in their listeners. The wisest musicians concentrated on making music that could cause God to fall in love with the musician.

Good music defies the thinking mind; good music has no literal meaning at all. Because music has the power to transcend the thinking mind, good music can help bring about an expanded state of consciousness. Listening to elevating music can prepare you for Nada Yoga.

Only bad music has meaning.
—***Alan Watts***[8]

One hears the sound of the unstruck resonance (anahata shabda); the quintessence of that sound is the (supreme) object (consciousness). The mind becomes one with that object of knowledge and it dissolves therein. That is the supreme state of Vishnu (sthiti).

—***Hatha Yoga Pradipika IV:100***[9]

We saw music raise consciousness during the 1960s when the Beatles unapologetically brought Indian music and spirituality to pop music. The Beatles

Since the 1960s, Indian philosophy and spirituality have entered our culture via music. Swami Satchidananda gave the opening talk at the Woodstock Festival in 1969. The theme of the Festival was Peace, Love, and Music, and Swami Satchidananda said:

> My beloved brothers and sisters, I am overwhelmed with joy to see the entire youth of America gathered here in the name of music. In fact, through music we can work wonders. Music is the celestial sound and it is sound that controls the entire universe, not atomic vibrations. Sound energy, sound power is much, much greater than any other power in the world.
>
> One thing I very much wish you all to remember—with sound we can make, and at the same time break. . . . We can break with sound, and if we care, we can also make with sound.
>
> So let all our actions and all our arts express Yoga. Through the sacred art of music let us find peace that will pervade all over the globe. The future of the whole world is in your hands. You can make it or break it.
>
> The entire world is going to be watching. The entire world is going to know what the American youth can do for humanity.[10]

movie *Help* included a scene with Indian musicians. The songs "Norwegian Wood" and "Rain" featured George Harrison's sitar playing. The Beatles even interjected Sanskrit mantra into their songs, singing "Jaya Guru Deva" in "Across the Universe" from the *Let It Be* album and "Guru Brahma, Guru Vishnu Guru Devo Maheshwara" on George Harrison's album *All Things Must Pass*. Ravi Shankar was introduced to the West by the very hip Beatles and so became hip himself.

Indian music is profoundly spiritual. As Ravi Shankar says, "Our tradition teaches us that sound is God—Nada Brahma. That is, musical sound and the musical experience are steps to the realization of the Self. We view music as a kind of spiritual discipline that raises one's inner being to divine peacefulness and bliss."[11] In most Eastern and African cultures, music and dance are spiritual practices. In our culture, music has been turned into a commodity.

As Ram Dass wrote in *Be Here Now*, "It was only when music was profaned that it became a vehicle for gratification of the senses. Prior to that it was a method of communion with the Spirit."[12]

The longing for a connection to the Divine was so great in our culture, however, that it exploded in the music of jazz and the lyrics of rock. Before Woodstock, the great jazz saxophonist John Coltrane had already made a powerful connection between music and spirituality with his monumental recording *A Love Supreme*.

> ***When [Coltrane] delved into the Indian and African cultures he saw music as a means to enlightenment not an end in itself. His drive to expand his musical horizons became a process of spiritual development, his playing and composing a probing of soul and spirit with his audience as active participants rather than passive witnesses.***
>
> ***—The World According to John Coltrane***[13]

Coltrane's embrace of Eastern philosophy permeated jazz, rock, and folk music. The philosophical ideals of God as love, peace, and nonviolence were celebrated in the music of Alice Coltrane, Sun Ra, Pharoah Sanders, Ornette Coleman, Miles Davis, Don Cherry, the Mahavishnu Orchestra, Santana, and the Beatles. These ideals radiated through the lyrics of Jimi Hendrix, the Beatles, George Harrison, Van Morrison, Bob Dylan, Donovan, and others. Exposure to Indian music had indeed caused a shift in consciousness in American popular music.

Words, sounds, speech, men, memory, thoughts,
Fears and emotions—time—all related . . .
All made from one . . . all made in one.
Blessed be His name.
Thought waves—heat waves—all vibrations—
All paths lead to God. Thank you God.
His way . . . it is so lovely . . . it is so gracious
It is merciful—thank you God.
One thought can produce millions of vibrations
And they all go back to God . . . everything does.
Thank you God.
Have no fear . . . believe . . . thank you God.
The universe has many wonders. God is all.
His way . . . it is so wonderful.
Thoughts—deeds—vibrations, etc.
They all go back to God . . . God is alive.
God is
God loves
May I be acceptable in Thy sight.
We are all one in His grace.
The fact that we do exist is acknowledgement
Of thee O Lord.
Thank you God.
—*John Coltrane,* A Love Supreme[14]

We hear in Indian music the soul's yearning to be reunited with the source of joy: God. Indian music is in a modal style that, producer Bill Laswell explains, "is based on hearing and repetition of hearing to bring about a trance state."[15]

Whenever two notes come together they create a mood. The moods that result from the interaction between the notes make up raga. A raga is that which colors

Alice Coltrane leading satsang at Jivamukti, 1998.
Photographer: Sharon Gannon

the mind. The state of mind of the listener is colored by the music, and the music itself is built on the concept of relationship.

The relationships implied by this music are not those of mundane love songs, and they elicit deeper emotions from the listener than mundane love songs do. These are the real love songs—songs of Divine Love, of a "Love Supreme." Listening to this type of music prepares one to delve within, moving into subtle and expanding realms of joy.

The late great trumpeter Don Cherry, with whom we had the good fortune to play when he was in our band Audio Letter, was a profoundly spiritual musician, committed to seeing all as One. There was no doubt in him that music was God and God was sound. Don loved to recite this quotation from the Sufi Master Hazrat Inayat Kahn:

> All religions have taught us that the origin of the whole creation is sound. The music of the universe is the background of the small picture, which we call music. Our sense of music, our attraction to music shows that there is music in the depth of our being. Music is behind the working of the whole universe. Music is not only life's greatest object, but it is life itself. What makes us feel drawn to music is that our whole being is music. Every person is music, perpetual music, continually going on day and night; and your intuitive faculty can hear that music.

Music has always been an integral part of Jivamukti Yoga. In our classes we especially like to play the music that has resulted from India's pollination of American music. The Indo-futuristic fusion of producer Bill Laswell, for example, who has thrown together Western jazz musicians like Pharaoh Sanders and Ornette Coleman with Indian masters like Zakir Hussain and Ustad Sultan Khan and recorded the extraordinary results, elicits a devotional mood that draws the listener inward.

Bill Laswell
Photographer: Thi-Linh Le

Composers and musicians like Laswell, Gabrielle Roth, Jah Wobble, Anisa and Roderick Romero, Deva Premal and Miten Sean Dinsmore, Cheb i Sabbah, Arjun Spinner, Wah, Krishna Das, Jai Uttal, Bhagavan Das, and Mike Diamond are creating an East-West fusion that is surging over the air waves and enlivening dance clubs and yoga centers around the world. This music communicates that devotion to the Divine is hip—that it's a good thing that it also makes you feel good. As

Laswell says, "This is music played in the spirit of devotion, it is not music for the sake of style. Like the Pakistani Kawali singer Nusrat Fatah Ali Kahn—he sang for God. He didn't perform for the audience. The audience might be there, but they were there to witness someone singing to the Divine. That's the difference."[16]

Listening to wonderful uplifting music is a good first step toward refining your ability to listen. The next step is to learn to allow external sounds to pass through your body and mind without affecting them.

Try this: Sit comfortably and close your eyes. Sitting still, don't do anything else; just listen. Usually, as soon as we hear something we stop hearing it and the judgmental mind categorizes it as good or bad. But as soon as we name something, we stop hearing it. When we think we know, we stop learning.

Try instead to just witness the external sounds, without naming them, without giving them a positive or negative quality. Allow them to sound. Hear the ticking of the clock, the sound of voices in the other room, the traffic in the streets, without blocking anything out. Just allow all sound to pass through your body and mind.

Mantra is a sacred syllable, particularly like the Vedic Pranavah OM, or it is a set of words beginning with OM whereby recitation and reflection occur for the attainment of a desired result, enlightenment, or spiritual realization.

—Swami Turiyasangitananda (Alice Coltrane)[17]

Now you are ready to practice listening *inside*. Just as mantra is used in pranayama to count the duration of the breath, we can use mantra in Nada Yoga to develop the ability to listen. The root sounds of mantras are not loaded with conventional meaning; they contain vibratory essential meaning.

Choose a mantra, such as *So Ham*, inhaling *So* and exhaling *Ham*. Or *Om Shri Durgayai Namah*, inhaling *Om Shri* and exhaling *Durgayai Namah*. Or *Shri Krishnaha Sharanam Mama,* inhaling *Shri Krishnaha*, exhaling *Sharanam Mama*. Or *Not my will, but Thy will, be done,* inhaling *Not my will*, exhaling but *Thy will, be done*. Silently chant the mantra, coordinating the repetition of the sound with the incoming and outgoing breath. The mantra doesn't necessarily have to be divided between inhale and exhale. You could also repeat the entire mantra on the inhale and then again on the exhale.

Whatever thoughts or distractions arise in the mind, let them come and let them go, give them no attention. Instead, give all your attention to the internal chanting of the mantra.

Work with this until your attention to the mantra is uninterrupted by any other thoughts, feelings, or sensations. At this point, allow the mantra sound to penetrate internally, then let go. Stop chanting the mantra and listen for the mantra to sound itself.

We vocalize a mantra externally or internally only to trigger the realization of the omniscient presence of the mantra. These sacred mantras permeate the external and internal atmosphere. They go on with or without the chanter. Mantras are the subtle forms of God.

I am Om.
***—Krishna in the* Bhagavad Gita *10:25*[18]**

Japa is the term used to describe internal or external mantra recitation. When japa begins to bear fruit, the yogi need not continue to chant mantra: the mantra will chant the yogi.

This will happen only after all the yogi's pride and arrogance have been resolved into humility. Once the body and mind of the yogi have been tuned, the mantra will play the yogi as its instrument. This happens only after much sincere and sustained practice over years and even lifetimes. Shyam Das tells a beautiful story about this in his book *The Lives of the Great Bhaktas of India:*

> One evening, two Bhaktas went to deliver some special items needed at the Krishna temple across the Yamuna River. It was late at night and there was no boat available. One of the devotees, whose name was Chachaji, explained to the other, who was traveling with him, "Wherever I place my feet on the water, you must step in exactly the same place. Then you will be able to walk on the water and we will both be able to cross the river and deliver the items to the temple."
>
> Chachaji walked on the water, taking Shri Krishna's name with every step. The other Bhakta placed his feet exactly where Chachaji put his, but when they were halfway across the river, the Bhakta thought, "Why should I place my feet where Chachaji puts his? I recite Shri Krishna's name just like he does."
>
> As soon as he placed his foot on the water where Chachaji had not stepped, he started to sink. Chachaji called out, "I told you to place your feet wherever I place mine. Why did you step elsewhere?"
>
> "I thought because I am also reciting Shri Krishna's name that I could place my feet on top of the water wherever I want."
>
> Chachaji explained, "Shri Krishna hears my recitation while he has yet to hear yours."
>
> Chachaji then took hold of his hand and pulled him out of the water and they both walked safely to the other side. On arriving at the temple they presented the necessary items to the storeroom manager. Then the Bhakta told the guru everything that had happened.

"What does it mean when Chachaji told me that Shri Krishna hears his recitation but has yet to hear mine?" he asked.

The guru explained, "Until Shri Krishna really accepts the soul, our remembrance and our sadhana remain unripe. Only when devotion is firm can one attain the reward of bhakti. Chachaji's recitation of mantra is solid. Its excellence has already been revealed to you."

"Can I see the greatness of Chachaji's mantra recitation?" the devotee asked.

"Go to his home, he will show you again," said the guru.

When the Bhakta went to Chachaji's home, he found Chachaji asleep, but he heard Shri Krishna's name resounding from every pore of his body.[19]

For the river of sound to flow freely through the yogi, the nadis must be clear and unblocked. To purify the nadis, sound current can be directed into the chakras, or energy vortexes, to cleanse them. In this purification technique, you concentrate your attention on each chakra, vocalizing its corresponding bija mantra, the sound essence of each chakra.

Bija means seed. When this seed sound is planted in the atmosphere it acts as a vibrational key that can open the chakra with which it is associated.

After externally sounding the bija mantra, silently chant the bija mantra while focusing on its associated chakra. The final stage is to listen for the sound of each bija mantra while meditating on each chakra. Once you hear it, move to the next level of consciousness, ascending upward toward Ajna Chakra.

Chakra	**Corresponding Location in Physical Body**	**Glands/Sense**	**Associated Element**	**Bija Mantra**
Muladhara	At the perineum	Suprarenal/ smell	Earth	LAM
Swadisthana	Below the navel	Gonads, prostate testicles, ovaries/ taste	Water	VAM
Manipura	Solar plexus	Pancreas, liver/ sight	Fire	RAM
Anahata	Heart	Thymus/touch	Air	YAM
Vishuddha	Throat	Thyroid/hearing	Ether	HAM
Ajna	Between the eyes	Pineal/intuition	Akasha	OM/(voiced)
Sahasrara	Crown of the head	Pituitary/I-AM	Akasha	OM/(unspoken)

Traditionally, the beginning stages of Nada Yoga require that the yogi forcefully shut out as many of the external sounds as possible. The *Hatha Yoga*

Pradipika advises the use of the hand position yoni or shanmukhi mudra to block out external distractions by closing the ears, eyes, nose, and mouth with the fingers and directing the attention inward (see page 216). You could also simply blindfold the eyes and use earplugs. Choose one of these two methods to help you draw the senses inward.

You will hear a sound. Once you hear it, don't classify it, don't judge it, go into the sound. Listen for the sound within the sound. Keep going inside each sound that you hear. Hear the sound inside your head that is most dominant. Let all other sounds go. Listen to that inner sound. Allow it to fill your entire consciousness, until your attention merges with the sound.

You will then become aware of another sound; repeat the process. Continue to delve deeper and deeper, uncovering layers of more and more subtle sound until you reach the innermost Nadam, the Pranavah, Om.

The *Hatha Yoga Pradipika* describes the sounds that a yogi may hear while practicing Nada Yoga. There are no rules governing which of these sounds the yogi may hear or how many or in what order. Shri Brahmananda Sarasvati describes these sounds in his book *Nada Yoga*:

> *Jhinjhin-nada:* This is a sound like the chirping of crickets or other grasshopper-like insects, like the sounds heard in the evening in the garden when the insects sing.
>
> *Vanshi-nada:* This is the sound of the flute, but it is different in frequency and charm from the flute of an orchestra.
>
> *Megha-nada:* This is the rumbling sound, similar to rumbling thunderclouds. Thus, it is called the thundering nada. It is frequently accompanied by clicking sounds so powerful that it can seem to the meditator that his bones are being realigned or even broken. Yet, with this sound, we experience a new electrical atmosphere.
>
> *Jharjhara-nada:* This is the sound like the rattle of a drum.
>
> *Bhramari-nada:* This is the sound like the humming of bees, quite musical and sonorous, as of certain beetles and bees.
>
> *Ghanta-nada:* This may be compared to the sound of church bells.
>
> *Turi-nada:* This is like the sound of gongs or large clanging cymbals.
>
> *Bheri-nada:* This includes sounds similar to the kettledrum, the trumpet, various other wind instruments, and high-pitched flutes.

Mrdanga-nada: This sound is like a military drum or a snare drum.

Tantri-nada: Various string instruments are heard in this state, like the violin, cello, sitar, vina, and harp.[20]

To the yogi, the world is quivering, vibrating energy moving in all directions. It is an unconventional act to witness vibration on such a profound level. It requires conviction and valor. To be a yogi means to step outside of the convention of "yours, theirs, and mine" and step into the heart, where unconditional Love resides.

Time and language are also conventions. Through common agreement, people decide to speak the same language. Time, also, is determined by local, national, and international convention. The yogi looks for the essential meaning behind these conventions.

Underlying time (kala), for instance, is pulsation. We feel pulsation in the step of our walk, in the movement of the breath, in the pounding of the heart and blood, and in the pulses of electricity through the nervous system. If we ground ourselves in these primordial rhythms and witness their circadian implications each day, the clock is relegated to its proper conventional usefulness and no longer dominates our existence.

The nada yogi longs to pulse with the inner pulse of life itself. The various yoga practices reveal where there is discord or disharmony in the body/mind. They are techniques for tuning this instrument, for rendering an ordinary body into an instrument for Divine Will. Through the practices of Nada Yoga, the yogi's mind becomes absorbed in the inner sound of Om, the bija mantra of the ajna chakra. Like a cobra attracted to the music of the flute, kundalini (consciousness), hearing Om, moves into the central channel, the sushumna nadi. The vibration of Om coming from the ajna chakra attracts kundalini upward, and she begins her ascent to higher consciousness.

The nada yogi is a virtuoso of life, a virtuous friend, with a sound body/mind harmonized with the Source. When the vehicle is tuned to Om, the true purpose of life is revealed: to surrender your individual self-centered will to the limitless realm of unconditional Love. Through this process the nada yogi becomes the embodiment of kindness, the liberator of countless beings.

Great is the intoxication of money, of physical power and strength, of name, fame and position. These are the ultimate intoxications of the relative world. But far greater still is the infinite bliss of anahata Nadam, which takes one beyond time and space and makes all temporal intoxications fade away, useless.

—Kabir[21]

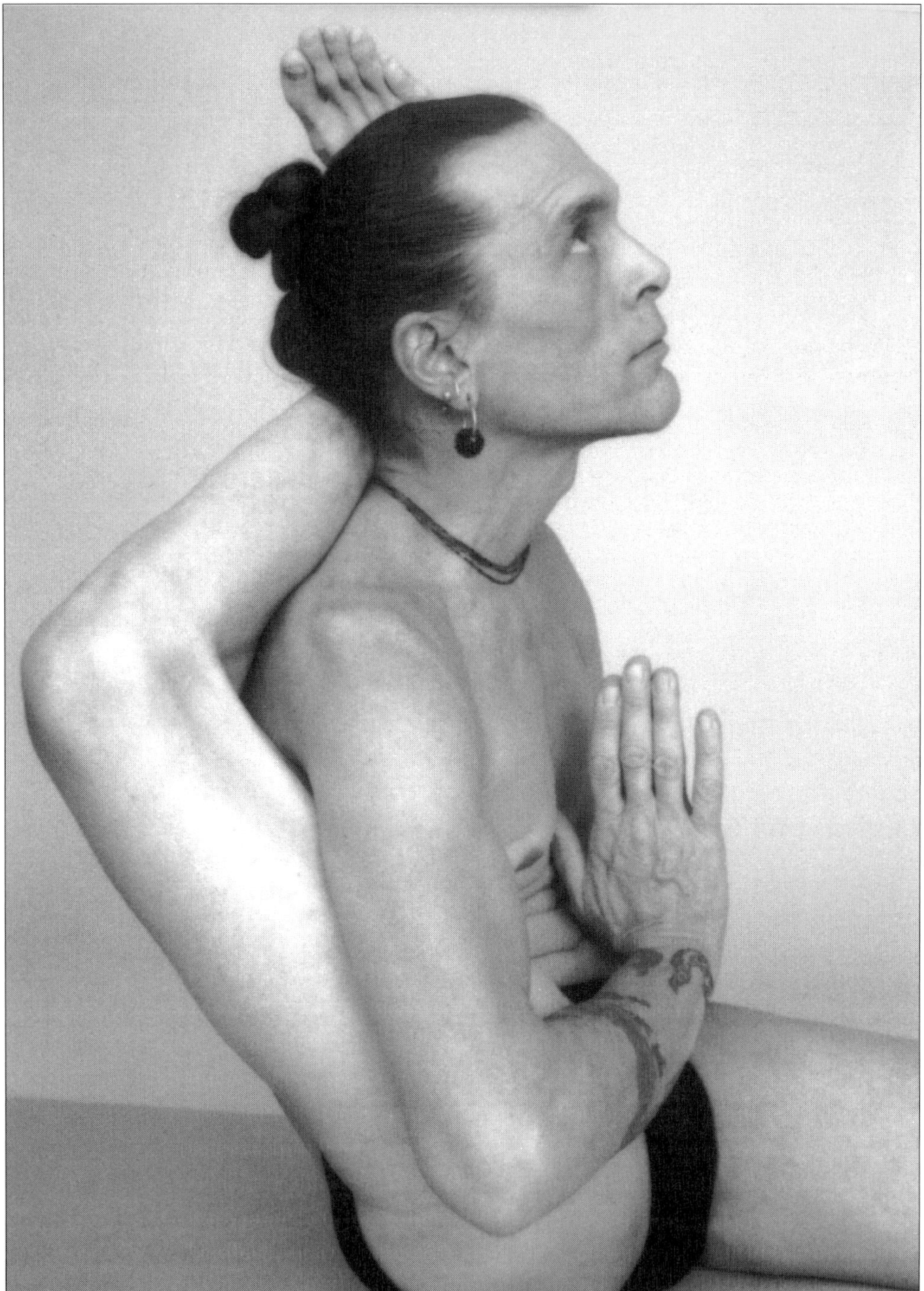

12

Bhakti: Becoming Love Itself

He was singing, dancing and shouting at a tremendous rate; now falling to the ground, now jumping up, and now twisting his body in varied contortions as if in convulsions; in a word, he was conducting himself in such a manner that anyone not acquainted with the manners of the Vaishnavas (those who worship the forms of Lord Vishnu) would think that the man had gone "daft." But the madder a Vaishnava is the holier he is deemed by the people.

—*Lal Behari Dey,* Bengal Peasant Life

Bhakti means "devotion to God." In Bhakti Yoga the practitioner cultivates desire for God. Bhakti Yoga is the most essential component of Jivamukti Yoga. To serve and get closer to God is the only reason to practice or to teach yoga. It was our desire to develop a devotional relationship to God that guided us over the years as we put together this method we named Jivamukti Yoga. We are bhakti yogis at heart. We felt from the beginning that without the desire for God, asana is meaningless exercise. Without devotion, Yoga cannot be attained.

The devotee longs only to love more and more, to enjoy eternally the lover/beloved relationship. Those who follow the path of devotion become purified through the intensity of their longing for God in whatever form appeals to them most.

—Krishna Das[1]

Devotion to God shows up several times in Patanjali's *Yoga Sutras* as Ishvara pranidhana.

Ishvara-pranidhanad-va. (YS I:23)
By giving your identity to God you attain the identity of God.

Tapah-svadhyaya-Ishvara-pranidhanani kriya yogah. (YS II:1)
Discipline, study of Self and devotion to God are the
actions taken for the attainment of Yoga.

Samadhi-siddhir Ishvara-pranidhanat. (YS II:45)
Union with cosmic consciousness is realized by devotion to God.

Patanjali says repeatedly that devotion to God is the most direct path to Self-realization. Devotion to God shows up again in Patanjali's second step, niyama, of the famous Ashtanga Yoga plan.

Patanjali is recommending the kind of faith that comes through complete surrender to God. There is an ancient Indian story from the *Mahabharata* that illustrates the power of total surrender to God.

Draupadi, the wife of the Pandava brothers, was humiliated in the court of a demon king in front of thousands of people when the king tried to pull off her sari. She lifted one hand upward to call on the Lord for help, but with her other hand she clutched her clothing. The Lord did not respond because her surrender was not total. Draupadi then lifted both hands toward heaven in a gesture of total surrender. Immediately God came to her assistance, wrapping her in an endless sari. If we devote ourselves completely to him, he will give himself completely to us.

Many modern yoga teachers and students contend that devotion to God is not important to yoga. They argue that these ideas are religious and that yoga is a philosophy, not a religion. We suggest that you familiarize yourself with the yogic scriptures such as the *Upanishads*, the *Yoga Sutras*, and the *Bhagavad Gita*, and arrive at your own conclusions.

One who has devotion for God is called a bhakta. It is through the method of Bhakti Yoga that the bhakta attains access to the form of the Divine that resides in his or her own heart. Devotion does not mean blind following. It means conscious seeking after the truth. How does one cultivate bhakti? Start by loving another being who is already near to you, such as your child or partner or friend. Make it a true love, a love that has the power to perceive the essential nature of this being you love. In Sanskrit, this kind of unconditional love is called *prem*, or Divine Love. To cause evolution of this prem inside yourself, use kindness. Begin to extend kindness to others who are not so near to you, to beings who don't resemble you, or who aren't even born yet.

If you can get that atmosphere of devotion going, then the spiritual path is fun and exciting. You won't even have to try, it will no longer be work but a part of your everyday life—a part of every moment.

—***Bhagavan Das,*** **It's Here Now (Are You?)**[2]

All relationships are important to the yogic practitioner because they provide an opportunity to feel love. They also provide opportunities to practice humility. Without humility, unconditional love will not arise. Working to perfect the relationships of everyday life helps the yogi to approach the ultimate relationship: the relationship with God.

Relationships can be cool and formal, or neutral, or hot and passionate. But all relationships take commitment and work to result in mutual happiness.

The relationships of life can be categorized as follows:

Servant and Master
Friend and Friend
Parent and Child
Lover and Beloved

These categories exist in ordinary daily life, but for the yogi they also exist in the subtle realms of the soul. According to your temperament and karmic imprints, one of these categories will appeal to you more than the others and dictate what type of relationship you could most readily cultivate with God.

Servant and Master: This is the relationship that most organized religions present to their followers. Worship God as if you were His servant and He was your Master. Or, as some more contemporary churches express it, as if you were working for Him and He was the Boss. This relationship may be a cool relationship, governed by fear and colored by power. For those whose tendency is to serve, however, this relationship offers a template for serving the Lord with humility. In this type of relationship, it is your humility that liberates you.

Friend and Friend: To have a relationship with God as a friend seems to be a little more relaxed than having God as your boss. Many people find this relationship uncomfortable, however, because it demands too much responsibility. Friendship takes work. You have to keep in touch on a regular basis. You have to be willing to share intimacies. In this type of relationship, it is this willingness to enter into an intimate friendship with God that liberates.

Parent and Child: To relate to God as if God were your child requires a pretty evolved soul. To cultivate this type of relationship, the bhakta has to be free from pride, like a loving mother who would sacrifice her own life for the life of her child. It seems that Mother Teresa might have had this relationship with God. She saw the sick and dying as Jesus and herself as a mother acting out of love to try to alleviate their suffering. She had tremendous strength because she had the strength that a mother has when she seeks to protect and care for her children. When you have this special kind of relationship with God, it brings out your tender aspects. You become tender and patient. You care for God, and this caring is what is liberating in this type of relationship.

The inverse of this relationship is when the bhakta becomes the child and sees God as the loving parent. The bhakta surrenders like a baby to God's care. These kinds of bhaktas have unwavering trust in God. They accept without question whatever happens in life, like a baby who sees the mother as the entire universe. Yogis who relate to God in this way see the whole universe as Divine. God provides everything and they live in a grace-filled world. The great saint Anandamayima was like this and always referred to herself as a little child. She would say things like "My body is aged but actually I am a small child."

Lover and Beloved: This is thought to be the most exalted relationship with God. As in the mundane world, we want to be loved by the perfect lover. The perfect love affair is one in which both parties feel equally desirous of the other. The yearning and desire for the other permeates and makes passionate the heart of the bhakta who is in love with God.

Love of God is not a duty for the bhakta who seeks to love and be loved; it is an obsession. The bhakta has a one-pointed focus, like one addicted; nothing can stand in his or her way. This is a hot relationship fueled by the fire of passion. This type of relationship, although most prevalent among

Vaishnavas (bhaktas who worship forms of Vishnu), is also found in other traditions. The Catholic mystic Saint Teresa of Avila had this type of relationship with Jesus. She said that he pierced her heart with a spear. Jesus was her lover, with whom she enjoyed ecstatic union. Rumi, the thirteenth-century Sufi mystic and poet, is another example. He described himself as a drunken lover intoxicated by the kiss of the Divine.

The nineteenth-century Indian saint Ramakrishna was ecstatically intoxicated with passionate yearning for the Divine. It was his closest devotee, Swami Vivekananda, who introduced yoga to the United States at the 1893 World Parliament of Religions in Chicago. Western practitioners owe a debt of gratitude to Vivekananda and ultimately to his guru, Ramakrishna, for this gift. Our heritage comes from a bhakti yogi, mad for God.

Ramakrishna was thought to be mad. His state was not ordinary madness, however, but mahabhava, or religious madness:

> In . . . the mood of erotic love he [Ramakrishna] identified with Radha [the beloved sweetheart of Shri Krishna] in her states of divine madness. He had a vision of Radha and wore a sari, gold ornaments, and artificial hair for six months. He regarded himself as one of the gopis of Vrindavan, mad with longing for their divine Sweetheart. In this love pursuit food and drink were forgotten. Day and night he wept bitterly.[3]

Ramakrishna further describes his experiences:

> Mahabhava is a divine ecstasy, it shakes the body and mind to their very foundations. It is like a huge elephant entering a small hut. The house shakes to its foundations. Perhaps it falls to pieces. . . . I was unconscious for three days in that state. I couldn't move. I lay in one place. When I regained consciousness, [my teacher] took me out for a bath. But my skin couldn't bear the touch of her hand; so my body had to be covered by a heavy sheet. Only then could she hold me with her hand and lead me to the bathing-place. The earth that had become stuck to my body while I was lying on the ground had become baked. In that state I felt as if a ploughshare were passing through my backbone. I cried out, "Oh, I am dying! I am dying!" But afterwards I was filled with great joy.[4]

Most of us are not as clear or as passionate about our devotion as Ramakrishna was. Most of us are still trying to decide where to direct our devotion—or whether we want to direct it anywhere at all.

You may be frightened of guru scenes or organizations. Or you may find it very easy to devote yourself wholeheartedly to a teacher. The panoply of Hindu deities may cause your heart to stir. Or you may still have affinity with an icon of the religion in which you were raised. Perhaps you do not believe in a god per se, but you have faith in enlightenment and the company of seekers.

It does matter to whom your devotion is directed. Your devotion should be directed to something higher than your own ego-self. Your devotion should stir your heart. Devote yourself to some form that, by mirroring your soul, shows you your inner wisdom, your highest potential for unconditional love.

Whatever form it takes, devotion is essential for the awakening of the soul. Because love is the nature of the immortal soul, do all you can to awaken your ability to love.

Bhava is the Sanskrit term used to describe the mood of one who is in love with God. This mood allows the practitioner access to deeper levels of the inner world of the soul. To the bhakta, the object of his or her love is God. The bhakta is in love with God and, like someone who is in love, can hardly wait for the next meeting with the beloved. As devotional singer Krishna Das describes this mood, "It's the evening. The sun is setting. My work is done. I am free now to turn to you again, my love. Come to me. Let me feel your touch on my cheek. Hold me in your arms and let me look into your eyes, your laughing, teasing, glowing eyes. Let me come to you, don't make me wait. I melt into you. I call your name."[5]

We all want to be known. God wants to know us. He wants us to know Him. There's a relationship here. It's romantic love. It's really simple. This is the truth. This is how it really works.

—*Bhagavan Das,* It's Here Now (Are You?)[6]

Although Patanjali clearly states that devotion to a form of God is necessary for Yoga, the sutras do not go into depth on the subject of God's nature. The *Srimand Bhagavatam*, an ancient text as old as the *Yoga Sutras*, does provide a detailed description of the nature of God. In this text He is referred to as Krishna, the all-attractive one who melts the hearts of His devotees. His mere glance is potent enough to fill the body with ecstatic waves of bliss. God is Bhagavan, a mischievous lover with mesmerizing seductive power.

This text personifies God quite differently from the *Bhagavad Gita*. In the *Gita*, God is on a dharmic mission, giving intellectual discourses on the nature of duty. But in the *Srimand Bhagavatam*, God shows us his heart. He is Krishna, the cow herder, the beloved who plays the flute and dallies with the soul. This charming Krishna turns the whole world into His *lila*, His playground. Krishna Das explains:

> The interaction of God and the devotee is called the Divine Lila. Lila is a Sanskrit term that roughly translates as "play." The moth, enjoying the light of the candle, flies closer and closer and finally is drawn into the flame. The devotee of God is the same, longing only to be closer and closer to the Divine Lover, to feel the warmth and ecstasy of that love. As the longing for the beloved grows more and more intense, the devotee experiences separation from the beloved so intensely that it obliterates all other suffering in life. Eventually, the devotee is drawn into the flame of Love and the mind dwells only on the beloved and sees Him/Her in everyone. This is Lila.[7]

As Krishna Das implies, devotion has two important elements: (1) identification, or a sense of belonging, and (2) separation, or a space within which to develop yearning and love.

Faith cannot exist without identification; no common ground is possible without an experience of the divine as something that is identifiable and potentially within our reach. At the same time, when there is no separation between the divine and the aspirant, there is no yearning; there is no "other" to be devoted to. In Buddhism, the compassion of the *bodhisattva*, the enlightened one, is not possible if merger is complete and no "others" exist to receive that compassion.

Others exist as an opportunity for us to practice kindness. When we are kind to others, we awaken our innate capacity to give, and it is this giving that liberates us. Kindness is the method for purifying the mind and thus liberating the soul. Looking to the welfare of others is the method for connecting to God.

To cultivate the desire to connect to God, bhaktas cultivate the sweetness of the pain of separation from God. We have all experienced separation from a loved one. We know the aching in the heart. We know the poetry that we hear in our yearning. We know what it is like to have visions of the beloved. From these experiences we can get a sense of what it must be like to yearn for closeness to God. The yogi fosters a sweet and sad yearning for the space of separation, knowing that it, too, is what is being searched for.

The yearning to transcend that space and reunite with the Divine fuels the efforts to move toward reunification and provides the landscape of spiritual life. Within the play of emotions between the longing for unification and the uncompromising surrender to the just-out-of-reach promise of it, the yogi finds equal reason to weep and seek total merger.

It is the yearning toward perfection, and the attainment of not-quite-perfection, that creates the chasm across which only the leap of faith can take us. The cultivation and savoring of yearning is essential to Bhakti Yoga. As Ramakrishna asked, "Wouldn't you rather taste sugar than become sugar?" When the quest is done there is no more yearning for the union, just union itself. To feel this yearning and understand that it is caused by isolation from the Source brings about the ecstatic vision of reunion.

When Swami Nirmalanda taught us to chant *Lokah Samasta Sukhino Bhavantu*, he tried to get us to sing it with a melancholy inflection. "When you sing to God there must be longing in your voice. A touch of sadness is good," Swamiji would say.

The best kirtan, or devotional, singers sing the blues. All the great kirtan singers we know have this lamenting quality in their voice. Their voice is deep, dark, and heavy. It's a sound characterized by the tamasic quality of stubbornness and the kind of intense attachment that leads to addiction.

In the mundane world of ordinary life and romantic love these qualities should be tempered or overcome. But when we move into the elevated world of spirit, these dark qualities take on a celestial sweetness that can result in addiction to God. To be addicted to God is to be possessed by ecstasy and boundless joy. The yearning in the voice that touches your heartstrings helps you recognize that the longing such singers express is the same longing we all feel in our hearts. It is the universal plea of the soul. It is the soul's yearning to go home.

Many times, I've wondered
If my heart will harden
Shadowed by the clouds
That hide the sun
A moment or a lifetime
Waiting in your garden
I see you in the distance
And I feel like crying out

—*Jai Uttal, Krishna Das, and Linde, "I Won't Ask for More"*

Kirtan is a yoga practice that reveals the heart. God lives within each of us, inside our hearts. Singer Jai Uttal says, "When we chant we are tearing open our chests, opening our hearts to reveal our true identity and finding God there."

We discovered the power of kirtan through Sharon's fascination with the ecstatic chanting of Bhagavan Das. She searched for all the information she could find about him. She discovered Ram Dass's classic 1971 book, *Be Here Now.* In this book we were introduced to the great bhakti saint, Neem Karoli Baba, or Maharaji, as his devotees called him. Even though Maharaji had left his body, there was a whole satsang of his Western devotees still around. Several of these devotees were mad with love for God and Guru and expressed their bhava, or mood of devotion, in the form of devotional singing or kirtan. Some kirtan recordings, which featured Bhagavan Das as well as Krishna Das and Jai Uttal, were available through the Hanuman Foundation.

Krishna says: I do not live in the eternal realms of Vaikuntha or in the hearts of jnana yogis. I go where my devotees sing my glories.

—Sirmand Bhagavatam[9]

Bhagavan Das singing
Photographer: Martin Brading

Soon we were practicing asanas while listening to devotional chanting by Maharaji's devotees. The music juiced up our own practice, so we felt it natural to share it with our students. We played this music to accompany the yoga classes we taught. Before long, we started to infuse our evening satsangs with devotional singing and kirtan. We never imagined, however, that these great singers would end up at Jivamukti Yoga Center someday!

Then one day a wild-looking American man, wearing a *dhoti*, a white piece of fabric tied around the waist like a skirt, got off a plane from India and walked into our yoga center, changing our lives forever. His name was Shyam Das. He was also a devotee of Maharaji. Shyam Das asked if he could lead a satsang at our yoga center. He led a wonderful kirtan-style satsang and

Shyam Das in Gokul, India
Photographer: Sharon Gannon

Jai Uttal
Photographer: Sharon Gannon

Krishna Das
Photographer: Carla Cummings

had us all singing Krishna's name with him in call and response. Still, only a few people were attending the satsangs at that time. The turning point came when Shyam Das suggested that we invite Jai Uttal to sing.

Jai had just released a CD on Triloka Records that we were playing in all the classes. We invited Jai to perform at our center and practically the whole student body showed up. There was a magical feeling in the air. Jai dazzled everyone as he walked in looking like a rock star, with long flowing hair and a voice that could croon as well as Sting's. Geoffrey Gordon accompanied him on drums and Charlie Burnham played violin.

Jai and "the band" were amazed to hear everybody singing along. "This doesn't usually happen when we play," Jai said, astonished. He didn't know that we had all been singing along to his tapes for years!

Krishna Das, who had produced Jai's CD, was in the audience that night. Unlike Jai Uttal, Krishna Das had concentrated for the past few years not on singing in public but on producing recordings for other people. He came to us with such humility and asked if he could come sing every week, adding that he used to chant in India at Maharaji's ashram. The next day Jai returned to California, but Krishna Das became the "house kirtan-wallah," leading kirtan at Jivamukti Yoga Center regularly on Monday nights.

A short time after the pivotal Jai Uttal concert, Bhagavan Das called us, at the urging of Shyam Das. Shyam Das had told him, "Hey, you should hook up with these nice people in New York. They have your picture on the altar and everybody stands on their heads while listening to you singing."

To be honest, we were a little apprehensive about meeting the man that Allen Ginsberg said, in his poem "Ah, Bhagavan Das Singing," "sits on floors to sing, closes his eyes and groans to God for hours, and can sing the blues, in Yogic Sanskrit like a perfect Virgin."[10]

Was the hype we had developed around Bhagavan Das for so many years going to match up to the real flesh-and-blood person? Well, Bhagavan Das came and gave the first of many concerts/satsangs at Jivamukti. He was everything and more than we had imagined.

With the help of these bhaktas, we developed a satsang at Jivamukti that was infused with such a mood of devotion that it made it easy for our students to feel comfortable joining in.

Never doubt that a small group of thoughtful, committed citizens can change the world; indeed, it is the only thing that ever does.

—Margaret Mead[11]

As Krishna Das says, "Whenever we enter into the heart we're all immediately in the same place together."[12] All you have to do at any kirtan is show up and listen, and perhaps you will sing spontaneously from your heart. You are not there to impress other people. This is a sadhana, a spiritual practice. It is an opportunity to reach into your own soul using the magic key that has been used for centuries to unlock the door to the heart: the name of God. The name of God is the same *as* God.

Jai Uttal adds, "We are all going on a journey together when we chant. The more each person reaches into his heart, the easier it is for the next person to do it. Because so many people have sung these chants for so many centuries, when we sing them, we plug into that energy field and are nourished by it. We derive strength, we're getting juice from centuries of people singing *Sita Ram*."[13]

Without the divine mood, none of this can happen. I think that's what's missing in the New Age movement. There's not a lot of divine mood going on. There's only a lot of hustle going on, more buying and selling.

—Bhagavan Das,* It's Here Now (Are You?)*[14]

Chanting the Names of God is one of the devotional practices that can dissolve the feeling of separateness from the Beloved. Chanting utilizes the body, mind and emotions. But here is the mystery: What we experience as the longing for God, is really God pulling us from within, pulling us into Him/Herself. There is only One and we are already part of that One, but we think we are separate.

—Krishna Das[15]

Song, dance, chanting and prayer have been throughout the ages traditional forms of Bhakti Yoga. *There are many levels at which you can participate in these rituals. At first such rituals are matters of curiosity and you are the observer. Then you arrive at the stage of peripheral participation—a "sing-along." Then in time you become familiar with the routines and you start to identify with the process. As your identification deepens, other thoughts and evaluations fall away until finally you and the ritual become one. At that point the ritual has become the living process and can take you through the door into perfect unity. To know that these stages exist does not mean that you can jump ahead of where you are. Whatever stage you are in, accept it. When you have fully accepted your present degree of participation, only then will you start to experience the next level.*

—Ram Dass, Be Here Now[16]

At first, the Sanskrit chants may seem too complicated to follow. If you drop your defensiveness, however, and open your heart, you will begin to pick them up. Listen, and allow yourself to respond.

What excites us most about having bhakti yogis visit is how they are able to charge the atmosphere. Even after they physically depart, a devotional vibe lingers that helps to elevate the mind of everyone who enters into the space they occupied.

This mood of love or bhava is essential to any yoga practice. To have this element taken away would leave us flat and without the inspiration necessary to continue. Any yoga practice has to be a labor of love. It has to turn your heart on or it's just not worth doing. For us, music expresses this yearning mood more than words ever could, so we have made music an important part of Jivamukti Yoga. The devotional chants sung by Bhagavan Das, Krishna Das, Jai Uttal, and others, whether live or recorded, permeate our classrooms, reminding our students of the deep sweetness of devotion.

All the saintly people we have ever met, regardless of what form of God they worshiped, chanted God's name. This chanting is called *nama-kirtana*. It is a powerful method of transforming the contents of the mind. Where your mind goes, so goes your reality. If your mind dwells on God from moment to moment, well, there you are!

Bhakti Yoga is cultivation of desire for God. Without this single-pointed desire, God remains a concept in the mind. Only the fire of emotion elevated to devotion can melt away the faithlessness of our hearts, which have been hardened by years of intellectual bondage. When the river of tears floods the mind, the soul is carried to the shores of the Divine Heart, there to drop into the embrace of the Beloved.

Home at last, Oh Lord, I's home at last.
—Traditional Black spiritual

Or, as Shri Brahmananda Sarasvati might have said, *"Home at last, Oh Lord, I-AM 'OM' at last."*

Appendix I: Asana Charts

In the charts that follow, each asana is assigned a number from 1 to 4. This is an indication of the relative difficulty of the asana when compared to others in the same group and across all groups. It is difficult to assign these values to the asanas because a particular posture may be difficult for one person and easy for another. You should give a relative value to the assignments according to your individual needs and proclivities. Our intent is not to provide an asana encyclopedia, but to provide enough information so that you can start putting together sequences.

Neutralizers

These postures help to neutralize the effect of an asana without moving the prana in the reverse direction.

Corpse—Shavasana	1
Child's Pose—Bheki	1
Standing forward bend—Uttanasana	1
Downward-facing Dog—Adho Mukha Svanasana	1
Mountain—Samastittih	1
Goddess Pose—Reclining Baddha Konasana	1
Squatting position	1
Star—Tarasana	1

Standing Postures

Mountain, Steady standing—Tadasana, Samastittih	1
Standing forward bend—Uttanasana	1
Seat of Isis	1
Tiptoe Asana	1
Triangle—Utthita Trikonasana	2
Extended side angle—Utthita Parsvakonasana	2
Rotated triangle—Parivritta Trikonasana	2
Rotated side angle—Parivritta Parsvakonasana	2
Standing forward bend, pulling toes—Padangusthasana	2
Standing forward bend, stepping on palms—Pada Hastasana	2
Standing straddle forward bend A, B, C, D—Prasarita Padottanasana A, B, C, D	2
Awkward Pose—Utkatasana	2
Rotated Awkward Pose—Parivritta Utkatasana	2
Warrior 1, 2—Virabhadrasana 1, 2	2
Standing forward bend over one leg—Parsvottanasana	2
Crocodile—Makarasana	3
Half bound Lotus forward bend—Ardha Baddha Padmottanasana	3
Tree—Vrksasana	3
Eagle—Garudasana	3
Standing Split—Urdhva Prasarita Ekapadasana	4
Standing on one leg balance—Utthita Hasta Padangusthasana	4
Warrior 3—Virabhadrasana	4
Balancing Marichyasana	4
Half Moon—Ardha Chandrasana	4
Standing forward bend, foot behind head—Ruchikasana	4
Foot behind head, standing up—Durvasasana	4

Sidebending

Seated sidebend	1
Standing sidebend, feet hip-width	1
Triangle—Utthita Trikonasana	2
Rotated triangle—Parivritta Trikonasana	2

Extended Angle—Utthita Parsvakonasana	2
Reclining side leg stretch	3
Sidebending Tree—Parsva	3
Vrkasana—Anantasana	3
Gate—Parighasana	4
Side inclined plane holding toe, leg straight—Vasisthasana	4

Forward Bends

Standing forward bend—Uttanasana	1
Dog Pose—Adho Mukha Svanasana	1
Standing forward bend—Padangusthana, padahastasana	1
Staff Pose—Dandasana	1
Standing forward bend over one leg—Parsvottanasana	1
Simple squat	1
Standing Split—Urdhva Prasarita Ekapadasana	2
Star—Tarasana	2
Seated forward bend—Paschimottanansana	2
Full Boat—Paripurna Navasana	2
Half Boat (knees bent, or back near floor)—Ardha Navasana	2
Head of knee down—Janu Sirsasana	2
Ankle to Knee	2
Standing Straddle—Prasarita Padottanasana A, B, C, D	3
Seated straddle forward bend—Upavistha Konasana	3
Cowface—Gomukasana	3
Great Seal—Maha Mudra, holding big toe, bandhas, janusirsasana	3
Seated half bound Lotus forward bend—Ardha Baddha Padma (A.B.P.) Paschimottanansana	3
Standing half bound Lotus forward bend—A.B.P. Padmottanansana	3
One leg straight, one knee up, arms wrap—Marichyasana A	3
One leg Lotus, one knee up, arms wrap—Marichyasana B	3
One leg straight twisting, one knee up, arms wrap—Marichyasana C	3
Cobbler's Pose—Baddha Konasana	3
Big toe standing balance—Ubhaya Padangusthasana	3
Reclining leg stretch toward head—Supta Padangusthana	3

Reclining leg stretch toward head—Supta Trivikramasana	3
One leg Virasana forward bend— Triang Mukha Haika Pada Paschimottanasana	3
Heron—Krounchasana	3
Compass Shooting Bow—Akarna Dhanurasana	3
Backward somersault—Chakrasana	4
Tortoise—Kurmasana	4
Sleeping Tortoise—Supta Kurmasana	4
Sleeping Yogi—Yoganidrasana	4
Garland—Malasana	4
Fetus in the Womb—Garbho Pindasana	4
Balancing forward bend—Urdhva Mukha Padangusthasana (open)	4
Balancing forward bend—Urdhva Mukha Paschimottanansana	4
One foot behind the head—Eka Pada Sirsasana	4
One foot behind the head, bend—Skandasana	4
Two feet behind the head—Dwi Pada Sirsasana	4
One foot behind the head reclining—Bhairavasana	4
Side inclined plane, foot behind head—Kala Bhairavasana	4
Moonbird—Chakorasana	4
Standing, bending forward, foot behind head—Ruchikasana	4
Standing, foot behind head—Durvasasana	4
Leg in Virasana, other knee up, arms wrap—Marichyasana E, F	4
Foot behind head, other knee up, arms wrap—Marichyasana G, H	4
Foot behind head, arms behind, sitting up—Buddhasana	4
Foot behind head, arms behind, forward bend—Kapilasana	4
Foot behind head, other leg in Lotus, arms behind—Viranchyasana A	4
Foot behind head, other leg in Virasana, arms behind—Viranchyasana B	4
Chinese Split—Samakonasana	4

Backbending

Goddess Pose—Reclining Baddha Konasana	1
Gathering Together—Crawling	1
Snake	1
Praying Snake	1

Warrior 1—Virabhadrasana 1	1
Locust—Shalabhasana	1
Lunge	1
Tabletop	1
Inclined plane—Purvottanasana	1
Hero—Virasana	2
Reclining Hero—Supta Virasana, with head on floor Paryankasana	2
Upward-facing Dog—Urdhva Mukha Svanasana	2
Fish—Matsyasana	2
Upward facing thunderbolt—Supta Vajrasana	2
Peacock—Mayurasana	2
Lotus peacock—Padma Mayurasana	2
Fish with straight legs and arms raised—Uttana Padasana	2
Frog—Bhekasana	2
Cobra—Bhujangasana	2
Lion—variation in full lotus, Simhasana	2
Bow—Dhanurasana	2
Bow on side—Parsva Dhanurasana	2
Dancing Shiva—Natarajasana without shoulder rotation	3
Camel—Ustrasana	3
Split—Hanumanasana	3
Bridge—Setu Bandhasana	3
Wheel, upward-facing bow—Urdhva Dhanurasana	3
Pigeon—Kapotasana	4
Full Bow—Padangustha Dhanurasana	4
King Pigeon—Rajakapotasana	4
Split Pigeon—Eka Pada Rajakapotasana	4
Dancing Shiva—Natarajasana with shoulder rotation	4
Pigeon in lunge—Kapotasana variation	4
Side inclined plane with one leg in full Bow—Kapinjalasana	4
Reclining Frog—Supta Bhekasana	4
Drop Back—Urdhva Dhanurasana 2	4
Wheel with arm and leg raised on one side—Eka Pada Urdhva Dhanurasana	4

Baby Wheel with hands to knees—Laghuvajrasana	4
Swan, peacock with fingers forward—Hamsasana	4
Tick-tocks—Viparita chakrasana	4
King Pigeon with back leg straight—Vilakhilhyasana	4
King Pigeon with leg in virasana—Eka Pada Rajakapotasana 3	4
Cobra holding knees with legs straight—Bhujangasana 2	4
Cobra holding knees with feet to head—Rajakapotasana	4
Half Frog, Half Bhekasana, half crossed dhanurasana—Gherandasana 1	4
One leg bound half Lotus, one in dhanurasana—Gherandasana 2	4
Grasshopper with feet to floor—Ganda Bherundasana	4
Locust with straight legs, feet on floor—Viparita Salabasana	4
Full Wheel (holding ankles)—Tiriang Mukhottanasana	4
Balancing on elbows/chin to palms—Sayanasana	4
Head stand with feet to head—Sirsa Padasana	4

Twists

Standing, hanging, Spinal Twist easy version, backbending counterpose	1
Reclining Spinal Twist with one knee bent	1
Reclining Spinal Twist with Garuda legs	2
Reclining Spinal Twist with straight legs	2
Seated Half Spinal Twist—Ardha Matsayendrasana	2
Seated Spinal Twist—Marichyasana C	2
Rotated Awkward Pose—Parivritta Utkatasana	2
Standing Spinal Twist—Parivritta Parsvakonasana	2
Rotated Triangle—Parivritta Trikonasana	2
Rotated Ankle to Knee	2
Standing Straddle Twist, holding ankle	3
Twisted Sidebend—rotated Janusirsasana	3
Twisted Sidebend—rotated Virasana leg open	3
Seated Spinal Twist—Marichyasana D	3
Spinal Twist squatting with legs together—Paschasana	3
Rotated Blossoming Lotus—Parivritta Vikasitakamalasana	3
Side Crow—Parsva Bakasana	3
Side Crow with both legs straight and together	3

Side Crow with both legs straight and top leg behind	4
Arm balance legs to side—Astavakrasana	4
Lotus Side Crow	4
Standing, hanging, Spinal Twist with back to legs	4
Twisting Forward Bend—Parsva Paschimottanasana	4
Full Spinal Twist (Lotus Pose)—Purna Matsayendrasana	4

Inversions

Downward-facing Dog—Adho Mukha Svanasana	1
Half shoulderstand—Viparita Karani	1
Fish—Matsyasana	1
Shoulderstand—Salamba Sarvangasana	2
Candle—Niralamba Sarvangasana	2
Shoulderstand with one leg in Halasana—Eka Pada Sarvangasana	2
Shoulderstand with one leg in Halasana, twisted—Parsvaika Pada Sarvangasana	2
Shoulderstand with hips twisting to one side, legs lowered to bridge—Parsva Sarvangasana	2
Shoulderstand with legs in Bridge—Setu Bandha Sarvangasana	2
Shoulderstand Bridge with one leg raised—Eka Pada Setu Bandha Sarvangasana	2
Shoulderstand with legs in Lotus—Padmasana in Sarvangasana	2
Shoulderstand with legs in Lotus, lowered to forehead—Pindasana in Sarvangasana	2
Plow—Halasana	2
Plow with knees to ears—Karnapidasana	2
Plow with legs straddle—Supta Konasana	2
Plow with knees to one side of head—Parsva Halasana	3
Inverted bow—Urdhva Dhanurasana	3
Bridge—Setu Bandhasana	3
Headstand—Salamba Sirsasana	3
Peacock Feather—Pincha Mayurasana	3
Headstand with legs lowered 90 degrees—Urdhva Dandasana	4
Arm variations in headstand, from tripod—Baddha Hasta, Mukta Hasta, 2, 3	4

Leg variations in headstand—Eka Pada, Parsvaika Pada, Urdhva Padmasana, Parsva Urdhva, Pindasana, Sirsa Padasana	4
Headstand with legs in Bridge—Dwi Pada Viparita Dandasana	4
Headstand with one leg in Bridge, one leg up—Eka Pada Viparita Dandasana	4
Headstand walking feet in a circle—Mandalasana	4
Peacock Feather with both feet in Bridge, holding heels—Chakra Bandhasana	4
Tick-tocks—Viparita Chakrasana in Urdhva Dhanurasana	4
Lotus Bridge—Uttana Padma Mayurasana	4
Scorpion—Vrschikasana	4
Handstand—Adho Mukha Vrksasana	4
Handstand Scorpion—Vrschikasana 2	4
Balancing on elbows, chin in hands—Sayanasana	4
Grasshopper with feet to floor on side of head—Ganda Bherundasana	4
Locust with feet over head, straight legs—Viparita Salabhasana	4

Balancing Postures

Tree—Vrksasana	1
Four-legged staff—Chaturanga Dandasana	1
Half Boat—Ardha Navasana back rounded or knees bent	1
Boat—Navasana	1
Reclining side leg stretch—Anantasana	2
Dangling Earring—Lolasana	2
Eagle—Garudasana	2
Half bound Lotus standing forward bend—Ardha Baddha Padmottanasana	2
Half Moon—Ardha Chandrasana	2
Balancing forward bend holding toes—Urdhva Mukha Paschimottanansana 1	2
Balancing forward bend chin to shin—Urdhva Mukha Paschimottanansana 2	2
Crow—Bakasana	2
Standing Split—Urdhva Prasarita Ekapadasana	2
Standing one-legged balance—Utthita Padangusthasana	2

Big toe standing balance—Ubhaya Padangusthasana	2
Warrior 3—Virabhadrasana 3	2
Arm balance, ankles crossed—Bhujapidasana	2
Side Crow—Parsva Bakasana	2
One leg over arm, one leg forward—Eka Pada Bhujasana	2
One-legged Tortoise Staff—Eka Pada Kurma Danda	3
Split—Hanumanasana	3
Firefly—Tittibhasana	3
Side Inclined Plane, holding toe—Vasisthasana	3
Side Inclined Plane foot in lotus—Kasyapasana	3
Side Inclined Plane, leg straight over arm—Visvamitrasana	3
Side Inclined Plane, foot behind head—Kala Bhairavasana	3
Rotated Half Moon—Parivritta Ardha Chandrasana	3
Crocodile—Nakrasana	3
Sage Astavakra balance—Astavakrasana	3
Embryo in the womb—Garbha Pindasana	3
Peacock—Mayurasana	3
Peacock Feather—Pincha Mayurasana	3
Flying Side Crow—Eka Pada Galavasana	3
Side Crow with both legs straight and together—Dwi Pada Koundinyasana	3
Side Crow with both legs straight and top leg behind—Eka Pada Koundinyasana 1	3
Side Crow with both legs straight and bottom leg behind—Eka Pada Koundinyasana 2	3
One leg Firefly, one leg Crow—Eka Pada Bakasana 2	3
Firefly 2—Tittibhasana 2	3
Lotus Peacock—Padma Mayurasana	4
Horse—Vatayanasana	4
Cowherd—Goraksasna	4
Flying Crow—Eka Pada Galavasana	4
Lotus Crow—Urdhva Kukkutasana	4
Lotus Side Crow—Parsva Kukkutasana	4
Lotus Crow with one knee inside arms—Galavasana	4

One-legged Crow—Eka Pada Bakasana 1	4

Seated Postures

Thunderbolt—Vajrasana	1
Easy Pose—Sukhasana	1
Half Lotus—Ardha Padmasana	1
Adept's seat—Siddhasana	2
Yogini's seat—Yoni Siddhasana	2
Dangling Earring—Lolasana	2
Balancing Lotus—Vikasitakamalasana	2
Hero—Virasana	2
Full Lotus—Padmasana	3
Scales—Tolasana (Lotus variation)	3
Yoni Mudra—Sanmukhi Mudra (Parangmukhi, Sambhava)	3
Heels up: forced arch—Yoni Asana	3
Mountain—Parvatasana	3
Rooster—Kukkutasana	3
Embryo in the womb—Garbha Pindasana	3
One foot in Mulabhandasana, one in Lotus—Vamadevasana 1	4
(from Pigeon) Press both feet in prayer to side—Vamadevasana 2	4
Yoga seal—Yoga Mudrasana	4
Yogi's staff—Yogadandasana	4
Sitting on feet, both heels forward—Mulabhandasana	4
(from Bhaddakonasana) Both feet to chest—Kandasana	4

Appendix II: Recommended Resources

Recommended Readings

A Garland of Forest Flowers, Swami Nirmalananda (Karnataka, India: Viswa Shanthi Nikethana, 1993).

Aghora, Vol. I, Robert E. Svoboda (Albuquerque, NM: Brotherhood of Life Inc., 1986).

Aghora, Vol. II, Kundalini, Robert E. Svoboda (Albuquerque, NM: Brotherhood of Life Inc., 1993).

Aghora, Vol. III, Karma, Robert E. Svoboda (Albuquerque, NM: Brotherhood of Life Inc., 1997).

A Gradual Awakening, Stephen Levine (New York: Doubleday Dell, 1979).

Animal Liberation, Peter Singer (New York: Avon Books, 1990).

A Path with Heart, Jack Kornfield (New York: Bantam Books, 1993).

Ashta Chhap, Shyam Das (Baroda, India: Shri Vallabha Publications, 1985).

Astavakra Samhita, Swami Nityaswarupananda (Calcutta: Advaita Ashrama Publications, 1994).

Ashtanga Yoga Primer, Baba Hari Das (Santa Cruz, CA: Sri Rama Publishing, 1981).

Autobiography of a Yogi, Paramanhamsa Yogananda (Self Realization Fellowship, 3880 San Rafael Avenue, Los Angeles, CA 90065; 1946).

Be As You Are: The Teachings of Sri Ramana Maharshi, David Godman, ed. (New York: Penguin, 1985).

Be Here Now, Ram Dass (Kingsport, TN: Hanuman Foundation, Kingsport Press, 1978).

Bliss Divine, Swami Sivananda (The Divine Life Society, PO Shivanandanagar Dist. Tehri-Garmul U.P. Himalayas, India; 1997).

Cats and Dogs Are People Too!, Sharon Gannon (New York: Jivamukti Press, 1999).

Diet for a New America, John Robbins (Tiburon, CA: H.J. Kramer, 1998).

Ethics for the New Millennium, His Holiness the Dalai Lama (New York: Riverhead Books, 1999).

Fundamentals of Yoga, Sri Brahmananda Sarasvati (New York: Harmony Books, 1995).

Foundations of Tibetan Mysticism, Lama Anagarika Govinda (New York: Samuel Weiser, 1971).

Four Articles by Shri Ramamurti, Shri Brahmananda Sarasvati (Monroe, NY: Bhagavandas Publications).

Grist for the Mill, Ram Dass (Berkeley, CA: Celestial Arts, 1987).

Hatha Yoga Pradipika (Ganga Darshan Munger, Bihar, India: Swami Muktibodhananda Sarasvati Bihar School of Yoga, 1993).

Health, Healing and Beyond, T.K.S. Desikachar (New York: Aperture Foundation, 1998).

Karma and Creativity, Christopher Chapple (Albany: State University of New York Press, 1986).

I Am That: Talks with Sri Nisargadatta Maharaj, translated by Maurice Frydman (Durham, NC: Acorn Press, 1973).

Inner Revolution, Robert Thurman (New York: Riverhead Books, 1998).

Interior Castle: St. Teresa of Avila, translated and edited by E. Allison Peers (New York: Doubleday, 1961).

It's Here Now (Are You?), Bhagavan Das (New York: Broadway Books, 1997).

Light on Yoga, B.K.S. Iyengar (New York: Schocken Books, 1966).

Light on Paranayama: The Yogic Art of Breathing, B.K.S. Iyengar (New York: Crossroad Publishing, 1999).

Nada Yoga, Sri Brahmananda Saraswati (Monroe, NY: George Leone Publication Center, Ananda Ashram Press, 1989).

Mandukya Upanishad, Sri Brahmananda Saraswati (Monroe, NY: George Leone Publication Center, Ananda Ashram, 1990).

Matri Darsham, translated by Atmananda, D. Schang, and Josette Herbert (Westerkappeln, West Germany: Mangalam Verlag S. Schang, 1988).

Miracle of Love: Stories about Neem Karoli Baba, Ram Dass (New York: Dutton, 1979).

Ramakrishna and His Disciples, Christopher Isherwood (Hollywood, CA: Vedanta Society of Southern California, 1965).

Sadhana, Swami Sivananda (The Divine Life Society, PO Shivanandangar Dist. Tehri-Garmul U.P. Himalayas, India).

Self-Analysis and Self-Knowledge, Ramamurti S. Mishra (Shri Brahamanada Sarasvati), (Monroe, NY: Baba Bhagavandas Publication Trust, 1977).

Sweet on My Lips: The Love Poems of Mirabai, Louise Landes Levi (Brooklyn, NY: Cool Grove Press, 1997).

The Compassionate Cook, PETA and Ingrid Newkirk (New York: Warner Books, 1993).

The Concise Yoga Vasistha, Swami Venkatesananda (Albany: State University of New York Press, 1984).

The Dreaded Comparison, Marjorie Spiegal (New York: Mirror Books, 1996).

The Elements of Yoga, Godfrey Devereux (Element, Inc., 42 Broadway, Rockport, ME 01966; 1994).

The Food Revolution: How Your Diet Can Help Save Your Life and Our World, John Robbins, (Berkeley, CA: Conari Press, 2001).

The Gospel of Sri Ramakrishna, Gupta Mahendranath, translated by Swami Nikhilananda (Mylapore, India: Sri Ramakrishna Math, 1980).

The Heart of Yoga, T.K.V. Desikachar (Rochester, VT: Inner Traditions, 1995).

The Inner Art of Vegetarianism, Carol Adams (New York: Lantern Books, 2000).

The Life and Teaching of Sri Anandamayima, Alexander Lipski (Delhi, India: Motilal Barnarsidass Publishers, 1977).

The Life of Milarepa, translated by Lobsang P. Lhalingpa (New York: Penguin, 1977).

The Living Gita, Swami Satchidananda (Buckingham, VA: Integral Yoga Publications, 1988).

The Yoga of the Bhagavad Gita, Sri Krishna Prem (Longmead, England: Element Books, 1988).

The Madness of Saints: Ecstatic Religion in Bengal, June McDaniel (Chicago: University of Chicago Press, 1989).

The Myths and Gods of India, Alain Danielou (Rochester, VT: Inner Traditions, 1964).

The Only Dance There Is, Ram Dass (New York: Doubleday, 1974).

The Ramayana, retold by William Buck (Berkeley, CA: University of California Press, 1976).

The Sunlit Path, The Mother, (Pondicherry, India: Sri Aurobindo Ashram Trust, 1984).

The Textbook of Yoga Psychology, Ramamurti S. Mishra (Sri Brahmananda Sarasvati) (Monroe, NY: Baba Bhagavandas Publication Trust, 1997).

The Tibetan Book of Living and Dying, Sogyal Rinpoche (New York: HarperCollins, 1993).

The Tibetan Book of the Dead, translated by Robert A. F. Thurman (New York: Bantam Books, 1994).

The Upanishads, translated by Juan Mascaro (New York: Penguin Books, 1965).

The Way of Compassion, Martin Rowe, ed. (New York: Stealth Technologies, 1999).

The World Is Sound, Nada Brahma, Joachim-Ernst Berendt (Rochester, VT: Destiny Books, 1983).

The Yoga of Spiritual Devotion, Prem Prakash (Rochester, VT: Inner Traditions, 1998).

The Yoga Sutras of Patanjali, Swami Satchidananda (Buckingham, VA: Integral Yoga Publications, 1978).

The Yoga Sutras of Patanjali, Georg Feuerstein (Rochester, VT: Inner Traditions, 1979).

The Yoga Tradition, Georg Feuerstein (Prescott, AZ: Hohm Press, 1998).

Vegan: The New Ethics of Eating, Erik Marcus (Ithaca, NY: McBooks Press, 1998).

Vegan Vittles: Recipes Inspired by the Critters of Farm Sanctuary, Joanne Stepaniak (Summertown, TN: Book Publishing Company, 1996).

Vegetarian Starter Kit (pamphlet), PETA, 501 Front St., Norfolk, VA 23510.

Who Dies?, Stephen Levine (New York: Doubleday, 1982).

Why Vegan? (pamphlet), Vegan Outreach, 211 Indian Drive, Pittsburgh, PA 15238.

Yoga Mala, Shri K. Pattabhi Jois (New York: Eddie Stern/Patanjali Yoga Shala, 1999).

Yoga, Alain Danielou (Rochester, VT: Inner Traditions, 1991).

Yoga the Iyengar Way, Silva, Mira, and Sham Mehta (New York: Knopf, 1990).

You Can Save the Animals, Ingrid Newkirk (Rocklin, CA: Prima Publishing, 1999).

Recommended Viewing

Diet for a New America, produced by EarthSave, Fox Lorber Associates, 419 Park Ave., New York, NY 10018.

Henry (Spira): One Man's Way, directed by John Swindells, produced by Peter Singer, 1997, Bull Frog Films, (800) 543-3764.

The Animals Film, directed and produced by Victor Schonfield and Myriam Alaux, 1987, SlickPics Int., Inc MPI Home Video, Oak Forest, IL 60452.

The Witness: Animal People Anthology Volume I, directed by Jenny Stein, produced by Tribe of Heart, Ltd., PO Box 149, Ithaca, NY 14851 www.tribeofheart.org.

What Is Yoga?, directed by Mary Bosakowski, produced by Jivamukti Yoga, distributed by Mystic Fire Video/Jivamukti, www.jivamuktiyoga.com, 1998.

Asana, Sacred Dance of the Yogis, choreography by Maher Benham and Sharon Gannon, film direction by James Carman, produced by Jivamukti, distributed by Mystic Fire Video/Jivamukti, www.jivamuktiyoga.com, 1998.

Recommended Listening

SPOKEN WORD: CASSETTES AND CDS

Moon over Morocco, audio drama by Tom Lopez, ZBS Productions, 174 N. River Road, Fort Edwards, NY 12828. ZBS@global2000.net.

The Fourth Tower of Inverness, audio drama by Tom Lopez, ZBS Productions, 174 N. River Road, Fort Edwards, NY 12828. ZBS@global2000.net.

Four one-hour Jivamukti Yoga classes with Sharon Gannon and David Life, produced by Jivamukti Yoga, 1997:

1. Intermediate/Advanced, music by Bhagavan Das, instructed by David Life.
2. Intermediate/Advanced, music by Krishna Das, instructed by Sharon Gannon.
3. Basic/Beginner, music by Bill Laswell, instructed by David Life.
4. Relaxation/Meditation, music by Bill Laswell, instructed by Sharon Gannon.

Chakra: The Seven Centers, story and music with David Life, Sharon Gannon, Willem Dafoe, Sarita Choudry, Bill Laswell, Zakir Hussain, produced by Janet Rienstra, Meta Records, 2000.

Jivamukti Lectures, recorded talks given at the Jivamukti Yoga Center:

The Silent Sage Speaks, Swami Nirmalananda, 1999.
Yoga and Buddhism, Robert Thurman, 1999.
Yoga and Buddhism Volume II, Robert Thurman, 2001.
Ahimsa and the Pig Story, John Robbins, 1999.
Ayurveda and Yoga, Robert Svoboda, 2001.
Opening the Heart, Krishna Das, 2001.
Telltale Heart, Krishna Das, 2001.
Why You Should Care About Animal Rights, Ingrid Newkirk, 2001.

Music: CDs

Bill Laswell, *Asana,* Meta Records, 1999.
Bill Laswell, *Asana II,* Meta Records, 2000.
Jai Uttal, *Beggars and Saints,* Triloka, 1994.
Bhagavan Das, *Bhagavan Das: Now!,* Mike D. Triloka, 2002.
Arjun Spinner, *Bhajananandi, Volumes 1, 2, 3,* People, People Int., 2001.
Gabrielle Roth, *Sundari,* Raven Records, 1999.
Deva Premal and Miten, *The Essence,* White Swan Music, 1998.
Alice Coltrane, *Turiya Sings,* Jowcol Music, 1982.
Alice Coltrane, *Divine Songs,* Jowcol Music, 1987.
Krishna Das, *One Track Heart,* Triloka, 1996.
Krishna Das, *Pilgrim Heart,* Triloka, 1998.
Krishna Das, *Live on Earth,* Triloka, 1999.
Krishna Das, *Breath of the Heart,* Karuna, 2001.
Jai Uttal, *Monkey,* Triloka, 1992.
Jai Uttal, *Shiva Station,* Triloka, 1997.
Sean Dinsmore, *Export Quality,* The Dum Dum Project, 2001.
Jai Uttal, *Footprints,* Triloka, 1990.

For a more complete listing of books, videos, CDs, and tapes, please contact Jivamukti for a free catalogue:

Jivamukti Yoga Center
404 Lafayette Street, 3rd floor
New York, NY 10003
1 (877) I AM YOGA
1 (877) 426-9642
www.jivamuktiyoga.com

Notes

Introduction: Putting It All Together

Epigraph: Walt Disney, "Walt Quotes," Walt Disney Company home page (www.Disney.com).

1. Robert Thurman, *Inner Revolution* (New York: Penguin Putnam, 1998), p. 281.
2. *Taittiriya Upanishad* 3:1–6, from *The Upanishads*, translated by Juan Mascarò (London: Penguin Books, 1965).

Introduction to Part 1

Epigraph: The Sky Cries Mary, "Chickaboom Cocktail," *Seeds,* Collective Fruit Records, 1999.

Chapter 1 Jivamukti Yoga: Putting Yoga Together in the West

Epigraph: Vidyaranya, *The Jivan-Mukti-Viveka,* quoted in "The Concept of Jivanmukti," by Paul Norman Cohen (Master of Arts in Religion thesis, McMaster University, Hamilton, Ontario, 1976), pp. 19–20.

1. Ishvarakrishna, *Samkhyakarika,* 2nd century B.C., as quoted on Internet.
2. Shri K. Pattabhi Jois, *Yoga Mala* (New York: Eddie Stern/Patanjali Yoga Shala, 1999), p. xiii.
3. His Holiness the Dalai Lama, *Life Space Death,* liner notes, produced by Bill Laswell, Meta Records, 2001.

4. Bhagavan Das, "I Was Born on the Wings of a Dove," *Bhagavan Das Live,* cassette, self-released, 1993.

Chapter 2 The Roots of Yoga . . . Back to the Source

Epigraph: Pandit Usharbudh Arya, *Yoga-Sutras of Patanjali with the Exposition of Vyasa (a Translation and Commentary)* (Honesdale, PA: Himalayan International Institute of Yoga Science and Philosophy of the U.S.A., 1986), vol. 1, p. 3.

1. Ramamurti S. Mishra (Shri Brahmananda Sarasvati), *The Textbook of Yoga Psychology* (New York: Julian Press, 1971), p. 173.
2. Ibid., p. 80.
3. The Mother, *The Sunlit Path: Passages from Conversations and Writings of the Mother* (Pondicherry, India: Sri Aurobindo Ashram Publication Department, 1984), p. 5.
4. Swami Nirmalananda, *The Silent Sage Speaks: Recorded Live at Viswa Shanthi Nikethan, BR Hills, South India,* cassette, released by Jivamukti Yoga Center, New York, 1999.
5. Deepak Chopra, *How to Know God* (New York: Harmony Books, 2000), p. 2.
6. Sankaracharya, *The Viveka Chudamani,* quoted in *The History of Yoga,* by Vivian Worthington (London: Arkana, 1989), pp. 117–118.
7. Swami Satchidananda, *The Yoga Sutra of Patanjali, Translation and Commentary by Sri Swami Satchidananda* (Buckingham, VA: Integral Yoga Publications, 1990), pp. 6–7.
8. Shri K. Pattabhi Jois, authors' interview, 1993.

Chapter 3 Karma: What You Think, Say, and Do

Epigraph: Shri Anandamayima, *Matri Darshar,* German-English ed. (Rastede, Germany: Mangalam Verlag S. Schang, 1983), p. 45.

1. Shri Anandamayima, *Matri Darshan,* p. 127.
2. Patanjali, *Yoga Sutras,* I: 33, translated by Ramamurti S. Mishra (Shri Brahmananda Sarasvati), *The Textbook of Yoga Psychology,* p. 148.
3. His Holiness the Dalai Lama, *Ethics for the New Millennium* (New York: Riverhead, 1999), pp. 162–163.
4. *Yoga Shikha Upanishad,* translated by Alain Danielou, *Yoga: Mastering the Secrets of the Universe* (Rochester, VT: Inner Traditions, 1991), p. 117.

Chapter 4 Ahimsa: Walking the Nonviolent Path

Epigraph: Martin Luther King, Jr.

1. False Prophets, "Baghdad Stomp," Alternative Tentacles Records, 1987.
2. His Holiness the XIV Dalai Lama, public lecture, Beacon Theater, New York City, 1999.
3. Ramamurti S. Mishra (Shri Brahmananda Sarasvati), *The Textbook of Yoga Psychology,* p. 205.
4. Swami Satchidananda, "Guided Relaxation and Affirmations for Inner Peace," cassette. Recorded at Satchidananda Ashram, Yogaville, VA. Integral Yoga Publications, 1986.

5. Thomas Edison, quoted in *Why Vegan?*, pamphlet (Vegan Outreach, 1999). Pittsburgh, PA.
6. *PETA Vegetarian Starter Kit* (Norfolk, VA: PETA, 2000).
7. John Robbins, author of *Diet for a New America,* from letter to authors, December 27, 2000.
8. Karen Davis, *Poisoned Chickens, Poisoned Eggs,* quoted in *Why Vegan?*
9. *Why Vegan?*, pamphlet (Vegan Outreach, 1999). Pittsburgh, PA.
10. John Robbins, letter to authors, December 27, 2000.
11. Excerpt from Associated Press article, September 20, 1996, reprinted in *Why Vegan?*
12. Mahatma Gandhi, quoted in *Why Vegan?*
13. Sting, "Fragile," *Nothing Like the Sun,* A&M Records, 1987, published by EMI Music/Magnetic Music.
14. George Bernard Shaw, *Living Graves,* quoted in *Why Vegan?*
15. Ingrid Newkirk, *You Can Save the Animals,* (Rockland, CA: Prima Publishing, 1999), p. xix.

Chapter 5 Guru: The Teacher You Can See and Feel

Epigraph: Indian proverb.

1. Georg Feuerstein, *The Yoga Tradition* (Prescott, AZ: Hohm Press, 1998), p. 20.
2. Shyam Das, conversation with authors, August 2000.
3. Robert Thurman, *Inner Revolution,* p. 33.
4. Swami Nirmalananda, *A Garland of Forest Flowers* (Bombay: R.V. Raghavan, Vindya Press, 1993), p. 19.
5. Ibid., p. 147.
6. Swami Nirmalananda, *The Silent Sage Speaks: Recorded Live at Viswa Shanthi Nikethan, BR Hills, South India.*
7. Swami Nirmalananda, *A Garland of Forest Flowers,* p. 153.
8. Ibid., p. 19.
9. Ibid., p. 147.
10. Shri K. Pattabhi Jois, conversation with authors, 1992.
11. Shri K. Pattabhi Jois, conversation with authors, September 2000.
12. Swami Vivekananda, quote seen by authors on old poster in India.
13. Ramamurti S. Mishra (Shri Brahmananda Sarasvati), *The Textbook of Yoga Psychology.*
14. Shri Brahmananda Sarasvati, *Keys to Nirvana-Tantram* (Monroe, NY: Baba Bhagavandas Publication Trust, 1998), pp. 14–15.
15. Shri Brahmananda Sarasvati, teachings heard by authors at Ananda Ashram satsangs.

Chapter 6 Prana: Freeing the Life Force

Epigraph: *Kaushitaki Upanishad* 3:2, quoted in Georg Feurerstein, *The Yoga Tradition,* p. 179.

1. *Hatha Yoga Pradipika: Light on Hatha Yoga,* translated by Swami Muktibodhananda

Saraswati (Ganga Darshan Munger, Bihar, India: Sri G. K. Kejriwal Honorary Secretary Bihar School of Yoga, 1993), p. 491.

2. Shri Brahmananda Sarasvati, *Nada Yoga* (Monroe, NY: ICSA Press, Ananda Ashram, 1989), p. 5.

Chapter 7 Asana: Giving Structure to the Desire for Yoga

Epigraph: Alan Watts, WBAI radio broadcast, October 1997.

1. *Ashtavakra Samhita,* I:18, translated by Swami Nityaswarupananda (Calcutta: Advaita Ashrama Publication Department, 1994), pp. 14–15.
2. Lama Anagarika Govinda, *Foundations of Tibetan Mysticism,* 3rd ed. (New York: Samuel Weiser, 1971), p. 76.
3. Bhagavan Das, *What Is Yoga?,* video, directed by Mary Bosakowski, produced by Jivamukti Yoga, distributed by Mystic Fire Video/Jivamukti, 1997.
4. "Is This a Bridge, Exactly?" *It Is This, It Is Not This,* Audio Letter, (Cityzens for Non-Linear Futures, 1987.)
5. Alan Watts, Upsala College lectures, broadcast on Upsala College radio.
6. Deepak Chopra, *How to Know God,* p. 147.
7. Bob Dylan, "I'll Keep It with Mine," *Bob Dylan, The Bootleg Series Volumes 1–3,* Sony/Columbia, 1991.

Chapter 8 Vinyasa Krama: The Forgotten Language of Sequencing Postures

Epigraph: Ramamurti S. Mishra (Shri Brahmananda Sarasvati), *The Textbook of Yoga Psychology.*

1. Ram Dass, lecture at Yuca Valley, CA, 1979.

Chapter 9 Kriya: Discipline, Study, and Devotion

Epigraph: The Mother, *The Sunlit Path,* p. 111.

1. Shri Brahmananda Sarasvati, *Terrestrial and Celestial Magnetism* (Monroe, NY: Baba Bhagavandas Publication Trust, 1996), pp. 4–5.
2. Robert E. Svoboda, *Prakruti: Your Ayurvedic Constitution* (Albuquerque, NM: Geocom Ltd., 1989), p. 4.
3. Ibid., p. 10.
4. Hugh Romney, quoted in *Diet for a New America: How Your Food Choices Affect Your Health, Happiness and the Future of Life on Earth,* by John Robbins (Tiburon, CA: H. J. Kramer, 1998), p. 284.
5. John Robbins, letter to authors, December 27, 2000.
6. Robert E. Svoboda, *Prakruti: Your Ayurvedic Constitution,* p. 10.

Introduction to Part 3

Epigraph: Audio Letter, "Is This a Bridge, Exactly," song, *It Is This, It Is Not This,* Cityzens for Non-Linear Futures, 1997.

Chapter 10 Meditation: Sitting in the Seat of the Soul

Epigraph: Swami Nirmalananda, *The Silent Sage Speaks: Recorded Live at Viswa Shanthi Nikethan, B.R. Hills, South India.*

1. Bhagavan Das, quoted in *Be Here Now,* by Ram Dass (New York: distributed by Crown Publishing, 1971), p. 10.
2. Bhagavan Das, *It's Here Now (Are You?)* (New York: Broadway Books, 1997), p. 307.
3. Ibid.
4. Ibid., p. 306.

Chapter 11 Nadam: Listening for the Unstruck Sound

Epigraph: Authors' translation.

1. *Chandogya Upanishad,* quoted in *The World Is Sound, Nada Brahma,* by Joachim-Ernst Brent, (Rochester, VT: Destiny Books, 1991), pp. 28–29.
2. Shri Brahmananda Sarasvati, *Nada Yoga,* p. 3.
3. Joachim-Ernst Brent, *The World Is Sound, Nada Brahma,* p. 137.
4. Bhagavan Shree Rajneesh, quoted in ibid., p. 141.
5. Robert Thurman, conversation with authors, October 19, 2000.
6. *Hatha Yoga Pradipika: Light on Hatha Yoga,* commentary by Bihar School of Yoga, 2nd ed. (Munger, Bihar, India: Bihar School of Yoga, 1993), p. 584.
7. *Plato's Republic,* translated with an introduction by Desmond Lee, 2nd ed. (London: Penguin Books, 1974).
8. Alan Watts, lectures, Upsala College, broadcast on Upsala College radio.
9. *Hatha Yoga Pradipika: Light on Hatha Yoga,* translated by Swami Muktibodhananda Saraswati (Gana Darshan Munger, Bihar, India: Sri G. K. Kejriwal Honorary Secretary, Bihar School of Yoga, 1993), p. 523.
10. *Sri Swami Satchidananda: Portrait of a Modern Sage,* edited by Dr. Prem Anjali and Sw. Sharadananda (Buckingham, VA: Integral Yoga Publications), p. 62.
11. Ravi Shankar, *My Music, My Life* (New York: Simon and Schuster, 1968), quoted in *The World Is Sound, Nada Brahma,* by Joachim-Ernst Brent, p. 154.
12. Ram Dass, *Be Here Now,* p. 74.
13. *The World According to John Coltrane,* director, Robert Palmer, Master of American Music Series, Toby Byron/Multiprises in association with Taurus Film, Munich, and Video Arts, Japan; BMG Video, a unit of BMG Entertainment, New York, 1993.
14. John Coltrane, *A Love Supreme,* liner notes, Jowol Music BMG, 1964.
15. Bill Laswell, interview with authors, October 12, 2000.
16. Ibid.
17. Swami Turiyasangitananda (Alice Coltrane), back cover of *Mantram* CD, Shaila Music (BMI), 1999.
18. Sri Swami Satchidananda, *The Living Gita* (Buckingham, VA: Integral Yoga Publications, 1997), p. 156.

19. Shyam Das, *The Lives of the Great Bhaktas of India,* unpublished manuscript.
20. Shri Brahmananda Sarasvati, *Nada Yoga,* pp. 16–17.
21. Kabir, quoted in ibid., p. 35.

Chapter 12 Bhakti: Becoming Love Itself

Epigraph: Lal Behari Dey, *Bengal Peasant Life,* quoted in *The Madness of the Saints: Ecstatic Religion in Bengal,* by June McDaniel (Chicago: University of Chicago Press, 1989), p. 29.

1. Krishna Das, *One Track Heart,* liner notes, Triloka Records, 1999.
2. Bhagavan Das, *It's Here Now (Are You?),* p. 308.
3. Mahendranath Gupta, *The Gospel According to Sri Ramakrishna,* translated by Swami Nikhilananda, quoted in June McDaniel, *The Madness of the Saints: Ecstatic Religion in Bengal,* p. 97.
4. Ibid.
5. Krishna Das, *One Track Heart,* liner notes.
6. Bhagavan Das, *It's Here Now (Are You?),* p. 305.
7. Krishna Das, *One Track Heart,* liner notes.
8. Jai Uttal, Krishna Das, and Linde, "I Won't Ask for More," *Monkey,* Triloka Records, 1992.
9. *From Sirmand Bhagavatam,* as told to authors by Shyam Das.
10. Allen Ginsberg, "Ah, Bhagavan Das Singing," liner notes to Bhagavan Das, *AH,* Bhagavan Das Music, 1971.
11. Margaret Mead, quoted in *Why Vegan?*
12. Krishna Das, conversation with authors, September 2000.
13. Jai Uttal, *Beggars and Saints,* liner notes, Triloka Records, 1994.
14. Bhagavan Das, *It's Here Now (Are You?),* p. 308.
15. Krishna Das, *One Track Heart,* liner notes.
16. Ram Dass, *Be Here Now,* p. 74.

Glossary

Note: In this book Sanskrit is rendered for general readership, without the use of diacritical marks for unseen letters. As for pronunciation, a few general rules are:

1. *a* is typically pronounced "ah."
2. *e* is typically pronounced like a long a ("hay").
3. The next-to-last syllable of a word typically receives the accent (example: abhinivesha is pronounced "abiniVAYsha").
4. *i* appearing at the end of a word is typically pronounced "ee" (example: shakti is pronounced "shaktee").
5. *c* is always pronounced "ch" ("chair").

abhinivesha excessive fear of death, one of the five *kleshas* or obstacles to Self-realization

abhyantara interior

Adisesha Endless, the serpent Ananta who gives support to Lord Vishnu

agami karma future karma

ahimsa nonharming; restraining your behavior toward others in such a way that you do not cause them harm with your thoughts, words, or deeds; the first yama from Patanjali's Ashtanga system. Ahimsa is the touchstone of all yogic practices.

ajna chakra the third eye center, located between the eyebrows; the abode of Shiva or Cosmic Consciousness

akasha space, subtlest ether

anahata chakra "unstruck wheel"; the subtle body energy center situated in the region of the heart and cardiac plexus, the fourth chakra

anahata nadam "unstruck sound"; the primal soundless sound

ananda bliss, ecstasy

Ananda Ashram spiritual center founded in 1964 by Shri Brahmananda Sarasvati; dedicated as a universal school for meditation and spiritual research; located about one hour from New York City in Monroe, New York

anandamaya kosha bliss body, causal (seed) body

anarchy Self-rule; true Self-rule means to be guided by the inner Divine Self, not motivated by the desires of ego. The philosophy of Self-rule is called anarchism.

anna food

annamaya kosha the physical body, which is composed of food; one of the five coverings of the soul

antar-kumbhaka "inward savoring"; inhale retention, holding the breath inside the body

apana downward-flowing prana or vital energy; one of the prana vayus, it flows from the navel to the feet; creative and eliminative energy

aparigraha non-hoarding, greedlessness; one of the five yamas from Patanjali's *Yoga Sutras*. Patanjali suggests that those who wish to attain Yoga restrain their behavior toward others by not being greedy and by sharing.

apocalypse the uncovering, the revealing

Arjuna a hero prince, one of the Pandava brothers, who is on the battlefield with his chariot driver, Shri Krishna. *The Bhagavad Gita* (The Song of the Lord) is the discourse between Arjuna and Shri Krishna.

asamprajnata without seed, *nirbija samadhi;* the second stage of *samadhi* or superconscious ecstasy

asana seat, posture, connection to the earth; the third limb of Patanjali's Ashtanga system

ashram forest retreat, place for spiritual practice

ashtanga eight-limbed

Ashtanga Yoga Patanjali's eight-limbed path, also called *Raja Yoga*; also the "brand name" for the style of yoga developed and taught by Shri K. Pattabhi Jois of Mysore, South India

Ashtavakra Samhita ancient scripture written by the sage Ashtavkra in the form of a dialogue between King Janaka and Ashtavakra. The teachings it expounds are pure monistic Vedanta.

ashwini mudra "mare seal"; contraction of the anal sphincter muscle (not *mulabandha*)

asmita ego identification, egoism, individualism; one of the five *kleshas* or obstacles to Yoga or Self-realization

asteya non-stealing; one of the five *yamas* from Patanjali's *Yoga Sutras*. If you wish to attain yoga, Patanjali suggests, don't steal.

astral bodies coverings of the soul more subtle than the physical body but not as subtle as the body of bliss. The three astral bodies are composed of vitality, emotions, and intellect.

Atha yoganushasanam The first sutra from Pantanjali's *Yoga Sutras*, in which the introduction to the exposition of yoga is stated: "Thus proceeds yoga as I have observed it in the natural world."

atithi the guest whose arrival date is unknown

Atman the Divine Self, the in-dwelling soul; that which identifies with the absolute *Brahman* rather than the limited form of body and mind

Atman jnana knowledge of the Self; identification with cosmic consciousness, not with ego personality

Audio Letter musical band founded in 1979 by guitarist Sue Ann Harkey and vocalist-violinist Sharon Gannon. "[Audio Letter] is not really an art band but an anti-rock performance group. All A.L.'s musical material is improvised. Its members do not sing; they intone and chant. Sharon Gannon repeats phrases until they become exempt from meaning, acting only as sounds or spells." (From an article by Gary Reel, *Art Express,* May–June 1981, p. 81). The group disbanded in 1988 after recording the album *It Is This, It Is Not This,* which featured musicians Denis Charles, Don Cherry, and David Life.

avidya misknowing; ignorance of one's true identity, which is the Divine Self

ayama unrestrained, expansion

ayurveda the science of life; the ancient Indian system of medicine and healing

bahya-kumbhaka "outer savoring"; exhale retention; holding the breath outside the body

bandha lock or tie; a psychokinetic energy lock used to direct the flow of *prana*

basti enema; one of the *shat karmas*, which are the six purification techniques of Hatha Yoga

Bhagavad Gita *The Song of the Lord,* written circa 200 B.C., is an episode from the epic *Mahabarata* composed by the sage Vyasa, in which Krishna explains to the warrior Arjuna the methods for attaining Yoga. Bhakti and Karma Yoga are emphasized. Alongside Patanjali's *Yoga Sutras*, and *Hatha Yoga Pradipika*, this is the essential reference book for the practices of yoga.

Bhagavan Das (1945–present) kirtan singer, devotee of the Divine Mother in the form of Kali Ma; featured in the book *Be Here Now* by Ram Dass; author of *It's Here Now (Are You?)*; disciple of Neem Karoli Baba

Bhagwan Shree Rajneesh (1931–1990) also known as Osho; Self-realized master

bhairavi mudra "Demoness seal"; Bhairavi is the name of one of the ten shaktis of Lord Shiva. She represents the power of death, which is continuously with us throughout life. This mudra helps to overcome abinivesha (fear of death).

bhakta one who is devoted to God

bhakti devotion to God, love of God

Bhakti Yoga the yoga that is attained through surrender and devotion to the Lord

bhava from the Sanskrit root *bha* meaning state, condition of being; a state or mood characterized by waves of intense emotions generated by a connection to the Divine

bija seed; the contained vibratory essence

bindu the point of immortality

Bodhananda, Swami spiritual name given to David Life after he was initiated into the order of *sanyaas* by Swami Nirmalananda. The name means the "bliss of higher intelligence."

bodhisattva a Buddhist term used to describe one who has attained Nirvana, or enlightenment; one who has realized the True nature of the Self but, instead of enjoying the ecstasy that accompanies *samadhi*, vows out of compassion to live among the unenlightened to assist them in their journey toward realization

bolo positive exclamation

Brahma the creative aspect of the Hindu trinity

Brahma bandha binding and directing the *prana* (life force) toward the Supreme Consciousness

brahma granthi "creator knot"; lowest blockage of energy, situated between *muladhara* (root) and *svadisthana chakra* (sexual center)

brahmacharya literally, reaching for *Brahman*; the fourth *yama* from Patanjali's *Yoga Sutras*, which refers to sexual conduct. The yogi's sexual relations should have an underlying intention of moving toward enlightenment and should not be engaged in to enhance power or ego.

Brahmadev, Swami director of Viswa Shanthi Nekethana, Swami Nirmalananda's Ashram in B.R. Hills, Karnataka, India

Brahman from the Sanskrit root *bri*, which means to expand; the eternal, changeless reality; that which transcends all forms

brahmin the priestly caste, the highest of the four castes of Hinduism

bri to expand, become large, to praise; the Sanskrit root sound from which the terms *Brahma* (God the creator) and *Brahman* (the Supreme Consciousness, God) are derived.

Buddha the awakened one; Gautama, the Buddha. Hindus consider him to be an avatar, an incarnation of Lord Vishnu.

causal body seed body; refers to the most subtle covering of the soul, the *anandamaya kosha*, which is made up of bliss

chakra "wheel"

Chandogya Upanishad one of the major *Upanishads*, which are the ancient foundation scriptures from which the philosophy of *Vedanta* is derived

chin mudra "awareness seal," performed by joining the thumb and forefinger together at their tips. This mudra coalesces *prana* and directs it toward realization.

chittam mind stuff

chitta-vritti the fluctuations and whirlings of the thinking mind

chutney Indian-style relish; may be sweet, salty, or hot; used as a condiment

darshana 1. sight or vision; 2. point of view or perception. Hinduism has six philosophical systems or *darshanas*.

das servant

deva one of the shining gods of Hinduism

devi one of the radiant goddesses of Hinduism

dhana to give, or direct toward; as in *pranadhana*, which means to give or direct the *prana* (life force)

dhara place

dharana concentration that leads to meditation, or *dhyana*

dharma-megha-samadhi rain cloud of knowledge; the highest form of *samadhi* or superconsciousness; from Pantanjali's Yoga Sutra IV:29

dhauti washing; one of the *shat karma kriyas*

dhoti traditional Indian male garment, usually made of white cotton cloth, wrapped around the lower body

dhyana the meditation state; absorption, continuous focus of attention on one object

diksha formal initiation into a spiritual practice or lineage

Divine transcendental, beyond the mundane world; heavenly, celestial

Divine Mother a title for god as Goddess

Divine Self highest Self, highest consciousness principal, *Brahman*

Divine Will Higher Will, devoid of selfish ego motive; God's will; the desire for that which is the most good

doshas "flaws"; the three humors of *ayurveda*: *kapha*=phlegm, *pitta*=bile, and *vata*=air

drishti gaze

dukha "bad space," limitation, suffering; opposite of *sukha* (happiness)

dvesa hatred, aversion for things unpleasant; one of the five *kleshas* or obstacles to Yoga or Self-realization, enlightenment

ego individual personality self

enlightenment Self-realization; liberation from individualization, the ecstatic experience of oneness with the Divine Source

Gautama (150 B.C.?) the name of the Buddha; also the name of the exponent of the Nyaya school of philosophy, one of the six philosophical systems of India

Geranda Samhita medieval source text for Hatha Yoga

God the Divine, the highest principal, *Brahman*

Gopal cow-boy; name for the youthful *Shri Krishna*

Gopi cow-girl. In Sanskrit *go* means cow, senses; *pi* means to move or to herd. In a mystical sense, a Gopi is a soul who can move the senses toward God; in a more esoteric sense, she can herd the cows.

granthi a block located in the subtle body that blocks the flow of prana, obscuring enlightenment. The three granthis must be pierced before realization can occur.

guna quality; three gunas make up the manifest world of Mother Nature: *sattva* (lightness), *rajas* (activity), and *tamas* (inertia)

guru the remover of darkness, teacher

Guruji affectionate name for a teacher or guru. Putting a *ji* at the end of someone's name shows familiarity and affection.

Ham *bija mantra* for the *vishuddha chakra*

Hanuman "jaw man"; Lord Shiva incarnated as *Hanuman*, the monkey god featured in the classical Hindu epic, *The Ramayana*. He exemplifies the perfect devotee, one whose heart and mind are always on God and whose every action is done out of love for God. The great saint Neem Karoli Baba was thought by his devotees to be an incarnation of Hanuman.

Harappa site of a second millennium civilization located in the Indus River Valley; in the present day this area is located in the northwest of India

Hatha Yoga *Ha:* sun; *tha:* moon; *yoga:* yoking; the yoking of the sun and the moon; the yoga that is obtained through forceful means of disciplining the physical body so as to cleanse the subtle nerve channels, the *nadis*. When the body is sufficiently purified, *kundalini shakti* or consciousness is awakened and ascends upward through the *chakras*, or levels of consciousness, to the seat of the Self, the abode of joy in the *ajna chakra*. Hatha refers to the dual state made up of all the pairs of opposites: male/female, pleasure/pain, good/evil, night/day, left/right. When these preferences are overcome, the boundless Self manifests in the yogi.

Hatha Yoga Pradipika *Light on the Sun and Moon Union;* fourteenth-century source scripture, a manual for Hatha Yoga written by Swatmarama

Himalayan pertaining to the Himalaya mountain range; sacred mystical mountains. The two most famous mountains are Mount Everest, the highest in the world, and Mount Kailash, home to Lord Shiva. Located at the junction of the Indian subcontinent and Eurasia.

himsa harm

himsic harmful, that which causes pain and suffering

Hindi language spoken in most northern states of India; uses the same script as Sanskrit

Hinduism Sanatana Dharma, the universal Truth, the religion of the people who lived near the Indus River Valley. Generally speaking, besides having been born a Hindu, there are four concepts that determine whether or not one is a Hindu: belief in moksha (liberation), the law of karma, reincarnation, and vegetarianism.

Hindustani someone or something of Indian descent or origin, from the subcontinent of India

homa fire sacrifice, ancient Vedic ritual; intended to purify the one who is performing it. Common offerings include grain and ghee, which are given to the fire while mantras are recited.

I-AM the supreme Cosmic Self

ida nadi "moon stream"; the left, cool energy channel

Ishvara the Lord; God in form

Ishvara pranidhana giving one's life force, *prana*, to the Supreme Lord; devotion to God; from Pantanjali's sutra I:23

Isis Egyptian goddess, wife-sister of Osiris, mother of Horus, the younger. She is the personification of what "Is." She is the earth, the world of manifestation. The worship of Isis was very popular not only with the ancient Egyptians but among the Romans as well.

jagrat the waking state of consciousness; the world of objective reality

jalandhara bandha "cloud-catching lock," commonly known as "chin lock"; one of the three bandhas used in Hatha Yoga practices

Jamini exponent of *Purva Mimamsa*, one of the six classical philosophical schools of India

japa mantra repetition, sometimes done with prayer beads *(mala)*

jaya victory to! Hail!

Jaya Gurudev "victory to the one who removes darkness and opens the door for enlightenment"

jiva the individual self, the unenlightened soul

jivanmukta one who is enlightened to the true nature of being, while still living

jivanmukti living liberated; the state of one who is a jivanmukta, who identifies with *Brahman*, not with body/mind consciousness

Jivan-Mukti-Viveka fourteenth-century text written by Vedanta philosopher Vidyaranya, whose work draws heavily from Valmiki's *Yoga Vaisistha*. The *Yoga Vaisistha* is the first major text expounding on the concept of *jivanmukti*.

jnana knowledge; could pertain to worldly knowledge, *jnana vritti,* or knowledge of the Divine Self, *atman jnana*

Jnana Yoga the yoga obtained through the discriminating power of the intellect and through *svadhyaya*, study of the Self; one of the four types of yoga, the others being Bhakti, Karma, and Raja

Jois, Shri K. Pattabhi (1914–present) one of the principal students of Shriman T. Krishnamacharya; lives and teaches in Mysore, Karnataka, South India; codified a system of yoga called Ashtanga Yoga

Kabir (1440–1518) bhakti poet born into a Muslim family of cloth weavers. He converted to Hinduism.

kaivalyam aloneness; the highest state of *samadhi* or enlightenment; absolute liberation from all that is not real

kala time

Kali fierce Hindu Goddess who destroys the devotee's attachment to ego *(asmita)*; aspect of the warrior goddess *Durga*

Kali Yuga "dark age"; our present era; according to Hinduism, it is the last of the four age cycles. It is generally thought to have begun with the death of Krishna, 3006 B.C. It is typified by spiritual decline. Satsang and chanting of the name of God are thought to be the most direct practices that lead to Self-realization in this era.

Kanada exponent of Nyaya, one of the six classical Indian philosophical systems

kapalabhati "skull shining"; a Hatha Yoga purification technique, using the exhaling of the breath; one of the six *shat karmas*

Kapila exponent of Samkhya, one of the six classical Indian philosophical systems

karma from the Sanskrit root, *kr,* which means action. Generally speaking, karma is any action: thought, word, or deed. The Law of Karma is the law of cause and effect: for every action there is a reaction.

Karma Yoga the yoga attained through selfless service, renouncing the fruits of one's actions, and performing actions with pure intention, devoid of selfish motive. The karma yogi realizes that God is the only "doer."

Kaushitaki Upanishad ancient scripture containing a detailed explanation of the doctrine of reincarnation. It also sheds light on the Divine nature of *prana.*

kevala kumbhaka "motionless savoring"; spontaneous cessation of breath

Khan, Hazrat Inayat (1882–1926) Sufi mystic, renowned master of north Indian music, a nada yogi who proclaimed that the knower of the mystery of sound knows the mystery of the whole universe; father of Vilayat Inayat Kahn, who carried on his father's work of spreading Sufism in the West

kirtan from *kir*, "to cut"; devotional singing in a call-and-response format, usually chanting the name of God or sacred mantras

klesha obstacle to liberation, an affliction of the mind. In the *Yoga Sutras*, Patanjali describes five *kleshas*: *avidya* (misknowing), *asmita* (ego identification), *raga* (attachment to pleasure), *dvesa* (aversion, hatred of that which is unpleasant), and *abinivesha* (fear of death).

kosha sheath or covering

kr to act

krama the succession (of transformations) that occurs from moment to moment

Krishna "the one who attracts"; beloved Hindu God, avatar of Lord Vishnu

Krishna Das (1947–present) devotee of Neem Karoli Baba (Maharaji); inspiring and much-loved kirtan singer who has been instrumental in infusing American yoga with the element of devotion or *bhakti*

Krishnamacharya, Tirumalai nineteenth–twentieth century South Indian yogi, scholar, doctor, bhakta. He is guru to four of the most influential yoga teachers of the twentieth century: K. Pattabhi Jois, B.K.S. Iyengar, T.K.V. Desikachar, and Indra Devi. Thought to be the greatest yogi of the twentieth century.

kriya from the root *kr*, which means action; a specific action taken for purification purposes

Kriya Yoga the yoga that is attained through the means of purification actions that cleanse the body and mind in preparation for Self-realization. According to Patanjali, Kriya Yoga is composed of *tapas*, *svadhyaya*, and *Ishvara pranidana*.

ksana a timeless moment

kundalini consciousness; in the unenlightened, said to lie in a dormant state coiled like a snake in *muladhara chakra*. As enlightenment begins to dawn, consciousness moves upward through the central channel, *sushumna,* and the energy vortexes called *chakras*; her destination is the abode of Shiva, the *ajna chakra* (third eye center).

lam *bija mantra* for the *muladhara chakra*

law of karma the law of cause and effect: every action has built into it a reaction

Laxmi Hindu goddess of affluence, abundance, wealth, prosperity, and beauty. She represents the bountiful aspect of Nature. Also known as "Shri"; consort to Narayana; associated with water. She is the ever-giving generous mother. Her devotees please her through acts of kindness, compassion, and generosity. She bestows power, pleasure, and prosperity on those who respect the laws of life and strive to live in harmony with all of existence.

lila "play"; divine manifestation or projection

madhyam medium

maha big or great

maha bandha a practice in which one applies the three *bandhas—mula bandha, uddiyana bandha,* and *jalandhara bandha*—on the exhale retention *(bahya-kumbhaka)*

mahabhava "the great mood," when one has become intoxicated with the ecstasy of union with God, *samadhi*

Maha Prabhu "Great Lord"; prefix commonly used for the great fifteenth-century *bhakti* saint Shri Chaitanya

manas mind. This term is thought of as heart/mind, as it includes the emotions.

manipura chakra "jewel-town-wheel"; energy center situated in the subtle body at the location of the solar plexus

manomaya kosha the mental sheath or covering of the *Atman*; one of the five bodies that cover the Self

mantra "mind traverser or protector"; a word or phrase that has transcendental power

marga path

maryada that which is limiting

maryada marga the path of effort or discipline

mauna silence; a yogic practice in which one refrains from external speech to begin to control one's thoughts

maya measure, condition; the illusory power of the Divine; that which veils, limits, and conceals

meditation *dhyana,* absorption, uninterrupted concentration on one object; the seventh limb of Patanjali's Ashtanga system

moksha liberation

Mother, The (1878–1973) spiritual collaborator with Sri Aurobindo, was simply known as The Mother to her devotees. In 1926 The Mother took full charge of the Aurobindo Ashram and remained as its head for almost fifty years. She conceived of and built Auroville, a utopian community outside of Pondicherry.

mudra seal

mukta one who is liberated from *avidya*

mukti the state of one who is liberated from *avidya*

muladhara root place

muladhara chakra the root *chakra* (energy vortex) located at the base of the spine; doorway to *sushumna nadi*

nada(m) sound current, primal vibration *(shabda)*, the sacred mantra *Om*

Nada Yoga the yoga that is attained by hearing the *nadam (Pranavah* or *Om)*; practiced by listening for the unstruck sound

nadi river, current, rushing, sounding, stream; subtle channels for the flow of *prana* (life force). There are 72,000 *nadis* in the subtle human body. The flow of *prana* through these channels is what animates the physical body. There are three main *nadis*: *ida* (left), *pingala* (right), and *sushumna* (center).

Nadi Shodhana "channel cleaning"; *pranayama* technique that purifies and balances the *nadis* through alternate nostril breathing

nama-kirtana *nama* means name; nama-kirtana means singing the names of God

namaskar formal greeting; way to acknowledge the shared sacred divinity within each being; performed by pressing both palms together at the heart center. In doing so, you are saying: "The divine that resides in my heart bows to the same God who resides in your heart."

namaste a less formal expression of the greeting *namaskar*

nauli one of the *shat karma* techniques of Hatha Yoga; the muscles of the abdomen are isolated and used to massage the internal organs

Navasana boat seat

Neem Karoli Baba (1900?–1973) twentieth-century Vrindavan saint known as an incarnation of Hanuman. This guru taught many people the value of a simple life of devotion and humility. He was continuously chanting "Ram." Guru to Bhagavan Das, Krishna Das, Jai Uttal, Ram Dass, Baba Hari Das, and Shyam Das. His life and teachings are presented in the books *Be Here Now* and *Miracle of Love* by Ram Dass.

neti "nose cleaning"; one of the *shat karma* techniques of Hatha Yoga. To perform *jala neti*, water is poured into one nostril and allowed to flow out the other. In *sutra neti* a string is inserted into one nostril and pulled out through the mouth.

nirbija samadhi literally: *samadhi* without a seed; the second level of *samadhi*; *Asamprajnata Samadhi*

Nirmalanda, Swami (1925–1997) Self-realized saint from Kerala, South India. After touring the world, he lived for over thirty years secluded in the forests of B.R. Hills outside of Bangalore, Karnataka, South India. His *sadhana* included the practices of *mauna* (silence), meditation, and *ahimsa* (nonviolence). His commitment to *ahimsa* motivated his active involvement in social action. Through his prolific letter writing, he communicated with heads of state on an international level. He took *prayopavesha* (self-willed death) on January 10, 1997.

nirodha restriction, ceasing, stopping

niyama observances; the second limb of Patanjali's Ashtanga system; actions that the yogi takes concerning himself or herself. There are five *niyamas*: *saucha, santosha, tapas, svadhyaya,* and *Ishvara pranidhana.*

Om the sound symbol for God *(Pranavah)*; the most powerful mantra, the primal sound, the *Nadam*

Om Namah Shivaya "I bow to Lord Shiva the benevolent, who has the power to transform through destruction."

Om Shri Durgayai Namah "I bow to the beautiful Goddess Durga, the one who is difficult to reach."

Padmasana lotus seat; seated asana performed by crossing the legs into the shape of a lotus flower. This pose stimulates the *nadis* so that *prana* can flow into *sushumna* during meditation practice.

parabda karma present karma

paramapara lineage

Pashupati "protector of the animals"; an ancient form of Shiva found on the Harappa seals discovered in the Indus river valley

Patanjali sage considered an incarnation of the divine Serpent, *Adisesha*, *Sesha*, or *Ananta*, who supports the whole universe; compiler of the *Yoga Sutras*, considered the founder of Yoga philosophy. There is disagreement as to when he lived, with speculations ranging from 3,000 B.C. to 300 B.C.

physical body the outer material body, composed of food, the *annamaya kosha*

pingala nadi "sun stream"; right, hot, male energy channel

Prakriti Mother Nature, composed of three qualities called *gunas*: *tamas*, *rajas*, and *sattva*

prana life force, vitality. There are five *pranas* called *prana vayus: prana*, *apana*, *undana*, *samana*, *vyana.*

pranamaya kosha the vital sheath, the energetic body

pranayama (life force) + *yama* (restriction), or *prana* (life force) + *ayama* (to set free); to restrict the life force and/or set it free; the fourth limb of Patanjali's Ashtanga system.

pratyahara the practice of pulling the senses inward toward their source in preparation for concentration and meditation; the fifth limb of Patanjali's Ashtanga system

pravahi worldly

prayopavesha self-willed death. As opposed to suicide, which is prompted by anger, despair, disappointment, or sadness, *prayopavesha* is performed by one who is in an elevated state of Yoga. The method used most often is to refrain from the taking of food and drink until the physical body ceases to function.

prem Divine Love

puja ritual worship through making offerings to the Divine, in the form of a deity or guru; an important devotional practice

puraka inhale

Purusha pure spirit, the transcendental Self

Purva Mimamsa one of the six classical philosophical systems of India; concerned with Vedic ritual

pushti well-nourished, fat, fat from grace

pushti marga the path of grace

raga (1) desire, excessive attachment to pleasure; according to Patanjali, *raga* is one of the five *kleshas* or obstacles to enlightenment. (2) from the root *ranj*, which means to color or to tinge with emotion. Indian music is based on *raga*, an order of notes and sound that elicits a certain mood or emotion in the listener.

rajas passion, dynamic activity, movement outward, external creativity; one of the three *gunas*

ram *bija mantra* for the *manipura chakra;* when capitalized, the name of the avatar of Lord Vishnu, hero of the *Ramayama: Ram*

Ram Dass born Richard Albert in 1931; American psychology professor at Harvard. During the 1960s he was active in research on consciousness with Timothy Leary. In 1967 Dass went to India, where he met Bhagavan Das and Guru Neem Karoli Baba; authored the classic book, *Be Here Now,* which profoundly shaped the Western spiritual awakening that emerged in the early 1970s; founded the Hanuman Foundation.

Ramakrishna (1836–1886) nineteenth-century Bhakti saint from Bengal, India; devotee of Mother "Kali." Through his chief disciple, Swami Vivekananda, the philosophies of Yoga and Vedanta were first brought to America in 1894.

Rama Mohan Brahmacharya nineteenth-century Shri T. Krishnamacharya's guru from the Himalayas

Ramana Maharshi (1879–1950) Self-realized *jnana* yogi from Tamil Nadu, South India. His method of Self-inquiry consisted of the search for the answer to the question "Who Am I?"

rechaka exhale

rishis forest-dwelling, Self-illuminated sages who acted as channels for the divine wisdom of the yogic scriptures. Their revelations came through in the form of hymns and poems.

roga illness

Rose, Tara (195?–present) New York–based yoga teacher, studied in the Sivananda lineage; Sharon Gannon's and David Life's first yoga asana teacher

Rudra tear; the one who cries, the wailer; one of the many names for *Shiva*

rudra granthi Shiva knot; uppermost energy blockage in the subtle body between the *vishudda* (throat) and the *ajna chakra* (third eye)

sabija samadhi literally, *samadhi* with seed; first level of *samadhi, samprajnata*

sadhana conscious spiritual practice

sadhu renunciate; one who has taken vows of *sanyaas*, renouncing the activities of the world to search within for *atman jnana* (knowledge of the Self)

sahasrara chakra "thousand-petaled lotus wheel"; energy center in the subtle body located at crown of head

sakshi "the one with eyes"; the witness

Salamba Sarvangasana *salamba* = supported + *sarv* = all + *anga* = parts, limbs + *asana* = seat; "supported all parts seat" (supported shoulderstand)

samadhi "same as the highest"; *sam* (same) + *adhi* (highest); ecstasy, bliss; enlightenment, Self-realization, cosmic consciousness

samana vayu "even breeze"; diffusive vital energy; one of the *prana vayus*

samavritti "same turning"; even breathing

Samkhya enumeration; one of the six classical systems of Indian philosophy; deals with the creation of matter descending from the most subtle to the gross. Yoga is the reverse, as it is concerned with ascending from the outer or grossest levels to the most inner, subtle level of being.

samprajnata first level of *samadhi*; *sabija samadhi*, with seed

samsara suffering individualization; the wheel of birth and death, suffering

samskaras grooves or impressions that are etched onto the covering of the soul by every karma or action taken

Sanatana Dharma the universal Truth, commonly known as Hinduism, based on the wisdom of the *Vedas*

sanchitta karma past karma that has accumulated over lifetimes

Sankaracharya (A.D. 788–820) one of the five great teachers *(acharyas)* or proponents of the Vedanta system of philosophy. His commentaries have been widely translated into Western languages. Because of this, most Westerners equate Vedantic philosophy with the views held by Sankaracharya and don't compare his with the views of the other four *acharyas*.

Sanskrit the ancient language of India; a potent vibrational language with the inherent power to invoke what is spoken

Sant Khesavadas Self-realized saint from Bangalore, South India; disciple of Swami Sivananda from Rishikesh

sanyaas initiation into a monastic order; one renounces worldly activities to seek within

Sarasvati the *shakti* or energy of *Brahma*, the creator. She is the goddess of learning, music, science, and the arts. She plays the celestial *vina*; her vehicle is a white swan.

Sarasvati, Shri Swami Brahmananda (?–1993) twentieth-century Self-realized saint from Uttar Pradesh, North India. At the height of a successful medical career he devoted himself to teaching the means to Self-realization primarily through the study and practice of yoga, Sanskrit, and meditation. He founded Ananda Ashram in Monroe, New York, and the Yoga society of San Francisco, Brahmananda Ashram. He is the author of the definitive text on the *Yoga Sutras* of Patanjali: *The Textbook of Yoga Psychology*. He left his body September 1993.

satchitananda true existence, knowledge and bliss; the attributes of the Supreme Self

Satchidananda, Swami (1914–present) twentieth-century Self-realized saint, disciple of Swami Sivananda from Rishikesh; Satchidananda founded the Integral Yoga Institute, which has centers throughout the United States; author of many books, including commentaries on the *Yoga Sutras* of Patanjali; gave the opening talk at the 1969 Woodstock Festival and was instrumental in bringing Eastern philosophy to the 1960s youth culture. He lives in Yogaville, Buckingham, Virginia; known for his gentle ways and exceptional extemporaneous speaking, which is a brilliant weave of wisdom and wit.

satsang *sat* = Truth + *anga* = attachment or limb; attachment to the Truth; association with those who remind you of your True potential

sattva balance, lightness, purity, movement toward the inner; one of the three *gunas*

sattvic having the qualities of *sattva*; lightness, purity, desiring to move toward that which is enlightening

satya "being real"; truthfulness, honesty

shakti feminine power of the Divine; force of nature or *Prakriti*

Shankarananda, Swami (1949–present) twentieth-century disciple of Swami Vishnudevananda. For many years Shankarananda was director of the Sivananda Yoga Ranch in upstate New York. Shankaranada is endowed with a deep understanding of the philosophy and science of yoga and its application to the modern world. He continues to be a charismatic and inspiring teacher.

shastra authoritative text on any subject, particularly science or religion

shastric taken from a teaching or a textbook of teachings

shat karma "the six acts"; Hatha Yoga techniques for cleansing

shauca "shining"; cleanliness

Shiva the destroyer; the third deity in the Hindu trinity of gods. He is the god who gave the teachings of yoga to the world through his first student, Matsyendranath

shraddha faith in God, guru, and scriptures

shravana "hearing"; to know or learn through hearing; real listening

Shree Ma twentieth-century Indian woman saint; lives at Devi Mandir, her ashram in Napa Valley, California

Shri (1) name for the goddess *Laxmi*: (2) divinely beautiful, used as a respectful preface to a name

Shri Anandamayima (1896–1982) twentieth-century female Bengali ecstatic *bhakta*

Shri Krishnaprem Western swami, devotee of Krishna; wrote commentary on the *Bhagavad Gita* that was a favorite among the Neem Karoli Baba *satsang*

Shri Krishna Sharanam mama "Sri Krishna, the beautiful attractor, is my refuge."

Shyam Das (1953–present) devotional singer, a devotee of Lord Krishna in the lineage of Shri Vallabhacharya; traveled to India, where he met his guru, Neem Karoli Baba; Sanskrit scholar, speaks Hindi as well as the ancient language of Shri Krishna, Braja Basha; one of the few English translators of the teachings of Shri Vallabhacharya and an initiate of the Pushti Marga lineage

siddha "finished one"; master with supernatural powers

Siddhasana "the master's seat"; after *Padmasana*, the most important asana, according to the *Hatha Yoga Pradipika*

siddhi "completion, accomplishment"; powers resulting from yoga practice

Sivananda, Sri Swami (1887–1963) Self-realized saint, founded the Divine Life Society in Rishikesh. As a medical doctor, he found that he was administering only to the symptoms of suffering, so he renounced his career and devoted himself to eradicating the cause of suffering through spreading the teachings of Yoga and Vedanta. He was a prolific writer and wrote in English. Among his many gifted disciples are Swami Satchidananda, Swami Vishnu-devananda, and Swami Sivananda Radha.

sloka a scriptural verse, could be a poem or a mantra

soul the essence of a being

speciesism a prejudicial regard for specific species of animals; a commonly held bias (among humans) that human animals are the only ones that have rights (or souls), and that all other animals are here to benefit human beings

Srimand Bhagavatam tenth-century Sanskrit scripture that relates Shri Krishna's life story. It is also known as the *Bhagavata-Purana*.

sthira steady, stable

sthit unmoving, stable, steady, unaffected by physical distraction or thoughts

sukha "sweet space"; spaciousness, happiness, opposite of *dukha* (suffering)

Sur Das fifteenth-century blind poet; one of the eight poets who formed Ashta Chhap, a group of bards founded by Vallabacharya to sing the praises of Shri Krishna

sushumna "sweet shrine"; central energy channel of the subtle body, most important *nadi* to the *hatha yogi*

sushupti unconscious deep sleep; one of the three states of normal consciousness

sutra "thread"; teachings given in terse concise statements

svadhyaya "moving toward one's own"; Self-study

swadhisthana chakra "her favorite standing place-wheel"; second lowest energy center of the subtle body, the creative and sexual center

swapna dream state, one of the three states of normal consciousness

Taittiriya Upanishad one of the principal *Upanishads*

tamas inertia, heaviness, darkness, obstinacy, stubbornness; one of the three *gunas* or qualities inherent in *maya*, the illusory world

tapas "to burn"; austerity, intense discipline

Tat tvam asi "That thou art"; refers to identification with the transcendental Self

Tibetan Book of the Dead (circa A.D. 8th century), original title was *Bardo Thodol*. This is a tutorial for the "in-between" states arrived at when one body is dropped and a new one is acquired.

trataka steadfast gazing at one object without blinking; one of the *shat karmas* of Hatha Yoga

triguna the three qualities of *maya* or *Prakriti*, the manifested world: *tamas* (inertia), *rajas* (activity), and *sattva* (balance)

Truth that which is absolute, beyond relative existence; *Brahman*

turiya "the fourth," *samadhi;* beyond the three normal states of consciousness

udana one of the *prana vayus*; vital energy moving up from the base of the throat to the top of the head

uddiyana bandha "flying-up lock"; lifting the diaphragm muscle up and under the ribs after *bahya-kumbhaka* (exhale retention)

ujjayi victorious

upadhi body, vehicle

Upanishad "sitting near"; ancient scripture written circa 800 B.C. The wisdom contained in these books was revealed to the rishis. There are said to be over a hundred, but there are twelve major *Upanishads*. The philosophy of Vedanta is founded on these scriptures.

Uttal, Jai (1951–present) devotee of Neem Karoli Baba; renowned student of Indian master musician Ali Akbar Khan; kirtan singer as well as multi-instrumentalist and recording artist. With his band, The Pagan Love Orchestra, Jai is an innovative force in world music.

vaikuntha the heavenly realm of Lord Vishnu

vairagya "dispassion"; detachment from anything that would lead one into *avidya* (ignorance, misknowing)

Vaisesika one of the six classical philosophical systems of India, usually paired with *Nyaya*. The founder was the sage *Gautama* (not the Buddha).

vajrasana "lightning bolt seat"

vam *bija mantra* of the *swadhisthana chakra*

vayu "wind"; vital air

Vedanta "the end of the *Vedas*"; the *Upanishads* are the distillation of the essential spiritual message of the *Vedas*. *Vedanta* is the name of the classical philosophical school derived from the *Upanishads*. The essence of *Vedanta* is that the Ultimate Reality, *Brahman,* is the essential nature of each being. *Vedantic* refers to ideas and practices that are based in the philosophy of Vedanta.

Vedas from the Sanskrit root *vid*, which means knowledge; ancient knowledge first passed as an oral tradition, then written; considered the oldest written scriptures. There are four: *Rig, Yajur, Sama,* and *Atharva Veda. Vedic* pertains to ideas and practices derived from the *Vedas*.

vegan (1) food or other products that are derived solely from plant sources; (2) one who is a strict vegetarian, abstaining from eating or using any products derived from animal sources.

vegetarianism the practice of not eating meat

vijnanamaya kosha one of the subtle sheaths that cover the soul, comprising higher intellect (intuition)

vinyasa linking mechanism

vinyasa krama the linked moments in the continuous process of change

Virasana "hero seat"

visamavritti unequal breathing; changing durational ratios of inhalation, exhalation, and retention

Vishnu "preserver." In the Hindu trinity *Vishnu* represents the *sattvic* force of preservation. He incarnates as an avatar when the world is in need of preservation. Krishna, Ram, Buddha, and, some believe, Jesus were all avatars of Lord Vishnu.

vishnu granthi "dweller knot"; energy blockage between the *manipura* (solar plexus) and the *anahata chakra* (heart)

Viswa Shanthi Nikethana Swami Nirmalananda's small ashram, deep in the forest of B.R. Hills, Karnataka, South India; a sanctuary for all bird, animal, and plant friends now directed by Swami Brahmadev

viveka discrimination between the real and the unreal; knowing what is True

Viveka Chudamani eighth-century text written by Sankaracharya, which expounds on the philosophy of *Advaita* (nondual) *Vedanta*

Vrindavan small town in northern India where *Krishna* spent his young adult years as a spell-binder to cows and enchanter of the *gopis*

vritti "turning, wave, whirling"; fluctuation

vyana vayu the all-pervasive vital air; one of the prana vayus

Vyasa sage who founded the *Vedanta* philosophy, one of the six classical philosophical systems of India; composer of the epic *Mahabarata*; wrote the ancient authoritative commentaries on Patanjali's *Yoga Sutras*

Yajur Veda one of the four *Vedas*; deals with sacrificial ritual

yam *bija mantra* of the *anahata chakra* (heart center)

yama (1) restriction; the first limb of Patanjali's Ashtanga Yoga system. The *yamas* are restrictions on the yogi's behavior toward others. Patanjali gives five restrictions: *ahimsa, satya, asteya, brahmacharya, aparigraha.* (2) When capitalized, *Yama* the Hindu god of death. Death of the body is a great restriction to the soul, for without a living body it is difficult to work out *karma*.

Yamuna one of the three sacred rivers of India; the other two are the Ganga and the Sarasvati. *Yamuna* is thought to be the female counterpart of *Shri Krishna*. Each goddess bestows a boon to the sincere devotee; Ganga gives *moska* (liberation), Yamuna gives *bhakti* (love).

yoga from *yuj*, to yoke; the yoking of the individual sense of self to the cosmic eternal Self; union with God, *samadhi*

Yoga Sutras scriptural source for the philosophical and practical system of yoga, or the method for attaining *samadhi*; compiled by the sage Patanjali; composed of short terse statements *(sutra)*, divided into four chapters dealing with *samadhi* (superconsciousness), *sadhana* (practice), *siddhis* (powers), and *kaivalya* (final enlightenment)

Yogash chitta-vritti-nirodhah the second sutra of Patanjali's *Yoga Sutras*, in which the definition of yoga is given: "Yoga is when one ceases to identify with the whirlings of the mind (the fluctuating thoughts)."

yogi one who practices techniques to bring about Self-realization, also one who has attained Self-Realization; in contemporary usage can be used to denote a male or female practitioner

yogin (male) older, more original term used to describe one who practices yoga or who has attained yoga

yogini a female yogin

yoni mudra also known as *shanmukhi mudra*; performed by using the fingers to close the seven gates of perception in the head

Yoni siddhasana *yoni* = vagina + *siddhi* = power + *asana* = seat; female power seat

Acknowledgments

We wish to acknowledge our Gurus, Shri Brahmananda Sarasvati, Shri Swami Nirmalananda, and Shri K. Pattabhi Jois. Without their love nothing would be possible.

Thanks also to Bhagavan Das for his steady voice and deep heart; Shyam Das for his joy, enthusiasm, zest for life, and Hari under all circumstances; and to Tulsi for never missing the beats of our hearts.

To Krishna Das for keeping on the track of the pilgrim and evolving into the heart. To Jai Uttal for tenaciously yearning for the Divine.

To Shri Neem Karoli Baba and Shri Anandamayima, we bow at your feet and your blanket. Shri Krishnamacharya, we strive to walk in the shadow of your lotus feet. Deep appreciation to Amma and Manju Jois, Sarasvati, Sharath and Shruthi Rangaswamy, for their boundless kindness.

Gratitude and love to Swami Shankarananda for his wonderful stories, wisdom, encouragement, and support.

Special thanks to Swami Satchidananda for his kindness, humor, and endearing saintliness. Thank you to Ram Dass for telling the truth, loving everyone, and telling us all about it. To Dharma Mittra for reminding us to "Think of God."

Thank you to Swami Ramananda for sharing Ma's blessings with us.

To Tara Rose for being our first yoga teacher. With appreciation, we give thanks to Peter Lamborn Wilson for putting us in touch with Swami Nirmalananda, and to Swami Brahmadev for taking care of Swami Nirmalananda's ashram.

Thank you to Radha, Bharati, Ma Ba, Joan, Manorma, Vidya, Krishna-devi, Bhavani, and Charka from Ananada Ashram for generously and joyfully continuing to share with us the wisdom of Shri Brahmananda Sarasvati.

We continuously bow to His Holiness the XIV Dalai Lama. We deeply thank Professor Robert Thurman and his mastermind consort, Dakini Nena, for their enthusiastic friendship, support, and encouragement.

To Lex Hixon for his sweetness and poetry.

To Geshe Michael Roach for giving us The Garden.

Much appreciation to the Beatles for turning us all on to India and all things magical and mystical. Special thanks to George Harrison for his devotion to Shri Krishna.

To our honorable and dear friends Maha Laxmi (Trudie Styler) and Stingji Maharaj for their unshakable love, kindness, and support, and to their ability to encourage our souls onward toward freedom.

Thank God for Bob Dylan and his daring to think differently, and to Van Morrison for his deep Irish heart and mystic vision. To John and Alice Coltrane for bringing the remembrance of God into American music. Thank you to the genius of Bill Laswell for his uncompromising continuation of that remembrance. Deep gratitude and amazement to Janet Rienstra for her ability to hold up the foundation and still infect us all with her sparkling contagious playfulness. To our friends Don Cherry and Denis Charles for playing music and Life with us.

To Joel Sneed for being living proof that yoga works.

To Gabrielle Roth for her passion for sacred music and dance.

To Louise Landes Levi for her Mirabai-like devotion to God.

To Sean Dinsmore for making groovy sounds.

To Cheb i Sabbah for spinning our hearts.

To Asha Puthli for her ability to listen and to sing what she has heard.

To Deva Premal and Miten for having the strength of a rose.

Thank you to Amachi for her hugs.

To The Mother and Shri Aurobindo for integrating the paths of yoga.

To Swami Sivananda for writing so many books on yoga and giving the world so much.

To Alan Watts for inspiring people to see that meditation and spirituality can be hip. Thank you, Robert Svoboda, for being so smart and so witty about it all.

Thank you to Sant Khesavadas for all the sweet blessings.

Thank you to Tom Lopez for the Fourth Tower of Inverness.

Thank you to Billy Forbes for keeping in touch from Nepal. We give thanks for the wit and enlightenment of U.G. Krishnamurti.

Thank you to Saint Theresa Lowrey for proving that sainthood is possible in these times.

With appreciation to Mike Diamond and Tamra Davis for their sincerity, humility, and courage in finding ways to worship God and contribute to reshaping our culture.

With deep appreciation, we thank the heroic courage and compassion of John Robbins, truly one of the most important people of our time.

To Ingrid Newkirk and PETA for their tireless work to eradicate speciesism.

To Russell Simmons for being a vegetarian and recognizing the link between vegetarianism and world peace.

We thank Dr. Martin Luther King, Jr., for having a dream and Robert and John Kennedy for helping him to share that dream with the world, and Rory Kennedy for continuing to dream.

Thank you to Michelle Hooten and Wes Doherty for giving their Body Electric as the place for our beginning.

Thank you to Mary Bosakowski for helping us find out What is Yoga?

To Maher Benham and James Carmen for being inspired by our asana dances and to Edward Clark for continuing to dance.

To Maria Rubinate for her musicality, humility, and patience.

To Willem Dafoe for his sincere dedication to yoga and his desire for realization.

To Christy Turlington for always being the grace-filled yogini.

Thank you to Donna Karan for daring to put realness into an unreal world.

Thank you to all the blessed people who run The Omega Institute for creating a place for space.

Thank you to Shiva (Marty) Shankar for teaching us how to die consciously.

To our family and steadfast friends who have always been treading the razor's edge alongside us, we bow humbly and embrace boldly: Evlyn and Joe Laslo; Fran, Bob, Richard, Leslie, Kerry, and Julie Kirkpatrick; Jules and Alex Fabre; Martin, Ivy, Brandon, Marti, April, Hilma, and Don Gannon; Laurel McGraw, Richelle Fisher, Ricky Schultze, Kathleen Hunt, Dr. Andrew Lange, Anisa and Roderick Romero, Beaver Chief, Kat Allen, Bill Wikstrom, Isabelle Kahn, Randy Hall, Glen Whiprud, Vyvyn Lazonga, Rodney and Lucy Hogan, Alex Auder, Pilar Limosner, Umananda Sarasvati, Anshula Kedar, Mamuska, Tai Tea, Miten, and Ursula.

To our entire staff at Jivamukti we owe a debt of gratitude, especially to Carlos Menjivar, and Amy Gail. To all our dedicated Jivamukti teachers, we honor and bow to your sense of adventure and willingness to make the practice of Jivamukti Yoga your life and to enrich our lives with your continuous evolution.

Without the direct efforts of the following people this book would not be:

Sue Ann Harkey for her creative design ideas.

Christopher Hildlebrandt for generously assisting with the glossary.

Deb DeSalvo for her brilliant writing, editorial skills, and relentless pursuit of excellence, and for directing this project from beginning to end.

Martin Brading for his magical skills that make photo images that vibrate with sound—much like the Grateful Dead, who could make sound that vibrated images—without which this book might just be a lot of words.

Joel Gotler for enthusiastically believing in us from the beginning.

Leslie Meredith and Maureen O'Neal for their mindful editing, and all the people at Ballantine for believing that people would be interested in reading a book like this.

Most importantly, Thank God.

INDEX

Page numbers appear in italic for illustrations.

About the Authors

SHARON GANNON's (Tripura Sundari) quest for Independence began with her birth on July 4th in Washington, D.C. Her interest in mysticism was nourished by her Catholic upbringing. She studied ballet, modern dance, classical Indian dance, music, and Eastern philosophy, and earned a bachelor's degree in dance from the University of Washington in 1979.

During the 1980s, Sharon was the vocalist and violinist for the jazz/rock band Audio Letter. She was also a regular contributor to the anthologies and journals of Semiotext(e) (Columbia University, New York). In 1984 she shifted away from performing and toward teaching yoga in an effort to offer practical methods that might benefit people more directly and immediately.

Sharon has always viewed art as a means for uplifting the soul. Through her various artistic pursuits, she sought to offer something that was not only inspirational but also educational, and that spoke of the spiritual quest for deep happiness that is shared by all.

"The success and happiness that we enjoy is a direct result of the kindness we have shown toward others," Sharon notes. She is an animal rights activist and an outspoken advocate of ethical vegetarianism and is the author of *Cats and Dogs Are People Too* (Jivamukti Press, 1999), an investigation of the insensitive attitudes that result in commercial pet food.

Since 1976, Sharon has studied yoga with many teachers around the world, the most noteworthy being Shri Brahmananda Sarasvati, Swami Nirmalananda, and Shri K. Pattabhi Jois.

David Life (Deva Das) was born in a small town in Michigan. He earned a bachelor of fine arts degree from Michigan State, with minors in poetry and psychology.

Throughout his life, David has been interested in metaphysics and spirituality. His Catholic upbringing inspired his devotion to Christian mystics like St. John of the Cross and Teresa of Avila. David spent three years as an initiate of a Shankaracharya lineage of yogic monks and has also received Bodhisattva and Kalachakra initiation by His Holiness the XIV Dalai Lama.

David moved to New York City in 1979, where he pursued his art career and opened Life Café, an East Village hot spot for music, art, and poetry.

While operating Life Café in the 1980s, David had close associations with Latino poets, old guard Beats like Allen Ginsberg, and Julien Beck and Judith Malina of the Living Theater, and was an influential performer, painter, and poet.

In 1984, David began studying yoga. He went on to study with many great teachers worldwide, including K. Pattabhi Jois, from whom he received certification in the advanced Ashtanga series. David's interest in yoga is supported by his artistic, literary, and metaphysical studies. He imbues his classes with metaphor, musicality, and spirituality, spiced with humor, vigor, and spontaneity.

About Jivamukti Yoga

Jivamukti Yoga Center
404 Lafayette Street
New York, NY 10003
(800) 295-6814

Jivamukti Yoga Center Uptown
853 Lexington Avenue
New York, NY 10021
(212) 396-4200

Beginning and intermediate/advanced Jivamukti Yoga classes are available on instructional CDs and tapes. The videos *What Is Yoga* and *Asana: Sacred Dance of the Yogis* are also available. To order, call (888) I AM YOGA for a free catalogue, or visit www.jivamuktiyoga.com.